The Shaping of Somali Society

Reconstructing the History of a Pastoral People, 1600–1900

Lee V. Cassanelli

University of Pennsylvania Press

Philadelphia   1982

This work was published with the support of the Haney
Foundation.

Library of Congress Cataloging in Publication Data

Cassanelli, Lee V., 1946–
  The shaping of Somali society.

  (Ethnohistory)
  Bibliography: p.
  Includes index.
  1. Somalis—History. I. Title. II. Series:
Ethnohistory (University of Pennsylvania Press)
DT402.3.C37   967'.7301   81–43520
ISBN 0-8122-7832-1   AACR2

Printed in the United States of America

The Shaping of Somali Society

Ethnohistory

A series edited by
Anthony F. C. Wallace
and Lee V. Cassanelli

Contents

Illustrations

Plates

Maps

Figures

Preface

      This book reconstructs and interprets certain aspects of Somali history in the three centuries before 1900, that is, before the start of the colonial period. The Somalis are a predominantly pastoral people who inhabit the semi-arid lowlands of the eastern Horn of Africa. While they have been the subject of several studies by anthropologists and political scientists, and have more recently drawn the attention of journalists, development experts, and international relief agencies, their precolonial history is virtually unknown. Part of the reason for this is the paucity of early written records on the Somali and the difficulties of interpreting those sources—primarily oral and ethnographic—which do exist. Moreover, there are real problems in trying to write the history of a nomadic population that has no tradition of centralized authority and no single geographical heartland. For these reasons, this book can be considered as much a study in the methodologies of nomadic ethnohistory—and oral history—as it is an attempt to add to our substantive knowledge of the Somali past.

      I have organized my material in a series of chapters which, though covering most of the period from 1600 to 1900, cannot be considered a strictly chronological record of the past. Rather each chapter aims to illuminate an aspect of Somali society through the analysis of certain historical events known to us from written or oral sources. In addition, each chapter contains some discussion of the problems of historical reconstruction and the reasoning used in analyzing the various types of evidence available. I have tried to provide sufficient cultural and geographical background in each chapter to render the historical analysis comprehensible to the general reader. In addition, in the Introduction I set out the specific theoretical concerns that have informed my approach to the book as a whole, and in the Appendix I describe the nature of the oral sources on which much of my analysis rests.

Large parts of this study are based on field work that I conducted in Somalia from December 1970 to November 1971, and again from September to December 1977. On both occasions my interviews and observations were made in southern Somalia, and it will be evident that many of my interpretations rely heavily on data from that region. Still, I have tried where possible to incorporate the findings of Somali and European scholars who have worked extensively in other parts of Somalia as well as in Kenya; and I have attempted to relate my analyses to some of the larger historiographical issues that have pervaded scholarship in the Horn of Africa over the past several decades.

There are many individuals and institutions who assisted me at various stages of my research, and to whom I am indebted. Chapters 3 through 6 contain material that was collected in the course of my research for the doctoral dissertation, prepared for the University of Wisconsin in 1973. That research was conducted in Italy and Somalia from September 1970 to December 1971 and was supported by a Fulbright-Hays Fellowship and by a supplementary grant from the Comparative Tropical History Program at the University of Wisconsin. A summer research grant from the University of Pennsylvania enabled me to go to Italy in 1976 to collect data for the second chapter. Grants from the Social Science Research Council and the American Council of Learned Societies gave me time to rewrite the various chapters and to undertake a second period of field research in Somalia in the fall of 1977.

I am extremely grateful to the Somali government and to my many Somali friends for the hospitality and help they extended during my visits to their country. The decade of the 1970s was a difficult one for Somalia. A prolonged drought, war with neighboring Ethiopia, and, recently, a staggering refugee problem have severely taxed the nation's material and human resources. Despite the inevitable restrictions that had to be imposed on foreign field researchers as a result of these crises, I never found the Somalis to be wanting in their generosity, their encouragement, and their unflagging interest in my work. It is to my numerous Somali teachers, informants, and friendly critics that I dedicate this book.

Special thanks go also to Professor B. W. Andrzejewski of the School of Oriental and African Studies, University of London, for his patient efforts to check my rendering of Somali place names and poetic fragments in the new national orthography; to Ahmed Ali Aboker, who taught me my first words of Somali and kept after me constantly (though not always successfully) to improve; and to Professor I. M. Lewis of the London School of Economics and Political Science, whose practical counsel was invaluable during my first visit to Somalia and whose scholarly advice has been invaluable ever since. I would also like to acknowledge the help of my tireless assistants in 1970–71, Aboker Ali Omar, Ahmed Shaykh Osman, and Muhammad Rinjele; my colleague and fellow traveler in 1977, Muhammad Mukhtar of the Somali National University; the staff at the Somali Academy of Arts and Sciences, and especially Sa'id Osman, Aw Jama Omar Isa, and Deeqo Jama; and Michele Pirone and Virginia Luling for generously sharing their research notes and firsthand knowledge of Somalia with me.

My brief forays into the archives of the ex Ministero dell'Africa Italiana in Rome would not have been as productive without the assistance of Dr. Mario Gazzini and his staff. Thanks go also to members of the Istituto Italiano per l'Africa and the Società Geografica Italiana in Rome, and to the staff at the Istituto Agronomico in Florence, for their help in locating early colonial publications and documents on Somalia.

I owe a unique debt of gratitude to the late Alphonso A. Castagno, who as much as anyone was responsible for my taking up the study of Somali history, and whose death in 1973 deprived Somali studies of one of its most committed scholars. I am also grateful to Professors Steven Feierman and Jan Vansina of the University of Wisconsin for reading earlier versions of this work and for offering many helpful suggestions, and to Debby Stuart and Lee Ann Draud for their editorial patience and precision. My colleagues in the Ethnohistory Workshop at the University of Pennsylvania were a continuing source of ideas and enlightenment, particularly in the anthropological sections of the study.

Finally, I want to acknowledge in a special way the friendship and support of Muusa Haji Isma'il Galaal, who died in Jidda in December 1980. Muusa was an outstanding poet, researcher, and recorder of Somali lore in his own right, and a source of inspiration to two generations of researchers on Somalia. All those concerned with the preservation of the Somali oral heritage must mourn his passing, for it is unlikely that we will see a cultural interpreter of his like again. I am particularly sad that he did not live to see the publication of this book which he so keenly encouraged during its long gestation. Not least for him, and for his memory, I am pleased to have brought it at last to fruition.

Note on Transcription

In 1972 a national orthography for Somali was introduced and is now uniformly used in all publications in that language. The salient features of this orthography are that the vowel letters have pronunciation values that approximate those in Italian; length is indicated by doubling the vowel letters. The pharyngeal consonants represented by Enrico Cerulli in *Somalia: Scritti vari editi ed inediti* (Rome, 1957) as ' ('ain) and *ḥ* correspond to *c* and *x* in the new orthography. For English readers, *c* is normally unpronounced (for Ceel Waaq, "Well of God," read *Eel Waaq*), and *x* corresponds to aspirate *h* (for *Xamar*, the local name for old Muqdisho, read *Hamar*).

In this book, I use the new orthography for all words except Somali personal names. The reason for this one important exception is that pronunciation in southern Somalia, where my fieldwork was conducted, often differs considerably from that of standard Somali. For example, the initial *c* is sometimes dropped from names like Cali and Cabdi. In the interests of clarity and consistency, therefore, and until such time as the transcription of southern Somali names can be standardized, I have chosen to anglicize all Somali personal names—hence, Ali and Abdi, Hassan rather than Xasan, and Muhammad rather than Maxamad, will be used throughout. For the word *Somali* itself, I follow standard English usage rather than the phonetically more accurate *Soomaali*.

In rendering Somali common nouns, proverbs and poetry, and place names, I have employed the official orthography. In most instances, the reader should have no difficulty identifying places whose names may be spelled differently in earlier works on Somalia (e.g., Muqdisho = Mogadishu, Mogadiscio; Baraawe = Brava; Baardheere

xiii

= Bardera). Where the new spelling may cause some confusion, I have included a more familiar older spelling in parentheses—Seylac (Zeila), Baydhabo (Baidoa). Alternate forms of the more important place names are listed in the index.

In translating passages from the Italian, I have taken the liberty of altering Somali clan and place names to conform to the new orthography. In quoting from English language sources, however, I use the spelling that appears in the original.

Finally, I have anglicized most words of Arabic derivation, although in a few instances I have employed the Somali equivalent of the Arabic word (e.g., *dikri* rather than *dhikr, qaaddi* rather than *qadi*). Somali and Arabic terms used in the book are listed in Appendix B, the Glossary.

Note on the Use of Geographical and Clan Names

In this book, the term *Somali* refers to any Somali-speaker, regardless of his geographical location. During the scramble for Africa at the end of the last century, the region inhabited by the Somalis was divided into several political units. Most Somalis became subjects of the British Somaliland Protectorate or of the colony of Italian Somalia. Many, however, were included within the boundaries of French Somaliland, the eastern Ethiopian provinces of Hararghe and Bale, and the Northern Frontier District of British Kenya, and in each of these places they form substantial minorities maintaining their Somali language and culture. In 1960, the former British and Italian territories received their independence and united to form the Somali Republic (renamed the Somali Democratic Republic in 1969). Both within and outside the country, the term *Somalia* is familiarly used, and I have used it throughout this study to refer loosely to the entire area that coincides with the modern Republic.

Similarly, in discussing regional developments in the past, I will refer to certain regions such as the Benaadir, Hiiraan, and Ogaadeen. Although these terms had certain territorial significance even in the precolonial period, they acquired specific boundaries only after the formal establishment of colonial rule. By referring to the map on p. 10, the reader can locate the regions in question but should bear in mind the indeterminateness of boundaries in the precolonial period.

The entire Somali-speaking community was divided in precolonial times into numerous clans and subclans, often called "tribes" in the early ethnographic literature. Since 1969, the Somali government has attempted to prohibit public discussion of clan or tribal affiliations in an effort to overcome what it sees as a major obstacle to national unity and development. Since this is a study of precolonial Somalia, however, I have felt free to use clan names for the sake of clarity and accuracy, even though this may cause some discomfiture to modern nationalists. I hope that the use of clan references will not unduly distract Somali readers from the main issues this book addresses.

Finally, I have used the word *Oromo* to refer to the people called Galla in most previous writings on the region. The people themselves favor the name Oromo, and it has been officially adopted by the mass media in both Somalia and Ethiopia.

The Shaping of Somali Society

Introduction

The ethnic configuration of the Somali Peninsula presents the student of African societies with a unique case. In contrast to most of the rest of Africa, where independent states seek to forge a common national identity from a multiplicity of ethnic groups within their boundaries, Somalia is essentially a one-nationality state whose population shares an ethnic identity with Somalis in three adjoining states. Since attaining their independence in 1960, the 3,000,000 Somalis in the Republic have been almost unanimous in their desire to unite with their fellow Somalis who form substantial minorities within Ethiopia (about 1,000,000), Djibouti—formerly French Somaliland—(about 100,000), and Kenya (250,000). What gives Somalis this strong sense of common identity, despite more than eighty years of political partition, is their long-time occupation of nearly four hundred thousand square miles of contiguous territory; a common language (albeit with regional dialect differences); a shared Islamic heritage; a widespread belief that all Somalis are ultimately descended from a small number of common ancestors; and a way of life that is overwhelmingly pastoral.

The Somali consciousness of a common cultural identity is also clearly the product of shared historical experiences; one of the central questions for historians concerns the relative importance of the Somalis' early history in the shaping of that identity. Modern scholarship on Somalia has tended to concentrate on the formative experiences of the twentieth century: the imposition of colonial administration over a previously segmented clan society; the creation, however short-lived, of an Italian East African Empire by Mussolini's Fascists (1936–41) and subsequent British efforts to form a "Greater

3

Somalia" out of the ruins; and the rise of territory-wide Somali political parties calling for the reunification of the Somalilands. Clearly these forces were critical to what I. M. Lewis has called "the long process of gestation from cultural to political nationalism."[1] However, the forces of the twentieth century operated on a Somali population that had already attained a certain cultural and historical unity. Unlike any other African territory, Somalia in 1900 was already an embryonic nation.

Contemporary students of Somali society have recognized that Somalia's modern national identity rests on a long history, but the details of that history are not well known. In part this is the result of the unusual circumstances in which twentieth-century Somali historiography developed. Colonial and postcolonial scholars were preoccupied, as I will show in chapter 1, with political and territorial issues, and therefore tended to neglect the underlying cultural and social processes that had their roots in the more distant past. More significant, however, is the paucity of traditional historical sources for the precolonial period. Somali-speakers have apparently occupied the Horn of Africa for at least two thousand years, but because most were nomads, they left few material artifacts and almost no permanent settlements to be investigated by archaeologists. The absence of any form of centralized government in the nomadic lowlands meant that there were no administrative records or official chronicles. And although most of the Peninsula's inhabitants were Islamized by the fifteenth century, few Arabic written records outside of the coastal towns have come to light.

Only with the linguistic and ethnohistorical advances of the past twenty years, along with the recent methodologies developed by Africa's oral historians, have researchers acquired the tools to probe more systematically into the Somali past. Even so, it is frequently impossible to find anything more than traces of past migrations in the distribution of clan groupings today, or to hear anything more than faint echoes of past battles in the oral poetry and clan traditions that survive. Broad patterns of social and cultural change often must be inferred from the fragmentary data available. Many of the reconstructions attempted in this work are, consequently, highly speculative; and much of the evidence on which they rest—ethnographic data, for example, or oral traditions taken down in the nineteenth and

1. I. M. Lewis, *The Modern History of Somaliland* (London, 1965), p. x.

twentieth centuries—is not contemporaneous with the events in question. For these reasons, I have given more than the usual attention to problems of methodology.

It may be worthwhile to set out at this point some of the larger considerations that informed the organization of the chapters that follow. One such consideration has to do with the nature of historical analysis in societies that are made up primarily of nomadic pastoralists. In the course of my Somali research, I continually ran up against the issue of how to translate the particular local histories of Somalia's numerous pastoral clans into some kind of historically significant patterns. The problem, common to all students of nomadic societies, was to find a unit of analysis appropriate for the historical study of a decentralized, geographically mobile population like the Somali. There are simply no fixed territorial boundaries to help delimit the social groups under study; and the groups themselves typically consist of clans and lineages that sometimes federate, sometimes break apart, according to the situation on the ground.

To resolve this difficulty, I approached the study of Somalia's pastoral history from a regional perspective, one which can incorporate many interacting clans in a single framework. This approach is suggested partly by the ecological and comparative literature on nomads, and partly by the historical evidence of social and political interaction among various groups of nomads over time. In chapter 2, I outline the characteristics of what I call "regional resource systems" and then attempt to demonstrate their utility for purposes of historical analysis. My aim there and throughout the book is to discuss social and political change at least partly in terms of the resources, both human and material, that are available within the region and that can be drawn upon by different corporate groups.

There is now clearly a trend toward integrative regional history in African studies. It is implicit, for example, in the recent works by Steven Feierman, Aylward Shorter, and John Lamphear.[2] Although these authors are concerned with three different types of East African societies, all demonstrate a sensitivity to environmental factors in

2. Steven Feierman, *The Shambaa Kingdom* (Madison: University of Wisconsin Press, 1974); Aylward Shorter, *Chiefship in Western Tanzania* (Oxford: Clarendon Press, 1972); John Lamphear, *The Traditional History of the Jie of Uganda* (Oxford: Clarendon Press, 1976). For a discussion of the peculiar problems that confront the historian of "stateless" societies, see the Introduction in John Tosh, *Clan Leaders and Colonial Chiefs in Lango* (Oxford: Clarendon Press, 1978).

their discussions of precolonial political economies. All analyze shifting power relations in the contexts of neighboring groups and of resource accessibility. And all draw on oral evidence not just from the centers of power but also from peripheral groups. By looking beyond the clan or locally defined corporate unit, these scholars have been able to point to processes of political or cultural change that are not confined to the historical experience of a single group, and not dependent on the historical consciousness of any one local community. If I have been more explicit than my predecessors in my exposition of the regional approach, it is because the Somali population is far more mobile and more widely dispersed than are other populations previously examined by this method, and hence the regional context in which the Somalis operated must be more expressly identified.

The advantage of the regional approach is not only that it allows us to study pastoral politics, trade, and migrations in their larger territorial setting, but also that it enables us to integrate the history of Somalia's nomads with the distinct but interrelated histories of those small urban and agricultural communities that played an important role in various phases of the history of the Somali Peninsula. The theme of nomadic/sedentary interaction is scarcely a novel one in the literature on pastoral societies.[3] But too often patterns of interaction have been examined exclusively from the point of view of the sedentary population, whence most of our standard historical sources invariably come. By taking the nomad's ecological and social universes as our starting points—and I will argue that these are regional rather than local in scale—I believe we can obtain fresh insights into the development of urban/rural and pastoral/agricultural relations over time.

The regional framework has one additional advantage: it permits us to eschew the categories of tribal and national history with which recent Somali historiography has tended to operate. It is, of course, undeniable that tribal and national identities have played an extremely important role in the twentieth-century history of Somalia.

3. To cite but a few of the many comparative studies: Cynthia Nelson, ed., *The Desert and the Sown* (Berkeley: University of California Press, 1973); William Irons and Neville Dyson-Hudson, eds., *Perspectives on Nomadism* (Leiden: E. J. Brill, 1972); Theodore Monod, ed., *Pastoralism in Tropical Africa* (London: Oxford University Press, 1975); L'Equipe écologie et anthropologie des sociétés pastorales, *Pastoral Production and Society* (Paris and Cambridge: Maison des Sciences de l'Homme and Cambridge University Press, 1979).

Nevertheless, I am persuaded that, for the precolonial period, the regional framework is more appropriate for examining the evolution of Somali social, religious, and political identity. I will try to demonstrate that in the years before 1900, processes of regional integration were far more significant than has heretofore been recognized.

Another theoretical consideration in the organization of this book stems from the nature of the sources used in the historical reconstruction. Many of the chapters rely heavily on Somali oral traditions, whose nature, content, and collection are discussed in Appendix A. Oral historians of Africa are coming increasingly to see traditions not primarily as direct records of the past, but also as reflections on that past by members of the society that preserves them.[4] I would go even further and say that history, as distilled in tradition, actually shaped the attitudes and behavior of the Somalis toward contemporary events. Thus I have suggested that Somali society was not only the product of a series of historical experiences whose impact can be described in terms of new institutions, networks, social relationships, and the like; it was also the product of beliefs about the past and of beliefs about the relationship of the present to the past. This subjective dimension of Somali history I consider particularly in chapters 3 and 4, where the relationship between tradition, belief, and history is discussed with examples from two distinct bodies of oral traditional material.

Finally, although I do not explicitly take up the twentieth-century issues of Pan-Somalism and Somali nationalism, these issues have invariably shaped the historiographical tradition from which the present study departs. I have sought to emphasize themes that I feel have not been systematically studied by modern scholars of Somalia, but their relevance to the twentieth century nevertheless seems to me unmistakable. If modern Somali nationalism is the product of the unique events and ideologies of the twentieth century, surely it draws its strength from the common traditions and shared experiences of the precolonial past.

Indeed, one of the implicit arguments of this study is that the interplay of environmental, social, economic, and religious forces produced a society which, though politically fragmented, was integrated

4. For a recent statement, see Joseph C. Miller, ed., *The African Past Speaks* (Folkestone, England, and Hamden, Conn.: Wm. Dawson/Archon Books, 1980), esp. pp. 21–52.

at various levels of structure, belief, and behavior. The processes I have in mind are the Somalis' common struggle against a harsh environment and the construction of regional networks of mutual aid to adapt to that environment (chapter 2); the periodic incorporation of Somali kinship groups into larger political structures, either territorial confederations or theocratic states (chapter 3); the diffusion of common Islamic institutions and practices, chiefly through the efforts of itinerant "saints" who became folk heroes in many parts of rural Somalia (chapter 4); the development of long-distance trade routes and regional economies that linked Somalia to the wider world of international commerce (chapter 5); and the resistance by Somalis to foreign invaders at various times in the distant and not-so-distant past (chapter 6). Each of these developments had its own peculiar antecedents and consequences, but all were interwoven into the history of Somalia from 1600 to 1900.

At the same time, a common fund of historical experience did not preclude the existence of deep social and political divisions within the Somali population. Clan loyalties, local saint cults, and various modes of economic activity divided Somalis into distinct and often fiercely competitive groups. Patterns of social, economic, and religious differentiation were also part of the precolonial heritage. As will become evident, many of those same processes that shaped the larger Somali society did so by sharpening the definitions of the subgroups within it.

In the first chapter I will describe the basic features of Somali society as they appeared at the start of the twentieth century, paying particular attention to regional variations in culture, mode of production, and sociopolitical organization. Then I will review both the historiography of Somalia as it developed in the present century and the issues that have molded our contemporary understanding of the Somali past. This will set the stage for the chapters that follow, each of which examines one or more of the processes that helped shape Somali society.

1 The Societal and Historiographical Background

If you don't know the country you will get lost;
if you don't know the people, you will go hungry.
—Somali saying

Aspects of Somali Society

Means of Subsistence

A well-known Somali poem by Salaan Arabay says, "Of every two problems that are discussed, the first must be on the subject of subsistence." And so it must be, for one of the most striking features of life in the Somali Peninsula is the difficulty of eking a living from its sunbaked, often barren soil. In a land where rainfall is generally scarce and unpredictable, and where the only vegetation one may see for miles is coarse desert grass or impenetrable thorn bush, life is a constant struggle. Somalis have adapted to their harsh environment in a number of ways, most notably through various forms of nomadic pastoralism. For as far back as we have written records, the peoples of the Horn of Africa depended on livestock for their basic subsistence needs. A ninth-century Chinese travel compendium noted that the people of Po-pa-li ("Berbera," as the Horn was then known) "do not eat any cereals but they eat meat: more frequently even they prick a vein of one of their oxen, mix the blood with

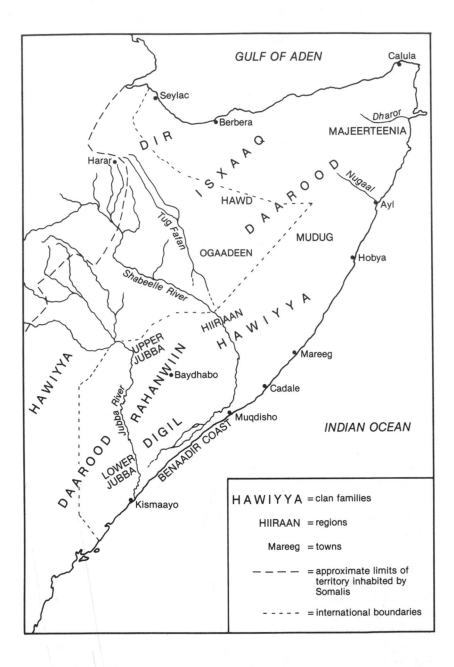

Map 1. *The Horn of Africa: Present distribution of Somali clan-families*

milk and eat it raw."[1] Since Somalis have not been known in recent times to drink the blood of their cattle, it is not clear whether this description applies to them. But another account, from the early thirteenth-century work of Chao Ju-kua, could have been written of the Somalis at the end of the nineteenth century.

> The country of Pi-p'a-lo contains four cities; the other places are all villages which are constantly at feud and fighting with each other. The inhabitants pray to Heaven and not to the Buddha. The land produces many camels and sheep, and the people feed themselves with the flesh and milk of camels and with baked cakes.[2]

Somalia is truly a nation of nomads with a long pastoral tradition. Virtually all Somalis own some livestock, and a glance at any Somali dictionary will reveal the vast vocabulary of specialized terms pertaining to the size, color, age, behavior, and habitats of domestic animals. Place names throughout the Peninsula typically reflect pastoral concerns: *Candho-qoys*, the place of "moist udders," *Tuur Caanood*, "hill of milk," *Dhiinsoor*, "the feed of cattle," *Adhi-gaba*, "betrayer of flocks," and *Geel-weyta*, the place that "weakens camels." There also exists an extensive body of folklore and specialized veterinary knowledge associated with breeding practices, transhumance patterns, and the relationship between the stars and the well-being of the domestic herds.[3] Somalis are extremely proud of their expertise as managers of livestock: "It is through animals that we learn to subsist," goes one proverb; "anything else we try to rear will be in vain."

Since the ecology of Somali pastoralism will be taken up in detail in chapter 2, we need here only take note of the major variations within the wider pastoral tradition of the Horn. Most Somali families keep several types of livestock, but certain regions of the country are better suited to the breeding and rearing of particular animals.

1. G. S. P. Freeman-Grenville, *The East African Coast: Select Documents* (Oxford, 1962), p. 8.
2. Ibid., p. 21.
3. The most comprehensive treatment of Somalia's traditional pastoral lore is an unpublished manuscript of the late Muusa H. I. Galaal, "Stars, Seasons and Weather in Somali Pastoral Traditions." It is an expansion of an earlier work by the author which is slightly more accessible: *The Terminology and Practice of Somali Weather Lore, Astronomy and Astrology* (Muqdisho, 1968).

In southern Somalia cattle husbandry is often practiced in conjunction with dry-land farming. The small settlement in the background is built around a small series of wars, or natural depressions, which collect rainwater.

Shallow wells dug at the bottom of wars conserve water for use during the dry season.

From the age of six or seven, children are expected to tend the herds of sheep or goats near the settlements. When they get older, they will assume responsibility for watching the camels or cattle.

Mud and wattle houses with conical roofs are characteristic of the agricultural villages along the Shabeelle River, which typically range in size from fifty to more than five hundred inhabitants.

Camel breeding predominates in the dry plains of northern and central Somalia and is supplemented in the rugged mountains and coastal zones of the extreme north by sheep and goat herding. Cattle breeding predominates where water is more abundant (and rainfall generally more reliable), specifically in most of the southern region between the Jubba and Shabeelle Rivers and in a small section of the northwest around Borama. Historically, certain clans were regarded as outstanding breeders of camels, others of cattle, though one could find all types of livestock in virtually all parts of the country.

The varying nutritional and watering requirements of the different animals produced diverse forms of pastoral adaptation. Nomads who annually travel hundreds of miles across the arid north with their camels and goats are called *reer godeed,* and those who travel more limited distances with cattle are called *reer nugul.* The importance of these distinctions for the social historian of Somalia will become apparent when we discuss patterns of social and political organization below.

Although pastoralism was the most common and most highly esteemed way of life in Somalia, it coexisted for centuries with pockets of agricultural activity, found mostly in the south. Along the Jubba and Shabeelle Rivers, which rise in the Ethiopian highlands and provide the Peninsula with its only source of year-round surface water, small villages of farmers subsisted on durra (grain), beans, and maize. Some of these farmers may have been descendants of Bantu-speaking peoples who settled in the river valleys of Somalia more than a millenium ago.[4] Even today, many of the farmers differ in physical appearance from their pastoral neighbors. And although they have been assimilated linguistically by the Somalis and, for the most part, consider themselves Muslims, they have retained a number of social customs and ritual practices that give southern Somali rural life a

4. On the subject of early negroid populations in Somalia, see Enrico Cerulli, *Somalia: Scritti vari editi ed inediti,* 3 vols. (Rome, 1957), 1: 54–57; (Rome, 1959), 2: 115–21; Vinigi L. Grottanelli, "The Peopling of the Horn of Africa," in H. Neville Chittick and Robert L. Rotberg, eds., *East Africa and the Orient: Cultural Syntheses in Pre-Colonial Times* (New York, 1975), pp. 61–68; V. V. Matveyev, "Northern Boundaries of the Eastern Bantu (Zinj) in X Century according to Arab Sources," *XXV International Congress of Orientalists* (Moscow, 1960). For a different interpretation, see E. R. Turton, "Bantu, Galla, and Somali Migrations in the Horn of Africa: A Reassessment of the Juba/Tana Area," *Journal of African History* 16 (1975): esp. 523–28.

decidedly different flavor than the strictly nomadic culture of the north.

Until recently, farmers were regarded as an inferior class by the Somali pastoral majority, probably in part because of the disdain most herdsmen had for the agricultural way of life. Beyond this, groups of farmers seeking military security and perhaps trading partners tended historically to attach themselves to powerful nomadic clans in the area, and thereby came to be seen as "clients" or dependents of the latter and therefore necessarily inferior. Finally, many local Somalis believed that the negroid farmers were the descendants of slaves. Although the evidence on this point is inconclusive, it seems likely that at least some of the ancestors of the modern farmers came originally as free settlers to the Somalilands. At the same time, there is no question that their numbers have been augmented in more recent times (certainly during the nineteenth century) by slaves imported into Somalia from neighboring parts of East Africa.[5] Whatever their origins, the farmers' success in the river valleys of southern Somalia gave rise to a mixed pastoral-agricultural economy that was not possible elsewhere in the Peninsula.

It ought to be remarked that the distinction between herdsman and farmer is not always clearcut, as the foregoing description might suggest. Many herdsmen practiced seasonal, dry-land farming, particularly in the fertile "black-earth" districts of the southern inter-river plateau. Following the spring or fall rains, family members would sow small quantities of grain in plots adjacent to their home wells. Women and older men would remain to tend the fields while the younger men took the livestock off in search of pasture. These dry-land farms, in contrast to those in the irrigable lands along the Shabeelle, offered little long-term security, and small agricultural settlements could disappear just as quickly as they had sprung up. For most Somalis, pastoralism was the only sure means of securing a living.

Patterns of Social and Political Organization

There is linguistic evidence that Somali-speakers have been in the Horn of Africa for at least two millenia, but their early political history is obscure. The word *Somali* first appears in an Ethiopic hymn

5. See chap. 5, pp. 168–71.

of the early fifteenth century celebrating the victory of the Ethiopian king Negus Yeshaaq (1414–29) over the neighboring Islamic sultanate of Adal, which apparently included a number of pastoral "tribes" among which the Somali are mentioned.[6] As early as the twelfth century, however, the geographer al-Idrisi (1100–1166) mentions a group known as the "Hawiyya" living in the central Peninsula near a river (almost certainly the Shabeelle); and a century later Ibn Sa'id (1214–87) identifies the coastal town of Marka as the capital of the Hawiyya.[7] The Hawiyya were one of the six major clan-families into which the Somalis were divided at the start of the twentieth century; in all probability, then, al-Idrisi and Ibn Sa'id provide the earliest direct evidence of a distinct Somali presence in the Horn. The word *Somali* itself does not appear in any Arabic documents before the sixteenth century,[8] but references to identifiable Somali clans appear occasionally in the written Arabic literature after 1300. This fact itself provides a clue to the nature of Somali political organization in the past: far from being a unified people, the occupants of the Horn were divided into several distinct communities.

In precolonial times, Somali political identity rested on membership in a discrete kinship group based on descent. The groups were named after their founding ancestors, and every individual maintained a genealogy that traced his ancestry back to the founder of the line. Descent was traced agnatically, that is, through the male line. At birth, each child received an original first name and took as surnames the first name of his or her father, grandfather, and so on back to the purported founder. In this way, lengthy genealogies *(abtirsiinyo)* were built up; and by comparing genealogies, two individuals could quickly determine how closely they were related. Many Somalis can reckon their ancestries back through twenty or twenty-five generations.

The ancestors of virtually all Somali kinship groups are said to be ultimately descended from Arab immigrants, whose arrival in the Horn of Africa can typically be dated, by counting generations, to the first half of the present millenium. Somali claims to Arab ancestry, whether real or fabricated, reflect the fact that trade and human migration have historically linked Arabia to the Somali Peninsula.

6. Cerulli, *Somalia* 1: 111–12.
7. Ibid., pp. 91–95.
8. Ibid., p. 112.

Probably most of the traditions of Arab ancestry date from the period when Somalis converted to Islam, a process that may have begun for some groups as early as the eighth century A.D. and continued for others into the early eighteenth century.[9] Locating one's ancestors in the homeland of Islam is characteristic of many African Muslim peoples and probably accounts for the emphasis in Somali traditions on their Arab origins.

Notwithstanding the profound attachment of all Somalis to a common Islamic heritage, it was their political division into distinct kinship groups and the formation and breaking of alliances among these groups that most influenced their precolonial political history. Somalia was, in the language of the anthropologists, a segmentary society, that is, a society made up of several structurally similar groups capable of combining or dividing at various levels according to the circumstances. In the absence of any higher authority, people have to combine for purposes of self-defense and economic survival. In a segmentary system, it is the opposition of balanced groups and coalitions that provides the fundamental source of order and security in the larger society.

By the time the first modern ethnographers studied Somalia in the late nineteenth century, the Somali-speaking population was divided into six major groupings which may conveniently be called "clan-families."[10] These were vast confederations of kinship groups whose members claimed descent from a common ancestor some twenty-five to thirty generations removed. At one time, the clan-families may have been discrete territorial entities occupying separate grazing lands. By the beginning of the twentieth century, however, pastoral migrations, uneven demographic growth, and political conflict had led to the dispersal of the components of these clan-families throughout the Peninsula. Thus segments of the Daarood, the largest clan-family, could be found spread from the northeastern tip of the

9. The best general overview in English of the impact of Middle Eastern Islam on Somalia is Ali Abdirahman Hersi, "The Arab Factor in Somali History: The Origins and Development of Arab Enterprise and Cultural Influences in the Somali Peninsula" (Ph.D. diss., University of California, Los Angeles, 1977), esp. chaps. 3 and 4. See also J. Spencer Trimingham, *Islam in Ethiopia* (London, 1965), esp. pp. 138–43, 209–16.

10. The terminology used here follows I. M. Lewis, *The Somali Lineage System and the Total Genealogy* (London, 1957), cyclostyled. It is summarized in Lewis, *Modern History*, pp. 4–12.

Figure 1. Genealogical relationships among Somali clan-families and clans mentioned in the text

General Relationship of Somali Clan-Families*

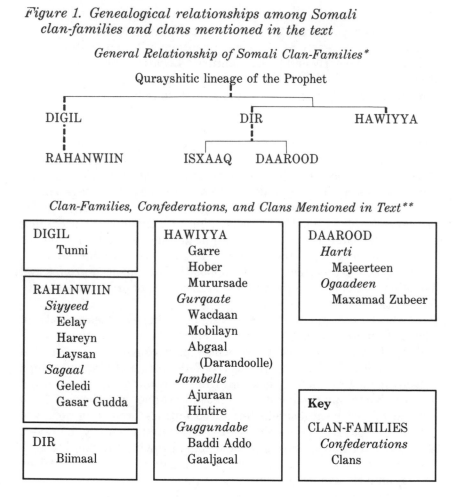

Qurayshitic lineage of the Prophet

DIGIL   DIR   HAWIYYA

RAHANWIIN   ISXAAQ   DAAROOD

Clan-Families, Confederations, and Clans Mentioned in Text**

DIGIL
  Tunni

RAHANWIIN
  Siyyeed
    Eelay
    Hareyn
    Laysan
  Sagaal
    Geledi
    Gasar Gudda

DIR
  Biimaal

HAWIYYA
  Garre
  Hober
  Murursade
  Gurqaate
    Wacdaan
    Mobilayn
    Abgaal
      (Darandoolle)
  Jambelle
    Ajuraan
    Hintire
  Guggundabe
    Baddi Addo
    Gaaljacal

DAAROOD
  Harti
    Majeerteen
  Ogaadeen
    Maxamad Zubeer

Key

CLAN-FAMILIES
Confederations
Clans

---

*Adapted from I. M. Lewis, *The Somali Lineage System and the Total Genealogy* (London, 1957), pp. 71–89.

**Most clan-families consist of several confederations, which in turn are made up of several clans. No attempt is made here to list all of the confederations or all of the clans within each, nor to portray the precise collateral or uterine relationships among them.

Horn to the western Ogaadeen, and from the Gulf of Aden coast to the wells of Wajir in northern Kenya. The Hawiyya, though concentrated in the central plains and eastern coastal regions of the Peninsula, were represented by clans that had made their way to pastures west of the Jubba River. The powerful Biimaal clan of Marka district claimed distant links with the Dir clan-family, most of whose constituent clans inhabited the harsh plains of the northwest, between Djibouti and Harar. Only the Isxaaq in the heart of what would become the British Somaliland Protectorate, and the Digil and Rahanwiin of the interriver region of southern Somalia, were confined to one section of the vast Horn (see map 1).

Even though every Somali belonged to one of these clan-families and could identify with a large number of people who claimed a common ancestor, these groupings were too large and too dispersed to be effective units of political action. Somalis identified more immediately with the clans into which each clan-family was subdivided. At least fifty major Somali clans could be identified at the end of the nineteenth century, numbering anywhere from a few thousand to ten or twenty thousand members. Some of the largest clans, like the Ogaadeen or Majeerteen, contained sub-clans and lineages which might themselves be larger than many neighboring clans. These large sub-clans themselves functioned as corporate political units, sometimes opposing one another, occasionally uniting against a rival clan.

Clans were typically the largest exogamous units in Somali society: marriage outside the clan was encouraged because it helped to widen the circle of potential allies that could be called upon in time of need. The clan was also a territorial unit. There were certain grazing areas associated with each clan and "home wells" to which clan members returned during the dry season. However, because nomadic movements were conditioned by unpredictable and widely scattered rains, and because pasture was regarded as a gift from God to all Somalis, herding units from different clans were often interspersed in the same district. Clansmen were often widely separated from one another through much of the year. Still, in times of scarcity or prolonged drought, kinsmen were more likely to join together to protect their customary grazing areas from encroachment by members of other clans. For ultimately it was the effective fighting strength of a clan that determined its right to territory.

The mobilization of kinsmen for joint military action or resource management usually occurred at yet another level of political segmentation, that of the *diya*-paying group. This was a group within a clan of patrilineal kinsmen—usually from the same or several closely related lineages—who agreed to work and fight together and, most important, to pay the *diya*, or bloodwealth, in common. Bloodwealth was the compensation, traditionally measured in numbers of animals, that was due to an aggrieved person and his kinsmen. If one member of a *diya* group killed or injured a person from another such group, the aggressor's group collectively paid compensation to the victim or the victim's kin, with the agressor himself paying the greatest share from his own herds. Similarly, the *diya* group distributed proportionately among its members any compensation received. For example, the amount of compensation traditionally assigned for killing a man was one hundred camels. The clan within which the murder took place would be expected to raise the bloodwealth from the members of the murderer's *diya*-paying group. The murderer himself might be asked to contribute fifty from his own or his brothers' herds; the rest of the *diya* unit would contribute the remaining fifty. Clan elders or religious notables usually oversaw the transfer of the bloodwealth to the victim's kin group and its redistribution within that group. Probably fifty camels would go to the victim's wife, children, and brothers and the remainder to more distant kinsmen.

In the absence of any external authority, the alternative to bloodwealth payments was almost always retaliation in kind for insult, injury, or homicide and, more often than not, the start of a prolonged feud between the two parties that could eventually draw in other *diya* groups and sometimes the entire clan. The institution of *diya* groups thus reduced the incidence of open conflict in Somali society. These groups also afforded each individual the moral and material backing of kinsmen pledged to support or to atone for fellow members' actions and helped to define more precisely the circle of kinsmen who could be called upon in times of stress. Typically numbering anywhere from a few hundred to a few thousand kinsmen, *diya* groups were considerably smaller than most clans and more likely to act jointly on a day-to-day basis. A man's "most binding and most frequently mobilized loyalty" was to his *diya*-paying group.[11]

While membership in particular *diya*-paying groups could

11. I. M. Lewis, *Modern History*, p. 11. The contract implied in the *diya* system is discussed more fully in I. M. Lewis, *A Pastoral Democracy* (London, 1961), esp. chap. 6.

change over time, they were the most basic political units in the larger segmentary society and could be found in some form throughout the Somalilands. Even the Somalis' centuries-long exposure to Islam, which holds individuals morally responsible for their own actions, did not erode the strength of the *diya* system. Only pressure from successive colonial and postcolonial governments has suceeded in diminishing the importance of though not completely eliminating the *diya* group as a unit of corporate responsibility in Somali pastoral society.

It is clear that the effective units of social and political cooperation in precolonial Somalia varied according to the circumstances. A man might identify with his entire clan when its wells or grazing lands were threatened by another clan but act on behalf of his own lineage or *diya*-paying group in a feud within the clan over access to dry-season grazing reserves or over the distribution of booty taken in a livestock raid. On still other occasions, a man's interest might compel him to join forces with his wife's kinsmen against a segment of his own lineage. Thus though kinship and the *diya* contract helped to define the range of people that might command one's loyalty at different times, friends of one occasion could easily become foes of another. The fluid and pragmatic nature of Somali politics is summed up in the proverb, "If you love a person, love him moderately, for you do not know whether you will hate him one day; on the other hand, if you hate someone, hate him moderately also, for you do not know whether you will love him one day." Even more succinct is the Somali proverb

> I and my clan against the world.
> I and my brother against the clan.
> I against my brother.

In later chapters I will describe the operation of Somali clan politics in some concrete historical situations. Here I want only to point out how the relationship between kinship and territoriality differed for northern and southern Somalia. In the south the relative abundance of ground water and cultivable land gave rise to a mixed farming/pastoral economy. The wide-ranging movements characteristic of nomadism in the north were more circumscribed in the inter-river area of the south, and pastoral life frequently revolved around small villages of riverine or dry-land farmers. In these circumstances, attachment to the land was correspondingly stronger and is reflected in the fact that the term *curad* ("first-born"), which in northern Somalia referred to a clan's senior lineage in terms of the order of birth of its founder, in the south was applied to that clan segment believed to have first occupied the land. The *curad* in the south typically had the privilege of initiating joint clan activities, leading clan warriors into battle, and ritually granting access to farm and pasture land for use by newly arrived pastoral immigrants.[12]

Indeed, it appears that many southern "clans" were formed by the coming together of nomadic groups of disparate genealogical origins over a considerable period of time.[13] The immigrants occupied adjacent tracts of grazing and farm land and made alliances with neighbors who were not necessarily agnatic kinsmen. The result was a series of confederated communities whose cohesiveness rested as much on territorial proximity as on genealogical affiliation. In contrast to the strictly pastoral regions of the north where clans could best be defined as kinship groups which might but need not be territorial units, the typical clan in the south was a territorial unit which might but need not be an actual kinship group.

Language and Society

The distinctions in the economic and sociopolitical organization of different parts of Somalia overlap to some extent with distinctions in the linguistic organization of the country. The Somali language is a member of the East Cushitic branch of the Cushitic subfamily of African languages. Within the East Cushitic branch, Somali seems to share the greatest number of linguistic features with Rendille—a language spoken today by pastoralists living east of Lake Turkana in Kenya—and with Boni, which is spoken by a few remnant populations of hunters and gatherers scattered throughout southern Somalia and eastern Kenya.[14] Neither of these peoples figures prominently in the later precolonial history of Somalia. Far more important historically have been speakers of Oromo (Galla), the largest of the East Cushitic language communities. The Oromo occupy a vast arc of territory along the western and southwestern margins of the Somali-

12. See I. M. Lewis, "From Nomadism to Cultivation: The Expansion of Political Solidarity in Southern Somalia," in Mary Douglas and Phyllis M. Kaberry, eds., *Man in Africa* (London, 1969), pp. 70–71.

13. Ibid., pp. 67–72. Massimo Colucci, *Principi di diritto consuetudinario della Somalia italiana meridionale* (Florence, 1924), pp. 49–62, 171–204.

14. Harold C. Fleming, "Baiso and Rendille: Somali outliers," *Rassegna di studi etiopici* 20 (1964): 35–96.

lands, and they form the largest single ethnic group in modern Ethiopia. The majority of Oromo along the Somali frontier were cattle-keeping pastoralists, who frequently came into conflict with their Somali neighbors over grazing land. Somali-Oromo interaction, which involved not only warfare but also trade and occasionally intermarriage, has been an important factor in the history of the Horn since at least 1500.[15]

The Somali language itself contains a number of regional dialects which have only begun to be studied by linguists.[16] Somalis themselves distinguish two major divisions within their language community, characterized by the different pronunciations of the question "What did you say?" Speakers of *May tiri?* are concentrated in the interriver area of the south. Their speech is not immediately intelligible to those who speak *Maxaad tiri?*, which is spoken everywhere else in the country. There are, however, at least three major subdialects within the *Maxaad* group: that spoken in the northern third of the country and to some extent in the area west of the Jubba River, where large numbers of northern Somalis have settled since the end of the nineteenth century; that spoken in central Somalia and which was in the past associated with members of the Hawiyya clan family; and a variant of the latter which is spoken in the towns of the Benaadir (southern Somali coast) and their immediate hinterlands.

We can only speculate now on the historical significance of these regional dialect differences. Current scholarship suggests that the two major divisions could have separated as long ago as two thousand years.[17] If this is true, then regional subcultures within the Horn may be older than many have suspected. Moreover, one Somali scholar has reported the existence of at least seventeen subdialects *(afguri)* within the *May tiri?* or southern division.[18] This suggests either that

15. The history of the Oromo/Somali borderlands has yet to be written. While there are many logistic, linguistic, and political obstacles to conducting field research in these areas, they should provide fascinating ethnographic and linguistic data.

16. Cerulli, *Somalia* 2: 171–75, and M. M. Moreno, *Il somalo della Somalia* (Rome, 1955), pp. iii–viii, provide overviews of the dialect situation in Somalia.

17. Personal communication from Harold C. Fleming. For an excellent discussion of recent linguistic work on the East Cushitic languages, see Bernd Heine, "The Sam Languages: A History of Somali, Rendille, and Boni," *Afroasiatic Linguistics*, vol. 9, no. 2 (1978), pp. 1–93.

18. Personal communication from Hussein Shaykh Ahmed "Kaddare" of the Somali Academy of Arts and Sciences, Muqdisho.

southern Somalia represents the earliest location of Somali-speakers
in the eastern Horn (and hence the area where greatest linguistic
differentiation has occurred) or that the interriver region was a refuge
area for diverse groups of nomads who migrated there from different
parts of the Horn. Current linguistic research may help to clarify the
historical picture. For now, we can only say that Somali society consisted of a great variety of subgroups whose linguistic diversity suggests a complex early history. Despite considerable interaction on the
ground, many Somali communities clearly retained their distinctive
linguistic characteristics.

Islam in Somali Society

If varied economic pursuits, clan loyalties, and linguistic
differentiation attest to the fragmented nature of the Somalis' historical experience, adherence to Islam seems to have offered a unifying
force. Virtually all Somalis are professed Muslims, and despite growing pan-African sentiments within the country, many continue to
point to their genealogies as evidence of a common Middle-Eastern
origin. At various times in the past Islam has been a rallying point for
Somalis. Members of several clans joined together to fight under the
banner of the sixteenth-century Muslim leader Ahmed Gurey, who
nearly succeeded in conquering the Christian kingdom of Ethiopia.[19]
In the early twentieth century, many Somalis responded to the call of
the dervish hero Muhammad Abdullah Hassan to shed their clan
loyalties and oppose the colonial invaders in the name of Islam.[20]
Somali religious leaders also figured prominently in the founding of
the first modern political party, the Somali Youth League, which
called for the submergence of clan and regional loyalties and for the
unification of the Somalilands.[21]

Nevertheless, though Islam has periodically served to unite So-
malis against foreign enemies, the history of its penetration into the
Horn of Africa actually militated against its totally transforming
Somali society. Islam spread by different means and at different rates

19. Hersi, "The Arab Factor," pp. 136–41, 205–12; Trimingham, *Islam in Ethiopia*, pp. 84–91.
20. See chap. 6, n. 1, for a list of the literature on the dervish movement.
21. Hersi, "The Arab Factor," pp. 287–89; I. M. Lewis, *Modern History*, pp.
121–22.

to different regions of the country. Its penetration through the agency of countless itinerant saints had the effect of localizing religious authority and religious practice. Moreover, the competition of the various Islamic Orders *(tariiqas)* which spread into the Somali interior in the later nineteenth century often worked against the development of a united Islamic front, even while their *khaliifa*s preached the brotherhood of the faithful.[22] Islam's universalism has certainly contributed to the Somalis' consciousness of their common identity as a people, but Somali society has in turn given Islam as practiced in the Horn a distinctly Somali character.

Town and Country

An introduction to Somali society must include some mention of the coastal towns which have played an important if often ill-understood role in the history of the Somali Peninsula. As early as the first century A.D., the *Periplus of the Erythraean Sea,* a traveler's handbook probably compiled at Alexandria by Greek traders, recorded the existence of trading emporia along the Somali coast. Then, as today, the coastal towns were outlets for the incense, aromatic woods, and ivory for which the Horn has always been famous.[23] However, our first real glimpses into town life date from the Islamic era, when religious refugees and traders from the Middle East founded or settled in towns along the Somali littoral. There they introduced Islamic institutions, forms of architecture, and some small handicraft industries that survived into the twentieth century.

The urban cultures which evolved in the largest of these towns —Seylac (Zeila) along the Gulf of Aden coast, and Muqdisho, Marka, and Baraawe along the Indian Ocean—contrasted with the nomadic culture around them. Their populations, though presumably always containing some local Somalis, were made up largely of Arabs, Persians, and Indians, who lived in one- or two-storied stucco dwellings with their kinsmen, dependents, and slaves. From the Arab traveler Ibn Battuta we learn that in 1331 Muqdisho was governed by a council of elders together with a religious hierarchy headed by a sultan.[24] The

22. See chap. 6, pp. 235–37.
23. For a recent reassessment of the evidence in the *Periplus,* see Gervase Mathew, "The Dating and Significance of the 'Periplus of the Erythraen Sea,'" in Chittick and Rotberg, eds., *East Africa and the Orient.*
24. Freeman-Grenville, *The East African Coast,* pp. 27–31.

same traveler's mention of a flourishing local textile industry suggests that Muqdisho was probably already housing an artisan caste of weavers. Six centuries later, the cloth industry was still in operation; Luigi Robecchi-Brichetti's careful census of 1903 revealed that nearly one-third of Muqdisho's population consisted of slaves, a pattern of social and economic stratification that in all likelihood had characterized town life from the beginning.[25]

During the nineteenth century, a period for which we have at least some written evidence, none of the coastal towns had more than a few thousand permanent inhabitants. Whether they were significantly larger in medieval times will only be known after more extensive archaeological investigation. We do know that Seylac was for a century or more part of the Islamic state of Ifat, and that Muqdisho under the Muzaffar dynasty (16th–17th centuries) was an outpost of the powerful Ajuraan confederacy.[26] But apart from these periods of political florescence, when the town populations may have been augmented through the presence of administrators and their dependents, the urban centers were essentially commercial entrepôts in the western Indian Ocean trading system.

Life in the coastal towns followed the rhythm of the monsoons. Townsmen depended for their livelihood largely on the arrival of dhows carried by the monsoon winds from Arabia and the shores of the Persian Gulf. The dhow trade brought prosperity to many urban traders. They were able to furnish their households with glassware, ceramics, silver, and tapestries from abroad. While we might consider these townsmen to have been the most cosmopolitan of the Peninsula's inhabitants in the precolonial period, the rural nomads often saw them as secretive and insular. The town dwellers' lack of sophistication about the customs of the countryside is proverbial and the subject of a common Somali jest: "If a man (of the town) lives long enough, he will get to see everything—even a camel being born!" There were undoubtedly many townsmen like the Indian merchant of Marka interviewed by an Italian governor in 1908 who had never set foot outside the town's walls, despite having lived there for twenty years.[27]

25. Luigi Robecchi-Brichetti, *Lettere dal Benadir* (Milan, 1904), pp. 67–92.

26. Trimingham, *Islam in Ethiopia*, pp. 66–76; Cerulli, *Somalia* 1: 40, 63–64; and 2: 245–49; Hersi, "The Arab Factor," pp. 194–98.

27. Tommaso Carletti, *Attraverso il Benadir* (Viterbo, 1910), p. 51.

Most Somali nomads shunned life in the treeless, cramped quarters of the coastal towns, but they nevertheless carried on a lively commerce with them. There were definite economic and social links between the rural hinterland and the urban centers of the littoral, and goods and information passed readily across the cultural divide between town and country. In chapter 2 we will see that Somali towns were important outlets for products from the pastoral sector and were places of refuge for nomads in times of drought. Most nomadic clans had allies within the towns who acted as their *abbaans* (host/protectors) when they came to trade there. Jewelry, weapons, and cloth fashioned by urban craftsmen were regularly exchanged for incense and ivory gathered far upcountry. The importance of the towns to the nomads of the interior is also witnessed by the ruins of numerous small settlements that dot the long coastline of Somalia and that can only have existed to supply them with imported dates, rice, and metal artifacts.[28] While far more ephemeral than larger centers like Seylac and Muqdisho, these ruined towns emphasize the extent of the Somalis' historical links with the world beyond the pasture.

On the eve of the colonial period, Somali society consisted of several distinct kin, language, and economic communities. Succeeding chapters will describe how these distinct communities gradually came to share a common genealogical idiom, an attachment to Islamic Sufism, and a growing sense of territoriality. It would be misleading, however, for the historian of precolonial Somalia to take the society I have described, with all its constituent parts, as a given—that is, as the starting point for a historical analysis. Rather, Somali society ought to be regarded as the product of interactions among small groups of herdsmen, farmers, itinerant shaykhs, and townsmen who came together under diverse circumstances in the past and whose modern sense of national identity derives less from primordial sentiments than from a set of shared historical experiences. The local and regional groupings identified by ethnographers in the early twentieth century were the progeny of history as well as agents in the making of it. What processes were most critical in giving form to those groups and to the larger identity they came to possess was the subject of considerable discussion in the early twentieth century. Then, as today, historical understanding was conditioned by contemporary concerns.

28. Hersi, "The Arab Factor," pp. 107–8, 155. See also chap. 2 below, pp. 72–75.

Previous Historiography

Before 1960, most historical writing on Somalia was the by-product of research conducted by colonial officials or by scholars in the employ of colonial governments. These researchers were concerned, explicitly or implicitly, with the kinds of questions that colonial authorities everywhere were interested in, namely, how more effectively to administer their colonial subjects, or how more smoothly to implement those economic and social reforms deemed essential to fulfilling their colonial mandate. Research directed to such ends was not without scholarly merit. Oral traditions and ethnographic information gathered by these early agents of colonial rule have provided modern historians with many fruitful insights into Somali culture and society. However, most colonial researchers were not historians by training, and their work could not be expected to deal systematically with historical problems that lay manifestly beyond the scope of colonial administration and development.

The predominance of colonial concerns in the early writing of Somali history is a characteristic common to the historiography of all excolonial nations. But research into the Somali past was also burdened with another problem. As the only African country to be partitioned twice in the past one hundred years—first during the late nineteenth-century "scramble" for Africa, and again after the collapse in 1941 of Mussolini's East African Empire—Somalia was beset with a continuing series of border disputes that absorbed politicians and scholars right into the 1970s and colored all contemporaneous historical scholarship.

As a result of this colonial legacy, two sets of issues came to dominate the twentieth-century historiography of Somalia. One concerns the nature of the Somali "conquest" of the Horn of Africa, the ways in which the Somali people came to occupy their present territory. The second set of issues, closely related to the first, concerns the evolution of Somali nationalism and irredentism. Scholarly focus on these two sets of issues has, to be sure, prompted some important historical research along with several lively academic debates. Both topics have extremely important political implications for contemporary Somalis and their neighbors in the Horn. However, preoccupation with them has diverted scholars from examining other important historical themes and from adopting alternative analytical perspectives in their study of the Somali past. The historical reasons for this preoccupation with territorial conquest and irredentism merit some comment.

The issue of Somali territorial expansion was not simply an academic question for those colonial officials sent to East Africa at the end of the last century. When the Imperial British East Africa Company assumed responsibility for the administration of the region between the Jubba and Tana Rivers in 1890, they found Somali nomads continually pressing into the area from the north and east. It soon became clear that most of the Somalis in the area known as Jubaland had arrived there only within the preceding fifty years. Their advance had driven the previous occupants of the region—chiefly Oromo (Galla) pastoralists—further south toward the Tana. By 1890, some Oromo had already fled across the Tana, and those who remained on the east bank appeared in danger of being annihilated by the hard-driving Somalis. After a prolonged campaign of military expeditions against (and occasional negotiations with) Somali clans, the British succeeded in halting the Somali advance near the Tana. It became commonplace for British officials to assert that without their intervention, Somali nomads would have overrun all of eastern Kenya.[29]

East of the Jubba, Italian authorities also found their new possessions in turmoil. Large numbers of Somali pastoralists recently departed from the Ogaadeen and Bale regions of "Ethiopia" were involved in countless conflicts with the existing Somali inhabitants of the interriver area, complicating Italian efforts to pacify the colony.[30] Both Italian and British officials realized that a major cause of these late nineteenth-century migrations was Ethiopian imperial expansion: a recently reunited Ethiopian state had been dispatching armed expeditions into the lowlands to seize livestock and grain. Even though the early colonial authorities recognized the particular causes of the Somali dislocations, they nevertheless viewed them as a natural tendency of the migratory and fiercely independent nomads. Whatever the causes, they still had to grapple with the problem of containing Somali territorial expansion.

29. Richard G. Turnbull, "The Wardeh," *Kenya Police Review* (July 1957); The Earl of Lytton, *The Stolen Desert* (London, 1966), pp. 34–35.

30. E. R. Turton, "The Pastoral Tribes of Northern Kenya, 1800–1916" (Ph.D. thesis, University of London, 1970), p. 342 ff., gives a detailed account of pastoral movements across the Jubba River and links several of them to disturbances along the Ethiopian frontier.

In an era when "effective occupation" was the objective of all governments that sought to establish their claims to African territory, the Ethiopian Emperor Menilek well knew the rules of the game. His aim was to secure European recognition of his political sovereignty in the "stateless" Somali lowlands by establishing a military presence there. The various treaties negotiated by Menilek with England, Italy, and France between 1894 and 1908 all effectively recognized Ethiopia's recent military conquests. In granting Menilek recognition, the Europeans also implicitly accepted Menilek's claim that he was simply retaking land lost to Somali nomadic encroachments in the past.[31] The treaty negotiations with Ethiopia—together with those conducted by the British to stabilize the boundary between Oromo and Somali in eastern Kenya—thus reinforced the notion that political stability meant the "containment" of Somali pastoral expansion. Given the colonialists' concern for orderly administration, it is scarcely surprising that the Somalis should have been viewed as a militantly migratory society whose hunger for territory could only be arrested by strong central government action.

As the pacification of the Somalilands proceeded, colonial ethnographers began examining Somali customs, folklore, and traditional histories. They found throughout the Peninsula oral accounts of past migrations, conflicts over wells and pastures, and raids into adjoining territories.[32] Somali traditions were also replete with references to Arab ancestors; virtually every clan could point to a founder purportedly descended from an Arab immigrant, and usually one who had reached the northern Somali coast at some point in the distant past and married into the local populace. The claims of Middle Eastern origins that are widespread among the peoples of Islamic Africa were generally accepted by European scholars in the early twentieth century as containing at least a kernel of historical truth.[33] In this particular case, Somali origin traditions helped reinforce the view that the

31. Saadia Touval, *Somali Nationalism* (Cambridge, Mass., 1963), pp. 47–48; John Drysdale, *The Somali Dispute* (London, 1964), pp. 26–31.

32. For example, Colucci, *Principi*, pp. 90–139 passim, 155–76; Corrado Zoli, *Oltre-Giuba* (Rome, 1927), esp. pp. 134–50; Giuseppe Caniglia, *Genti di Somalia* (Munich, 1921), p. 95 ff. A good summary of local oral traditions regarding the Somali occupation of the south is Enrico Cerulli's "Le popolazioni della Somalia nelle tradizione storica locale"; first published in 1926, it is reprinted in *Somalia* 1: 51–69.

33. See, for example, Cerulli, *Somalia* 1: 60.

earliest Somalis had lived in or near the northern coastal districts of the Peninsula and that their descendants must have expanded gradually over the centuries to occupy the whole of the eastern Horn. Thus the Somalis' own oral record added to the emerging historical portrait of the Somalis as an ever-expanding population.

The rich corpus of Somali oral traditions enabled colonial officials to piece together the earliest outline histories of the Somali migrations. Building to a great extent on the earlier general ethnographies of Paulitschke and Ferrand,[34] these amateur historians attempted to trace the movements of the major clan-families and clans. Some of the best efforts at historical synthesis were made by little-known district officials in both the Italian and British colonies. Some of their work was summarized in colonial publications; some was never published and can be found only in the ex-colonial archives. Yet these manuscripts seem to have been read in colonial circles, and they provided the foundation for later historical analyses. Almost all early twentieth-century reconstructions stressed territorial movements as a major theme of precolonial Somali history.[35]

Unquestionably the most influential early work on the occupation and settlement of the Somali Peninsula was that of Enrico Cerulli, an eminent orientalist who also served in the Italian colonial

34. P. Paulitschke, *Beitrage zur Ethnologie und Anthropologie der Somal, Galla, und Harari* (Leipzig, 1888); G. Ferrand, *Les Comalis: Matériaux d'études sur les pays musulmanes* (Paris, 1903).

35. One of the best early efforts to outline the migration history of the Somalis can be found in an unpublished manuscript by Giacomo Trevis entitled "La Somalia italiana." I saw it in the *Archivio storico dell'ex Ministero dell'Africa Italiana* (hereafter *ASMAI*) in Rome, position (pos.) 66/2, folder (f.) 20. Pt. 1, entitled "Gli habitanti della Somalia," was a carefully reasoned reconstruction of the historical relations among the various clan families of Somalia. Trevis had hoped to publish a major study on the Somali, but he was killed by a Somali in Marka in 1897, thus becoming one of the earliest casualties in colonial efforts to occupy the country.

Other noteworthy attempts by Italian officials to write Somali history on the basis of local oral sources include Gherardo Pantano, *La citta di Merca e la regione Bimal* (Leghorn, 1910); and the works cited in n. 32 above. Luigi Robecchi-Brichetti, an engineer and frequent traveler to Somalia, published a small collection of traditions from the region of Hobya as early as 1891: *Tradizione storiche dei Somali Migiurtini* (Rome).

On the British side of the border with Kenya, an important summary of Somali traditions was published by Richard G. Turnbull, "The Darod Invasion," *Kenya Police Review*, Oct. 1957, pp. 308–13.

service. Cerulli's interests included Oromo and Islamic studies as well as Somali. Between 1916 and 1948, he published nearly three dozen articles on Somali history, language, and culture, many of which must be considered seminal. Cerulli's interpretation of the Somali occupation of the Horn was based on a careful synthesis of multiple clan and local traditions and emphasized the almost incessant movement of pastoral populations through the region.[36] To be sure, Cerulli also argued that such movements rarely involved large-scale military conquests; more typically, they consisted of small clan segments infiltrating the grazing lands of other groups and attracting further migrations of kinsmen to the area. Cerulli's work also provided considerable evidence of assimilation, resource sharing, and peaceful trade between groups of pastoral immigrants and the previous hunting or agricultural occupants of the land.[37] Yet these aspects of his work received little attention in later historical writing on Somalia, which continued to focus on the origins of the Somali and the chronology of their pastoral expansion.[38]

In the period between the two world wars, colonial officials continued to collect clan traditions. Their aim was not so much to reconstruct the Somali past as to facilitate the tasks of administration and adjudication among their Somali subjects. Disputes between clans

36. A major statement of his interpretation of the Somali migrations appeared in an article first published in 1926 and reprinted in Cerulli, *Somalia* 1: 60–61:

The Somali tribes departed from the territory situated between the Gulf of Tajura and Cape Guardafui and proceeded to conquer from the Galla the central and southern regions of what is now Somalia—that is, the lower Ogaadeen, southern Italian Somalia, and the Somali portion of "Kenya Colony." These successive invasions followed two diverse routes: either along the river valleys and hence in a NW-SE direction perpendicular to the [Indian Ocean] coast; or along the chain of coastal wells situated a short distance from the Indian Ocean in a NE-SW direction. As can be seen, the invasion routes indicated in the traditions correspond to lines of resting places where permanent ground water can be found, and this is a fact which the natural configuration of the region renders absolutely certain; also perfectly credible are what traditions say about the region adjacent to the great bend of the Shabeelle River, which over the centuries has been the main object of invasions coming from the northwest as well as the place from which succeeding movements toward the south have been launched. [trans. from Italian by L.V.C.]

37. Ibid., 2: 29–30; (Rome, 1964), 3: 75–84.
38. See, for example, I. M. Lewis, "The Somali Conquest of the Horn of Africa," *Journal of African History* 1 (1960): esp. 219–21, 224–28.

over boundaries or watering rights often prompted local administrators to gather oral evidence from the disputing parties.[39] The transfer of Jubaland from the British to the Italian government in 1925 (as partial payment for Italy's contribution to the Allied effort in World War I) led to the preparation by Corrado Zoli of a substantial collection of oral traditions from the clans that had come under Italian suzerainty.[40] And the renewed efforts by the Fascist regime to develop agriculture in southern Somalia after 1923 led to increasingly detailed studies of the southern Somali clans. The strange combination of politics and ethnography typical of this period found expression in such works as that of Pietro Barile, *Colonizzazione fascista nella Somalia meridionale* (Rome, 1935). Despite its title and its opening and closing paens to Fascist vigor, tenacity, and sacrifice, the bulk of the work is a remarkable collection of oral and descriptive material not found elsewhere in the colonial literature on Somalia.

The fact that research into the Somali past was closely tied to colonial political objectives was revealed in a singularly portentous way on the eve of the Italian occupation of Ethiopia. In the early 1930s, Italian administrators posted to districts near the provisional border with Ethiopia were instructed by the colonial governor to collect detailed traditions from Somali clans whose traditional lands straddled that border. They were asked to take particular note of those clans whose seasonal movements took them along and across the territorial frontier, and whose history might support claims to pastures and wells in Ethiopian territory. The results of the inquiry were published in a top-secret document circulated to selected officials in 1932.[41] Two years later, the Italian government claimed that Walwal, a small cluster of wells situated about sixty miles west of the provisional frontier, lay in Italian territory. In December 1934, Italian and Ethiopian forces openly clashed at this desert outpost, and thus precipitated the chain of events that culminated in the Fascist inva-

---

39. For example, I. Gasparini, "Delimitazione confini sultanato Obbia," Nov. 1918, *ASMAI*, pos. 89/9, f. 32. For a published example, see Colucci, *Principi*, pp. 164–66. As late as the 1950s, during the period of Italian Trusteeship Administration in Somalia, traditions were being collected to help determine the historical relationship between feuding clans: "Rapporti fra Averghedir Saad e Soliman," by Michele Pirone, Regional Commissioner, Galcaio, 22 June 1952, AFIS Ufficio Affari Interni.

40. Zoli, *Oltre-Giuba*.

41. Regio Governo della Somalia, *Direttive per l'oltre confine*, Gubernatorial Circular n. 400 (Mogadiscio, 1932). Only 150 copies were issued.

sion of Ethiopia. Part of the Italian justification for the invasion was the desire to include Somalis beyond the border as part of "La Grande Somalia"; many clansmen from the border region were used as military auxiliaries.[42] In this instance, historical and ethnographic research nicely served the ends of empire.

The political uses made of Somali clan history by the Italians in the 1930s foreshadowed the political emphasis that would continue to dominate Somali historiography after World War II. The Italian East African Empire lasted less than five years, but its dissolution left a legacy of territorial problems that came to obsess European, Ethiopian, and Somali statesmen, and their scholarly supporters, for the next two generations. Debates over how to dispose of the former Italian colony of Somalia, and what to do with the Ogaadeen region, vexed the caretaker British Military Administration and fledgling United Nations throughout the 1940s. The frontier issue also became a major concern of the Somali Youth League, the first modern Somali political party, founded in 1945.[43] In the end, the proposal of British Foreign Minister Ernest Bevin to form a "Greater Somalia" uniting all the Somalilands was scrapped in favor of a less imaginative solution: Britain retained its northern Protectorate, the Ogaadeen was returned to Ethiopia, and former Italian Somalia became an Italian Trust Territory under United Nations supervision for a period of ten years. The Ethiopian government believed that it had successfully thwarted British schemes to "fabricate" a pan-Somali movement for its own neo-imperialistic ends. Yet Somali nationalists felt betrayed. Through the 1950s and after Somali independence in 1960, virtually all Somali political parties included in their platforms the goal of "reunification" of the Somali territories.

To the Somalis the border question was not resolved. This simmering issue naturally influenced the historiography of the late 1950s and 1960s, particularly among those writing from the Somali perspective. The most important books had a contemporary focus; indeed, they were not the works of historians but of journalists, political scientists, or former administrators. They included *The Somali Dis-*

---

42. See, for example, George W. Baer, *The Coming of the Italian-Ethiopian War* (Cambridge, Mass.: Harvard University Press, 1967), pp. 311–13.

43. The League grew out of the Somali Youth Club which was founded in 1943. On the rise of Somali nationalist political parties, see I. M. Lewis, "Modern Political Movements in Somaliland," *Africa* 28 (1958): 244–61, 344–64.

pute, by John Drysdale (London, 1964); *Somali Nationalism,* by
Saadia Touval (Cambridge, Mass., 1963); and *The Stolen Desert,* by
the Earl of Lytton (London, 1966). All of these works included chapters on Somali history presented primarily as a backdrop to discussions of the Somali drive for national unification. These influential
books helped frame the terms of the debate over Somali claims to the
Ogaadeen and, to a lesser extent, to portions of northern Kenya. The
authors saw the problem as having been caused by colonial rule.
Somali nationalism was viewed as a justifiable response to colonial
neglect of Somalia's nomads on the one hand, and to colonial boundary
manipulation on the other. Some recognition was given to the religious and cultural roots of Somali nationalism; but the greatest emphasis lay on the sense of Somali identity that had begun to emerge
at the beginning of the colonial period.

The only book-length effort by a modern historian to examine the
precolonial history of the Somali Peninsula in detail unfortunately fell
prey to the polemics of the "national" question. Jean Doresse's *Histoire sommaire de la Corne orientale de l'Afrique,* published in
1971, took the offensive against those the author viewed as apologists
for Somali irredentism. Doresse, who viewed the history of the Horn
from a distinctly Ethiopian state perspective, argued that Italian and
British colonialists had created the myth of a Somali nation to serve
their own (anti-Ethiopian) ends. Doresse's book made an effort to
refute the notion that Somalis were a distinct people before the medieval expansion of Ethiopian rule into the lowlands. He interpreted the
extremely ambiguous evidence from Ethiopian chronicles and Arab
travel accounts to argue that the ancestors of today's Somalis were
essentially a congeries of primitive tribes whose participation in the
sixteenth-century Islamic conquest of Ethiopia provided their first
experience of a larger identity. Moreover, he contended, Somali expansion into the central and southern Horn began only in the sixteenth century aided by the militant zeal of Islamic preachers and
warriors. Although Doresse was correct to argue that Somali political
unity is a relatively recent phenomenon, his refusal to acknowledge
the possibility of a precolonial cultural or political heritage in the
lowlands seriously diminishes the value of the book as an interpretation of Somali history. Admittedly his sources, which are limted to the
standard travelers' and explorers' accounts and to the official Ethiopian chronicles, have little to say about the Somalis. But he completely ignores the linguistic and ethnographic evidence of Harold C.

Fleming (1964) and Herbert S. Lewis (1966), who argued rather persuasively for an original Somali homeland in southwest Ethiopia and a Somali presence in the southern Horn long before the documented migrations of the sixteenth century.[44] What was potentially an important study of the peoples on the periphery of the Ethiopian highlands can best be considered an apologia for Ethiopia's "civilizing mission" and as yet another installment in the modern political debate over the origins of nationalism and political sovereignty in the Horn.

Most modern Somali scholarship has adopted the framework of the nationalist historiography. Since 1970, Somali historians have concentrated on documenting and interpreting their country's struggle against colonialism and imperialism, be it European or Ethiopian. Much has been written and continues to be written about the Somali national hero Muhammad Abdullah Hassan.[45] This warrior, poet, and religious leader led a twenty-one year resistance against British, Ethiopian, and Italian forces beginning in 1899; and the focus on his life and times reflects the attempts by Somali intellectuals to overcome the clan divisions of the past and to build a history around those personalities who sought to unify the nation. One consequence of this approach, however, has been a neglect by Somali scholars of the precolonial period. Only the unpublished 1977 doctoral dissertation of Ali Abdirahman Hersi—"The Arab Factor in Somali History"—departs from the territorial and nationalist framework to examine an important theme in the social and cultural history of precolonial Somalia.[46]

Conclusion

Historical writing on Somalia, both in the earlier colonial period and since Independence in 1960, has been dominated by political concerns. Colonial historians directed their attention to historical processes of expansion, occupation, and conflict—processes which affected orderly administration and the stabilization of frontiers. While the causes and nature of Somali pastoral movements *are* important themes in Somali history, attempts to document them do not tell

44. Fleming, "Baiso and Rendille"; Herbert S. Lewis, "The Origins of the Galla and Somali," *Journal of African History* 7 (1966): 27–46.
45. For references, see chap. 6, n. 1.
46. For full citation, see n. 9 above.

us very much about how Somalis adapted to the lands they came to occupy. Linguistic research over the past fifteen years has revised the view that Somalis originated in the northern regions of the Horn and have been expanding southward ever since. It is now widely accepted that the earliest Somali-speakers lived in what is today southwestern Ethiopia and that subsequent migrations have taken groups of them both north and south at different points in the past. Despite what this suggests about the long-term presence of Somali communities in the Horn, there is still a tendency to emphasize the expansionary movement of the Somali population as a whole, at the expense of the less dramatic processes of social and economic change that took place within various regions of the Peninsula. Colonial historiography, preoccupied with frontiers of expansion, has produced a somewhat unidimensional image of early Somali history. The regional diversity of the Horn suggests that it is time to look at patterns of change over more circumscribed areas and to supplement migration studies with greater attention to social history.

On the other hand, the nationalist perspective displayed in more recent writing on Somalia has tended to condense Somali history into a series of episodes that point toward a nascent political unity and to impose a certain uniformity on precolonial society that is not supported by the linguistic, ethnographic, or oral traditional evidence. The nationalist perspective frequently overlooks the distinct regional traditions within Somalia that are themselves the product of a long historical development. Moreover, by stressing the anticolonial dimension of Somali nationalism, this perspective can obscure the older, deeper, perhaps less conscious roots of Somali identity. The evidence for these deeper roots is, to be sure, fragmentary and often difficult to interpret. When it is assembled and analyzed, however, I believe it speaks eloquently of the richness and diversity of the Somali experience. One need not dismiss the very important contributions of previous historians to argue that more can be done to illuminate that experience.

2 Toward a Regional Approach to Somali Pastoral History

A warrior approaches an elder seeking guidance on how to deal with a rival clan:

Warrior: I come to ask your advice about how we may best defend ourselves.
Elder: Which of the two clans has the greater numbers?
Warrior: Ours.
Elder: Which has the better warriors?
Warrior: Ours.
Elder: Which has the stronger relations through marriage?
Warrior: Theirs.
Elder: And which lives in the direction of the wells and of the towns where water, cloth, and foodstuffs are available.
Warrior: Theirs.
Elder: Seek peace from them, then, for they have the upper hand.
    —A legendary Somali dialogue

The numerous clan traditions that provide the basic sources for our study of the Somali past are unquestionably rich in cultural insights and historical information, but the view of the past they provide is restricted; trying to make sense out of them is frequently frustrating. Somali oral traditions, like those of most African

38

societies, are concerned primarily with the social and political relationships that particular descent groups have formed with other groups in the larger society. They deal with the origins and structure of alliances, enmities, and social relations from the point of view of the clan that preserves them, and they take for granted—unlike the elder in our dialogue—the environmental constraints under which politics must operate. The historian who seeks to reconstruct larger patterns of historical change must find a unit of analysis that takes into account both the data provided by tradition and the setting in which the events described took place.

The following attempt to identify such a unit of analysis will be made in two parts. First, using evidence from the colonial period, I will describe the typical ways in which Somalis use the environmental and social resources available to them. Since it is in times of crisis that access to such resources is most vital, and recourse to them most apparent, I will focus on the herdsmen's response to drought. By drawing on recorded observations of nomadic behavior during several droughts in the first half of the twentieth century, I will construct a model of the sequence of adaptations made by herdsmen under conditions of worsening drought. The model in turn helps to illuminate the extensive networks of kinship and exchange that underpin the pastoral enterprise in the Horn.

In the second part of the chapter I will apply the regional framework derived from the drought/response analysis to the precolonial period and suggest how such a framework can help explain certain recurrent patterns of political and economic change that are only hinted at in the historical record. This chronological leap naturally raises a problem, one familiar to all historians of precolonial Africa: How appropriate is it to employ models derived from twentieth-century data to help interpret evidence from earlier periods? If I have not satisfactorily answered this question, I have at least explicitly engaged it by juxtaposing the two parts of the chapter.

Pastoralism and Drought: Adaptive Strategies in the Twentieth Century

Ecology and Transhumance

Most of the Somali Peninsula is a semi-arid lowland plain that rises almost imperceptibly into plateau country as one moves from the coast of the Indian Ocean to the interior. At first, the land-scape may appear monotonous: vast stretches of brown or red sand covered in some places by tufts of coarse grass, in others by sprawl-ing thorn bush. Here and there, lonely, flat-topped acacia trees and giant anthills stand out against the sky. Away from the well sites and rain basins, the land appears almost devoid of human habitation ex-cept for occasional clusters of beehive-shaped houses surrounded by fences made of brush. These are the hamlets of Somalia's pastoral nomads. Erected on flexible branches and covered with woven mat-ting or animal hides, the houses (aqals) are designed to be moved from place to place by their occupants, who must continually seek fresh pastures and water for their livestock.

There are many factors that influence pastoral movements across this rugged, seemingly inhospitable terrain. Rainfall is the most critical. Throughout most of the Somali Peninsula, there are two rainy seasons, which coincide roughly with the transition between the two annual monsoons. Rains are usually heaviest from late March to early June, the Somali season of gu. Gu is the ideal time for the bearing and weaning of calves, for pasture and water are abundant almost everywhere. A period of lighter rains occurs toward the end of the summer monsoon, between September and December, the Somali season of dayr. Between these two rainy seasons, there are frequently months when no rain at all falls. Particularly harsh is the jiilaal, spanning the months from December to March when water shortages almost invariably bring some livestock deaths and place great stress on the pastoral population as a whole.

Rainfall is highly variable from year to year and from place to place. It can reach 600–700 mm. per year on the southern interriver plateau and in the higher altitudes of the northern Ogo mountain range, while some parts of the northeast average less than 30 mm. per year.[1] But it is the unpredictability of the rains from year to year in any particular locale which makes pastoral life in the Horn so precari-ous. Localized droughts occur somewhere in Somalia virtually every

1. Virtually all the meteorological data that was recorded at different locales throughout Somalia from the early 1900s to 1958 is assembled and analyzed in Amilcare Fantoli, *Contributo all climatologia della Somalia* (Rome, 1961). The author kindly provided me with a copy of this massive and difficult-to-obtain volume.

A concise survey of Somali climate and rainfall patterns in English is "The Horn of Africa," in J. F. Griffiths, ed., *World Survey of Climatology*, vol. 8: *Africa* (New York, 1972).

Somali nomads rarely ride their camels, but use them to transport their household goods—and even the frames of their houses—from one grazing site to another.

When a suitable campsite is found, the portable houses (aqals) are erected in a cluster and surrounded by a thorn fence. (Courtesy of Alphonso A. Castagno)

year; and at least six times in this century alone, droughts lasting two years or more have produced famine over extensive regions of the country.[2] In general, rainfall totals occur below the annual mean more often than they occur above it, and so the typical pattern for most districts is one in which a year of exceptionally high rainfall is followed by several relatively dry years.[3]

It is these conditions that make geographical mobility a necessity for the majority of the country's inhabitants. Only along the Jubba and Shabeelle Rivers is permanent cultivation possible. In certain high rainfall areas between the rivers, dry-land farming is practiced; but even here, it is estimated that rain-fed farmlands experience crop failure on the average of two years in every five because of inadequate or unseasonal rainfall.[4] To the herdsman, this makes agriculture an even riskier enterprise than herding. "The farmer cannot drive his fields to the place where the rain is falling," states a popular proverb, and for this reason, even those Somalis who engage in seasonal cultivation maintain livestock as a form of mobile capital.

Although each region of Somalia has particular land forms and vegetational features that influence the patterns of pastoral movement, there are certain general features of Somali nomadism.[5] Through most of the year, the basic herding group, or *reer*, which typically consists of one hundred or more animals and two or more herdsmen and their families, moves as a discrete unit. During the *gu*

2. Brief descriptions of the major Somali droughts in the twentieth century, including that of 1973–75, can be found in I. M. Lewis, ed., *Abaar: The Somali Drought* (London, 1975), esp. pp. 1–2, 11–14, 20–22, 26–29.

3. J. F. Griffiths and C. F. Hemming, *A Rainfall Map of Eastern Africa and Southern Arabia*, East African Meteorological Department Memoir, vol. 3, no. 10 (Nairobi, 1963).

4. Thomas P. Ahrens, *A Reconnaissance Ground Water Survey of Somalia, East Africa*, U.S. Economic Co-operative Administration (Rome, 1951), p. 13.

5. There are a number of excellent regional studies of pastoral transhumance in the Horn. For the area of former British Somaliland, see John A. Hunt, *A General Survey of the Somali–land Protectorate 1944–1950* (Hargeisa, 1951), esp. pp. 121–75; and I. M. Lewis, *A Pastoral Democracy* (London, 1961), pp. 31–89. For the Majeerteen region, there is T. M. Bettini, *L'Allevamento del bestiame in Migiurtina* (Florence, 1941); the central peninsula receives excellent coverage in Gian Antonio Triulzi and Alberto Bassoni, "Relazione zootecnica ed idrologica del Mudugh, 1952–53," Somalia, no. 1571, Centro di Documentazione, Istituto Agronomico d'Oltremare (Florence), cyclostyled. The early study of Francesco Provenzale, *L'Allevamento del bestiame nella nostra Somalia* (Rome, 1914), remains the classic work on cattle nomadism in southern Somalia.

season, the *reer*s leave their home wells to take advantage of the fresh grass that springs up almost miraculously following the onset of the rains. In the north and center of the Peninsula, they trek away from permanent coastal wells and mountain springs toward the rain-fed grasslands of the interior (the Hawd, Ogaadeen, and Mudug plains). Some *reer*s may travel several hundred miles in a single season. If the rains are sustained, the camel-herders of these regions will remain in distant pastures through the summer months and await the shorter autumn *(dayr)* rains. In the cattle-breeding regions to the south, there are two annual movements away from home wells or riverbanks (where the dreaded tse-tse fly multiplies during the rains) to the rich pastures of the interriver plateau. The distances traversed by the cattle nomads are considerably shorter than those covered by the camel nomads and permit them to return to the home watering sites twice a year. After the fall rainy season, herdsmen throughout the Peninsula make their way back to the home wells to wait out the long, dry *jiilaal*. During these winter months, the component *reer*s of a given clan tend to concentrate around the wells with their flocks of sheep and goats, or with their herds of cattle. Young men, however, periodically drive the camels out on long forays in search of whatever nourishment the parched land can still offer. *Jiilaal* is the harshest season of the year. Forage is scarce and water jealously measured out; tempers are short and conflicts more likely to erupt.

Home wells and rainy-season pastures are the major foci of the nomads' annual migratory orbits, but, in the course of their migrations, nomads must take into account other climatic, ecological, and political factors. Among these are the quality and distribution of ground water en route; the quantity and nutritional value of browse and grass; the presence of salt licks; the variable distribution of the seasonal rains; the proximity of kinsmen whose military assistance might be required to exploit disputed terrain; the potential for conflict with nomads of other clans; and in some areas, the dangers of insect-borne diseases.

Much specialized botanical and meteorological knowledge is conserved in traditions specific to each region of the country. Virtually every nomadic clan has its recognized weather-lore experts *(cilmi curraaf)*. These are usually older men who have inherited knowledge of astronomy, meteorology, and animal husbandry from their forebears and who, during their own lifetimes, keep records of drought, rainfall patterns, and the changing qualities of the grazing areas frequented by their kinsmen. Their advice is often encapsulated in poetry or sayings of the following sort:

> If the *gu* rains fall
> And are successful,
> My herd should be taken
> To the red sand country
> Which is best for grazing.[6]

The weather-lore expert also calculates the arrival of certain propitious times such as *dambasamo,* the night in the middle of autumn when the rams are let loose to mate with the ewes. Lambs conceived on that night will be born about 150 days later, which should be in the middle of the *gu* (spring) rains.

Although most of the calculations of the weather-lore expert are grounded in experience and empirical observation, he is also usually something of a forecaster and astrologer. The following saying from the Mudug region of central Somalia is typical of the expert's predictions:

> The year of the successful rains is that in which *Dirir* [the star Arcturus] is slightly behind the moon in the early part of the night but in which the two become parallel in the sky throughout the second half of the night.[7]

In the calculus of pastoral decision-making, the weather-lorist is frequently consulted and his wisdom highly regarded. His expertise helps insure that nomadic groups are operating in an environment that has been well-charted by experience and tradition.

In moving over the land, each *reer* tends to choose campsites that are included within the territory of its particular clan. This territory is vaguely bounded by the clan's home wells and by its most distant rainy-season pastures, which may be shared with a number of other clans. Within each clan territory, individual *reer*s pursue their seasonal rounds, periodically merging with and separating from other (usually related) *reer*s alongside whom they erect their *aqal*s. Pastoral movements typically are adjusted to produce a minimum of friction between herding units and between the larger lineage segments

6. Muusa H. I. Galaal, "Stars, Seasons and Weather in Somali Pastoral Traditions," unpublished ms., p. 60.
7. Ibid., p. 29.

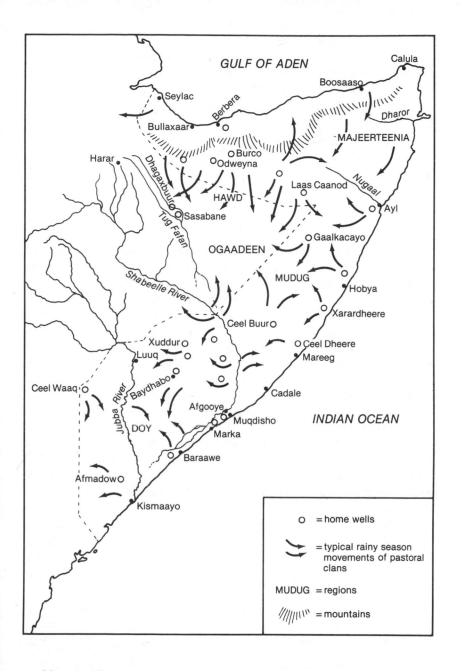

Map 2. *Major patterns of Somali transhumance (twentieth century)*

of which they form part, but even a local drought can have repurcus-
sions on the nomads of adjacent districts. Interaction between *reer*s
is inevitable. Such interaction may take the form of temporary sharing of pasture or water resources; of formal treaties of protection and
clientship; or of conflict leading to feud. Entire lineages may be drawn
into treaties or disputes involving their component *reer*s. The situation on the ground is never completely stable, and as a result, political
conditions in a grazing area will vary from year to year.

Pastoral Trade and Commerce

Unlike many of the better-known pastoral societies that
have been described by anthropologists, the Somalis historically could
not be considered large-scale traders of livestock. Although they were
outstanding breeders of camels, cattle, and horses, they never raised
animals specifically to meet the needs of any large nonpastoral population. Periodically a few Somali camels were exported across the Gulf
of Aden to Arabia, and Duarte Barbosa includes horses in his list of
trade goods in Muqdisho in the early sixteenth century.[8] In addition,
the Garre, who were renowned as breeders of burden camels, did
supply the Somali and Oromo caravaneers of the Jubba Basin in the
eighteenth century and probably much earlier.[9] But the regular export of livestock for foreign consumption, even on a modest scale,
does not appear to antedate the establishment of a British outpost at
Aden in 1839. Along the Benaadir, the export of animal products in
substantial quantities dates from the rise of Zanzibar as a major
international emporium in the early nineteenth century.[10]

8. Duarte Barbosa, *A Description of the Coasts of East Africa and Malabar
in the Beginning of the Sixteenth Century*, trans. E. J. Stanley (London, 1866), p. 16.
    9. The early political history of the Garre is summarized in E. R. Turton, "Bantu,
Galla, and Somali Migrations in the Horn of Africa: A Reassessment of the Juba/Tana
Area," *Journal of African History* 16 (1975): 528–31. On the role of the Garre as
caravaneers, see Ugo Ferrandi, *Lugh: Emporio commerciale sul Giuba* (Rome, 1903),
pp. 113, 150–51, 341–67 passim.
    10. Livestock on the hoof is not listed among the prominent exports of northern
Somalia in any of the medieval sources examined by Ali Abdirahman Hersi, although
the renowned traveler Ibn Battuta saw livestock from Muqdisho in the Maldive Islands
in the fourteenth century. See Ali Abdirahman Hersi, "The Arab Factor in Somali History: The Origins and Development of Arab Enterprise and Cultural Influences in the
Somali Peninsula" (Ph.D. diss., University of California, Los Angeles, 1977), pp. 142–76.

The pastoral economy of the Horn was subsistence-oriented and almost self-sufficient in most years even during the *jiilaal,* when camel's milk frequently provided the sole sustenance for young herdsmen in the camel camps. Somali nomads occasionally traded goats, hides, or clarified butter to obtain such nonpastoral products as rice, tea, tobacco, cloth, and jewelry. In the northern part of the country, these goods were available annually at the winter bazaars in the coastal towns and periodically from itinerant traders who set up makeshift shelters near water holes or *wadi*s in the interior.[11] These petty traders had to adjust their operations to the movements of the nomads, for external markets had little influence on the pastoral cycle.[12] Even in the better-watered areas of the south, where small permanent villages dotted the local landscape, trade between nomads and farmers seems to have been more a by-product of the pastoral cycle than a vital part of it. As nomads gathered near riverbanks and well sites for the dry season, they might part with a few head of livestock in exchange for beans, durra, or maize, providing the *dayr* rains had produced a sufficient harvest. Something of a symbiotic relationship does seem historically to have evolved between a few pastoral clans and groups of "client-cultivators" along the middle Shabeelle River.[13] But there is no evidence of the large-scale production of livestock for sedentary markets that typified, for example, the

11. I. M. Lewis, "Lineage Continuity and Modern Commerce in Northern Somaliland," in Paul Bohannan and George Dalton, eds., *Markets in Africa* (Evanston, 1962).

12. Analyzing the livestock trade of Somalia just before World War I, an Italian economist starkly wrote, "The sale of livestock is never determined by demand and by (market) prices but rather by the seasons and by the necessity of providing for everyday needs—that is, predominantly according to the supply." Romolo Onor, *La Somalia italiana* (Turin, 1925), p. 256.

Paul Baxter groups the Somali with a number of other East African pastoral populations which he calls "pure" pastoralists, i.e., those in which productive efforts are devoted almost entirely to stock management, in which little nonpastoral food is consumed, and where few alternative occupations are available outside the nomadic sector. Of these "pure" pastoralists, Baxter says, "There seems to be no evidence that their annual cycles or the division of labour were affected in any way by a need for non-pastoral products, or any need to coordinate their movements to the requirements of sedentary people." See P. T. W. Baxter, "Some Consequences of Sedentarization for Social Relationships," in Theodore Monod, ed., *Pastoralism in Tropical Africa,* p. 214.

13. Enrico Cerulli, *Somalia: Scritti vari editi ed inediti,* 3 vols. (Rome, 1959), 2: 115–21; (Rome, 1964), 3: 75–84, 87–89.

regional economies of the West African Sahel or the mixed economies of South Persia.[14]

Nevertheless, despite the low level of commercialization that characterized Somali pastoralism right up to the 1950s, Somali nomads were never isolated from external markets. There is considerable evidence to show that caravan routes have long linked remote parts of the nomadic interior to the old towns of the Indian Ocean and Red Sea coasts.[15] Livestock may have formed only a small fraction of the goods carried along these routes; but incense and aromatic woods from the north, and ivory and rhinoceros horn from the south were always in great demand as far away as India and the Persian Gulf. Ivory was typically gathered by small groups of specialized hunters, but the many varieties of incense were harvested and marketed by nomads in conjunction with their normal dry-season activities.[16] Many pastoral lineages specialized in the transport of these products and thus were tied into the regional commercial networks that annually carried goods from far upcountry to the coast.

Furthermore, the exigencies of the pastoral cycle itself brought many nomads into contact with the major trading centers of the Peninsula. Every year between January and March the sleepy coastal towns of Berbera and Seylac came to life. Their populations doubled and trebled as nomads from the interior moved in and erected their portable *aqal*s around the outskirts of the towns. The occasion was

14. Gellner formulates the distinction as "simple" vs. "symbiotic" nomadism, and he sees the latter as characteristic of Middle Eastern pastoralists. Ernest Gellner, "Introduction: Approaches to Nomadism," in Nelson, ed., *The Desert and the Sown*, p. 2. For an example of nomadic-sedentary exchange in Iran, see Fredrik Barth, *Nomads of South Persia* (Boston: Little, Brown, and Co., 1961), esp. pp. 93–111. On the Sahel, see Paul E. Lovejoy and Stephen Baier, "The Desert-Side Economy of the Central Sudan," *International Journal of African Historical Studies* 8 (1975): 551–81.

15. Hersi, "The Arab Factor," pp. 171–76, 234–35; Mordechai Abir, "Caravan Trade and History in the Northern Parts of East Africa," *Paideuma* 14 (1968): 103–20; J. M. Watson, "The Historical Background to the Ruined Towns in the West of the Protectorate," *Somaliland Journal*, vol. 1, no. 2 (Dec. 1955), pp. 120–25.

16. For the harvesting and trade in incense, see Rolando Guidotti, "L'Incenso nella Migiurtinia," *L'Agricoltura coloniale*, vol. 24, no. 10 (1930). Other resins and woods that were periodically collected for sale in coastal markets are discussed by Andrea Branca, "Le piante spontanee della Somalia e la loro utilizzazione economica," *Rivista di agricoltura subtropicale e tropicale*, vol. 54, nos. 4–6, 7–9 (Apr.–Sept. 1960), pp. 608–51.

the annual bazaar, which was made possible by the convenient convergence of two perennial phenomena: the onset of *jiilaal,* which drove nomadic *reer*s to their dry-season wells along the coast, and the northeast monsoons, which carried the dhows of Asian traders to that same coast in search of incense, ivory, ostrich feathers, and animal hides. These seasonal traders brought with them dates, rice, and sugar—all welcome supplements to the nomads' customary diet of milk and meat.[17]

The well-established historical links between pastoralists and merchants are attested to by the social composition of many of the Somali coastal towns. The small urban populations typically consisted of Somalis of diverse clan and lineage affiliations, together with a number of foreigners who had intermarried with local women. There were both social and economic ties between townsmen and the nomads. Town residents frequently possessed camels that were grazed in distant pastures by agnates or affines; as part of *diya*-paying groups, they paid their share of the costs incurred by kinsmen's marriages, homicides, or injuries.[18] Townsmen also acted as *abbaan*s (host/protectors) to inland traders when the latter needed to transact business at the coast; and reciprocally they enjoyed protection and assistance as guests *(marti)* when they traveled upcountry.[19] Such customary ties, though barely manifest in normal times, could be extremely vital in situations of economic hardship, as will be seen below.

Herd Size and Management Strategies

It has been estimated that an average Somali family (a man, his wife, and three children) required 10–20 camels, 50–60 sheep and goats, or 15–20 head of cattle to subsist in the normally harsh environment of the Horn. Many family herds, however, were three or four times this size, and a few holdings were much larger

17. Nineteenth-century descriptions of market-season activities in Seylac (Zeila) and Berbera are conveniently collected in Richard Pankhurst, "The Trade of the Gulf of Aden Ports of Africa in the Nineteenth and Early Twentieth Centuries," *Journal of Ethiopian Studies* 3 (Jan. 1965): 36–63 passim.

18. I. M. Lewis, *A Pastoral Democracy,* pp. 92–95.

19. For a fuller discussion of the role of *abbaan*s and brokers, see chap. 5, pp. 156–59.

still.[20] Given the low level of commercialization noted above, the accumulation of livestock recorded by many observers of the Somali scene can best be explained as a form of social capital used in bride-wealth payments, in collective *diya* compensation, and in attracting allies or clients, or as a hedge against hard times.

Most recent analyses have stressed the importance of large herds as a form of disaster insurance.[21] The reasoning here is that by "hoarding" large numbers of animals in good years, *reer*s insured that at least some livestock would survive the bad. Moreover, in good times, herdsmen could lend some of their surplus animals to friends or neighbors or use them to contract a favorable marriage for a family member—both forms of alliance-building. The social alliances built up through these transactions could then be called upon in time of need. Individual families whose herds were lost to drought could approach affines or allies for assistance in replenishing their breeding stock, or a group of brothers could sell some of their surplus animals to obtain rice or dates from a trading center to help see them through a period when milk supplies were low.

There is evidence that many Somali nomadic groups not only maintained large herds to hedge against the possibility of natural disaster but also practiced a limited form of range management. In the relatively densely populated plains of southern Somalia, for example, herdsmen avoided pastures containing certain varieties of hardy grasses during the rainy seasons in order to insure their availability for the livestock during *jiilaal.*[22] In the Mudug (central region), particular pastures were set aside exclusively for dry-season use by

20. Estimates on basic subsistence requirements and actual herd sizes can be found in a number of sources. See, for example, I. M. Lewis, *Peoples of the Horn of Africa* (London, 1955), pp. 67–68; Leo Silberman, "Somali Nomads," *International Social Science Journal* 11 (1959): 570–71; Z. A. Konczacki, "Nomadism and Economic Development of Somalia," *Canadian Journal of African Studies* 1 (1967): 170. Estimates of herd size from the early colonial period (e.g., Provenzale, *L'Allevamento del bestiame,* pp. 157–58) are consistent with the more recent figures, suggesting that both ideal and actual domestic livestock holdings per family have remained fairly constant through the twentieth century.

21. This argument is most fully developed by Mark Karp, *The Economics of Trusteeship in Somalia* (Boston, 1960), pp. 49–70. The notion of "precautionary hoarding" is also employed by Konczacki, "Nomadism and Economic Development."

22. Adriano Fiori and T. M. Bettini, *Contributo alla conoscenza di alcuni pascoli della Somalia italiana,* Relazioni e Monografie agrario-colonial, no. 66 (Florence, 1941), pp. 33, 39, 56.

mutual consent of several contiguous clans.[23] In the extremely arid north, Majeerteen clan treaties recognized a strict prohibition *(xirmo)* against the use of certain coastal tracts of land for six to eight months every year. The opening of these areas to grazing, late in *jiilaal,* coincided with the period when people and livestock were most concentrated around the home wells and commercial centers of the northern littoral.[24]

Apart from those rudimentary range-management practices, the Somali herdsman had other techniques to see him through the typical dry season. The most basic, of course, was his physical mobility; both his family and his capital (livestock) could move to the places where water and grass were most abundant. A second technique was exchange, not only exchange of livestock for supplementary foodstuffs, but also exchange of support and service for the right to share another clan's water and pasture land. Temporary alliances were common even in normal years, and sometimes formal treaties of submission and clientship *(sheegad)* had to be entered into by militarily weak and economically impoverished lineages to insure their survival as livestock-holding groups.[25] A third alternative open to pastoralists in certain regions of the Peninsula was the opportunity for temporary subsistence outside the pastoral sector—in agriculture, for example, or incense gathering or fishing. This third option, however, was rarely and reluctantly employed by Somali nomads, even in the drought conditions of the early twentieth century.

These basic modes of adaptation to a marginally productive environment were in operation throughout the year but were depended on more frequently in the dry season. The best way to study these fundamental forms of adaptation, however, is to look at how they were used in times of drought. The evidence from several major droughts of the early twentieth century shows that the Somalis responded to drought with their normal dry-season strategies and that they had a definite preference for certain of them.

---

23. Franco Giuliani, "Alcuni aspetti e problemi della pastorizia somala: I pascoli e le acque di abbeverata," *Rivista di agricoltura subtropicale e tropicale,* vol. 43, nos. 7–9 (July–Sept. 1969), p. 323.

24. Bettini, *L'Allevamento del bestiame,* pp. 17–18. Cf. Cerulli, *Somalia* 2: 70–71, where tradition records that in addition to declaring certain pastures as *xirmo,* the sultan of Majeerteenia could also prohibit the cutting of trees for firewood for a given period of time.

25. See below, pp. 75–78.

The Incidence of Drought

Meteorological records and oral recollections from this century alone indicate that the Somali Peninsula is visited by serious drought at least once every twenty to twenty-five years and that less severe or briefer periods of dryness can be expected once or twice in the interims.[26] A serious drought is one that is both prolonged (two or more rainy seasons with inadequate or no rainfall) and widespread (preventing *reer*s from exploiting pasture reserves in districts adjacent to their customary grazing grounds). Serious drought typically produces livestock losses in excess of 40 percent of a clan's composite holdings, particularly of sheep and cattle, and individual families may lose much more. Famine may result, particularly among the very young and very old, though actual cases of death by starvation are probably fewer among nomads caught up in drought than is commonly assumed. On the other hand, some local districts experience severe shortfalls of rain every three or four years, and other natural disasters such as locust invasions or animal epidemics may produce famine conditions even in years when rainfall is perfectly adequate.[27]

Widespread droughts occurred in former Italian Somaliland in 1910–12, 1921–22, 1931–33, 1943–44, 1951–52, and 1963–65. For British Somaliland, the incidence of reported drought is much greater: 1911–12, 1914, 1918, 1925, 1927–28, 1933–34, 1938, 1943, 1950–51, 1955, 1959, 1968–69, and 1973–74.[28] Although the nature of the evi-

26. Evidence from adjacent regions of East Africa over the past century suggests a pattern of cycles of wetter and drier years, with perhaps three or four cycles per century: S. J. K. Baker, "A Background to the Study of Drought in East Africa," *African Affairs,* vol. 73, no. 291 (1974), p. 9; D. L. Gunn, "Consequences of Drought Cycles in East African Climate," *Nature* 242 (13 Apr. 1973): 457.

27. Locust invasions during the colonial period alone have been documented for 1905, 1912–13, 1927, 1938, 1942, and 1949. In each instance, the locusts remained to do damage for three or four years after the initial invasion. Salvatore Sozio, "La lotta contro la cavalletta del deserto in Somalia," *Rivista di agricoltura subtropicale e tropicale,* vol. 47, nos. 7–9 (July–Sept. 1953), pp. 356–85. Traditional animal diseases known to the Somalis are discussed by Provenzale, *L'Allevamento del bestiame,* p. 240 ff.

28. Dates for the northern Somaliland droughts are listed by Jeremy Swift, "Pastoral Development in Somalia: Herding Cooperatives as a Strategy against Desertification and Famine," in Michael Glantz, ed., *Desertification* (Boulder, 1977), pp. 278–79; among his sources are Hunt, *General Survey,* and Isabel Boothman, "A

dence makes it difficult to determine the full geographical extent of these droughts, it appears that in this century only the drought of 1910–12 affected the entire Somali Peninsula. The terrible drought and famine of 1931–33 seems to have been confined to the southern and central regions of the country, and the widely reported drought of 1973–74 most seriously affected the northern two-thirds of the Peninsula. The extent of any given drought is an extremely important consideration in studying the strategies available to its victims and in probing the historical causes of the long-term southerly migrations of Somali pastoralists.[29] Ongoing climatological research in adjacent regions of East Africa may someday provide us with correlations between periodic rainfall shortages in certain latitudes and abundant rainfall in others. It might reveal, for example, that periods of prolonged drought in the northern Horn frequently coincide with periods of average or above average rainfall in the south. Such a finding would support the hypothesis that the steady southerly migrations of Somali nomads during the past millennium are drought-related. In the absence of any definitive evidence, however, we must be content to examine the Somali response to drought within the particular regions where drought is known to have occurred.

The Response to Drought: Some Examples

An examination of colonial district records and reports for the drought years 1910–12, 1921–22, and 1931–33 turns up remarkably few references to the existence of crisis conditions among the nomadic clans of the then Italian colony of Somalia.[30] Admittedly most colonial officials were posted to centers of cultivation and

---

Historical Survey of the Incidence of Drought in Northern Somalia," in I. M. Lewis, ed., *Abaar*, pp. 26–29. Information on droughts in the southern region was gleaned from a variety of sources, among them A. Fantoli, *Contributo alla climatologia*, pp. lxxxiii–xcviii, passim; and the annual *Bulletino d'informazioni* published from 1913 on by the Ufficio Affari Economici, Ministero delle Colonie, Rome.

29. See below, pp. 78–82.

30. District reports were consulted at *ASMAI*. Occasionally these reports were summarized in the official *Bulletino d'informazioni*, whose name changed in 1922 to *Bulletino di informazioni economiche*. After 1927, the relevant information can be found in the *Rassegna economica delle colonie* published by the Ministry of Colonies in Rome.

were concerned almost exclusively with the vicissitudes of the agricultural sector, on which they built their hopes for a prosperous colony. Both practically and philosophically, Italian officialdom before World War II was inclined to leave the nomads alone. Even so, droughts that are vividly remembered by Somali elders received scant attention in contemporary written records. One can infer from this that the effects of drought, at least in its early stages, were absorbed largely by the pastoral population itself and intruded very little into the agricultural regions which the colonials were able to observe at first hand.

What the records do indicate for all three droughts under scrutiny is the movement by pastoral clans to dry-season wells and pasture reserves earlier than usual. Such movements led to unusual concentrations of men and livestock around a few permanent wells and in a few favored pastures. Inevitably, controversies erupted and the colonial authorities were forced to intervene. Thus, one indirect colonial source of evidence for the severity of drought are the records of litigation conducted to resolve rival claims over grazing and watering rights. The incidence of such claims rose remarkably, for example, in 1911. Following the failure of the fall rains the preceding year, officials in the Benaadir province were dispatched to intercede in a number of disputes involving the spread of herding units beyond the normal limits of their recognized grazing areas. Pastureland normally considered open to the herds of all became the source of contention among contiguous clans.[31]

A good example of the disputes that arose in periods of exceptional drought occurred in the interriver area in November 1921. Both the spring and autumn rains had been sparse. A section of Clan X

31. A typical example was recorded in the bimonthly report of the Italian Resident at Baraawe (Brava):

> For reasons of pasture and water, a few Biimaal reers have been forced to expand along the coast beyond their own territory and to occupy that of the Tunni near the wells of Ceel Hurr and Torre. For some years they co-existed alongside the Tunni of Torre; but recently they have come into conflict. The two groups have exchanged blows, and without our intervention the problem would have become serious. Four Biimaal elders and the leaders of the Tunni have met to discuss the problem and hopefully resolve it.

Resident G. Piazza to the Regional Commissioner at Giumbo, Bimonthly report, Jan.–Feb. 1911, *ASMAI,* pos. 75/12, f. 136.

claimed the right to use a permanent well situated in the territory of neighboring Clan Y.[32] The section of X based its claim on the fact that, fifty-two years earlier, it had accepted temporary clientship with Clan Y and had subsequently received permission from Y's elders to sink a well on Y's territory. Some years later, the section of X had renounced its client status and relocated its herds some distance away on land occupied by fellow clansmen. In 1921, some leaders of X revived their claim to the well their forebears had dug. Clan Y rejected the request on the grounds that the well had been excavated while X had stood in a dependent status. Moreover, Y's spokesmen argued that they could not permit X to share the well even temporarily for fear that the surrounding plain would be eroded by too-heavy concentrations of livestock. Similar incidents could be cited in the Mudug and Hiiraan regions during each drought under study (providing, incidentally, a useful source for local history). It is evident that drought conditions typically prompted nomadic groups to resurrect old claims of alliance and clientship as they sought fresh pastures for their deteriorating herds.

Another manifestation of the severity of conditions in the countryside was the influx of refugees into the market centers of the colony. Rural nomads turned up in greater numbers and remained longer than usual in the farming villages and coastal towns of the Benaadir and Lower Jubba regions. In the most extreme circumstances, nomads even attempted to clear and farm small plots of land for one or two seasons. Official records of the severe drought of the early 1930s mention small groups of nomads working in the agricultural harvests along the Lower Jubba and Shabeelle Rivers.[33] Oral recollections of this period tell the same story: inhabitants of the fertile Afgooye area vividly recall the *Isniin Eelay-daad*—"Monday year [1932–33] of the flood of Eelay"—which refers to the large numbers of Eelay nomads who poured into the district seeking to share in the works and fruits of the harvest, which unfortunately was meagre even there. Italian authorities hoped that the crisis would

32. The incident is related in Massimo Colucci, *Principi di diritto consuetudinario della Somalia italiana meridionale* (Florence, 1924), pp. 164–66.

33. *Rassegna economica delle colonie*, vol. 21, nos. 9–10 (Sept.–Oct. 1933), pp. 1017–18. See also Ruggero Tozzi, *Cenni sull'agricoltura e l'economia degli indigeni del Basso Giuba* (Florence, 1941), p. 8.

induce the nomads to stay on the land. However, the process of sedentarization proved temporary. From all indications, as soon as conditions permitted, the majority of nomadic refugees resumed their
pastoral pursuits, and the populations of the larger coastal towns also
decreased noticeably.[34]

The resiliency of pastoralism following each of the droughts of
this century is not hard to understand if one realizes the rationale of
the nomads' drought-confrontation strategy. A primary objective of
that strategy was to maintain the herd's capacity to reconstitute
itself, to preserve a viable number of the best breeding stock for the
recovery period. For nomadic *reer*s, this meant reducing the number
of animals that the land had to support and reducing the number of
people who depended directly on the herds for their subsistence. A
consideration of this latter point suggests that the movement of nomadic families into towns and villages need not be interpreted as an
indication that the family herds were being wiped out; rather, the
process of sloughing off dependents was intended as a temporary
measure to reduce the pressure on the herds and thus improve the
chances for their survival. The old, the infirm, women, and children
were sent to stay with urban kinsmen or agricultural allies for the
duration of the drought, while a small group of younger men continued to watch over the livestock.[35]

Some human lives were lost to drought. Undernourishment, long
treks in search of nonexistent forage, diseases spread near over-
crowded watering sites—all took their toll. While such circumstances
produced great suffering, the existence of extensive kinship and socioeconomic networks helped minimize the impact, in terms of human
subsistence, of the disaster. In addition to absorbing refugees from
drought-afflicted regions, towns and marketplaces provided supplementary foodstuffs and sources of credit. Pastoral trade was clearly
brisker in times of drought than in times of plenty. A cursory look at
statistics on livestock exports during the three droughts confirms the
impression that exchange was an important element in the larger
pastoral strategy for coping with hard times. Figure 2 shows the total

34. For example, *Bulletino di informazioni economiche*, vol. 11, no. 4 (July–
Aug. 1923), p. 411; *Rassegna economica delle colonie*, vol. 21, nos. 9–10 (Sept.–Oct.
1933), p. 1017.
35. Ibid. See also Egidio Lipparoni, "Rilievi sul nomadismo nelle sue correlazioni
nosografiche ed epidemiologiche in Somalia," *Archivio italiano di scienze mediche
tropicali e di parassitologia* 3 (Mar. 1954): 137.

numbers and value of live animals and animal hides exported from the southern ports of Muqdisho, Marka, and Baraawe in the years 1908 to 1914, which include the drought years of 1910–12.[36] The data reveal that, in the first full year of drought, there occurred a modest increase over the two preceding years in the numbers of cattle and of sheep and goats exported, and a considerable increase in the number of camels exported. Figures on the total value of these exports indicate that the market price of livestock remained high, evidence that the animals were still in good condition and their supply still limited. As the drought persisted through the following year, the numbers of cattle and of sheep and goats exported remained high, increasing

Figure 2. Exportation of livestock and hides from southern Somali ports, 1908–14

LIVE ANIMALS

	Cattle		Sheep and Goats		Camels	
	Number	Value (lira)	Number	Value (lira)	Number	Value (lira)
1908–9	1959	98,650	8280	51,670	143	7630
1909–10	1507	66,990	7361	43,710	150	8290
1910–11	1694	109,780	7642	53,470	266	17980
1911–12	1948	98,180	7113	49,790	76	5110
1912–13	1733	80,000	5533	57,020	174	12200
1913–14	1794	96,070	7704	64,710	163	11860

ANIMAL HIDES

	Cow Hides		Sheep and Goat Skins		Camel Hides	
	Weight (×100 kg)	Value (lira)	Number	Value (lira)	Weight (×100 kg)	Value (lira)
1908–9	4232	459,730	105,480	122,070	387	20,700
1909–10	1955	551,310	532,896	326,530	470	22,950
1910–11	2852	619,330	612,612	243,590	773	32,570
1911–12	5327	637,130	850,668	320,140	714	25,030
1912–13	5400	736,304	271,726	187,710	542	20,550
1913–14	2942	518,945	243,152	172,000	433	18,210

36. The statistics come from the annual *Bullettino d'informazioni,* which began in 1913. Volume 1 contains trade statistics from the preceding seven years.

markedly for cattle—this despite a drop in market value. The number of camel exports fell to only 30 percent of that of the preceding year, and to half the number exported in the last normal year.

Certainly these aggregate figures need to be treated with caution, not least because they involve relatively small numbers and because they take no account of internal trade, which in southern Somalia could involve the exchange of surplus livestock for agricultural products. Nonetheless, statistics on the exportation of cattle from Italian Somaliland after 1920 (when the numbers involved become considerably more significant) reveal a similar trend, namely, an increase in the numbers of live animals marketed during the drought years of 1921–22 and 1931–33 (fig. 3).[37]

In addition, during all three droughts, exports of animal hides of all types rose significantly. Combined figures on hide and live animal exports from British Somaliland (a more strictly pastoral colony) reveal the same dramatic increases during the northern peninsular droughts of 1927–28 and 1933–34 (fig. 4).[38] These gross export

*Figure 3. Exportation of cattle
from Italian Somaliland,
1921–34*

	Number	Value (lira)
1921–22	9,582	874,597
1922–23	4,504	452,624
1923–24	2,155	261,312
1924–25	4,631	521,378
1925–26	10,539	1,332,137
1926–27	11,958	1,126,434
1927–28	7,583	858,055
1928–29	17,922	1,245,680
1929–30	18,390	2,073,376
1930–31	18,896	2,217,395
1931–32	21,329	——
1932–33	13,993	509,370
1933–34	5,294	230,420

37. Robert L. Hess, *Italian Colonialism in Somalia* (Chicago, 1966), appendix 5, p. 211.
38. Hunt, *General Survey*, pp. 123–24.

figures tell us little about the particular factors that influenced the decisions of individual herdsmen, but they are revealing of a generalized response to drought that is consistent over time, that is, the removal of substantial numbers of animals from the pastoral system, which reduced the pressure on the land as it reduced the nomads' accumulated holdings. The least hardy (cattle) and the least valued (sheep and goats) elements of the livestock population were the chief victims of drought. Camels, because of their ability to tolerate drought and to provide transportation when other means failed, were slaughtered only as a last resort.

The reduction of herd size through slaughter and sale not only improved the chances that the remaining livestock would survive but also provided the herdsman with the means to obtain food substitutes. Data on imports during the drought years show marked increases in the purchase of dates, rice, and durra which tended to replace the luxury imports of normal years: tobacco, coffee, and imported cloth. This shift in imports, most of which came from the Persian Gulf and India, reflected the sensitivity of the local merchant community to the needs of the pastoral populations in the interior.[39]

Figure 4. Exportation of livestock products from British Somaliland, 1927–35

	Total sheep, goats, and their skins	Total cattle, camels, and their skins
1927	1,882,092	3,332
1928	3,856,140	21,006
1929	1,047,848	24,980
1930	896,093	4,675
1931	1,117,817	1,802
1932	1,237,030	1,328
1933	1,856,539	2,110
1934	1,957,277	2,111
1935	1,198,587	3,643

39. Fluctuations in the quantities of "luxury" goods imported were also related to the cost of grain produced locally. As early as 1899 a colonial administrator noted: "When the price of durra reaches a certain maximum, there is a decline in the consumption of luxuries, which for the local people are cotton, tobacco, molasses, coffee, and

Indeed, the cooperation of Arab and Somali importers was crucial to the nomads' struggle to survive periodic drought. Their willingness to advance foodstuffs on credit or in exchange for the nomads' surplus skins and hides was frequently commented upon in colonial reports. Of course, merchants who supplied emergency foodstuffs also helped themselves economically. For in times of drought, they bought hides and skins in large quantities at low prices and dried and stored them until the crisis was over. Then, as supplies diminished and foreign demand rose, they sold the hides at higher prices and insured themselves a handy profit.[40]

The Response to Drought: A Model

Having outlined the basic patterns of Somali pastoral transhumance and trade, and having examined nomadic behavior during three specific droughts in this century, I will now offer a model of the Somali response to drought as a recurrent phenomenon. This response consisted of a series of strategies designed to cope with the various stages of drought from its onset to its conclusion. While resort to these strategies could vary in time or intensity from district to district in the drought-afflicted area, they were generally taken up by nomadic *reers* in a specific sequence which tended to correspond with progressively worsening conditions on the ground. This sequence, together with its consequences, can be outlined as follows:

1) If anticipated rains are scanty, herding units tend to evacuate their seasonal grazing grounds and return toward home wells earlier than they normally would. If the rains have failed altogether, they might not move out to distant pastures at all. In either case, alteration

---

sugar." Commissioner Dulio to Benadir Company Directors, 4 July 1899, *ASMAI,* pos. 80/1, f. 1.

In 1910–11, it was noted that about 40,000 quintals of durra and maize were imported into Somalia, and that this was accompanied by a "notable reduction in cotton imports." Imports of dates, a frequent substitute for dairy products and local grain, also rose during these years. *Bullettino d'informazioni,* vol. 1, no. 4 (Oct. 1913), pp. 220–21.

40. "When hide prices are low, the local merchants prefer to hold them in deposit until the market improves." *Bullettino d'informazioni,* vol. 1, nos. 2–3 (Aug.–Sept. 1913), p. 95; see also Dulio to Benadir Company Directors.

in the transhumant cycle results in the rapid deterioration of pastures located near permanent ground water reserves. Lineage groups tend to limit access to these watering sites more rigorously than usual, primarily to prevent overgrazing of nearby grasslands.

2) In response to the conditions described in (1), herds are divided into smaller, more specialized units. Camels or cattle are separated from sheep and goats, and each is handled according to its capacity to cope with worsening conditions. In this attempt to exploit every possible ecological niche, herdsmen may cross traditional clan boundaries and provoke conflict with segments of neighboring clans. At this point, old alliances may be tested and new ones forged.

3) As drought persists, women, children, and the elderly are commonly sent to stay with kinsmen or allies in towns or farming villages. They may take a few sheep and goats with them. This movement is usually temporary, though it depends on well-established networks of mutual help.

4) The slaughter or sale of large numbers of animals indicates that the herdsmen perceive the drought to be serious. Sheep and goats are slaughtered first, then cattle, and finally camels. Hides are sold to traders or promised to coastal merchants in exchange for imported foodstuffs.

5) A lineage segment may be compelled to accept client status (sheegad) to a clan in a nearby district. Under this arrangement, the client group agrees to work and fight alongside the "patron" clan in exchange for protection and regular access to the latter's water and pasture. By surrendering its political autonomy, the client group assures its survival as a stock-holding unit. In general, this measure is adopted by herdsmen with great reluctance after previous alternatives have been tried and proven inadequate, although lineages that are militarily weak, geographically dispersed, and economically poor may be forced into clientship early in the drought cycle.

6) The adoption of cultivation by nomadic reers is not a typical or widespread response to drought even in those areas of southern Somalia where a symbiotic relationship between pastoralists and agriculturalists has long existed. Nomadic movement into cultivable regions in times of drought generally represents a temporary sloughing off of nomadic dependents rather than an abandonment of

pastoralism altogether, although the very poorest families may be forced to remain on the land even when drought conditions subside.[41]

7) In a few instances, prolonged drought may induce nomads to seek to relocate their herds in new grazing areas, although the occupation of new territory generally involves the possibility of conflict with other clans, the abandonment of traditional alliances, and the hazards of adaptation to a new microenvironment. It is an option more likely to be undertaken by an isolated *reer* or lineage segment, which then faces the prospect of accepting the status of client in the new grazing area.

8) With the breaking of the drought, many of the processes outlined above are reversed. *Reer*s are reunited, pasturelands reoccupied, and the normal patterns of transhumance resumed. Over the next several years, herds must be rebuilt, debts resolved, alliances of convenience formalized or rejected. During the recovery process, richer families typically lend animals to poorer ones, thereby creating new balances of power and patronage within the clan. Boundaries between clans may undergo readjustments that recognize the uneven demographic and economic consequences of the drought. A new equilibrium is gradually established, but the resultant political and territorial landscape is invariably different from what it had been before the drought.

In the continuum of responses enumerated above, one can discern the three basic objectives of the Somalis' drought-confrontation strategy, in descending order of importance: *(1)* the survival of the family and the lineage group; *(2)* the preservation of the reproductive potential of the family livestock; and *(3)* the conservation of the grazing and water resources of the clan. In normal years, the nomads generally succeed in realizing all three objectives. With the onset of drought, environmental conservation becomes secondary to family and herd maintenance. Then, in the most severe crises, herds may have to be sacrificed to insure the survival of the family group. In a

41. Where Somali nomads have gradually taken up cultivation in response to drought, it has been as a supplement to pastoralism and not as a replacement for it. See Ben Wisner, "An Example of Drought-Induced Settlement in Northern Kenya," in I. M. Lewis, ed., *Abaar*, pp. 24–25. Cf. Cerulli, *Somalia* 3: 82–84, for an analysis of pastoral-agricultural interaction along the middle Shabeelle River.

land where drought is a recurrent phenomenon, Somali herdsmen continually face difficult choices: they must subordinate certain goals to others they deem more important.

The process of pastoral decision-making can be described in economic terms. Under normal conditions, Somalia's nomads accumulate livestock in numbers generally estimated to be far in excess of basic subsistence requirements. The aim of this "hoarding" is to build up capital assets as a form of insurance against the inevitability of hard times. Even when the rains fail to come at the end of the dry season, the hoarding principle continues to operate as *reer*s rely on the mechanism of herd dispersal and on adjustments in the timing of grazing movements to maximize resources and minimize risk. As drought intensifies, however, the *reer* shifts its strategy from one of hoarding to one of selective depletion. The deliberate slaughter and sale of livestock is one indication of this shift. Increased reliance on trade to obtain food substitutes is another. At a certain point, the strategy of depletion becomes more effective as a way of maintaining the best stock and of insuring human survival. By removing some animals from the land, the *reer* seeks to maintain the minimal conditions under which renewed capital accumulation can take place when the drought is past. Only when the strategies of hoarding/dispersal and depletion/exchange are perceived to fail in sustaining herd viability and economic security is the *reer* constrained to employ less palatable options: clientship, territorial migration, or the adoption of cultivation.

Evidence from the present century suggests that the first four strategies have indeed been adequate to sustain the pastoral enterprise through at least three major droughts. There have been no large-scale pastoral migrations since 1910, and, until very recently, no evidence of any major trend toward sedentarization despite the numerous incentives offered by successive colonial and post-independence regimes to encourage nomadic settlement.[42] The percentage of pastoralists in the total Somali population has remained at about 65 percent since the beginning of the century, and the total livestock population of the territory has at least doubled, and probably tripled,

42. An interesting exception can be found among the Somali in the Borama district of northwest Somalia, who may have been influenced to take up farming by their sedentary Ethiopian neighbors. See I. M. Lewis, *A Pastoral Democracy,* esp. pp. 106–26.

since the first reasonably serious censuses were made in the 1920s.[43] Some of this growth must be attributed to improved veterinary services, exploitation of new ground water reserves, and the opening of new overseas markets for Somali livestock products. Nonetheless, the continued expansion of the livestock sector owes much to its capacity for recovery from each of the major droughts of this century. This resiliency is all the more remarkable if it is realized that no central government until the present one intervened in any but a marginal way in the practices of the nomads.[44] There were no attempts to introduce range management schemes or selective breeding practices (except at a few experimental stations), and drought intervention was limited to providing relief supplies to refugees.

Thus, before the 1970s, the strategies for dealing with drought were entirely those developed and implemented by the nomads themselves. The drought-response model outlined above, though derived from observations made in the first third of the twentieth century, can be considered applicable up through 1974. What remains is to assess

43. Figures on the overall livestock population of Somalia are notoriously unreliable. But for some estimates, see United Nations Food and Agricultural Organization, *Agricultural and Water Surveys: Somalia, Livestock Development Survey* (Rome, 1967), p. 50; International Labour Office, Regular Program of Technical Assistance, *Report to the Government of the Somali Democratic Republic on the Integrated Development of the Nomadic Zones* (Geneva, 1972), pp. 4–6. Cf. Irving Kaplan et al., *Area Handbook for Somalia*, 2d ed. (Washington, D.C., 1977), pp. 267–70.

44. The decision by Italian colonial officials to refrain from significant economic action in the pastoral sector was almost certainly influenced by the recommendations of Romolo Onor, whose study of Somalia's economy was published posthumously in 1925 as *La Somalia italiana*. In this influential work, Onor contended that government efforts to promote livestock production for export would have only a marginal impact on the colony's economy, and that the Somalis' traditional tendency to hoard animals for domestic use could not be overcome with the limited resources available to the Italian regime. He concluded, "in sum, we do not see what can be gained from a program of specialized zootechnics which, if anything, would simply be a by-product of an agricultural program" (p. 38).

Thirty-five years later, a veterinary expert would argue for government intervention in the pastoral economy on the grounds that virtually nothing had changed from the earlier period. Luigi Bozzi, "L'immobilismo della pastorizia somala," *Rivista di agricoltura subtropicale e tropicale*, vol. 54, nos. 4–6, 7–9 (1960), pp. 403–10.

In 1975, the Somali government, with the assistance of a Russian airlift, attempted to relocate nearly two hundred thousand nomads in farming and fishing villages hundreds of miles from their traditional homelands. This mass relocation project was accompanied by the initiation of several range management schemes in the drought-afflicted regions of the country.

its validity as a description of nomadic behavior before 1900 and then to ask how it can enrich our understanding of the history of Somalia's pastoralists.

Historical Applications

Methodological Considerations

There are inevitably problems in attempting to project back into the past a model of adaptation derived from data gathered in a more recent historical period. There is, first, the danger of viewing the past solely in terms of the model (when in fact the model is no more than an abstract description of selected kinds of behavior in certain kinds of situations) and thereby oversimplifying it, and, further, there may be a tendency to use fragmentary historical data as evidence for the historical operation of the model as a whole. Such applications easily convey the impression that Somali society in the early twentieth century was no different than it had been in the eighteenth or the sixteenth century.

With regard to the first problem, the historian who begins with an ecological approach clearly needs to beware of falling into a kind of environmental determinism. The study of social processes in the past should be conducted with an eye toward the material conditions that all groups had to deal with; but other explanatory models must not be discarded when seeking to interpret the historical evidence. In this study I have pointed out the particularly harsh conditions Somalia's nomads have had to face and the adaptive mechanisms they have developed. An appreciation of these adaptive mechanisms, however, ought to enrich rather than constrict our understanding of Somali history. Philip Gulliver has made precisely this point in a recent article discussing the shortcomings of an approach to pastoral movements that stresses ecological factors to the exclusion of other kinds of social and cultural motivations.[45]

There is no danger that fragmentary historical data will be used to argue for the operation of our model in times past, because there is no direct evidence of the Somali response to drought in precolonial times. My assumption that the model is a valid description of past

45. Philip H. Gulliver, "Nomadic Movements: Causes and Implications," in Monod, *Pastoralism in Tropical Africa*, pp. 369–84.

behavior rests in part on data from comparative studies of disaster-response in other pastoral societies and in part on the model's capacity to order and make sense of other pieces of historical evidence indirectly related to drought. The model cannot be proved by evidence from the precolonial period, but it can help to clarify and interpret that evidence.

The argument can be made, of course, that the advent of colonialism in northeast Africa significantly altered the range of options open to nomads in times of drought. For example, colonial policy imposed new limits on the territorial movements of pastoral *reer*s. In an effort to prevent conflicts arising from nomadic encroachment, colonial arbitrators sought to define by treaty the limits of each clan's grazing domains and thereby diminish the Somalis' reliance on the principle that might makes right. The effect was to discourage Somali pastoral expansion into new territories and, one might assume, to hinder the nomads from escaping the ravages of drought. However, our evidence clearly indicates that other mechanisms were widely employed by Somalis in the droughts of 1910–12, 1921–22, and 1931–33. Given the growth of the Somali livestock sector in the twentieth century, it is difficult to argue that colonial policies destroyed all of the traditional mechanisms of pastoral adaptation. Common sense suggests that there were important continuities with the past.

The comparative literature on nomadism supports the conviction that our model reflects a pattern of response to drought widespread in both time and space. Among other things, comparative analysis helps to identify the range of variations that one can expect to find in the structural and behavioral manifestations of an institution, a particular type of social or economic unit, or, in this case, a set of responses to recurrent drought. Although most of the rich comparative literature on nomads has tended to focus on their social, political, and economic organization, a few authors have recently examined the dynamics of response to drought over a wide range of pastoral societies. Studies by Paul Baxter, John C. Caldwell, Douglas Johnson, and Gudrun Dahl and Anders Hjort reveal a range of responses similar to those we have identified for the Somali: dispersal, depletion, exchange, and temporary resettlement outside the pastoral sector seem to be characteristic responses of pastoralists confronted by drought.[46]

46. Baxter, "Some Consequences of Sedentarization"; John C. Caldwell, *The Sahelian Drought and Its Demographic Implications*, Overseas Liaison Committee

On the other hand, migration to or settlement in new grazing areas were not typical responses and, in fact, were rarely employed by the pastoral peoples in question.[47] The major impression derived from these comparative studies is that most nomads tend to rely on proven strategies for coping with drought even where external assistance may be available. Centralized administration, improved transportation, and more accessible markets may help to soften the impact of drought; but they do nothing to alter the underlying causes of recurrent drought or to alter the nomad's perception of the need for proven mechanisms to cope with it. The comparative data suggest that the Somali response to drought is analogous to the response of most pastoral populations that are subject to similar environmental constraints. The Somalis' perception of disaster and of their options in the face of it are therefore typical of the pastoral situation and may be considered relevant in times and places other than those directly observed. In fact, I have assumed that the insights to be gained by applying the model to earlier historical periods far outweigh any possible distortions that such an endeavor may entail.

Toward a Regional Perspective in Somali History

If our description of the Somali response to drought can be considered applicable to the period before 1900, its usefulness for purposes of historical analysis has yet to be demonstrated. As I will try to show, the drought-response model suggests to the historian both a way to organize his fragmentary historical data and a tool for helping interpret that data. Although I have been stressing certain

---

Paper No. 8 (American Council on Education, Dec. 1975); Douglas L. Johnson, "The Response of Pastoral Nomads to Drought in the Absence of Outside Intervention," United Nations Secretariat, Special Sahelian Office, Paper ST/SSO/18 (Dec. 1973); Gudrun Dahl and Anders Hjort, *Having Herds: Pastoral Growth and Household Economy* (Stockholm, 1976).

47. Based on evidence from four pastoral populations in the Sahel and North Africa, Johnson ("The Response of Pastoral Nomads to Drought," p. 12) notes: "Surprisingly, in conditions of deepening drought the pressure situation frequently encourages restricted movement rather than abrupt departure for distant areas. This inhibition against long-distance movement . . . is based on quite rational motives. Because nomads possess a detailed understanding of local pasture and water resources, there is a reluctance to move to zones where their local knowledge is less intimate. . . ."

structural aspects of nomadic adaptation to the environment, it has been preparatory to explaining processes of political change, institutional evolution, and long-term population movements in Somali history.

To begin with, our description suggests a workable unit of historical analysis, one that permits nomadic activities to be studied in a context broader than that of the individual clan yet narrower than that of Somali pastoralism as a whole. That unit is the region containing the complex of resources necessary to insure the nomads' survival not only in good years but also in bad. A regional complex includes both the natural resources—permanent ground water, wet- and dry-season pastures, salt licks—that sustain the *reer* in its normal pastoral rounds, and the complementary nonpastoral resources—agricultural, commercial, social—to which the *reer* must resort in times of drought and famine. These dispersed natural and socioeconomic resources are linked into a set of functional systems by regional networks of kinship and credit, clientship and alliance. Each of these regional systems is identifiable by a major market town or towns, by a series of well complexes that serve herdsmen from several clans, and by caravan trails that link these two nodes of pastoral activity. Within each regional system, any number of *reer*s carry out their seasonal rounds, forge alliances of marriage or of convenience, establish exchange relationships, and, not infrequently, fight with one another.

While the boundaries of a particular regional resource system cannot be fixed with precision, they can be seen to coincide roughly with the outermost limits of a *reer*'s pastoral, commercial, and social activities, the maximum extent to which its pursuits in all these spheres may take it. As we have seen, this maximum extension, both geographically and socially, tends to be reached in times of drought, when livestock must be dispersed or marketed, foreign goods must be imported, and distant kinsmen and allies called upon for assistance. Thus the regional unit is most discernible in times of environmental crisis when the full range of the nomads' supportive systems must be activated. Droughts highlight the truly regional, rather than purely local, nature of pastoral activity in the Horn.

By focusing on a region and its resources, the historian can study processes of ecological adaptation through the recorded experiences of any number of clans that have occupied that region. He can fruitfully use individual clan traditions by placing accounts of migration, war, and alliance in the tangible matrix of a specific resource system, whose boundaries can often be delineated from evidence in the traditions themselves. Through the juxtaposition of numerous clan traditions, then, a regional history becomes possible. That history will consist of more than just the sum of the histories of the various clans that occupy (or once occupied) it. A regional history will include the history of drought and famine in the area, the development of caravan trade in the region, the growth and decline of local market towns, and successive political struggles for control of the region's resources. In the remainder of the chapter, I will present examples of some historical inferences that can be drawn from this regional approach.

Regions as Social and Political Units

In the first place, the existence of distinct regional resource systems may have some bearing on the form and historical evolution of the larger sociopolitical groupings that have been recognized in the Horn of Africa. As we have seen, each basic herding unit partakes in a variety of kin, contractual, and socioeconomic relationships with other herding groups in the territory they mutually inhabit. Such relationships are the means by which the natural resources spread over a given region are shared among the occupants of the region; they provide the institutional framework within which economic activities are carried out. In a few instances, a single Somali clan may control a strip of territory that contains all necessary resources.[48] In such instances, those who share resources also share agnatic affiliation, an ideal arrangement in the quest for economic security. However, where demographic or military factors make it impossible for a single agnatic group to control all of the resources essential to its survival, alliances must be made with its neighbors in the region. One would expect that interclan marriages and other forms of contractual alliance are more frequently sought within a given resource system than outside it. Predictably, patterns of social and economic interaction are denser within than outside the system.

48. Such seems to be true for those northern Somali clans—like the Habar Awal, Habar Toljaclo, and Warsangeli—whose home wells lie in part along the coastal littoral and provide them with access to coastal markets as well as dry-season grazing resources. See the illustrations in Hunt, *General Survey*, p. 155.

The formation of social ties within regions of shared resources may help to explain the evolution of the large clan confederations into which the Somali-speaking population was historically divided. It might even be postulated that, at one time, the ancestors of the six major clan-families occupied discrete territories, each a resource system within which much of their history was played out and in which their sense of a common historical identity evolved.[49] Population growth and the pastoral migrations of the last five hundred years have, to be sure, altered the geographical picture. Segments of the Hawiyya clan-family have penetrated the territory of the Rahanwiin, and numerous Daarood clans in the Jubaland area have for at least a century been separated from their northern kinsmen.[50] Yet even in the twentieth century, the regional variations in material culture, social organization, and linguistic usage noted by anthropologists continued to coincide roughly with recognized clan-family divisions. In the present age of mass communications and bureaucratic centralization, however, it becomes increasingly difficult to detect the formation of regional subcultures in areas where resources are regularly shared.[51] We can merely speculate on the working out of this process in the past.

A slightly more tangible application of the regional resource model may be made in the historical study of pastoral politics. Until this century, the peoples of the Somali Peninsula never came under the control of a single political authority. However, there periodically emerged throughout Somali history regional sultanates whose leaders claimed authority over many clans and over large tracts of territory. Examples include the medieval sultanates of Adal, Ifat, and Harar on the eastern fringes of the Ethiopian highlands; the Ajuraan sultanate in the sixteenth century (discussed in chapter 3); the Majeerteen sultanate in the extreme northeast, which arose in the eighteenth century; and the nineteenth-century sultanates of Hobya and Geledi. While it is impossible to determine with any precision the boundaries of these pastoral polities, it is apparent that they encompassed well

49. While there is no way of knowing for certain, it is extremely probable that widely dispersed clan-families like the Daarood and Hawiyya at one time occupied the regions where their clan ancestors' tombs are found.

50. See below, pp. 77–78.

51. Linguistic studies of speakers of Eastern Cushitic languages being conducted by Chris Ehret of UCLA and Bernd Heine of the African Institute in Cologne may help to identify the core areas where such regional subcultures developed.

sites, trade routes, and market towns shared by many different clans. I am confident that a careful reading of the evidence would reveal that their leadership controlled some or all of the critical pastoral resources we have been discussing and used this control to exert power over the peoples of the region. By dominating the well sites or *wadi*s to which the nomads always returned at some point in their annual movements, an ambitious lineage could impose tribute or exact political favors from several nomadic groups. A good example of the way in which pastoral leadership could be exercised over a wide, sparsely settled region comes from this description of the sultanate of Hobya in the late nineteenth century:

> At the wells of Xarardheere, a source of water the year round, all the herds of this region used to and still do converge. By occupying this locale with a few of his armed followers, Yusuf Ali constrains the surrounding tribes to recognize his authority, arrogating to himself the right to collect tribute when he deems it appropriate. Using the same method, he thus spread his authority much further into the interior, from the west of Hobya all the way to Eraniale and in the northwest all the way to Gaalkacayo in the Mudug region.[52]

The fact that leaders like Sultan Yusuf Ali were able to acquire firearms in the later nineteenth century no doubt made the task of dominating watering points much easier. But even before the revolution in firearms, militarily strong lineages could use the same strategy of occupying critical watering sites to stake their claim to an area, as will be seen in our discussion of Ajuraan domination in the next chapter.[53]

To suggest that the periodic emergence of regional sultanates in the history of Somalia is related to the takeover of integrated regional resource systems is not to deny the importance of other factors such as religious ideology and interclan marriages in the rise of such sultanates. The recognition of resource systems is important chiefly because they appear to make the exercise of extra-clan author-

52. Report of Pestalozza, 2 January 1900, quoted in *Somalia: Memoria sui possedimenti e protettorati italiani,* Commando del Corpo di Stato Maggiore (Rome, 1908), pp. 22–23.
53. Most of the ruins associated in popular tradition with the sixteenth-century Ajuraan dynasty are located near important concentrations of wells.

ity possible in a pastoral setting. Thus, to claim control over neighboring pastoral clans it was not necessary to subjugate them militarily or occupy their land. One needed only to dominate some of the central nodes of pastoral activity, notably those associated with herd maintenance in the dry season.

The resource system also set limits on the size of regional polities in the past, since centralizing authority could be exercised only as far as the resource base used by its subjects extended. Pastoral populations beyond the limits of any given resource system could not be made subject to a sultanate without further incentives or military action. This fact explains why certain regions of Somalia were easier to control than others and why they became the sites for successions of sultanates through time.[54] It also explains why, despite cultural and linguistic similarities over wide areas of the Peninsula, the historical sultanates were generally rather circumscribed in their areas of effective authority.

Nomads in Town Life

There are some other historical questions that a regional framework may help to illuminate. One concerns the internal development of regional market towns, which we have seen to be important to Somali pastoralists particularly in times of drought. By indicating the economic importance of towns in the overall strategy of nomadic adaptation, the model provides a fresh perspective on the history of urban-rural relations in the Horn. We have noted how each of the old commercial towns along the Indian Ocean and Red Sea coasts served, among other things, as outlets for pastoral produce, suppliers of

54. Thus the populations living along the commercial corridor from Seylac to the Awash valley were successively incorporated into the Islamic principalities of Shewa (not to be confused with the Christian highland state of the same name), Ifat, and Adal between the tenth and sixteenth centuries; the Majeerteen region in the northeastern corner of the Peninsula was the site of a sultanate from as early as the fourteenth century into the twentieth; while the Shabeelle bend witnessed the successive dominance of the Ajuraan, Silcis, and Geledi sultanates (fifteenth through nineteenth centuries). See Ulrich Braukämper, "Islamic Principalities in Southeast Ethiopia between the Thirteenth and Sixtèenth Centuries (Part I)," *Ethiopianist Notes* 1 (Spring 1977): 22–38; Charles Guillain, *Documents sur l'histoire, la géographie et le commerce de l'Afrique orientale*, 3 vols. (Paris, 1856), 2: 440 ff.; I. M. Lewis, *Peoples of the Horn*, pp. 99–102. See also chap. 3 below.

imported foodstuffs, and occasional refuges for drought-stricken nomads. Every pastoral clan was linked in some way to a market town. Even where such links appeared to be minimal, the evidence suggests that they were used in times of drought-induced crisis. In essence, the establishment of commercial, credit, and kinship ties with townsmen was one of the basic forms of pastoral adaptation to a given region of the country.

Thus when we read accounts of the "bedouinization" of old coastal trading towns like Berbera and Muqdisho,[55] we can reasonably interpret them as evidence of the incorporation of the towns into the regional resource systems of nomadic groups. For example, clan traditions indicate that the Abgaal Darandoolle (a section of the Hawiyya clan family) began to arrive in the hinterland of Muqdisho while the Muzaffar dynasty was ruling that town, sometime in the sixteenth century.[56] Manuscripts from Muqdisho record about the same time the appearance of Abgaal nomads in the immediate interior, and shortly thereafter Somali (Abgaal) names begin to appear in the previously Arab- and Persian-dominated genealogies of the town's leading families.[57] Toward the end of the seventeenth century, an imam of Abgaal descent took up residence in the Shangaani quarter of Muqdisho. Members of the imam's lineage, which was known as Yaaquub, intermarried with the BaFadel and Abdi Semed, famed merchant families of Yemeni origin, and soon became renowned as *abbaan*s in the trade between coast and interior.[58] While this process of Abgaal penetration into town life did have political implications—the Abgaal, it is said, were responsible for assassinating the last Muzaffar governor of Muqdisho—it can also be interpreted as part of an effort by a

---

55. Cf. I. M. Lewis, *The Modern History of Somaliland* (London, 1965), pp. 34–39, who concludes his summary of precolonial Somali history by saying: "Thus by the middle of the nineteenth century the Somali coast was no longer isolated, and locally it was now rather the nomads of the hinterland who controlled the ports than the other way about. To a large extent the coastal and hinterland traditions had merged, and the centre of political pressure had swung from the coast to the interior." See also Hersi, "The Arab Factor," pp. 173–74, 227–35.

56. Abgaal traditions are recorded by Cerulli, *Somalia* 2: 243–51; Guillain, *Documents* 2: 524 ff.; and Gualtiero Benardelli, "L'Annello dell'Imam: Leggenda di El Uergadi," *Somalia d'Oggi*, vol. 1, no. 1 (1956), pp. 24–25.

57. Cerulli, *Somalia* (Rome, 1957), 1:10–40 passim.

58. Emilio Rovatti, "Mogadiscio," Report dated 22 November 1907, *ASMAI*, pos. 87/1, f. 7, esp. pp. 14–16.

recently arrived nomadic group to assure itself access to the commercial networks of the region. There is no evidence that Abgaal nomads forcibly overran the town; the Yaaquub imams shared the governing of Muqdisho with the town's traditional leading families while continuing to exercise titular leadership over their rural Abgaal kinsmen.[59]

As other (predominantly Hawiyya) pastoral clans came to occupy pastureland in the environs of Muqdisho, the process of urban-rural economic integration repeated itself. By the later nineteenth century, a French traveler could report that each of three market places in town was frequented by the nomads of one particular clan to the exclusion of all others.[60] Each *suuq* (market) had its own *abbaan*s, brokers, and *qaaddi*s (legal experts), with the entire scene mirroring the complex clan makeup of the adjacent hinterland. Analogous urban-rural links evolved in the regions of Marka and Baraawe to the south; around Seylac and Berbera, on the Gulf of Aden coast; and even in the environs of the interior towns of Harar and Luuq.[61] None of these commercial centers relied for its prosperity exclusively on trade in pastoral products; the collection and export of gums, incense, ivory, and the like were generally more important to their commerce. None was ever governed wholly by men with pastoral roots; authority was typically exercised by councils of elders representing the leading mercantile, religious, and property-owning families in town. Yet these towns were each part of a regional exchange system, and their social histories invariably reflected the vicissitudes of the nomadic world around them.

The close historical relationship between Somali pastoralism and town life is perhaps best evidenced in the existence of towns that were founded or sustained through the initiatives of pastoral populations.

59. Guillain, *Documents* 2: 527; Cerulli, *Somalia* 1: 21–24; Carlo Rossetti, *Tre note sulla citta di Mogadiscio* (Rome, 1907), pp. 10–13.

60. Georges Revoil, "Voyages chez les Benadirs, les Comalis, et les Bayouns en 1882–1883," *Le Tour du Monde* 49 (1885): 38; 50 (1886): 199–200.

61. For the Benaadir towns of Muqdisho, Marka, and Baraawe, see chap. 5 below, pp. 158–59. For Seylac and Berbera, see I. M. Lewis, "Lineage Continuity," pp. 368–70; Robecchi-Brichetti, *Somalia e Benadir* (Milan, 1899), pp. 632–33; and Pankhurst, "Trade of the Gulf of Aden Ports," pp. 36–37, 44–46. On Harar, see Enrico Cerulli, *L'Islam di ieri e di oggi* (Rome, 1971), pp. 325–27; Bruno Francolini, "I Somali del Harrar," *Annali dell' Africa italiana* (Rome), vol. 1, nos. 3–4 (1938), pp. 114–30. For Luuq, see Ugo Ferrandi, *Lugh*, pp. 283–87, 341–43.

Kismaayo, originally a small fishing village, became a major center of livestock trade after Harti pastoralists settled in its hinterland in the later nineteenth century.[62] Mareeg, Hobya, and Boosaaso appear to have been established as coastal outposts of various sultanates which emerged among Somali pastoralists between the fifteenth and nineteenth centuries.[63] Bullaxaar, the sister port of Berbera, owes its early nineteenth-century origins to a dispute between segments of the Habar Awal clan, whose members had traditionally traded through Berbera.[64] While none of these towns ever attained the size or stature of cosmopolitan centers like Muqdisho and Seylac, their existence clearly reveals the importance of fixed points of exchange in the highly mobile world of Somali nomadism. The rise and decline of small market towns must have been a constant process in the past, as successive groups of nomads established their dominance in the regions behind the towns.[65]

Pastoral Clientship

Another aspect of Somali social organization whose development may be illuminated by a regional ecological approach is that of formal clientship. In precolonial Somali society there were several different types of corporate patron-client ties, including those between pastoralists and farmers (described in chapter 5) and those which bound specialized artisan groups to particular Somali line-

62. Corrado Zoli, *Oltre-Giuba* (Rome, 1927), p. 146.

63. Apparently founded as an administrative outpost during the ascendancy of the Ajuraan sultanate in the sixteenth century, Mareeg was virtually deserted during Robecchi-Brichetti's visit in 1891. G. Benardelli, "Uno scavo compiuto nella zona archeologica di Hamar Gergeb, nel territorio di Meregh durante l'agosto 1932," *Somalia d'Oggi*, vol. 2, no. 1 (Jan.–Feb. 1957), pp. 28–35; Robecchi-Brichetti, *Somalia e Benadir*, pp. 150–51. Hobya, which may have been a small dhow haven in earlier times, became prominent as the fortified capital of Yusuf Ali, who rebelled against the Majeerteen Sultan Osman Mahmud and founded his own sultanate in 1878. Guillain, *Documents* 2: 404–5, 441–43; Robecchi-Brichetti, *Somalia e Benadir*, pp. 197–201.

64. See Pankhurst, "Trade of the Gulf of Aden Ports," p. 57.

65. Ali Hersi has noted that only along the extreme peripheries of the Somali coast—at Seylac and along the Benaadir—did extensive Arab settlement contribute to the growth of hybrid "Arab-Somali" subcultures in the coastal towns. The vast intervening coastal areas show little evidence of foreign settlement. This suggests that most of the small towns north of Muqdisho and east of Berbera were sustained, if not actually founded, by Somalis. See Hersi, "The Arab Factor," pp. 107–8, 155.

ages.[66] A third type of clientship, which has been alluded to previously in this chapter, involved formal treaties entered into by pastoral lineages seeking access to the grazing and water resources of other lineages or clans. Under this arrangement, the dependent group *(sheegad)* surrendered a degree of political autonomy to a richer or more powerful clan in exchange for protection and the use of the latter's wells and pastures.

It has been widely noted that the practice of pastoral clientship is more widespread in southern Somalia than elsewhere in the Peninsula.[67] This has generally been interpreted as a reflection of the high degree of heterogeneity in clan composition characteristic of the southern interriver region, which has long been a refuge area for nomads fleeing environmental pressures or Ethiopian military raids in the lands to the north and northwest. From a strictly socioanthropological perspective, clientship can be viewed as a way of incorporating lineage segments of diverse origins into larger political confederations; it is seen as a way of increasing the strength and cohesion of social groups in a region where agnatic ties are weak or diffuse.

Genealogical heterogeneity, however, is only one characteristic that distinguishes southern Somalia from the rest of the country. Because of its more abundant rainfall and less widely separated sources of permanent ground water, the south can support denser concentrations and a greater variety of domestic livestock than the more arid zones to the north. It is the only region where cattle husbandry is practiced on a large scale, and, as a result, the south has historically been an area where cattle nomads and camel nomads interpenetrate to a great extent. This leads us to consider the ecological ramifications of the institution of clientship.

Somali nomads in the south distinguish clearly between pasture suitable for camels *(geel-geel,* "many camels") and that suitable for cattle *(dibi).* The former consists typically of brush-covered prairie broken by high thorny thickets; the latter is open meadowland pocked by shallow rainfall basins which retain subterranean water. Camels and goats can thrive on both kinds of terrain, whereas cattle must

66. The several varieties of patron-client ties are discussed in I. M. Lewis, *The Somali Lineage System and the Total Genealogy* (London, 1957), cyclostyled, pp. 58–65, 69–70.

67. Ibid., p. 58. See also Colucci, *Principi,* pp. 45–59. In the Italian literature, the term *arifa* (from the Arabic *halif*) is commonly used to refer to client groups.

have access to *dibi*, particularly in the dry seasons when they must be watered every other day. In every dry season, and particularly in times of drought, the fertile *dibi* pastures attract large concentrations of livestock of all types. Since camels and goats crop the grass much closer than do cattle, they can in a season or two of uncontrolled grazing render the pasture unsuitable for cattle.[68] Thus the cattle nomads of the south, many of whom also engaged in seasonal agriculture on farms adjacent to *dibi*, had to restrict access to local pasture to prevent its long-term deterioration. It was here that the institution of clientship, with the formal restrictions it imposed on the dependent party, played a crucial role. For pastoral clients were typically prohibited from sinking wells and erecting permanent settlements without the approval of the clan whose land they had contracted to share. The effect was to limit unwanted concentrations of people and livestock in certain grazing areas; we have noted how such concentrations were part of the dispute which arose between clans during the drought of 1921.[69]

During the periodic migrations of Somali nomads from the drier central plains of the Peninsula into the interriver area, the incidence of contractual clientship multiplied. For the nineteenth century, oral traditions provide ample evidence of the frequency with which incoming Daarood nomads entered into the status of *sheegad* with the long-established residents of the Benaadir.[70] Not surprisingly, most of these newcomers were camel and goat nomads who had been driven from the Ogaadeen by military conflicts on the Ethiopian fron-

68. Asmarom Legesse has suggested that the gradual encroachment by Somali camel and goat herds into pasturelands previously grazed by Oromo (Galla) cattle may help to explain the displacement of Oromo by Somali nomads in the Bale and Sidamo provinces of Ethiopia since the late nineteenth century. In times of drought, Oromo cattlemen move west toward the lake districts, while Somalis move their camels and goats into the abandoned territory. The result is frequently overgrazing, which renders the pastures unsuitable for use by cattle in succeeding seasons. The Somali thus can be seen to have occupied the plains by default; and Somali expansion at the expense of Oromo assumes an ecological rather than a strictly military dimension. Asmarom Legesse, *Gada: Three Approaches to Galla Society* (New York, 1973), pp. 15–17.

69. See above, pp. 54–55. For the restrictions customarily imposed on *sheegad* groups, see Colucci, *Principi*, pp. 197–204; Zoli, *Oltre-Giuba*, pp. 176–78; and E. Cucinotta, "La proprieta ed il sistema contrattuale nel *Destur* somalo," *Rivista coloniale* 16 (1921): 244–45.

70. For example, Zoli, *Oltre-Giuba*, pp. 141–44; Giuseppe Liprandi, "La residenza di Iscia Baidoa," *La Somalia italiana*, vol. 7, nos. 1–3 (Jan.–June 1930), p. 53.

tier or had been attracted by the prospects of fertile pasturelands west of the Jubba. In the course of their southerly migrations, these camel nomads entered into the regional economies of the dominantly cattle-keeping peoples of the south. The result was either conflict, of which traditions record a great number for the nineteenth century, or the acceptance of temporary clientship. Far from being assimilated into the political confederations of the southern region, which might be expected had their pastoral economies been compatible, the nomadic immigrants were kept in a subordinate client status.[71] Most eventually renounced the bonds of *sheegad* and by the end of the nineteenth century had crossed the Jubba and were pressing into what soon would become eastern Kenya. While the conflicts of the past century were no doubt exacerbated by clan differences—most of the migrants were Daarood, most of the local inhabitants Hawiyya or Rahanwiin—it can be argued that the camel-cattle dichotomy underlay much of the trouble. In the delicately balanced regional economies of the south, the large influx of camel and goat herds held the potential for environmental disaster. We must assume that the cattle nomads of the region clearly perceived the danger; evidence comes from the frequency with which they invoked their privileges as patrons and, that failing, the militancy with which they defended their lands.

Regional Strategies, Drought, and the Somali Migrations

The Somali migrations are perhaps the best-known aspect of Somali pastoral history. Recent linguistic studies have established rather conclusively that the Somali originally spread into the Horn from a homeland in what is today southern Ethiopia.[72] If we accept this reconstruction, we must conclude that at least some types of Somali pastoralism are relatively recent adaptations. That is, in their first millennium (or earlier) migrations from the better-watered re-

71. Traditions record that the Kablallax severed their ties of clientship with the Eelay about 1855 because the latter refused to accord them a fair share of the spoils after a joint raid against the Warday. Zoli, *Oltre-Giuba*, pp. 141–42.

72. H. S. Lewis, "The Origins of the Galla and Somali," *Journal of African History* 7 (1966): 38 ff.; Christopher Ehret, *Ethiopians and East Africans* (Nairobi: East African Publishing House, 1974), p. 34; and Bernd Heine, "Notes on the History of the Sam-Speaking People," Department of History Staff Seminar Paper No. 9, University of Nairobi, 12 Jan. 1977, cyclostyled, 14 pp.

gions of the Omo and Jubba basins toward the more arid northern and eastern parts of the Horn, some ancestors of today's Somali moved from an environment where mixed agriculture and (cattle) pastoralism was possible to one where only pure pastoralism was practicable. Whether they came by choice or constraint, the first Somalis who occupied the Horn had to adapt to progressively drier conditions.

Only in more recent times (perhaps since the start of the present millennium) has the overall trend been reversed, as groups of Somali-speaking nomads moved southward to occupy the fertile pasturelands south and west of the Shabeelle River, where the cattle-keeping ancestors of the Digil clan-family were probably already established. While most of these more recent migrants remained pastoralists, they interpenetrated with the farming peoples of the south and produced the complex of cattle, camel, and farming economies characteristic of the interriver area today.

This second great migratory process, which generally ran in a north to south direction, is the only one for which we have any oral or written documentation.[73] The process does not seem to have occurred at a uniform pace but rather as a series of major movements lasting a generation or more and separated by periods in which only small groups of nomads occasionally migrated from one region to another. The causes for these migrations will probably never be known with certainty. Among the explanations that have been put forward are climatic change and progressive desertification in the northern and central Peninsula; demographic growth and population pressure augmented by continuous immigration from Arabia; the militant expansion of Islam; and domestic political conflict leading periodically to forced emigration.[74] A knowledge of Somali ecological adaptation cannot resolve the question of causes, but it can assist us in weighing the various hypotheses that have been advanced.

For one thing, scholarly preoccupation with long-term processes of Somali territorial expansion and "conquest" has tended to obscure the adaptations made by Somali nomads in those regions that they

73. Cf. Cerulli, Somalia 1: 57 ff.; I. M. Lewis, "The Somali Conquest of the Horn of Africa," Journal of African History, vol. 1, no. 2 (1960), pp. 213–30.

74. See, for example, I. M. Lewis, "Somali Conquest," p. 220; Merid Wolde Aregay, "Population Movements as a Possible Factor in the Christian-Muslim Conflict of Medieval Ethiopia," in Symposium Leo Frobenius (Cologne, 1974), p. 275; and, for a somewhat controversial interpretation, Jean Doresse, Histoire sommaire de la corne orientale de l'Afrique (Paris, 1971), p. 339ff.

have historically inhabited. This study has pointed out the variety of regional strategies the nomads have evolved to sustain their livelihood, their livestock, and their land under marginal environmental conditions. These strategies have proved remarkably effective in mitigating the worst consequences of periodic drought and, for the most part, in enabling the nomads to survive without being forced to abandon the land of their ancestors or to resort to permanent sedentarization. Given the intimate knowledge of the region's resources necessary for nomadic survival, any decision to migrate was fraught with great risks. Such a decision entailed the search for new home wells, the possibility of conflict with nomads of other clans, the separation from traditional allies and sources of aid, and the prospect of clientship. It involved the nomadic *reer* in an uncertain effort to establish new social and economic networks and to learn a new set of microenvironmental facts. These were steps not lightly undertaken. It was not a conservative pastoral ethic that compelled Somali *reer*s to stay and struggle on the land they knew, but rather the calculation that the risks of migration usually outweighed any potential benefits.

These considerations should caution us against assuming that periodically adverse climatic conditions typically produced a response that led to the abandonment of old lands for new. If the responses of this century are any indication, Somalia's herdsmen confronted drought within the regional ecosystems they occupied. Unless we assume that droughts of an earlier period were more prolonged than those experienced in this century, or that the consequences of past droughts were somehow more severe—assumptions that have as yet no evidence to support them—we would do better to look to other causes for the periodic migrations of Somali nomads in the past.

There are in fact several other possibilities that could more plausibly account for Somali territorial migrations, again within the framework of the regional resource system: the forcible occupation of a clan's home wells, either by rival clans or by expansionary governments seeking leverage over the nomads for purposes of taxation; the domination of a regional market center by an enemy, rendering it inaccessible to the nomads at critical periods of the year; chronic raiding of one group's herds by a militarily stronger group. Any of these situations could disrupt the mechanisms essential to the nomads' long-term security and prompt an outmigration. Other factors of a psychological nature might also account for territorial migrations: the desire to avoid political subordination or to sever a *sheegad* tie, the urge to follow a religious leader whose motives for migration might have little to do with pastoral concerns, and the lure of booty. These in fact are the motives most often cited in the oral traditions of past migrations.[75]

It must be remembered, however, that oral traditions tend to preserve relevant social and political facts longer than meteorological ones. Warfare resulting in outmigration is more likely to be remembered than drought, particularly if the enmity between the clans involved persists after the migration. Relationships of subordination are recalled more readily than famines because of their propaganda value, or because they can be the basis of future claims for aid. Indeed, since drought is a recurring phenomenon, it tends to be subsumed under the category of "weather lore," whereas political and military events, more discrete in their perceived causes and consequences, go down in traditional history. Nevertheless, the oral sources tend to support a political and religious interpretation of Somali migrations rather than a strictly environmental one.

Of course, recurrent drought operating in conjunction with other historical forces could produce the conditions under which territorial migration might take place. Competition for scarce resources in times of drought resulted in the breakdown of old alliances and the formation of new ones; the resulting political arrangements could leave smaller clans indefensible and prompt them to depart. Certain clans were hit harder than others by drought: a succession of devastating losses could weaken the economic or demographic position of a dominant clan and tempt others to occupy their territory. In the recovery period following each drought, certain wealthy clans or individuals enhanced their prestige and power by assisting others to build up their herds and thus might well have altered the balance of power within a region as well as prompted an outflow of less fortunate *reer*s. It should be realized that large-scale movements to new areas rarely took place without previous reconnaissance of those areas. Most migrations were spearheaded by traders, itinerant preachers, or a small group of *reer*s whose successful adaptation to the new envi-

---

75. I hope to publish these traditions elsewhere, along with a discussion of their implications for understanding Somali notions of causality.

ronment became a magnet for their kinsmen, who might migrate a generation later. Thus the displacement of an entire clan from one region to another was a complex phenomenon; a number of different forces could affect the various stages of the migratory process. In fact the number of historical instances in which large clans migrated from one part of the Peninsula to another is very small. A more common pattern was for small clan segments to move to new pastures; under favorable conditions, these groups grew and could eventually become distinct clans in themselves.

From the evidence at our disposal, then, it appears that the consequences of most droughts could be absorbed within the regional resource systems we have discussed. Pastoral survival strategies were not typically built around the uncertain prospects of large-scale migration, though unfortunate combinations of circumstances might ultimately compel this course. Still, in speculating on the causes of the Somali occupation of the Horn, it behooves us to steer away from simplistic or monocausal explanations. We should assume that recurrent drought, a fact of life for most Somalis, was coped with in familiar, tested ways and should perhaps consider more carefully the unpredictable forces of religion and politics in the history of the Horn.

Conclusion

If the notion of regional resource systems has any heuristic value, it should allow us to delineate certain historical processes more sharply than can a framework that is either less inclusive (clan histories) or more inclusive (Somali national history). Although this regional approach is derived from a study of Somali response to drought, it seems to me to offer a lens of the proper curvature to magnify many other aspects of Somali history, such as the processes of group formation, political centralization, urban-rural interaction, and pastoral migration.

Moreover, I am increasingly convinced that a regional approach to Somali history is more than simply a heuristic exercise. In the mobile and highly volatile world of traditional Somali pastoralism, knowledge of conditions beyond one's own grazing lands was essential for survival. The grazing cycles, kinship networks, and exchange systems which underpinned pastoral activity in the Horn extended over wide areas. The specialized weather lore, topical poetry, and saint cults which lay at the heart of Somali culture were regional rather than strictly local in scope.[76] The Somalis' social universe was an expansive one, and that fact suggests that a regional framework may most accurately reflect the Somalis' own conceptualization of their world. A student of comparative pastoralism made precisely this point in a recent article describing nomadic perceptions of space.

> The nomad, despite returning periodically to the same dry season well sites, is far less place specific and locale conscious than a farmer or village dweller.

> ... the precise location of a pastoral group in space, and determination of the territorial range occupied in a given year, is an ambiguous enterprise. The more variable the environment, the less rigid the spatial constraints placed on individual and group behavior. Even in relatively secure habitats ... the ... end of each tribal territory is devoid of boundary; controlled space can be extended as far as the group concerned has either inclination, ability, or need.[77]

By utilizing the notion of the regional resource system we can delimit the scope of pastoral history without losing sight of the fluidity which characterized nomadic spatial and social relationships in the past.

76. Based on differences in the astronomical calculations of various weather lore experts and in the terminology employed by them, Muusa Galaal has suggested that there are at least seven distinct "weather lore districts" in the Somali territory. See Appendix 6 of his "Stars, Seasons and Weather."

77. Douglas L. Johnson, "Nomadic Organization of Space: Reflections on Pattern and Process," in Karl W. Butzer, ed., *Dimensions of Human Geography* (Chicago: University of Chicago, Department of Geography, 1978), pp. 38, 40.

3 Pastoral Power:
The Ajuraan in History and Tradition

Power is a treasure that should be
Guarded wisely and prudently.
The man who uses it against people
Unjustly will soon lose it.
 —Qaaje-Gurey of Burco

I do not object to the idea of sharing our property;
What I object to is your eating what is mine as well as
  what is yours.
 —Fragment of *gabay,* anonymous

People, know your leaders;
Leaders, know your limits.
 —Proverb

  Power is both fragile and dangerous: such seems to be the
import of the Somali proverbs and poetic fragments quoted above. In
this chapter I will examine the nature of power and domination in
Somali society by analyzing a corpus of oral traditions about the
near-legendary Ajuraan dynasty, which is said to have dominated a
large part of southern Somalia from the late fifteenth to the mid-
seventeenth centuries. The power that these rulers purportedly exercised over the peoples of the region stands in striking contrast to most
characterizations of the Somali as an extremely egalitarian and democratic people with few notions of political hierarchy and a marked

84

aversion to any formal institutionalization of authority.[1] Thus traditions of Ajuraan domination, like other Somali accounts of supposedly historical "tyrannies" that operated in different regions of the country in the past,[2] present us with both historical and anthropological questions. Do these traditions record actual historical experiences? Do they tell us anything about the structure of regional pastoral polities in the past? Under what conditions can power be accumulated in Somali society? And why are traditions of Ajuraan domination preserved centuries after the demise and disappearance of the dynasty?

The remarkable story of the Ajuraan must be understood in the context of traditional Somali political culture.[3] Before the twentieth century, Somalis were never united under a single political authority. The largest effective political units were corporate kinship groups. As we have seen, day-to-day pastoral activities were conducted by small herding units or *reer*s. Whenever more manpower was needed—at dry-season watering sites, for example, or in feuds—several *reer*s could combine forces or call for assistance from members of their *diya*-paying group. Only on rare occasions did entire clans act as units, typically in military encounters with neighboring clans or in support of a major territorial movement. On such occasions, decisions were taken in the *shir*, or assembly of all adult males, often in consultation with the clan's religious specialists.

1. The most important studies in political anthropology on the Somali are I. M. Lewis, *A Pastoral Democracy* (London, 1961); and various essays by Enrico Cerulli, *Somalia: Scritti vari editi ed inediti*, 3 vols., esp. 2: 1–94 and 3: 47–113. It should be noted that the egalitarian model is most applicable in the northern regions of the Somali Peninsula where Lewis conducted most of his field work. Cerulli's research in former Italian Somaliland pointed up the existence of certain hereditary titles and forms of tribal authority that suggest a limited tendency toward political stratification in the past. Other examples of the development of embryonic types of hereditary politico-religious authority in the recent Somali past can be found in two unpublished case studies: Virginia Luling, "The Social Structure of Southern Somali Tribes" (Ph.D. thesis, University of London, 1971), and David H. Marlowe, "The Galjaal Barsana of Central Somalia: A Lineage System in a Changing World" (Ph.D. diss., Harvard University, 1963).

2. The tyrannical ruler is a frequent figure in Somali folklore, but there are also many historical figures who appear in traditions as having overextended their authority. Among them are Geedy Ababow, Mudawa, and Dubka Palow from the interriver area, and the legendary Hersi "Wiilwaal" from northern Somalia.

3. For a recent overview, see David D. Laitin, *Politics, Language, and Thought: The Somali Experience* (Chicago: University of Chicago Press, 1977), esp. pp. 14–42, 132–36.

Leadership in Somali society was fluid and informal. Personal bravery, skill in oratory and political mediation, or economic largesse could propel an individual to a temporary position of prominence within the clan or lineage; but this conferred no permanent authority on the man or his lineal successors. Clan assemblies occasionally elected sultans to represent their kinsmen to outsiders, but here again the sultans had no inherent powers to enforce their decisions, which had to be taken back to the *shir* for approval. Any leader's authority was based on successful performance rather than inherited right. And while certain titles connoting military or ritual preeminence were often passed down through particular lineages,[4] the individuals holding them gave the positions whatever real authority they had.

Religious power, on the other hand, could be transferred from one person to another. In the Somali view, *baraka* (spiritual power) might be inherited by the descendants of a holy man, a practice which helps explain the existence in Somalia of religious lineages. Moreover, certain kinds of mystical powers, particularly those associated with the written word of Islam, could be transmitted through instruction by a skilled practitioner. However, spiritual authority did not of itself constitute a basis for the exercise of secular leadership. In Somali thought, the power of the saint was counterpoised to that of the warrior and clan leader.[5] Wheras the former was seen as having the capacity to divine, bless, and mediate, the latter alone could defend, secure, and expand the material well-being of the clan. Most religious lineages were in fact neither numerically nor militarily strong, and hence not powerful in a secular sense.

It is against this segmented, antiauthoritarian and dualistic political heritage that the periodic emergence of regional power centers in Somalia must be interpreted. Over the past several hundred years, Somali traditions record a number of instances of domination by one clan over another. Such instances typically involved the unequal distribution of grazing resources, which compelled certain herding units and sometimes entire clans to accept a subordinate status within the grazing domains of clans that held better lands. On other occasions, charismatic leaders managed to secure recognition from a number of

4. Cerulli, *Somalia* 3: 53–60.
5. I. M. Lewis, "Dualism in Somali Notions of Power," *Journal of the Royal Anthropological Institute* 93 (1963): 109–16.

clans in opposition to a perceived external foe, Somali or foreign. However, the oral record reveals only a few instances where a ruling group managed to establish its control over many different clans and over extensive tracts of territory and to sustain that control for more than a generation or two. The Ajuraan provide one of the earliest and most striking examples that are still recounted by clan historians.

In this chapter I will examine the oral record for the insights it can provide into events, structures, processes, and ideas about domination in Somali history. After outlining the basic elements of the Ajuraan story, I will discuss their utility as historical sources in an effort to determine whether the Ajuraan dynasty was a historical reality. Then I will suggest what these traditions can tell us about the forms of domination that are possible in a pastoral setting and about the processes through which power is gained and lost. Finally, I will offer some thoughts on the meaning of the Ajuraan traditions for the contemporary society that preserves them.

The Ajuraan in Oral Traditions

In my research, I did not come across any one tradition that related the whole of the Ajuraan story. Accounts published by European and Somali authors over the past one hundred years as well as several variants which I gathered more recently in the field provided only fragments. When I asked my most knowledgeable Somali informants to tell me what they knew of the Ajuraan, they would recount particular, usually brief episodes about Ajuraan origins, the nature of their rule, or their ultimate defeat. Whether these pieces ever formed part of a single narrative tradition I cannot say—certainly most Somali oral history is episodic rather than epic in form.

There are descendants of the Ajuraan living today near Wajir in northeastern Kenya, and others along the upper Shabeelle River in Ethiopia. Some of my local informants thought that among these communities were elders who knew the entire history of Ajuraan ascendancy in southern Somalia; to my knowledge, however, they have never been identified or interviewed.

Nevertheless, fragments of the Ajuraan story are known throughout most of southern Somalia, and certain common episodes are known to Somalis from different and widely scattered clans. What follows, therefore, is a composite portrait of the Ajuraan era drawn from the testimonies of more than a dozen informants, including some from the Hintire, a clan genealogically close to the Ajuraan.[6] I have included in the narrative only those elements common to at least two independent sources. The extracts indicate excerpts from individual testimonies that can be considered typical of the kinds of accounts that are still recounted locally. Important variants appear to exist only for certain events, and these will be taken up in my subsequent analysis.

Like the origins of many Somali clans, Ajuraan origins are traced to the marriage of an Arab immigrant and the daughter of a local Somali leader. The immigrant is remembered as Balad and his bride as Faaduma, daughter of Jambelle, one of six "brothers" descended from the eponymous ancestor of the Hawiyya clan family. The fullest account of their union comes from a tradition collected by Cerulli and is translated here in full.

There once lived in the country six men born of two different women, three of one mother and three of another; and all of a single father. Their father was Hawiyya. Jambelle Hawiyya, Gurqaate Hawiyya, and Guggundabe Hawiyya are sons of a single mother. Haskulla Hawiyya, Rarane Hawiyya, and Karan-

6. The most important testimonies were those taken at a group interview in Mereerey on 26 August 1971, which included Shaykh Abow Yunis Shaykh Ashir, Shaykh Yusuf Muhyeddin, and Ali Begedow. Additional information came from interviews with Abdelqadir Abokor Ashir, Dundumey, 16 Aug. 1971; Muddey Haji Geeley, Muqdisho, 9 June 1971; Ahmed Shaykh Osman, Muqdisho, 19 July 1971; and Shaykh Aliow Mahad Emed of Bulow Eelay, whose testimony was recorded by Muhammad Rinjele, 29 July 1971.

I also had the opportunity to consult an Arabic manuscript in the possession of Shaykh Abow Yunis of Mereerey. This document contained a number of oral traditions dealing primarily with Hintire clan politics and personalities in the nineteenth century; the section on Ajuraan history came toward the beginning of the manuscript. The copy I saw was written on an old Italian ledger, suggesting an early twentieth-century transcription. Two separate translations from the Arabic were made for me by Ahmed Shaykh Osman and Muhammad Rinjele. The excerpts contained in my narrative are drawn from a combination of the two translations.

The most important published traditions on the Ajuraan are found in Cerulli, *Somalia* 1: 61–67, and 2: 243–58; Charles Guillain, *Documents sur l'histoire, la géographie et la commerce de l'Afrique orientale,* 3 vols. (Paris, 1856), 1: 287 ff., and 3: 140–42; Pietro Barile, *Colonizzazione fascista nella Somalia meridionale* (Rome, 1935), pp. 65–72; and Gualtiero Benardelli, "Uno scavo compiuto nella zona archeologica di Hamar Gergeb nel territorio di Meregh durante l'agosto 1932," *Somalia d'Oggi,* vol. 2, no. 1 (1957), pp. 34–35.

le Hawiyya are sons of a single mother. Jambelle begat
Faaduma Jambelle. She herded goats, pursuing them through
the bush. While wandering through the bush, she spied a man
perched up in a tall tree, like a sycamore. She said, "Come
down." "No," he replied, "let your brother and the brothers of
your father, those of your tribe, call me." Then she summoned
them. They came to the place and said to the man, "Come down."
He said, "I will descend if you will give me three things." "What
are the three?" they asked. "For the first, Faaduma Jambelle;
then a hundred camels with black humps; finally, a slave." Then
he added, "If you accept these three, I add another: I must
descend unto the back of a man." The six Hawiyya thought. The
people of ancient times were few. What they desired was help.
If the stranger should have sons while he remained among them,
they could seek his help. Then they said to him, "We accept,
come down." Guggundabe said, "Let him descend upon my
back." Gurqaate said, "No, we who have given Faaduma and a
hundred camels—should he now also descend upon our backs.
No!" he said, and refused. Then the man descended upon the
back of Rarane, the man. He married Faaduma Jambelle and
begat Ajuraan. This man, who knows who he was? He was seen
up in a tree.[7]

We will have occasion to return to the origin story below. For now,
it suffices to note that the auspicious appearance of a stranger who
marries the daughter of a local lineage or clan head is a common
theme in Somali oral traditions.[8] It is typically employed to enhance
the prestige of a clan's ancestry and often to link clan origins with the
religious prestige of immigrant Arab shaykhs. The question of possible Arab antecedents for the Ajuraan is an important one, but it

7. Cerulli, *Somalia* 2: 252–53.
8. See for example, I. M. Lewis, "Historical Aspects of Genealogies in Northern
Somali Social Structure," *Journal of African History* 3 (1962): 44–47; I. M. Lewis,
"Sharif Yusuf Barkhadle: The Blessed Saint of Somaliland," *Proceedings of the Third
International Conference of Ethiopian Studies held at Addis Ababa* (1969), 1: 75–81;
Ali Abdirahman Hersi, "The Arab Factor in Somali History: The Origins and Develop-
ment of Arab Enterprise and Cultural Influences in the Somali Peninsula" (Ph.D. diss.,
University of California, Los Angeles, 1977), pp. 121–31.
        The motif of the "wise stranger" is not confined to Somalia. See, for example,
R. S. O'Fahey, "Slavery and the Slave Trade in Dar Fur," *Journal of African History*
14 (1973): 29–31.

cannot be resolved strictly on the basis of this tradition, typical as it is of origin accounts elsewhere in the Horn.

According to most accounts, the Ajuraan appeared in the inter-river area of southern Somalia some sixteen to twenty generations ago. Traditions are vague and contradictory about the provenance of the earliest rulers. Some sources say that they came from Berbera, on the northern Somali coast; others, that they came from the sea via Muqdisho, on the southern coast; still others, that they arrived from the Ogaadeen region of central Somalia.[9] Once established in the southern plains, however, the Ajuraan are said to have ruled the country from Qallaafo, on the upper Shabeelle River, to the shores of the Indian Ocean; and from Mareeg on the central Somali coast to the Jubba River in the south.

> The Ajuraan were very strong and governed the country by force [xoog]. They had a powerful army that enforced the decrees of the imams of Ajuraan. The enemies of the Ajuraan were put in stone-lined prisons beneath the ground, and were forced to work as slaves of the imam.[10]

> The Ajuraan were very religious, and their law was that of the Shari'a [the law of Islam]. Their leader was the imam, who was always chosen from the family [or lineage] known as Gareen. When a new imam was to be chosen, the senior counselors consulted the stars and selected the wisest and most able of the representatives of Gareen.[11]

The imams, it is said, lived at various places in the interior and were surrounded by personal followings of advisers and slave soldiers. Most accounts mention that emirs were posted to govern the various districts of the realm, which included vast grazing areas and some of the more important trading centers along the Indian Ocean littoral. The Ajuraan leaders were said to have been allied to the Muzaffar (a

9. Shaykh Yusuf Muhyeddin, Mereerey, 26 Aug. 1971; Muddey Haji Geeley, Muqdisho, 9 June 1971. Cf. Michele Pirone, "Leggende e tradizioni storiche dei Somali Ogaden," *Archivio per l'antropologia e l'etnologia* 84 (1954): 119–22.

The difficulty here is that some sources appear to be tracing the ancestry of Balad, who may well have had Arab antecedents; while others locate the ancestors of Ajuraan among the Hawiyya, that is, through the maternal line.

10. Ali Begedow, Mereerey, 26 Aug. 1971.

11. Ahmed Shaykh Osman, Muqdisho, 19 July 1971.

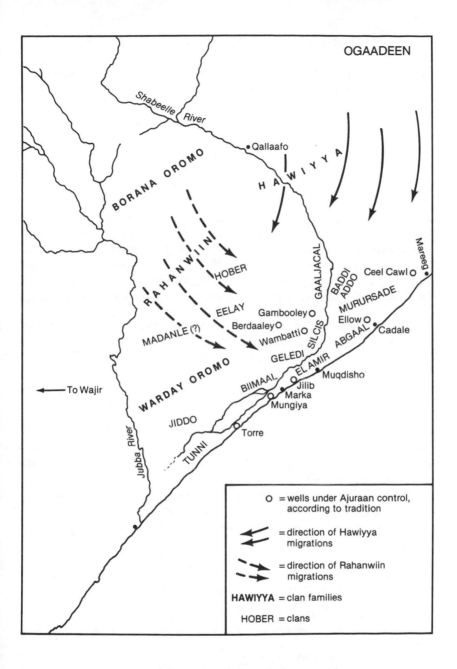

Map 3. Southern Somalia, ca. 1650

dynasty of mixed Persian-Somali ancestry that is known to have ruled the coastal town of Muqdisho from the early sixteenth century to the mid-seventeenth)[12] and to the Madanle (a legendary race of giants who traditions say preceeded the Rahanwiin as inhabitants of the southern interior between Baydhabo and the Jubba River).[13] Some sources say that the imam and his allies possessed horses and firearms, which would have been unusual, as both items were relatively uncommon in southern Somalia before the twentieth century.

The Ajuraan collected tribute in the form of durra and *bun* (coffee beans roasted in butter) from the cultivators who farmed the alluvial land along the lower Shabeelle River. They also demanded cattle, camels, and goats from the nomads of the region. (Some informants commented that the name Ajuraan came from the Arabic root *ajara*—"to tax"—and a few claimed that the Ajuraan were mercenaries paid by the Gareen imams to extort tribute from their subjects.)

> The people under Ajuraan rule were forced to dig canals for irrigating the land along the river and storage pits for preserving the grain that was taken in tribute. They dug wells for the imam's livestock and built fortifications for the imam's soldiers. They shepherded the camels and sheep and horses of the Ajuraan.[14]

(Many of the deep, stone-lined wells still in use in parts of southern Somalia are attributed by local tradition to Ajuraan construction; and abandoned fortifications in stone were still in evidence in the early twentieth century.)[15]

The population was large in Ajuraan times, according to tradition. A popular account says that the birth of an imam's son at Marka was reported the same day at Mareeg, on the northern confines of the "state."[16]

> The imam had wives in every district, and he remained in each part of his dominions for one or two months of every year. The

12. Cerulli, *Somalia* 2: 13–14, 62–64.

13. Shaykh Aliow Mahad Emed, Bulow Eelay, 29 July 1971; cf. Colucci, *Principi*, pp. 158–60.

14. Mss. of Shaykh Abow Yunis (see n. 6 above).

15. See, for example, Giuseppe Stefanini, *In Somalia: Note e impressioni di viaggio* (Florence, 1922), pp. 295–96.

16. Cerulli, *Somalia* 2: 63.

custom in Ajuraan times was for the ruler to spend seven nights with every new bride before she went to the bed of her husband. The imam also collected half [some sources say all] of the bridewealth normally given by the husband's kinsmen to the father of the bride. The bridewealth was in those days 100 camels.[17]

Ultimately, the people rose up against the tyranny of Ajuraan rule. According to most accounts, the first to rebel were the pastoral Darandoolle whose descendants today live on the outskirts of Muqdisho and in the pasturelands north of it. Sometime between 1590 and 1625—the approximate dates appear to be corroborated by a Portuguese document dated 1624[18]—these nomads ambushed and killed the Muzaffar governor of Muqdisho, who was an ally of the Ajuraan rulers.[19] A few years later, these same Darandoolle challenged the authority of the Ajuraan imam directly.

> After entering Muqdisho, the Darandoolle quarrelled with the Ajuraan. They quarrelled over watering rights. The Ajuraan had decreed: "At the wells in our territory, the people known as Darandoolle and the other Hiraab cannot water their herds by day, but only at night." . . . Then all the Darandoolle gathered in one place. The leaders decided to make war on the Ajuraan. They found the imam of the Ajuraan seated on a rock near a well called Ceel Cawl. They killed him with a sword. As they struck him with the sword, they split his body together with the rock on which he was seated. He died immediately and the Ajuraan migrated out of the country.[20]

In another variation of the story, a young Darandoolle warrior was born with a gold ring on his finger, a sign of his future preeminence. The Darandoolle then rallied around their young leader, who eventually assumed the title of imam of the Darandoolle and took up residence in Muqdisho.[21]

After the successful rebellion of the Darandoolle, other clans

17. Mss. of Shaykh Abow Yunis.

18. Cerulli, *Somalia* 1: 65, 2: 250.

19. Cerulli, *Somalia* 2: 245–51; Emilio Rovatti, "Monografia sul Mogadiscio," *ASMAI*, pos. 87/1, f. 7; Guillain, *Documents* 2: 524–25.

20. Cerulli, *Somalia* 2: 248.

21. The fullest account of this tradition I have seen is G. Benardelli, "L'Anello dell'Imam: Leggenda di El Uergadi," *Somalia d'Oggi*, vol. 1, no. 1. (1956), pp. 24–25.

began to challenge Ajuraan hegemony. Along the middle reaches of the Shabeelle valley, the pastoral Gaaljacal and Baddi Addo waged several unsuccessful campaigns before they eventually united to drive the Ajuraan out of the area.[22] In the region of the Shabeelle bend, the Geledi clan formed an alliance with the Wacdaan to expel a group of tyrants known as the Silcis, who were either allies of the Ajuraan or their immediate successors in that district.[23] Similarly, the Ajuraan lost control of the town of Marka to a people known as the El Amir (perhaps the followers of a rebellious regional governor), who then ruled that town for thirty-four years.[24] Toward the end of the seventeenth century, the El Amir were in turn defeated and driven out by the Biimaal, whose descendants today occupy the hinterland of Marka.

Most traditions agree that the Ajuraan fought long and hard to preserve their position of dominance, but in the end they were defeated and scattered throughout the country. Some of the survivors went to the upper Shabeelle, where a group of cultivators still claimed, in the early twentieth century, to be descendants of the slaves of the Ajuraan. Other Ajuraan crossed the Jubba where they today pursue a pastoral existence in the district of Wajir, in modern-day Kenya.[25] According to popular accounts, the Ajuraan declined because their tyranny became insupportable, because they abandoned the law of Islam, or because they were excessively arrogant. If pride alone brought success, goes one proverb, the Ajuraan would never have left the country.

The foregoing narrative contains the major elements of the Ajuraan saga, which can be related in greater or lesser detail by

22. Cerulli, *Somalia* 2: 256–57.

23. Ali Omar Haji "Goyle," Afgooye, 10 June 1971; Yusuf Nur, Muqdisho, 17 June 1971; Aw Abdullah Hassan, Afgooye, 16 Oct. 1971.

24. Guillain, *Documents* 3: 141–42, 127 n. 1. If Guillain's calculations are accurate, the El Amir would have seized Marka in the 1650s.

25. Massimo Colucci, *Principi di diritto consuetudinario della Somalia italiana meridionale* (Florence, 1924), p. 96; Cerulli, *Somalia* 1: 64. Within the territories of virtually all those clans who claim that their ancestors defeated the Ajuraan, there could be found, in the early twentieth century, lineages or lineage segments which also claimed descent from the Ajuraan or from "the slaves" (subjects?) of the Ajuraan. See, for example, Colucci, *Principi*, p. 110; Gherardo Pantano, *La citta di Merca e la regione Bimal* (Leghorn, 1910), pp. 13–15; G. Cerrina-Ferroni, *Benadir* (Rome, 1911), p. 24: Enrico Russo, *La residenza di Mahaddei-uein* (Rome, 1919), pp. 19–20.

informants from any number of clans today resident in southern Somalia. There appear to be no glaring discrepancies among the accounts obtained in different districts, nor have there occurred any notable distortions or deletions in the story since Guillain first recorded it in the 1840s. The most significant variations occur in accounts of Ajuraan decline, for which traditions are generally much fuller than those dealing with Ajuraan origins and with the nature of their rule. The significance of this last observation will be discussed below. The point here is that oral traditional accounts of the Ajuraan period are generally consistent through space as well as time. Such consistency regarding events that purportedly occurred more than three hundred years ago suggests that the Ajuraan saga has become part of the folklore of southern Somalia. It clearly contains a number of stock cultural and literary themes which must be recognized before one can assess the historicity of the episode as a whole.

Some of the more readily apparent stock themes in the preceeding narrative are the auspicious appearance of a stranger whose marriage into a local family holds out the promise of a large and supernaturally gifted progeny; the *ius primae noctis* enjoyed by the imam, a practice commonly attributed to tyrants in northeast Africa; the imam's possession of "wives in every district," a literary exaggeration of the polygamy customarily practiced by a few prominent Somali sultans in more recent historical times; and the supernatural sign—in this story, a golden ring—attending the birth of a challenger to the existing ruling order. These and other formulaic representations of Ajuraan oppression found in some of the variant versions clearly have didactic functions in a society known for its egalitarianism and its suspicion of all forms of centralized authority. One can reasonably argue that the preservation of the Ajuraan legend (whatever its historical foundation) served to remind Somalis of the dangers of autocratic rule. The Somali proverbs cited at the beginning of the chapter, and many others, speak to this same concern.

The Ajuraan saga also contains a number of eteological elements designed to explain the origins of stone ruins found scattered through southern Somalia. Many deep wells and large abandoned earthworks are popularly attributed to Ajuraan technology. While there is no reason to assume that the Ajuraan period could not have witnessed considerable construction in stone, the historian must be wary of attributing all such remains to a single historical period. Ruins have been discovered (though, unfortunately, rarely investigated) in many parts of the Somali Peninsula; the dates of their original construction probably span the past millennium.[26] Until more systematic archaeological work is carried out, we cannot regard these ruins as definitive evidence of Ajuraan engineering accomplishments.

Finally, it was noted above that traditions that describe the downfall of the Ajuraan are generally richer and more varied than those that describe the nature of Ajuraan rule. A number of clans preserve accounts of incidents which led to rebellion against Ajuraan hegemony. Some incidents are caused by conflict over resources; others appear to have religious or political causes. These will be discussed shortly. What should be noted here is that most accounts of Ajuraan decline end in military defeat for the former rulers. The decisive battles are typically described as having occurred in places which today are within the territories of the clans concerned and thus can be seen as helping to legitimize a clan's occupation of territory by referring that occupation back to an earlier, almost legendary era. Memories of having defeated the Ajuraan embellish a clan's history. In addition, certain long-standing clan alliances—the Gaaljacal and Baddi Addo, the Geledi and Wacdaan (see p. 215)—assume a sense of permanence by having begun in rebellion against a common oppressor. It is worth noting that many southern Somali clans which make no claims of ever having defeated the Ajuraan nevertheless have traditions of expelling other tyrannical leaders from the lands they occupy today.[27]

The Ajuraan in History

Given the many folk stereotypes in the Ajuraan saga, as well as the several legitimizing and didactic functions it performs, is

26. Benardelli, "Uno scavo compiuto"; A. T. Curle, "The Ruined Towns of Somaliland," *Antiquity* (Sept. 1937), pp. 315–27; H. Neville Chittick, "An Archaeological Reconnaissance of the Southern Somali Coast," *Azania* 4 (1969): 115–30; H. Neville Chittick, "An Archaeological Reconnaissance in the Horn: The British-Somali Expedition, 1975," *Azania* 11 (1976): 117–33.

27. For example, the Eelay claim to have defeated first the Madanle and then the Warday under the famed Barambara before occupying Baydhabo and Buur Hakaba; the Geledi of Afgooye record their expulsion of the Silcis rulers in the eighteenth century; and Biimaal traditions speak of their rebellion against Wakil Samow of Marka, perhaps the representative of Ajuraan authority in that district. See Colucci, *Principi,* pp. 158–61; Barile, *Colonizzazione fascista,* pp. 67–70; and n. 23 above.

Local traditions attribute this and several other pillar tombs in the vicinity of Marka to the sixteenth century, when naa'ibs *ruled the district as part of the Ajuraan state.*

it possible to arrive at a sound judgment about the value of these traditions as historical sources? Could a pastoral dynasty in fact have dominated the politically segmented and territorially dispersed populations of southern Somalia in the sixteenth century, given the limited means of coercion available at that time and recognizing the tendency of Somali nomads to resist any form of political authority imposed from outside the clan? I have answered a cautious yes to each of these questions, but not on the basis of the traditions alone. Where a purported historical episode has so clearly undergone literary elaboration and a change in motivational structure, the historian must look for external corroboration of the recorded episode. At the same time, traditions can provide clues about the special circumstances in which the supposed events took place. Such clues are typically found in the language (sometimes archaic) of tradition and in certain symbols that appear in the traditions but not in contemporary discourse.

To give an example: the traditions we have summarized indicate that the Ajuraan ruled according to a theocratic (Islamic) model. Most accounts refer to the Ajuraan leaders as imams, a title rarely used to identify Somali religious figures in more recent times. Oral accounts further allude to *emirs* and *naa'ibs* as agents of Ajuraan government, in contrast to the much more commonly used Somali titles of *boqor, islao,* and *malaakh* to indicate special military and ritual leaders. Furthermore, unusual toponyms which purportedly date from Ajuraan times—*Awal el-amir* ("tomb of the emir") and *Cusk Naa'ib Samow* ("the seat of Naa'ib Samow")—further convey the impression of a distinctly theocratic polity. Lest it be thought that such titles are simply glosses added in the process of the traditions' transmission, we have external corroboration in a Portuguese letter of 1624, which refers to a ruler in the southern Somali interior as an imam.[28]

With this evidence from the traditions in hand, we can turn to the wider religious history of the Horn of Africa in the fifteenth and sixteenth centuries for clues to the Ajuraan phenomenon. Briefly, the two centuries after 1400 witnessed the immigration into northeast Africa of substantial numbers of Hadrami and Yemeni Muslims. Brad Martin has shown how many sayyids and sherifs came with the hope of spreading Islam and assuming positions of leadership among

28. Cerulli, *Somalia* 2: 250.

newly converted populations.[29] They were drawn to the Somali low-lands by the revival of militant Islam on the eastern fringes of the Christian state of Ethiopia; and Arab migrations reached their peak in the fifty years after 1490, when a series of *jihad*s (holy wars) pushed the frontier of Islam into the Ethiopian foothills. The success, however ephemeral, of the Muslim offensive must have affected many of the pastoral tribes of the Ogaadeen, including some sections of the Hawiyya who are mentioned in chronicles of the period.[30] A string of roughly contemporaneous Islamic principalities emerged along the eastern borders of Ethiopia. Although some disappeared after the reversal of Muslim fortunes in 1543, others shifted their bases east-ward into the lowlands.[31] This evidence suggests a historical context for the Ajuraan "theocracy": it very probably was the southernmost in a series of Islamic polities that were inspired if not founded by zealous Muslim clerics from Arabia.

The link between the activities of these immigrants on the fron-tiers of Ethiopia and the founding of the Ajuraan state in the Sha-beelle Valley may be the Gareen lineage. As local traditions indicate, the imams of Ajuraan came from the Gareen. In Ogaadeen traditions, the Gareen are remembered as having been rulers of a small "state" near the upper Shabeelle River before they settled farther south.[32] The idea of theocratic government may have been planted in the south by this displaced lineage. On the other hand, one may not have to look any further than the Benaadir coast for the origins of the Ajuraan theocracy. The Islamic city-state of Muqdisho had been governed as a sultanate since the twelfth century by a series of Arab and Persian dynasties. The last of these, the Muzaffar, were allies of the Ajuraan rulers and apparently provided officials in Ajuraan administration.[33]

29. Brad G. Martin, "Mahdism, Muslim Clerics, and Holy Wars in Ethiopia, 1300–1600," in Harold Marcus, ed., *Proceedings of the First United States Conference on Ethiopian Studies* (East Lansing, 1975), pp. 91–100.

30. Chihab ed Din Ahmed, *Histoire de la conquête de l'Abyssinie*, translated by René Basset (Paris, 1897), pp. 35–36, 168–69, 206–7.

31. Ulrich Braukämper, "Islamic Principalities in Southeast Ethiopia Between the Thirteenth and Sixteenth Centuries," *Ethiopianist Notes*, vol. 1, no. 1 (Spring 1977), pp. 23–24.

32. Michele Pirone, "Leggende e tradizioni storiche," pp. 120–21.

33. Cerulli, *Somalia* 1: 40, 63–64; and 2: 245–49; Hersi, "The Arab Factor," pp. 194–98. While the Muzaffar are generally regarded to be of Yemeni origin, I was told by one informant that some members of the dynasty came from Daafeed (part of the interriver area controlled by the Ajuraan) and that they provided *wakil*s (local gover-

Whatever the antecedents of the Ajuraan polity, its development seems to have been aided by the religious and legal expertise of Islamic immigrants. Many Arab families today resident in the Benaadir have traditions of arriving there in the sixteenth century. Along the lower Shabeelle River, they are known by the local Somalis as *gibilcaad* ("white-skins"). Most continue to live in distinct endogamous communities and even today retain a certain aura of religious prestige.[34] While their precise role in the Ajuraan period cannot be determined with certainty, we can surmise that they aided the Ajuraan rulers in judicial matters and perhaps in tax collection. Literate in Arabic, versed in the imperatives of the Shari'a, these holy men appear to have helped institutionalize Islam in the Shabeelle Valley.

A second clue provided by oral tradition about the circumstances in which the Ajuraan state emerged concerns the role of the pastoral Hawiyya clans. Both the origin story (p. 88) and the scattered references to the components of the Ajuraan confederacy suggest that Hawiyya-related clans formed the core of the polity. External evidence indicates that the present pattern of Hawiyya settlement along both sides of the middle Shabeelle River took shape between 1300 and 1600. Apart from Hawiyya clan traditions, which provide us with a rough chronology of particular clan movements, we find corroboration in Arabic accounts from the coast, which document the spread of Hawiyya trading settlements along the Indian Ocean littoral, and also in Muqdisho town chronicles, which record the intrusion of Hawiyya pastoralists in town life from the mid-fifteenth century.[35] Hawiyya pastoral migrations involved the occupation of strategic well sites and trading centers as well as extensive grazing areas on both sides of the Shabeelle River. The process of occupation was almost certainly carried out by successive, small-scale advances of herding units and lineage segments over a period of several generations,[36] but the end

---

nors) for several districts under Ajuraan administration. This may reflect intermarriage between Arab immigrants and local Somali families.

34. For the *gibilcaad*, see Michele Pirone, *Sguardo alla società somala e ai suoi problemi in generale*, pt. 3 of *Appunti di sociologia generale* (Muqdisho, 1965), pp. 10–11; Colucci, *Principi*, pp. 105–6; Barile, *Colonizzazione fascista*, pp. 117–19; Rovatti, "Mogadiscio," *ASMAI*, pos. 87/1, f. 7. I am also grateful to Virginia Luling for information on the *gibilcaad* of Afgooye district.

35. Cerulli, *Somalia* 1: 23–24, 91–95, 136; Hersi, "The Arab Factor," pp. 231–33.

36. Cerulli, *Somalia* 1: 61–64; and 3: 75 ff.

result was the establishment of Hawiyya territorial dominance over a large region. Their control of key pastoral resources provided the economic foundations for an extensive pastoral polity. Indeed, the places identified in tradition as centers of Ajuraan power are without exception sites of important clusters of wells; and most of the ruins attributed to the Ajuraan era lie near well complexes which were central nodes in the annual grazing cycles of the region's nomads. The inference is that the Ajuraan ruled as a pastoral aristocracy, with the control of wells being the source and symbol of their power.[37]

These roughly contemporaneous population movements—the religiously inspired immigration of Arab clerics, and the predominantly pastoral migrations of Hawiyya Somali from the center of the Peninsula toward the south—can both be seen as contributing to the consolidation of a regional polity that fits well with what we know of the Ajuraan from traditions. While the traditions can do no more than indicate the general circumstances in which Ajuraan power was exercised, they do help us weigh the external evidence from the period. By juxtaposing oral sources with other fragmentary evidence, it has been possible to suggest a historical explanation for the appearance of the Ajuraan "state" around 1500.

The Structure of Ajuraan Rule

The oral sources also provide us with recurrent themes that point to certain structural features of Ajuraan rule. In the origin story cited above, Ajuraan is seen as the descendant of the extraordinary outsider Balad and the Jambelle line of Hawiyya. The descendants of the Ajuraan (among which are the Gareen imams) can therefore be understood to have inherited the spiritual (Islamic?) power of Balad and the secular (numerical) power provided by the alliance of the first three Hawiyya "brothers," who in the story contribute gifts to seal the marriage of Jambelle's daughter Faaduma. Ajuraan power reposed on the twin pillars of spiritual preeminence and Hawiyya kinship solidarity, a potent combination in the Somali cultural context. In historical terms, a theocratic ideology superimposed on an extensive network of Hawiyya-affiliated clans helped uphold Ajuraan dominance over a wide region.

The centrality of the Gareen lineage (from which, traditions

37. Cf. chap. 2, pp. 70–72.

agree, the imam was always chosen) is also a recurrent theme. While sources assert that the "tribes of the Ajuraan confederacy" did not intermarry, they also state that the imams had "wives in every district" of the realm and took a portion of the bridewealth for every marriage contracted. In such images the imam is portrayed as husband and father to all: he assumes in tradition a unique place at the apex of the Ajuraan political and social system.[38]

The straightforward interpretation of the foregoing is that the primary cohesive force in the Ajuraan polity—as in virtually all pastoral polities—was the network of agnatic and affinal ties that linked the leading lineages of the region. We can effectively view the boundaries of this pastoral "state" as coincident with the outer limits of the alliance system. Such an interpretation makes it easier to comprehend how Ajuraan authority could be said to have extended from Mareeg (the territorial center of the Darandoolle, a segment of the Gurqaate Hawiyya) to Qallaafo (the probable homeland of the Jambelle Hawiyya, where their clan ancestor is buried), when in fact it is evident that the polity was not an integral territorial one. In the vast grazing areas between these nodes of Hawiyya control lived sizable numbers of Biimaal, Digil, and Oromo pastoralists who do not appear to have been incorporated fully into the alliance system.

Like many of the pastoral polities that periodically emerged in the Sahara and central Arabian deserts, the Ajuraan state was not a cohesive territorial entity; rather it consisted of several clan territories joined together by the kin, marriage, and patron/client ties of the inhabitants. Wherever a Hawiyya group had settled and could be incorporated into the alliance system, the "state" could be said to exist. On the local level, lineage segments might opt into the larger confederation for military, labor-sharing, or resource-sharing rea-

38. Traditions suggest that in times past many Hawiyya clans were preferentially endogamous; that is, where possible, marriages were contracted between members of different lineages within the same clan. This practice helped maintain political cohesiveness within large, territorially dispersed clans; it also helped to keep livestock within the extended kinship group. The assertion that the imams of Ajuraan "violated" the norms of clan endogamy and collected bridewealth from many different clans (see quotation above, p. 93) highlights the dominant position of the Gareen lineage in economic as well as political terms. Interviews with Muddey Haji Geeley, Muqdisho, 16 May and 9 June 1971; Aliow Mahad Emed, 29 July 1971; and Sherif Hassan Sherif Muhammad, 6 Sept. 1971. Cf. Cerulli, *Somalia* 2: 301 ff., and Marlowe, "The Galjaal Barsana," pp. 31, 38.

sons; others might be compelled to pay tribute in order to gain access to watering sites controlled by the Ajuraan. The state also incorporated groups of riverine cultivators that were settled at various places along the Shabeelle from Qallaafo in the north to Torre in the southeast, near Baraawe. These cultivators probably formed the bulk of the servile labor force that was conscripted to construct the dikes and canals popularly attributed to the Ajuraan period. Although they are remembered in tradition as the "slaves" of the Ajuraan, they probably resembled the communities of client-cultivators known from more recent times.[39] In exchange for supplying grain and labor to the dominant pastoral stratum, the cultivators corporately received the latter's patronage and "protection." Thus a series of local and regional alliances underpinned and legitimized the apparent concentration of power in the hands of the Gareen imams.

From this perspective, the phenomenon of Ajuraan "domination" represented not a break with the typical Somali system of clan alliances and patron/client links but an extension and elaboration of it. What gave the polity its overall cohesiveness and unusual longevity were the rudimentary administrative procedures and the theocratic ideology introduced by the Gareen. The taking of tribute, for example, is one of the most salient features of Ajuraan rule recorded by tradition. There is no reason to doubt that this practice actually occurred in the sixteenth century, particularly having noted the presence of literate Muslim record-keepers and "slave soldiers" during that period. The posting of *naa'ib*s to the various districts and the conscription of labor for public works are other indications from tradition of an embryonic bureaucracy at work. Alliances contracted at the local level continued to be based on mutual interest; but now techniques of Ajuraan administration and the titles and practices of an Islamic hierarchy—a new technology and ideology so to speak—were grafted on to these various local arrangements to produce an overarching political structure.

Determining whether there were any links between the Ajuraan and the wider Islamic world is problematic. There is no evidence to date that the Ajuraan state was known to Muslims outside of Somalia.[40] At the same time, the muskets and luxury goods associated

39. See chap. 4 below, pp. 163–65.
40. Personal communication from Ali Abdirahman Hersi, Department of History, Somali National University. In the course of his research for "The Arab Factor,"

with the governing elite were almost certainly imported from the Ottoman Empire or its neighbors. The Gareen alliance with the Muzaffar dynasty of Muqdisho must have given the former access to engineers and architects from abroad. If the Muslim advisers of the imams corresponded with statesmen elsewhere in the Islamic world, no record of their contact has come to light. On the basis of the evidence presently available, we must assume that the Ajuraan state was essentially Somali-oriented, more concerned with domestic developments than with international politics.

To sum up our historical reconstruction: the Ajuraan appear to have been a confederation of Hawiyya clans led by the Gareen lineage, which was believed to possess religious power and a sound genealogical pedigree. This politico-religious leadership drew on the warrior strength of the predominantly pastoral Hawiyya and the ideology of an expanding Islam to establish a series of administrative centers in and around the well sites and irrigated riverbanks of southern Somalia. Marriage alliances reinforced ties of agnatic and religious loyalty among the leading families of the region. Perhaps with the aid of literate Arab scholars and mercenaries, the Gareen evolved a rudimentary administration which oversaw the collection of tribute from cultivators, herdsmen, and traders and which conscripted a servile labor force to undertake an unprecedented program of construction of wells and fortifications. Alliances with the leading families of Muqdisho and Marka bolstered the imam's power by providing an outlet for surplus grain and livestock[41] and a source of the luxury goods that symbolized the imam's high status.

Details on the period of Ajuraan domination are sparse, and we have been forced to conjecture about many aspects of their political structure and ideology. As has been suggested, surviving oral traditions tend to elaborate the more stereotypic features of Ajuraan rule; as such, they alone cannot be taken as indisputable evidence for the existence of a fully developed autocracy. The primary value of these traditions is to reveal the principles on which the Ajuraan polity was

---

Hersi reviewed numerous Arabic manuscripts on medieval Somalia in Egypt and the Middle East.

41. Duarte Barbosa noted of Muqdisho in 1500 that it was well-supplied with meat, wheat, barley, horses, and fruit. See Duarte Barbosa, *A Description of the Coasts of East Africa and Malabar in the Beginning of the Sixteenth Century*, trans , E. J. Stanley (London, 1866), p. 16.

constructed, the sources of power and authority believed to have underpinned the system. These principles—clan solidarity, religious *baraka,* political alliance (chiefly through marriage), control of natural resources—are the major forms of political capital in the Somali pastoral setting. To a greater or lesser degree, these same principles have been employed by virtually every leader or dynasty that has attempted to consolidate his or its authority over any portion of the Somali Peninsula in the past. The Ajuraan are unusual because, as traditions suggest, they exploited all four sources of power. It is the extent of Ajuraan domination and the range of techniques used to sustain it that probably account for the elaborate traditions associated with this period, as I will argue in the concluding section. The extent of Ajuraan domination may also account for the widespread traditions concerned with the overthrow of the dynasty. These we will consider next.

Variant Traditions and Historical Processes

Traditions of Ajuraan rule reveal more about general political principles than about specific historical events, and so the historian must seek to reconstruct the concrete historical circumstances in which these principles operated. Traditions of Ajuraan decline, on the other hand, present the historian with a different problem. Here he is confronted by a multiplicity of episodes, many of them restricted to certain locales and set in specific circumstances, from which he must extract some notion of the general processes at work in the declining years of the Ajuraan era.

Most clans that today occupy tracts of land adjacent to the west bank of the Shabeelle River have traditions of being subject to and ultimately expelling the Ajuraan. As was suggested above, the memory of having overthrown an oppressive regime helps a clan to embellish its history, to legitimate its present territorial claims, and to explain the origins of its alliances with other clans. At the same time, many of these traditions are sufficiently varied in structure and content to suggest that they are less a part of a general folklore tradition than a record, however embellished, of specific clan exploits. While the fact of defeating the Ajuraan is a shared feature of all the variants, there is no one standardized account of the process of that defeat. Rather there exists a variety of motifs which may in fact mirror the complexity of historical processes on the ground. Moreover, the processes of conflict and its resolution preserved in these traditions are not improbable ones given the nature of the Ajuraan polity sketched above.

Clan traditions about Ajuraan decline can be grouped into several categories. Some describe military encounters and include place names and, occasionally, the names of prominent leaders (Darandoolle rebellion, p. 93). Others recount the emergence of rivals to Ajuraan leadership and leave the actual downfall of the Ajuraan unstated (the El Amir takeover of Marka). Still others are elaborate stories detailing despicable acts wrought by Ajuraan officials together with plots of revenge contrived by the wronged parties.[42] Finally, there are traditions (like that about Shaykh Hassan Buraale, discussed below) which attribute Ajuraan decline to the loss of their religious authority and powers. The variety of style and structure in these accounts leads one to suspect that a number of different motives lie behind their formulation and transmission. At the core of each tradition lies the undisputed belief that the Ajuraan fell from power; yet each has elaborated the story of the fall to make particular points about the fragility of power. An analysis of the various types of traditions enables us to view the decline of the Ajuraan on different levels. From all indications, the demise of the dynasty was not a sudden event; it was a lengthy process involving both internal and external challenges to Ajuraan supremacy. Although these traditions are specific enough to establish a rough chronology—the erosion of Ajuraan power seems to have begun about 1620 and was complete by 1690—I will be less concerned here with particular events than with the various processes that altered the structure of Ajuraan domination.

In the first place, Ajuraan decline needs to be seen against the background of continuous pastoral migrations out of the arid central Peninsula toward the better-watered regions of the interriver plain, which was the heartland of the Ajuraan dominions. Hawiyya-affiliated clans and sub-clans—Gaaljacal, Baddi Addo, Murursade, Abgaal—continued to filter into the grazing areas opened up by earlier Ha-

---

42. Barile, *Colonizzazione fascista*, pp. 67–70, records a tradition in which an Ajuraan emir compels some of his recalcitrant subjects to eat the cooked flesh of one of their kinsmen who had been killed in punishment for his refusal to hand over his wife to the emir's henchmen. This macabre episode then becomes justification for the subsequent rebellion of the victim's descendants.

wiyya migrations. By 1600, clans of Hawiyya ancestry controlled most of the pasture land along both banks of the middle Shabeelle River.[43] At the same time, numerous pastoralists known in more recent times as Rahanwiin began to occupy the lands west of the Hawiyya.[44] While herding units in the vanguard of these two migratory waves could be incorporated into the Ajuraan polity through arrangements of pastoral clientship, their growing numbers—the result of additional migrations and natural reproduction—must have posed a threat to their hosts. Thus, on one level, the challenge to Ajuraan supremacy came from newly arrived nomads seeking to stake a claim to the region's resources and forming new alliances to do so. The Darandoolle settlement of well sites north and west of Muqdisho; their subsequent rebellion against restrictions imposed by the Ajuraan on the use of the wells; the Gaaljacal desire to extend their grazing areas: all are examples of the continual on-the-ground conflict between the established occupants of the area and the newer arrivals, chiefly over questions of access to natural resources. Accounts of such conflict, exemplified by the Darandoolle episode, may well be a record of actual historical events. On the other hand, they may be generalized descriptions of recurrent pastoral conflicts which characterized relations between the dominant Ajuraan and their erstwhile subjects. In either case, traditions of this sort point to a distinctly ecological/economic dimension in the challenge to Ajuraan supremacy.

Along with this competition for grazing resources there apparently occurred a series of struggles for political ascendancy among the various factions of the Ajuraan confederacy. This struggle is most clearly signaled in the story (alluded to on p. 93) of the auspicious birth of the future Darandoolle (Abgaal) imam, who would in time come to challenge the authority of the Gareen imams. In a related tradition published by Enrico Cerulli, the Gareen imam hears a prophecy that the descendants of his son-in-law (Osman Darandoolle) were destined to outnumber the sons of Ajuraan and to expel the latter from the land.

The mother of Hiraabe was Faaduma Karanle. The mother of Abgaal was Faaduma Sarjelle, who was an Ajuraan. She was

43. Cerulli, *Somalia* 1: 64. This was roughly the distribution of Hawiyya clans at the start of the twentieth century.

44. Cerulli, *Somalia* 1: 65–66. Cf. Colucci, *Principi*, pp. 104–7, 125–39.

married by Osman Darandoolle. They had a son who was called
Ali Osman. Sometime later a wise elder went to Sarjelle Gareen,
and said: "O noble Sarjelle, I have seen in the books that the
descendants of the son born to your daughter Faaduma will
drive your descendants from the land. I have seen this in the
books." "You have seen these things?" "Yes, I have seen them,"
he replied. "So be it!" responded the noble Sarjelle.[45]

The account goes on to tell of the Gareen imam's plan to poison the
young Ali, only to poison his daughter Faaduma by mistake. The
marriage relations cited at the beginning of the tradition are critical
to an understanding both of the nature of Ajuraan rule and of its
subsequent fragmentation.

The Darandoolle, it should be noted, were part of the Gurqaate,
a clan section collateral to the Jambelle Hawiyya from whom Ajuraan
(and Gareen) is said to have been descended. Intermarriage among the
descendants of these uterine brothers on the one hand helped reinforce the solidarity of the Hawiyya. On the other hand, competition
between collateral lines was very common in Somalia, particularly
where the titular leadership of a larger clan-confederation was at
stake. Such a struggle for the dominant place within the Hawiyya-
dominated Ajuraan confederation may also be reflected in the rise of
the Silcis and El Amir (see above, p. 94) in the later years of Ajuraan
rule. Both are said to have been descendants of Gurqaate Hawiyya,
as were the Abgaal Darandoolle. Thus it can be argued that the
dominant groups which appeared toward the end of the Ajuraan era
—the Darandoolle near Muqdisho, the Silcis near Afgooye, and the El
Amir in Marka—represent the partition of the Ajuraan imamate
among collateral Hawiyya sections. Or perhaps one branch of the
Hawiyya—namely the Gurqaate—forcibly replaced another (the Jambelle) as leaders of the confederation. This second hypothesis better
explains the apparent "disappearance" of the Ajuraan by suggesting
that the line of Gareen Jambelle was eclipsed politically by the more
numerous and widespread Gurqaate. In the Somali setting, power
ultimately comes from the fighting strength of a clan and its allies;
and domination most often depends on the relative numerical superi-
ority of the dominant. Thus the decline of Ajuraan power in political
terms conceivably resulted from shifts in the demographic structure

45. Cerulli, *Somalia* 2: 243–44.

of the original alliance network. Indeed, clans of Gurqaate and Guggundabe affiliation were the dominant representatives of the Hawiyya
clan family in the Shabeelle valley area at the beginning of the twentieth century. The bulk of Jambelle Hawiyya (including the Ajuraan)
are today located west of the Jubba River.[46]

Religious stories dealing with Ajuraan decline are abundant and
suggest yet another level at which the process can be studied. In the
formative years of the Ajuraan polity, the Gareen appear to have
enjoyed a religious preeminence which stemmed partly from their
purported Arab ancestry on the paternal side and partly from the
prestige associated with their early period of rule in the Ogaadeen.
The unique position of the Gareen as sole inheritors of Balad's religious authority was soon eroded, however, by the spread of Islam and
by the Gareen's own policy of political marriages with collateral Hawiyya clans. We have seen, for example, that the first Abgaal imam
was a direct descendant of a Gareen imam's daughter. Such unions
transmitted to their progeny some of the *baraka* and religious prestige of the Gareen, thus helping to validate the Abgaal's claims to
religious preeminence in their own right. With the diffusion of
spiritual gifts among the various descendants of the imam's family,
the unique religious position of the Gareen rulers was gradually un-
dermined. A series of religio-political dynasties replaced the former
imamate: each had a localized power base and exercised spiritual
influence over a limited area.

Related to the foreging level of analysis, local traditions popularly attribute the demise of the Ajuraan to excessive pride and neglect of the commands of Islam. Indeed, a challenge to the moral
authority of the imams appears to be a central theme in the following
account about Shaykh Hassan Buraale, who appears to have died
toward the end of the seventeenth century.

When the family of Gareen had expelled their saint and religious
adviser, Shaykh Hassan Buraale, as the family of the Quraysh-
ites did to their brother Muhammad, they said many bad things
about him. They said that he practiced *sixir* [sorcery] and that
he wished to command all of the Ajuraan from east to west by
his knowledge of *asraar* [sacred mysteries]. The imam was
angry; and his name was Omar. He sent messengers to bring

46. I. M. Lewis, *Peoples of the Horn of Africa* (London, 1955), p. 20.

Shaykh Hassan Buraale to him. He asked the shaykh, "Why do you put yourself above us? Why do you seek to sever the federation of the Ajuraan? You have divided in two the family of the Ajuraan which I command. You ought to act like the others, you should be a servant." The imam's *wazir* ordered Shaykh Hassan Buraale to feed the royal animals. Shaykh Hassan replied that he could not carry out the imam's orders. The latter demanded, "Why won't you obey me? Why do you act like my superior?" Shaykh Hassan Buraale responded, "I am not a slave of the Ajuraan. I am not your superior and I am not among the honored. I am a slave of God."

To demonstrate his sacred power, Shaykh Hassan Buraale brought grass to feed the imam's horses. It was late afternoon when the animals arrived for feeding. When they entered the *zariba* [animal enclosure], they ate all but the grass brought by Shaykh Hassan Buraale. When the imam returned to the *zariba,* he was speechless; the animals had not eaten the grass cut by Shaykh Hassan, although it was still green. The imam became angry and said, "In truth you are a sorcerer—you will be put in jail." The shaykh replied, "I am not a sorcerer, but I will tell you the reason that the animals have left the grass: they are beasts of God; they know truth, and you do not know it."[47]

This account is typical of the religious interpretations that many notable events in Somali traditions undergo in the course of their transmission. They persist alongside straightforward narratives of grazing disputes and military conflicts and frequently find their way into written form in books of Arabic prayers and religious genealogies. These religious interpretations have greatly influenced the telling of the Ajuraan story even by nonreligious informants; they are a good example of the didactic elements which have been grafted on to the story of Ajuraan decline.

The picture which emerges, then, is of a chain reaction of rebellions which eventually drove the Ajuraan leaders from power and ultimately from the middle Shabeelle valley altogether. Traditions suggest that they were succeeded in a few areas by a number of smaller polities, notably the Darandoolle, Silcis, and El Amir alluded to above. Oral accounts of the Silcis and El Amir occasionally seem

47. Translation from mss. of Shaykh Abow Yunis.

to be confused with accounts of the Ajuraan proper. For example, local traditions in the Afgooye district speak of the Silcis as despotic rulers. Their sultan enjoyed the *ius primae noctis*. He exacted tribute from the surrounding populations—by then largely consisting of the ancestors of the present-day Geledi and Wacdaan—in the form of durra and *bun*, and taxed all livestock which came to water at the river's edge. The peoples subject to the sultan were compelled to pray at the mosque in Lama Jiidle, the center of Silcis administration. Apparently the Silcis co-opted a segment of the local population; traditions recall that allies of the ruling dynasty placed *saab* (conical wicker baskets) on the roof peaks of their houses to indicate their immunity from Silcis raids.[48]

Some informants said that the Silcis were actually that section of the Ajuraan which governed the Afgooye district; others that they succeeded the Ajuraan as rulers of the area. In any case, the Silcis, too, were ousted from the lower Shabeelle valley by the combined forces of the Geledi and Wacdaan, whose present-day alliance is said to date from the end of the Silcis sultanate in the early eighteenth century. As with the accounts of Ajuraan decline, a number of different stories purport to explain the end of Silcis rule.[49]

In the vicinity of Marka, a mysterious group known as the El Amir made its appearance in the years between 1650 and 1700. According to an account collected by Guillain in 1847, a leader known as Amir formed a following which invaded the territory of Marka and expelled the Ajuraan. The El Amir then ruled for thirty-four years until the Biimaal definitively occupied Marka.[50] It is tempting to view this Amir as a warrior-administrator who seceded from the Ajuraan confederacy and formed a small principality of his own. Biimaal traditions, which associate the end of Ajuraan rule with the defeat of an *emir*, tend to support this hypothesis; but again, there is a tendency for traditions to confuse the demise of the Ajuraan with that of the El Amir. Guillain suggested that the El Amir were Abgaal; if this

48. Ali Omar Haji "Goyle," Afgooye, 10 June 1971; Yusuf Nur, Muqdisho, 17 June 1971. Cf. Luling, "Social Structure," pp. 30–32.

49. Luling, "Social Structure," p. 36.

50. It is possible that Guillain wrote "El-Amir" for *El-Hamar* ("people of Hamar," the Somali name for Muqdisho). Since the people of the environs of Hamar were by 1690 largely Abgaal, the rendering "El-Hamar" would not be unreasonable. See Guillain, *Documents*, 3: 141–42, 147, n. 1. Cf. Pantano, *La citta di Merca*, pp. 13–20; Barile, *Colonizzazione fascista*, pp. 66–70.

were true, their brief period of rule would fit the pattern of Gurqaate ascendancy following upon Ajuraan decline.

Rule by the Silcis and El Amir thus appears to represent the last phase of a period of theocratic government initially imposed by the Gareen. These small polities maintained for a time the form and some of the substance of Ajuraan rule, which helps account for their indistinguishability from the Ajuraan in many (particularly non-Hawiyya) traditions. With the disappearance of the El Amir and the Silcis—the Darandoolle imam remained as a titular clan leader in the Muqdisho area right into the twentieth century—the age of theocracy in southern Somalia came to an end. By the beginning of the eighteenth century, a new pattern of political alliances began to take shape, and the Ajuraan passed into memory and into oral tradition.

The long-lived and apparently effective rule of a theocratic dynasty would not be repeated again in the history of southern Somalia. The sources of power exploited by the Gareen imams were, to be sure, exploited also by subsequent leaders in the interriver area, notably the sultans of Geledi who managed to establish a sizable sphere of influence in the early nineteenth century.[51] But neither they nor the zealous Muslims of Baardheere (who for a time extended their authority all the way to Baraawe)[52] combined all the elements of pastoral power which characterized Ajuraan rule. The Geledi lacked the theocratic superstructure and administrative hierarchy, and the Baardheere reformers lacked the network of alliances and the resource base which in combination sustained Ajuraan domination for more than a hundred years. The interriver area of Somalia was never again brought under the control of a single dynasty.

In speculating about the long-term significance of the Ajuraan for the history of southern Somalia, we can see their era as one that promoted economic change in the interriver area. Before the establishment of Hawiyya hegemony in the Shabeelle Valley, the farming communities of the area most probably consisted of Bantu-speaking settlers who traded only casually with the cattle nomads who were their immediate neighbors. The coming of the Ajuraan, who systematically exacted tribute from the farmers in exchange for protec-

---

51. Luling, "Social Structure," pp. 169–76.; Lee V. Cassanelli, "The Benaadir Past: Essays in Southern Somali History" (Ph.D. diss., University of Wisconsin, 1973), pp. 100–123.

52. See below, chap. 4, pp. 137–40.

tion, may have helped institutionalize relations between farmer and nomad, creating ties of patronage and clientship that persisted into the twentieth century.[53] Moreover, by mobilizing an agrarian labor force to construct irrigation works, the Ajuraan probably contributed to the expansion of agricultural production. And by dominating major well sites and river crossings, the Ajuraan and their allies could readily control trade routes from the interior to the Benaadir Coast. The diversity of economic activity in sixteenth-century southern Somalia is attested to in Duarte Barbosa's list of products traded in Muqdisho (ca. 1500): ivory, wax, cereal, and horses.[54] Whether the Ajuraan were the creators or beneficiaries of this productive agricultural/pastoral regime is not clear. But it is certainly plausible to argue that the Ajuraan contributed to the integration of numerous local economies in the interriver area.

In the spread of Islam, the Ajuraan also played an important role. To be sure their polity may have been theocratic more in structure than in substance—for clan loyalties almost certainly continued to override allegiance to the imam as spiritual leader. But the presence of an Islamic power in the southern Somali lowlands drew Muslim jurists and preachers to the area and laid the foundation for the further penetration of Islam to the interior. Evidence for conversions during the Ajuraan era comes from Hawiyya genealogies; some of these show marked shifts from strictly Somali to distinctly Muslim names anywhere from fourteen to eighteen generations ago, that is, roughly during the period of Ajuraan hegemony.[55] Beyond this, Ajuraan traditions mention a number of military expeditions undertaken against the *gaal madow* (black infidels), presumably Rahanwiin or Oromo tribes that lay beyond the frontier of Ajuraan Islamic administration.[56]

53. See chap. 5, pp. 163–66.

54. Barbosa, *Description of the Coasts*, p. 16.

55. I am indebted to, among others, Elias Haji Omar, librarian to the National University in Muqdisho in 1971, for this information.

While a shift to Muslim names does not always mark the point of initial conversion, it does indicate an increasing use of an Islamic idiom. Somalis commonly have two first names, one given at birth and one descriptive (*naanay*s, or "nickname"). Even after the genealogies become distinctively Islamic, the Somali nickname gets appended to the Muslim name—for example, Ahmed "Dheere" Muhammad (Ahmed "the tall" Muhammad).

56. Sherif Hassan Sherif Muhammad, Muqdisho, 6 Sept. 1971; Shaykh Abdelqadir Abokor Ashir, Dundumey, 16 Aug. 1971.

Finally, we might speculate that both religiously and militarily the Ajuraan confederation provided a bulwark against the Oromo who, from the middle of the sixteenth century, were expanding dramatically in all directions from their homeland east of Lake Abbaya. Ajuraan power extended at least as far as Qallaafo on the upper Shabeelle River, giving the Somali an advanced position along the frontier of Oromo expansion. We can speculate that the spearhead of the Oromo migrations might have been toward the Benaadir coast—rather than toward Ethiopia and the Jubba River—had not the Ajuraan been at the peak of their power at the same historical moment.[57] Paradoxically, the diversion of Oromo movements to the northeast may have forced a number of Hawiyya groups in the Ogaadeen to migrate southward along the line of wells that parallels the Shabeelle. Eventually, these Hawiyya pastoralists crossed the river and entered the domains of the Ajuraan, challenging and displacing them.

Traditions as Ideology

It seems appropriate in conclusion to speculate about the possible significance of the Ajuraan traditions for contemporary Somalis. It has become commonplace to say that oral traditions are basically a form of ideology which uses history to explain, legitimate, or embellish the claims of certain groups to territory, political office, or privileged status in the larger society. The Ajuraan traditions we have been discussing, however, cannot be regarded as ideology in this narrow sense, because they deal with a situation of domination that no longer exists. Clearly they no longer mask or maintain the interests of any dominant stratum; if anything, they explain and justify the overthrow of a historical tyranny and thereby glorify the histories of the clans that rebelled. In some instances, the traditions also establish the circumstances in which two or more clans allied for a common purpose and therefore may be recalled to buttress or renew the alliance.

Another way in which these traditions may be considered ideologies derives from their role as a "charter" of Hawiyya solidarity. The Hawiyya are one of the six large clan-families into which the Somali nation is divided; they are today represented by some two dozen clans spread throughout the Somali Peninsula, though the majority occupy

57. Cf. Cerulli, *Somalia* 1: 65–67.

a contiguous stretch of territory in the south-central plains. Hawiyya informants in general possess more detailed and elaborate traditions of the Ajuraan period than sources from other clan-families do. This is to be expected, since Hawiyya ancestors were the major protagonists in the events we have related. More important, though, is the fact that the Ajuraan era represented a period of political consolidation that perhaps initiated and undoubtedly furthered the process of Hawiyya clan formation. Political consolidation in conjunction with the spread of Islam provided scattered nomadic groups with a genealogical and territorial identity that they have maintained (with certain adjustments) to this day. The Ajuraan story thus can be seen as an account of group formation for the Hawiyya.

Despite the contributions that Ajuraan traditions can make to clan solidarity and to the embellishment of clan history, the fact remains that they have little functional utility in the contemporary context. Most of the clans which relate accounts of their ancestors' victories over the Ajuraan have enjoyed uncontested rights to the lands they occupy for at least a century. Alliances purportedly made at the time of Ajuraan domination have been either broken or reinforced by more recent events. And claimed links with the long-dispersed Ajuraan appear to carry little prestige or practical value in the region today. In sum, the preservation of the Ajuraan saga in Somali traditions is in no way fundamental to the present-day exercise of rights over land and pasture or to the enjoyment of any political prerogatives. Why, then, does it remain as one of the two or three early episodes narrated by virtually every knowledgeable southern Somali informant when he is asked about the old days?

Apart from its intrinsic interest as an account of a unique experiment in political consolidation—must we assume that nonliterate peoples preserve only those historical memories that have an immediate instrumental value?—the Ajuraan saga has been conserved, I think, as a reflection on the dangers of institutionalized domination. It is a body of ideas, drawn from historical experience, which is counterpoised to the popular ideology of segmentary opposition that gives Somali politics its flexible and fluid character. It is a statement of what can, and does, happen when the inequalities that emerge periodically in pastoral society are formalized and solidified.

Despite the widely held notion that traditional Somali society was completely democratic and egalitarian—a notion generated partly by the Somalis' own firm adherence to a genealogical idiom that

stresses balance and complementarity among opposed lineage groups
—inequalities of power were inevitable. Somali clans and lineages
have always shared unequally in the scarce resources of the land and
consequently in the power conferred by access to such resources.[58] In
the ceaseless competition for pasture, water, and wives, clans with
larger numbers and better geographical location had a decided advantage over others. They used this advantage to build up their herds
(through raiding, tribute-taking, or gifts from client groups) and to
contract favorable marriages for their children.

These situations of differential wealth and power were mitigated
by the fact that the imbalances were neither all pervasive nor permanent. Rarely in a nomadic setting could a dominant clan impose its will
totally on the herdsmen of other groups. Tribute could be extracted
and grazing areas restricted, but seldom could powerful clans prevent
others from making those basic pastoral decisions that involved the
survival of livestock and of the lineage. Nomads who found their
options too severely restricted could usually find allies among rivals
to the dominant group; they could distribute their livestock among
distant kinsmen; or they could emigrate. Thus power was inherently
unstable, since the ecological and demographic realities that supported it were themselves in constant flux. Total oppression—which,
following Philip Salzman, I will define as the monopoly of the means
of coercion, of production and of decision-making[59]—was virtually
impossible under typical conditions of nomadic life.

Despite these limits to domination, which are found in most
nomadic societies, there have been historical occasions when the convergence of circumstances made it possible for certain ascendant
groups to solidify their positions at the top. For example, some of the
recent literature on nomads has discussed the intrusion into nomadic
society of a state apparatus. Whether one is dealing with the Otto-

58. This is apparent from the numerous traditions and oral poems that deal with
the subjects of prepotent clans, pastoral clientship and dependence, and conflict over
access to resources. For comparative and theoretical approaches to the question of
inequality in nomadic societies, see Talal Asad, "Equality in Nomadic Social Systems?"
Critique of Anthropology 11 (1978): 57–65; Jacob Black, "Tyranny as a Strategy for
Survival in an 'Egalitarian' Society: Luri Facts versus an Anthroplogical Mystique,"
Man 7 (Dec. 1972): 614–34; Philip C. Salzman, "Inequality and Oppression in Nomadic
Society," in L'Équipe écologie et anthropologie des sociétés pastorales, eds., *Pastoral
Production and Society* (Paris and Cambridge, 1979), pp. 429–46.
59. Salzman, "Inequality and Oppression," pp. 436–38.

mans, with European colonial regimes, or with the modern Iranian state, the pattern has been the same. To extend order and administration into the countryside, the state threw its force behind lineages or clans that appeared to be dominant at the time, thus enabling the latter to solidify their position of dominance.[60] These favored groups used their access to state-administered resources to expand the range and enhance the techniques of control over their countrymen while they ensconced themselves as agents of the state.

With the exception of a few Somali clans that have periodically been subject to Ethiopian imperial control, Somalis did not experience the intrusion of state power until the establishment of colonial rule in the early twentieth century. However, in the precolonial setting, other forces could play a similar role. Militant Islamic clerics, often backed by nomadic mercenaries, represented a form of power that stood outside the nexus of clan alliances; they claimed an authority which transcended that produced by the realities of warrior strength and resource control. When the introduction of theocratic notions of power coincided with (and helped consolidate) territorial control by a cohesive tribal entity, the conditions were present for the emergence of institutionalized domination.

The Ajuraan appear to have represented such a convergence of forces in the sixteenth century. Traditions assert that rule by the Ajuraan dynasty pervaded many areas of life: the Ajuraan controlled the means of coercion (through slave-soldiers and, perhaps in their later years, access to firearms from outside); the resources essential to production (through domination of well sites over a large region); and the decision-making apparatus (by the imposition of a theocratic model of leadership on a segmentary society). How effective and long-lasting Ajuraan domination was in reality cannot be known. It is conceivable that their exercise of power was not everywhere exploitative but rather integrative. Traditions do suggest, however, that the Ajuraan institutionalized pastoral power to a greater degree than any subsequent "desert strongmen" were able to.

To conclude: many stateless societies like the Somali project

---

60. See, for example, J. P. Mason, "Desert Strongman in the East Libyan Sahara (ca. 1820): A Reconstruction of Local Power in the Region of Augila Oasis," *Revue d'histoire maghrebine* 6 (July 1976): 180–88; Philip C. Salzman, "Tribal Chiefs as Middlemen: The Politics of Encapsulation in the Middle East," *Anthropological Quarterly* 47 (1974): 203–10; and references in n. 58 above.

through their proverbs and their genealogical charters an ideology of egalitarianism that may obscure the realities of inequality in the society. Such egalitarian ideologies may be regarded partly as ideals, partly as guides to the way the system of balanced and shifting alliances sometimes works. At other times, however, individuals and factions succeed in accumulating more power than can be counter-balanced by their neighbors; and more important, they use that power to exploit and oppress others. Historical traditions—however embellished or elaborated—often relate such instances of oppression. In contrast to the normative ideology of proverbs, they provide indications of the periodic tendency for groups within the society to attempt to formalize relations of inequality and domination. Thus, among other things, traditions are statements about the excesses to which power, when institutionalized, can be put.

4 Saints, Sultans, and Sectarians: Islamic Themes in Southern Somali History, ca. 1600–1850

The Islamization of the Somali people must be considered one of the central formative processes in their history. More than 95 percent of contemporary Somalis are professed Muslims, and many claim that their ancestors were converted more than a millennium ago. A visitor will not venture too far into the countryside before encountering a small circle of children sitting under a tree reciting verses from the Quran with a bearded shaykh; or before spying one of the many square, whitewashed buildings that mark the tombs of venerated saints from the past. These everyday scenes, which are observable from one end of the Peninsula to the other, reveal a common heritage that has an even more profound dimension: the belief by many Somalis that their remote ancestors are all ultimately descended from the Qurishi clan of the Prophet Muhammad himself.

Despite the centrality of Islam in Somali life and thought, however, very little is known about its actual diffusion in the countryside before the second half of the nineteenth century. Indeed, before the rapid spread of Islamic brotherhoods to the Somali interior in the later 1800s, there are few signposts to mark the progress of Islamization at the local level. Written records from the seventeenth and eighteenth centuries, whether Arabic or European, tend to be preoccupied with the competition among Turkish, Omani, and Portuguese interests for control of the Somali coast, or with the migration of Hadrami and Yemeni families to the coastal towns. They tell

119

us nothing about the interplay of coastal Islamic culture with the Somali interior.[1]

Indigenous written sources are only slightly more helpful. Enrico Cerulli has annotated and analyzed several documents on the history of Harar, the most famous center of Islamic learning in the Horn.[2] However, the history of that unique town is something of a self-contained one after 1577, when the ruling dynasty of the once-powerful Adal sultanate transferred its capital from Harar to the oasis of Aussa in the Danakil desert.[3] Harari records reveal little about life in the nomadic world beyond its walls. Similarly, chronicles from Muqdisho on the southern Somali coast do occasionally reflect the intrusion into town life of the various groups of pastoralists that inhabited the hinterland.[4] But on social change in the hinterland itself, again there is silence.

To help fill this gap in the social history of Islam in Somalia, the historian must turn to local oral traditions. For our purposes, the most important of these belong to a genre that can be called saint stories. Saints are historical personalities widely respected and even venerated by Somalis for their personal piety, miraculous works, or contribution to the spread of Islamic learning. Their tombs, which dot the countryside, are frequently the sites of annual religious celebrations held to commemorate the life and works of the deceased saint. Somali pilgrims often come from great distances to make personal petitions, material offerings, and common prayer with other believers.[5]

1. These sources and much of what they tell us about the lowland populations of northeast Africa are discussed in J. S. Trimingham, *Islam in Ethiopia* (London, 1965); Jean Doresse, *Histoire sommaire de la Corne orientale de l'Afrique* (Paris, 1971); and Ulrich Braukämper, "Islamic Principalities in Southeast Ethiopia Between the Thirteenth and the Sixteenth Centuries," *Ethiopianist Notes*, vol. 1, nos. 1 and 2 (1977).

2. These have been assembled in Enrico Cerulli, *L'Islam di ieri e di oggi* (Rome, 1971), esp. pp. 135–206, 281–327.

3. Shortly after the transfer of the capital, the *amir*s of Harar broke off their allegiance to Aussa, and henceforth their politics revolved primarily around local issues. See ibid., pp. 311–15.

4. Enrico Cerulli, *Somalia: Scritti vari editi ed inediti*, 3 vols. (Rome, 1957), 1: 12–13, 39–40; Ali Abdirahman Hersi, "The Arab Factor in Somali History: The Origins and Development of Arab Enterprise and Cultural Influences in the Somali Peninsula" (Ph.D. diss., University of California, Los Angeles, 1977), pp. 223, 231–33, 240–41.

5. A good introduction to the subject of saints in contemporary Somali society is I. M. Lewis, "Sufism in Somaliland: A Study in Tribal Islam," *Bulletin of the School of Oriental and African Studies* 17 (1955): 581–602, and 18 (1956): 146–60; and I. M.

During these annual pilgrimages *(siyaaro)*, the travelers exchange stories about the life of the saint, and in this way saint stories
become part of popular tradition. They are often told informally on
other occasions as well. Whenever I asked local elders about prominent personalities in the history of their village or locale, I invariably
received accounts of holy men. Stories of saints' lives do sometimes
find their way into written form in manuscripts kept by their descendants, though these are not easily accessible to the foreign researcher.

As one of the most popular forms of Somali oral literature, saint
stories provide valuable insights into local perceptions of religion and
society. In a recent article, B. W. Andrzejewski has pointed out the
great variety of motifs that run through this genre of folk tradition
and the attitudes toward religion and religious life that they typify.[6]
Traditions of the saints also represent a potentially rich source for the
reconstruction of local history. But they must be treated with caution.
It is, for example, often difficult to separate out the didactic and
hagiographic elements in the accounts from actual historical happen-
ings. Like most oral traditions, they lack chronological precision and
often tend to confuse process with interpretation in the narration of
events. This is particularly problematic in traditions about Islam,
whose historical impact is so inextricably linked in Somali thought
with its present place in Somali culture. Thus traditions about saints
from the past typically emphasize those miraculous feats that inspire
the continued veneration of these men; and they often attribute to a
single saint the introduction of Islamic institutions or rituals which
probably evolved over several generations.

Nevertheless, I believe it is possible to discover in the saint
stories, and in other local traditions, evidence of certain recurrent
patterns associated with the spread of Islam in rural Somalia. In this
chapter I will give particular attention to three aspects of the local
history of Islam before 1850. First I will consider the several roles
played by the saint in Somali society insofar as these can be historically reconstructed from oral traditions and second, the impact of the
saints and of the practices they introduced on Somali political thought

---

Lewis, "Shaikhs and Warriors in Somaliland," in Meyer Fortes and Germaine Dieterlen,
eds., *African Systems of Thought* (London, 1965), pp. 204–23.

    6. B. W. Andrzejewski, "The Veneration of Sufi Saints and Its Impact on the
Oral Literature of the Somali People and on Their Literature in Arabic," *African
Language Studies*, 15 (1974): 15–54.

and behavior. Finally, I will examine an extensive but little-studied war for religious supremacy that took place in southern Somalia in the 1840s: in it were manifested many of the tensions that had been generated during the preceding period of Islam's penetration into Somali life and society. The limitations of the oral data make it difficult to pinpoint these developments in years or even decades. But as I will try to show, the influence of the saints, and the Somalization of their Islamic Sufi tradition, were ongoing processes whose significance was not restricted to any one historical period.

The Saint in Somali Society

A survey of southern Somali oral traditions suggests that saints played an important role in the histories of many clans resident there today. For some clans, it appears that their initial exposure to Islam came through the arrival among them of itinerant holy men. For others, the saints figure significantly in tradition as protectors from enemy raids; as mediators in intra-clan disputes; or as initiators of customs that helped insure the prosperity and cohesiveness of newly formed confederations. Many traditions provide indirect evidence of the turbulent political conditions in which the saints found themselves. Those conditions could have been associated with the breakup of the Ajuraan sultanate;[7] with Oromo-Somali conflict following the historic expansion of the former from a homeland near Lake Abbaya in the mid-sixteenth century; and with the subsequent arrival in the interriver region of elements of the Rahanwiin clan family, many of which probably had had little previous exposure to Islam.[8]

The following account, narrated by a religious elder in Wanle Weyn, typifies the actions attributed to a saint. This one is called Omar "Arag" (Omar "the Seer"):

Omar "Arag" helped to organize the Rahanwiin tribes around Saramaan [an important cluster of wells north of Baydhabo].

7. See chap. 3, pp. 93–94, 106–12.
8. This interpretation accords not only with the most recent linguistic evidence, which suggests that the Oromo expansion was the most recent of those movements involving speakers of East Cushitic languages; it also fits with the oral traditions of many Rahanwiin clans that refer to periodic warfare with Oromo herdsmen before or during the period of their acceptance of Islam. See Bernd Heine, "Notes on the History of the Sam-Speaking People," Department of History Staff Seminar Paper No. 9, University of Nairobi, 12 Jan. 1977, pp. 3, 12–13.

The people then were divided into two sections and were always fighting with the Arussi and Borana [Oromo]. Omar "Arag" appointed *malaakh*s to lead the army, organized peaceful exchange among the tribes, and set boundaries for each.

He was the first to divide the 114 suras of the Quran among the various local tribes. Even today, the various clans come together at his tomb every year. Each brings with them a *loox* [piece of wood on which Quranic verses are written]. Then one of the descendants of Omar Arag washes the verses off the *loox* and the water which runs off is divided among the various clans to protect them.[9]

This same Omar "Arag" was also the subject of a testimony by another informant (see below, p. 124) from the Baydhabo district, some eighty miles from Wanle Weyn, evidence that some saints enjoyed more than simply a local reputation.

Another such widely remembered saint was Haran Medare, who is the subject of a tradition collected by a former Italian colonial official from the Eelay clan. The tradition refers to the period when the Eelay were beginning to occupy their present lands between Baydhabo and Buur Hakaba, around the middle of the seventeenth century. It records that while the Eelay were engaged in prolonged fighting with the forces of the legendary Geedy Ababow, a fierce pagan (Oromo?) warrior, there came among them a prophet called Haran Medare. He encouraged the recently converted Eelay in their new Islamic faith and foretold that before long a shaykh of great learning would come and lead them. The prophecy was fulfilled in the person of Shaykh Mumin Abdullahi, whose descendants (the Reer Shaykh Mumin) came to exercise considerable spiritual influence over much of the region between Baydhabo and Buur Hakaba. The great shaykh himself was reputed to have had power over the birds of the field, and even today his descendants are summoned to protect the harvests of those Eelay who cultivate durra and maize.[10]

Saints such as Omar "Arag" and Haran Medare worked along the frontier of Islam, backed by no authority other than God's and armed only with their Faith and an array of supernatural powers.

9. Haji Abdullahi Shaykh Ibrahim, Wanle Weyn, 27 Nov. 1977.

10. From the notes of Michele Pirone, former colonial official and then professor of sociology at the Somali National University. Cf. Massimo Colucci, *Principi di diritto consuetudinario della Somalia italiana meridionale* (Florence, 1924), pp. 141–42.

Indeed, with the decline of the Ajuraan theocracy toward the end of the seventeenth century, the itinerant shaykh became the foremost representative of the "great tradition" of Islam in the Somali interior. There commenced a new phase of southern Somali religious history, a phase characterized by the spread of Sufi mysticism, popular saint cults, and the growth of religious lineages. To a large extent, this probably replicated a process that had occurred several centuries earlier in the northern regions of the Somali Peninsula.

As in the north, the saints represented a tradition of Islam quite removed from the theocratic version with its formal hierarchy and legalistic practice.[11] In rural traditions, the saints were characterized not so much by their capacity to uphold Muslim law as by their possession of special religious gifts. Among these were *aziimo* (sacred knowledge), *tacdaar* (sacred magic), and *wardi* (the capacity to receive divine revelation). Access to *asraar* (sacred mysteries) was commonly associated with the saints' ability, however rudimentary, to read and write Arabic. With these gifts, the saints were enabled not only to perceive the forces of the supernatural world but also, in a limited sense, to control them. The following two examples are typical.

> Omar "Arag" wandered throughout the country pointing out places where the people should dig wells and *war* [natural depressions cleared out to collect rainwater]. He could see into the future and used *aziimo* to help the people make decisions. He buried four black oxen, one in each direction, to protect the people from the Abyssinians [probably means the Oromo] who raided the area almost every year.[12]

> Shaykh Abdullahi Isaaq wrote religious poetry. Before the *tariiqa*s [Islamic orders], people knew nothing about *dikri* [the liturgical chants of the orders], and so they used his poems when they beseeched God. He was a man who could speak of the future. He said:

11. I have developed this theme more fully in "Migrations, Islam, and Politics in the Somali Benaadir, 1500–1843," in Harold Marcus, ed., *Proceedings of the First United States Conference on Ethiopian Studies,* 1973 (East Lansing, 1975), pp. 101–15. For some comparative studies, see Nikki R. Keddie, ed., *Scholars, Saints, and Sufis* (Berkeley and Los Angeles: University of California Press, 1972), esp. Introduction and essays by Leon Carl Brown, Ernest Gellner, and Vincent Crapanzano.

12. Sayyid Haji Nurow Jennay, Baydhabo, 7 Aug. 1971, recorded by Muhammad Rinjele.

Kabtan iyonay Kommisarioko koy-doonan
Kitkaas ma roogow keleen Abokay hal kabalay
Kufka been-eh kamiiska been-eh kufiyada been-eh
Kulibta Kussow kufar idowda inkalme yeh.

Captain and Commissioner will come
When I am no longer here and the words of my God are
    read in haste.
Sandals, and robes, and *kofi*s [caps] will all be lies;
For the infidels will gather up the people
    and the people will help them.[13]

From these and other accounts it is clear that the religion of the saints
was associated in the popular mind with the practices of astrology,
divination, and magic. The accommodation of such practices within
the Sufi tradition of Islam was a common development throughout the
Muslim world.[14]

Veneration cults developed around many of these holy men after
their deaths. Pilgrimages *(siyaaro)* were made to the tomb of the
deceased saint, where his initiates or lineal descendants led prayers
and offerings to commemorate his name. If the saint had acquired
great reknown through his piety or *karaamo* (miracle working), his
tomb might draw pilgrims from many clans over a wide area to the
annual ceremonies.

Many of the saints—Omar "Arag" buried at Saramaan, Shaykh
Hassan Buraale at Jesiira, and Shaykh Mumin at Buur Hakaba—
came from small religious lineages, and their genealogies show them
to have lived anywhere from eight to fourteen generations ago. Other
figures whose tombs became the objects of *siyaaro* were clan or
lineage ancestors, such as Haji Yusuf of the Handab (a Geledi lineage)
and Shaykh Muhammad Dheere of the Garre. Still others, like Aw
Mahad (guardian of the harvest) and Aw Hilter (who protected men
from attack by river crocodiles) appear to be timeless. They may be
personages from pre-Islamic belief who were transformed in popular
tradition into Muslim saints.

One can discern here the outcome of a long process which involved the Islamization of the cults of all those personalities who

13. Shaykh Muhammed Nur Massak, Muqdisho, 17 July 1979.
14. See for example J. S. Trimingham, *The Sufi Orders in Islam* (Oxford, 1971),
p. 28.

Saint's tomb in the Daafeed region reflects the historical importance of Islam to the peoples of the countryside. Many tombs are the sites of annual pilgrimages (siyaaro) *drawing worshipers from the surrounding districts.*

represented the political and social cohesiveness of Somali groups. Over time, not only itinerant saints but also lineage ancestors (and perhaps traditional gods and folk heroes) were sanctified through their association with Islam. I. M. Lewis has suggested, for example, that traditional animal sacrifices made to founding ancestors by living clansmen were over time transformed into religious pilgrimages cloaked in Islamic prayers and rituals. In a similar way, apparently pre-Islamic ceremonies held to insure good rains and abundant harvests (such as the *Dab-shid,* or "fire-lighting," ceremonies to mark the Somali New Year) became Islamic festivals in which the saints were beseeched to intercede with Allah.[15]

In time, the descendants of the saints formed extended kinship

15. I. M. Lewis, "Sufism in Somaliland," 18: 147–48, 151–52, 154–55.

groups similar to those of the Somali warrior clans and, in most places, attached themselves to the clans in whose territory they resided. At times, the genealogical affiliation was tenuous and represented no more than an association of a lineage of shaykhs with a more powerful warrior clan. In other instances, however, a saint's descendants could become fully incorporated into the structure of a clan, forming in essence a lineage collateral with others in that clan. Whatever the strength of the association, the religious families enhanced the prestige of the entire clan by augmenting its spiritual resources.[16]

The founding of lineages of shaykhs was not the only legacy of the saints. They had a profound effect on the organization of Somali society itself and on Somali perceptions of that organization. In the turbulent conditions of the seventeenth and eighteenth centuries, countless newly arrived pastoral groups jostled for control of the grazing, watering, and limited agricultural resources of the interriver area. Herding groups and lineage segments of diverse origins had to adapt not only to new terrain but also to coexistence with their neighbors. Traditions suggest that the saints helped mediate countless situations of intergroup conflict, thus providing a precedent for their future influence in community affairs. As we saw above, Omar "Arag" is said to have organized exchange and demarcated boundaries among the numerous groups in the Saramaan area, and to have initiated the annual custom of bringing all the clan heads together for the ritual washing of the Quranic tablets. A similar integrative role is attributed to Shaykh "Sagaal Hajile" ("of the nine *hajj*'s," or pilgrimages):

> The real name of "Sagaal Hajile" was Yaqub. His wife was called Kadige and was from Muduun. She bore Sagaal Hajile nine sons and a daughter Halima, who died as a baby. . . .
>
> Sagaal Hajile told the ancient people about the pilgrimage to Mecca. He organized the people into various groups, such as the Sagaal [the "nine"] and Siyeed [the "eight"], the Bay and Argaan, and pointed out the *gebiibe* and *adableh* [various types of

16. Ibid., 17: 597–98. See also I. M. Lewis, "Conformity and Contrast in Somali Islam," in I. M. Lewis, ed., *Islam in Tropical Africa* (London, 1966), pp. 261–62. For an example of a religious lineage that was incorporated into a larger clan, see David Marlowe, "The Galjaal Barsana of Central Somalia: A Lineage Political System in a Changing World" (Ph.D. diss., Harvard University, 1963), esp. chap. 5.

cultivable soil]. He fixed many local customs [*xeer*] still in use, and showed people how to solve disputes without [formal] government. He preserved the peace by not allowing any [Hawiyya] to settle there; and he defended the people from attacks from Abyssinia. He also directed the settlement of many towns and well sites such as Cunka Madow and Gowdown, where he is buried.[17]

The Sagaal and Siyeed, and the Bay and Argaan, are territorial confederations found today in southern Somalia. They are believed to consist of clans and clan segments of diverse genealogical origins and are typical of the mixed clan communities found throughout the region. What gives them their cohesiveness, apart from territorial contiguity, are these traditions of early saintly mediation and, in some instances, their continued allegiance to the descendants of the saints, who are recognized as nominal spiritual leaders. The "Shanta Aleemo" ("five branches") of Dafeed have similar traditions of being consolidated through the efforts of the seventeenth-century Shaykh Osman Sherif Dalwaaq.[18]

Beyond these very specific contributions to the consolidation of multi-clan communities in southern Somalia, the saints may also have aided the development of a wider Somali consciousness. As I. M. Lewis has noted, most ordinary Somalis can trace their genealogies back to a founding clan ancestor, real or mythical. Also, some political leaders are familiar with the genealogical antecedents of those neighboring or allied clans whose assistance is periodically required.[19] It is unlikely, however, that rural Somalis in the past saw themselves as part of a larger Somali nation. Despite sharing a language, culture, and pastoral heritage with other groups in the Horn, most Somali communities occupied a social universe bounded by those neighboring communities with which they interacted in some direct way.

One can reasonably argue that it was the Muslim shaykhs, both Arab and Somali, who first planted the notion of a wider Somali identity. They propagated stories of Arab ancestry and facilitated the construction of genealogies that linked the ancestors of the various

17. Ma'allin Abdullahi Hassanow, Dhanfurur, 14 Aug. 1971, recorded by Muhammad Rinjele.

18. Group interview with elders of Wanle Weyn, 11 Nov. 1977.

19. I. M. Lewis, *The Somali Lineage System and the Total Genealogy* (London, 1957), pp. 71–73.

clans they served to the Qurayshitic lineage of the Prophet or to some prestigious immigrant from Arabia. Only the shaykhs maintained written Arabic manuscripts that recorded the genealogical connections, at the highest levels, among various clan founders.[20] The practical effects of such links were, of course, limited since there existed in Somalia no large-scale political organization to give substance to the concept of a total Somali genealogy; yet the ideological basis for the recognition of a larger Somali community was there.

We might speculate that through their activities of political mediation, social consolidation, and religious propagation, the saints helped both to forge and to reinforce the notion of a shared religious heritage among the Somalis. They provided to the various groups on the ground a sense of common history; and they encapsulated that history in the genealogies which every Somali maintained to define his place in the social system. To this extent, then, the work of the saints contributed to the fusion of Islamic and Somali identities. If today one can almost automatically say that to be a Somali is to be a Muslim, historically it can be said that to accept Islam was to accept membership in a larger Somali nation.

Sufism and Somali Politics

We have examined the role of the saint in Somali society, and to some extent in Somali social thought, but what are the implications for Somali political culture? In answering this question, I will focus on three integrally related developments: *(1)* the development of a mystically oriented, locally based political tradition that contrasted with an earlier theocratic tradition; *(2)* the incorporation of mystical arts and techniques into the exercise of local political leadership; and *(3)* the localization, or "somalization," of the means for legitimating Islamic religious authority.

As we have suggested, the spread of Islam through the work of itinerant saints coincided with and perhaps contributed to changing political conditions in Somalia. In the south, the Ajuraan imamate fragmented into a series of smaller Hawiyya-dominated principalities, and these in turn disappeared under pressure from Biimaal and Rahanwiin confederations. By 1750, the theocratic tradition represented by the Ajuraan was no longer dominant in the inter-

20. Ibid., pp. 73, 78–80. Cf. Hersi, "The Arab Factor," chap. 4.

river area.[21] Within the Rahanwiin and Hawiyya confederations of
the interior, leadership was exercised by politico-religious authorities bearing Somali titles such as *ugaas, waber,* and *islao.*[22] *Wazir*s,
*wakil*s, and *emir*s—titles with an Islamic flavor—had disappeared.
In the northern regions of the Peninsula, a similar process of decen-
tralization had occurred. Traditions collected by Michele Pirone suggest that the great Harti confederation which had dominated the
northeastern Horn from perhaps 1300 began to fragment in the
eighteenth century; the sultan of Majeerteenia, once the nominal
head of the entire confederation, retained authority only over his
own subclan, while new leaders emerged at the heads of smaller
tribal groups to assert their independence from the sultanate. These
new leaders, known as *islaan,* apparently enjoyed power "of a sort
more religious than truly political" as they sought to settle feuds
among competing local lineages.[23]

As power devolved to local leaders, customary rather than
Sharia'atic law dominated political relations at the local level. We saw
in the previous section how the saints of Somali tradition contributed
to the evolution of *xeer* (customary law) in the various communities
where they settled. They mediated disputes, helped assess bloodwealth *(diya)* payments, and assisted at rituals of reconciliation. Such
mediation was particularly critical in the evolving Rahanwiin confederations, which typically consisted of lineages of diverse genealogical
origins and perhaps different marriage and inheritance customs.

The basis of the saints' political mediatorship was the same as
that of their intercession between man and God, namely, their perceived ability to marshall supernatural forces. These forces could be
summoned to help reconcile opposing points of view if in no other way
than through the implicit threat of a curse upon an unwilling party
or of the withdrawal of customary blessings for its land or herds. In

21. See chap. 3, pp. 111–12.

22. The title *iman* (Arabic, imam) was conserved only within the family of the
Yaqub Abgaal, whose leader took up residence in the Shangaani quarter of Muqdisho
toward the end of the seventeenth century. By the nineteenth century, this titleholder
enjoyed prestige but little real power outside his own clan. See Cerulli, *Somalia,*
2: 249–51, and 3: 56–58; Charles Guillain, *Documents sur l'histoire, la géographie et
le commerce de l'Afrique orientale,* 3 vols. (Paris, 1856), 2: 524–25; and Carlo Rossetti,
Tre note sulla citta di Mogadiscio (Rome, 1907), pp. 10–13.

23. Michele Pirone, *Appunti di storia dell'Africa.* vol. 2, *Somalia* (Rome,
1961), pp. 67–68.

one account from the upper Jubba region, some shaykhs from an Ashraf lineage (presumed descendants of the Prophet) are said to have counseled a clan leader to avoid warfare with a rival clan. The Ashraf warned that if he ignored their advice, he would suffer defeat for seven years. In fact, the leader and his followers lost seven important battles. Only then, on the advice of a wise elder, did the repentant leader go before the Ashraf, apologize for his refusal to heed them, and pay them one hundred young camels for their services. The shaykhs were appeased and according to tradition said to him, "Go, you will conquer your enemy forthwith." The tradition then goes on to recount the clan's ultimate victory.[24]

The functions the saints performed were essentially political: advising elders in the application of *xeer*, mediating disputes, and defending clan territory. They used the techniques of the Islamic mystic and ritual leader to assist the performance of Somali politics. In return they received material support from the clan. These reciprocal relations produced a society in which shaykh and warrior provided complementary sources of power, often symbolized by the incorporation of religious lineages into the clan's genealogical structure.

The full implications of such a development can be seen in the case of the Gobroon, the religious lineage of the Geledi clan-confederation which came to dominate southern Somali politics shortly after 1800. The Gobroon provide an example of a lineage which was not merely incorporated into the clan structure but which came to stand as its political center.[25] Since the second half of the eighteenth century, the Goobroon have supplied the Geledi confederation with its sultan, who is both religious and political head. The adoption of the Gobroon into a political community consisting of two groups of lineages (Tolweyne and Yebdaale) is described in the following tradition recorded by a recent anthropologist.

The Gobroon originally traveled and lived with the Yebdaale. At this time, the villages of the Yebdaale enjoyed sunlight as they do today, but those of the Tolweyne lived in constant twi-

24. Sherif Aden Yusuf, Saramaan, 15 July 1971, recorded by Muhammad Rinjele. The tradition is translated in full in Appendix A, pp. 268–69.

25. I am grateful to Virginia Luling for providing me with detailed information on the Gobroon sultans, as well as the tradition cited below. Much of the data she collected was corroborated by Abokor Ali Omar, who introduced me to several elders of the Geledi community.

light or mist. A member of the Adawiin [a lineage of purported Arab descent] saw how to remedy this. By reading his Quran, he perceived that the Gobroon would have a great future. If the Tolweyne could get the Gobroon to stand with them, they too would have the sun.

One day the young men of the two groups were playing in an open field near their villages. Among them was Alin Warre of the Gobroon. A member of the Abikerow lineage sent two of his slaves to capture the young Alin. They carried him off to the Tolweyne village. Then the sun rose over the Tolweyne group.

The Tolweyne made an offering of peace to the Yebdaale. The two groups then accepted the situation, and to this day, the Gobroon stand with the Tolweyne.

The importance of divining (by the Adawiin shaykh) and mediation (over the question of Gobroon affiliation) comes through clearly in the story; these were critical techniques in the building of any political community. The emergence of the Gobroon lineage as a dominant force can be dated to the second half of the eighteenth century. Gobroon genealogies show that Alin was the grandfather of Ibrahim, who became sultan of the Geledi following the final defeat of the Silcis dynasty.[26] The process described in the tradition thus seems to have occurred toward the end of the period of Silcis domination. We can infer that this was a period of considerable political ferment, and that the saintly Gobroon were incorporated into the confederation at a time when the Geledi lineages were in need of reconciliation among themselves.

The religious preeminence of the Gobroon was transformed into political power through the solidarity of the now united Geledi lineages and through the submission of several neighboring clans who apparently sought the protection of Gobroon *tacdaar* and the benefits of its *baraka*. A succession of Geledi military victories over other clans in the early nineteenth century only strengthened the belief in the Gobroon's superior techniques.[27]

Also in the late eighteenth or early nineteenth century, Shaykh

26. Information provided by Abokor Ali Omar. For the Silcis, see chap. 3, pp. 110–11.

27. For further details, see Lee Cassanelli, "The Benaadir Past: Essays in Southern Somali History" (Ph.D. diss., University of Wisconsin, 1973), pp. 103–20.

Madow Ma'allin assumed the leadership of the united Hintire and Hober clans, neighbors of the Geledi. Shaykh Madow was a reputed descendant of the famed Shaykh Hassan Buraale; tradition says he was the first of the line since Hassan Buraale seriously to take up the study of *asraar* (religious secrets). This study was undertaken at Baraawe, which had become a major center of Sufi learning. Armed with religious books which contained the prayers and formulae necessary for the practice of the mystical arts, Madow returned to Mereerey (the center of the Hintire) as a major rival of the aforementioned Gobroon shaykhs.[28]

Although two examples scarcely constitute conclusive proof, they suggest that by the nineteenth century a knowledge of the mystical arts had become an important component of political leadership. A clan leader who sought to extend his authority over other clans could be aided by an education in the "secrets" of religion, to supplement a prestigious patriline and strong numerical backing (from clansmen or affines). The exercise of mystical powers gave him added prestige and a source of authority that originated outside the lineage framework.[29] This mystical authority was seen to improve his ability as a mediator, as a diviner, and as a protector of his followers. It is no coincidence that the most renowned leader in nineteenth-century southern Somalia—the sultan of Geledi—was believed to be a superior practitioner of all three arts.

The supernatural powers of clan leaders like the sultan of Geledi and the shaykh of Mereerey were partly inheritable, as they were in the saintly lineages proper. However, such inherited powers could also be augmented. Leading rituals at the tombs of ancestor-saints endowed the clan head with an additional aura of sanctity; the consul-

28. Ahmed Shaykh Osman and Shaykh Yusuf Muhyeddin, Mereerey, 26 Aug. 1971.

29. In an analogous case, Marlowe records how the perceived ability of members of the Barsana lineage to make rain and to cast the evil eye on their enemies gave them *dirinji* (status): the entire lineage was regarded as quasi-sacred. Although it stood outside the normal *diya* (compensation) system, the Barsana provided the *ugaas*, or titular head, of the entire Gaaljacal clan. See Marlowe, "The Galjaal Barsana," pp. 35–36.

For the importance of the mystical tradition as an added source of prestige in other settings, see C. C. Stewart, "Saints and Scholars in Mauritania," paper presented to the Middle East Studies Association Conference, Denver, 12 Nov. 1971.

tation of sacred books (probably Arabic works on astronomy and astrology) gave him added wisdom;[30] and visits to the centers of Sufi learning at the coast elevated and legitimated his mystical authority.

Although the mystical tradition assimilated by local Somali leaders was, it seems, recognized as Islamic, that tradition had become largely "somalized." This is evident from the change in the way Islamic authority was legitimized. The authority of earlier Muslim Somali political leaders, such as the imams of Ajuraan, had rested on their claims to primacy in conversion to the Faith and on the prestige resulting from their ancestors' intermarriage with Arab immigrants. There was a marked emphasis on the legitimating power of an "alien" (i.e., Arab) tradition.

By the early nineteenth century, however, legitimation was available locally: by periodic visits to the country's religious centers, through rituals performed at the local tombs of deceased saints, and in the otherwise restricted access to the family's sacred books. In effect, Somali society had absorbed an Islamic tradition by evolving its own bases of Muslim religious authority. Religious legitimation came from within rather than from outside Somali society.

In Somali thought, there is a clear distinction made between the sources of religious authority (which are otherworldly) and the sources of secular authority (which rest on warrior strength and the control of pastoral resources).[31] Nevertheless, the two could on occasion become fused, and the mystical tradition facilitated the link. By the nineteenth century, if not earlier, the power of the saints and the power of the clan heads had joined in the person of the Geledi sultan. The source of his authority as a clan head—personal character, genealogical pedigree, and the numbers of kinsmen he could mobilize—mirrored the sources of the saint's authority—personal charisma, inherited *baraka,* and the numbers of those who believed in his mystical power. Thus it was only natural that in the nineteenth century

30. In a personal communication, Brad Martin of Indiana University has suggested that knowledge of *asraar* (religious secrets) is very commonly associated with the possession of astrological treatises. Indeed many of the books donated by Somali shaykhs to the Garesa Museum in the early colonial period were these types of works. See *Museo della Garesa: Catalogo* (Mogadiscio, 1934), p. 21, entries 77, 78; and p. 28, entry 218.

31. Cf. I. M. Lewis, "Dualism in Somali Notions of Power," *Journal of the Royal Anthropological Institute of Great Britain and Ireland,* vol. 93, no. 1 (1963), p. 111.

people looked for leadership to those who were able to combine the gifts of the Sufi saints with the tools of lineage politics.

The Baardheere Jihad

Not all believers in Somalia subscribed to the interpretation of Islam propagated by the saints and adopted by such prominent leaders as the shaykh of Mereerey and the sultan of Geledi. The accomodation of Sufi Islam within the existing framework of Somali society produced for some Muslim purists a rather too comfortable conformity. In their eyes, the values of Islam were being distorted by the continued reliance on Somali *xeer,* by the anthropomorphic tendencies of the saint cults, and by the residue of pagan and magical practices that persisted despite the Somalis' voiced adherence to the Faith of the Prophet.

The tensions between these divergent interpretations of Islam —together with many other stresses in nineteenth-century Somali society—were strikingly revealed by the circumstances surrounding the Baardheere *jihad* (holy war), an event still vividly remembered in southern Somali historical traditions. This nineteenth-century attempt at radical reform was inspired by a group of Somali shaykhs who founded the Jubba River *jamaaca* (religious settlement) which eventually became the town of Baardheere. From its modest beginnings in 1819 as a retreat for fewer than one hundred pious believers, the *jamaaca* grew steadily in numbers and influence. It drew adherents from a great many Somali clans; at its peak in about 1840 the movement probably counted twenty thousand supporters.[32]

32. The following account of the Baardheere *jihad* relies on the testimonies of a number of informants, most importantly *Laashin* Abiker Osman of Afgooye, Shaykh Yusuf Muhyeddin of Mereerey, Mustafa Shaykh Hassan of Baydhabo, and Ma'allin Abdullahi Abdirahman Aden of Tagal Molimad; on an unpublished manuscript containing notes and excerpts from the diary of the Italian explorer and administrator Ugo Ferrandi, "Prima spedizione Ferrandi in Somalia" (no. 777 in the National Museum Library, Muqdisho); and on the following published works: Ugo Ferrandi, "Gli scek di Bardera," *Bollettino della Società africana italiana* 11 (1892): 5–7; William Christopher, "Extract from a Journal by Lieut. William Christopher," *Journal of the Royal Geographical Society* 14 (1844): 90–93; Guillain, *Documents* 3: 35–39; Ludwig Krapf, *Reisen in Ost Afrika* (Korntal, 1858), pp. 206–7; Otto Kersten, ed., *Baron Carl Claus von der Decken's Reisen in Ost Afrika in den Jahren 1862 bis 1865,* vol. 2 (Leipzig, 1871), pp. 317–19; and I. M. Lewis, "La Communità ('Giamia') di Bardera sulle rive del Giuba," *Somalia d'Oggi,* vol. 2, no. 1 (1957), pp. 36–37.

Although there exist many local traditions surrounding the military aspects of the *jihad,* its origins remain somewhat obscure. Baardheere itself was founded in 1819 by Shaykh Ibrahim Hassan Jeberow, a native of Dafeed, who had been refused permission to establish a reformist religious community in his home district. Dafeed sources claim that Shaykh Ibrahim was affiliated with the Ahmediya Order,[33] which developed out of the reformist teachings of Sayyid Ahmed ibn Idris al-Fasi (1760–1837) at Mecca. The religious zeal of the community, its militant emphasis on augmenting the number of its adherents, and the concentration of authority in the hands of its head shaykhs clearly fit J. S. Trimingham's characterization of the Ahmediya Order's branches elsewhere in Northeast Africa.[34] However, Ali Hersi and Trimingham himself identify Baardheere as an early Qadiri settlement.[35] The Qadiriya brotherhood is known to have had some followers at Baraawe as early as the eighteenth century; but it is not generally believed by Somalis to have penetrated the southern interior before the efforts of Shaykh Uways Muhammad al-Barawi (1847–1909) in the last two decades of the nineteenth century.[36] The Qadiriya, moreover, had a reputation in Somalia of being a teaching order, emphasizing liturgical and mystical instruction rather than radical social reform. Finally, several early European explorers identified the Baardheere Muslims as Wahhabis, a militant fundamentalist sect that conquered much of the Arabian peninsula in the early years of the nineteenth century.[37] However, despite the known sympathies of the Ahmediya's founder with Wahhabi ideas, and the known presence of Wahhabi reformers

33. Haji Abdullahi Shaykh Ibrahim, Haji Yahya Ma'allin Aden, and others, Wanle Weyn, 27 Nov. 1977.

34. Trimingham, *Islam in Ethiopia,* pp. 234–35; Cf. I. M. Lewis, "La Communita," p. 36.

35. Hersi, "The Arab Factor," pp. 249–50; Trimingham, *Islam in Ethiopia,* pp. 240–41.

36. Sherif Herow Hassan Aliow, Muqdisho, 9 July 1971; Shaykh Omar Isa Haaq, Muqdisho, 17 Mar. 1971. The former was a local *khaliifa* of the Qadiriya Order, the latter a member of the Ahmediya. Cf. Cerulli, *Somalia* 1:187–89.

37. Christopher, "Extract from a Journal," p. 93; Krapf, *Reisen,* pp. 206–7; Georges Revoil, "Voyages chez les Benadirs, les Comalis, et les Bayouns en 1882–1883," *Le Tour du Monde* 56 (1885): 392; G. Ferrand, *Les Comalis* (Paris, 1903), p. 227. European observers in the nineteenth century commonly attributed Wahhabi origins to any radical reformist Islamic movement.

on the island of Socotra about 1800,[38] there is no concrete evidence that Wahhabi zealots ever reached the Somali interior. It is possible that Baardheere was from the beginning an independent religious congregation with no specific *tariiqa* (order) affiliation, or one which incorporated radical Muslims from different *tariiqas*, as Massimo Colucci suggests.[39] In sum, there is not a consensus on Baardheere's religious antecedents. The question merits further investigation, since Baardheere produced the only *jihad* in modern Somali history apart from the famous anticolonial holy war of Sayyid Muhammad Abdullah Hassan (d. 1921), which was directed largely against foreign infidels.

The Baardheere Muslims aimed their reforms at their Somali neighbors. As part of their plan to purify Islamic practice, the reformers had outlawed the use of tobacco, abolished popular dancing and excessive social intercourse between the sexes, and instructed the women of Baardheere to wear the veil. They also prohibited the ivory trade through their district, because they considered the elephant one of the unclean animals.[40] Some of my Somali sources suggested that the reformers were opposed to the numerous local cults of saint worship; but these sources could not identify any tombs that had been destroyed (as happened, for example, during the Wahhabi occupation of Socotra). Other informants mentioned that the *qiil* (local interpretation of Shari'atic law) of Baardheere countenanced divorce and inheritance practices that ran counter to the prevailing Shafi'ite tradition that had begun to penetrate the country.[41] Again, there may exist Arabic texts that would shed some light on the nature of the religious controversy; to date, none has been found.

In the mid-1830s, the Baardheere movement entered a militant phase, first under Shaykh Ali Duure (d. 1836) and Shaykh Abiker Aden Dhurow (d. 1838 or 1839), then under the renowned Sherif Abdirahman and Sherif Ibrahim. The decision to expand the *jihad* was probably aided by the reformers' alliance with large numbers of migrating nomads that had recently arrived in the vicinity (see below,

38. Trimingham, *Islam in Ethiopia*, pp. 112–13, 242. For the Wahhabis on Socotra, see Guillain, *Documents*, 2: 368.

39. Colucci, *Principi*, pp. 80–81.

40. Christopher, "Extract from a Journal," pp. 90–92; Guillain, *Documents* 3: 36–37; Kersten, *Baron C.C. von der Decken's Reisen*, p. 317. See nn. 45–47 below.

41. Group interview with elders of Wanle Weyn, 24 Nov. 1977.

pp. 140–41). Expeditions of armed warriors fanned out through the Doy pasturelands southeast of Baardheere and overran farming settlements just east of Baydhabo. Shaykh Abiker also led expeditions against the Warday (Oromo) west of the Jubba and attacked the trading town of Luuq on the river to the north. In 1840, the reformers reached Baraawe and sacked it, forcing its inhabitants to submit to the new regulations. This event is significant in that Baraawe was a noted center of Sufi learning; both Ahmed Yusuf of the Gobroon and Shaykh Madow Ma'allin of the Hintire had studied there.[42]

The dramatic success of the jihadists ultimately provoked a concerted response from the clans of the interriver area. The focal point of the ensuing counteroffensive was Yusuf Muhammad, the sultan of Geledi and a direct descendant of that Gobroon shaykh whom tradition remembers as having united the Geledi and driven out the Silcis. In *sannad Arbaca Baardheere* (the "Wednesday year of Baardheere"—1843), Yusuf set out from Afgooye with an army of warriors from the Geledi and its allied clans. Swinging in a great arc through Dafeed and Baydhabo, his expedition gathered men from virtually every clan along its route.[43] It is said that an army of forty thousand arrived and camped before the walls of Baardheere. After a siege which lasted several days, Yusuf's forces stormed the town and burned it to the ground. Its inhabitants fled or were killed; there were so many huts in Baardheere, said one informant, that the fires remained warm for a month. With the deaths of Sherif Abdirahman and Sherif Ibrahim in battle, the one notable instance of *jihad* in southern Somalia came to a swift end.

As a glance at map 4 will show, the geographical area encompassed by the *jihad* was sizable—approximately a semicircle of a one-hundred-mile radius from Baardheere. Likewise, the distribution of the counterforces mobilized by Yusuf—"the towns were emptied of men of fighting age," I was told—indicates the extent of the area that felt threatened by Baardheere's expansion. The scale of the *jihad*

42. See above, pp. 132–33.

43. Guillain's informant described the route taken by Yusuf's expedition: *Documents* 3: 42–43. Traditions of most clans that participated in the battle still recall the expedition. For example, the elders of Wanle Weyn told me that Yusuf is remembered as having stayed only one night in their town; after recruiting warriors there, he moved on toward Baardheere. It was also recalled that the Geledi sultan was riding a white camel with an ornamented saddle, an uncommon practice among Somalis, who rarely ride their camels. Group interview, Wanle Weyn, 24 Nov. 1977.

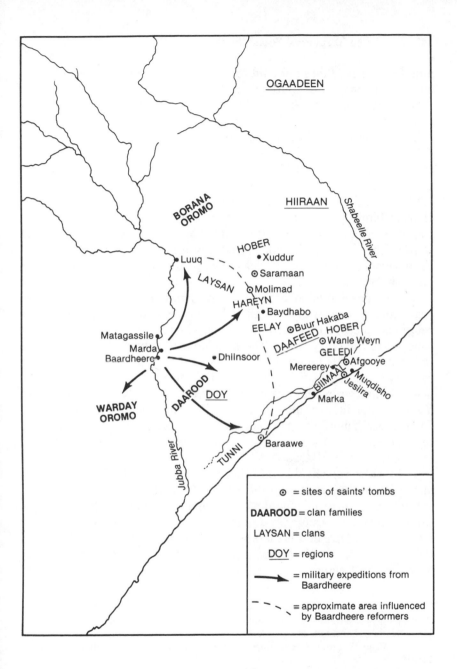

Map 4. The Bardheere Jihad *in the nineteenth century*

and its ultimate failure should tell us a good deal about the religious climate of nineteenth-century southern Somalia.

First of all, that the *jihad* originated in Baardheere proves that contemporary currents of Islamic reform reached far into the Somali interior. The founder of the Baardheere *jamaaca*—Ibrahim Hassan Jeberow—came from Daafeed, a district located only forty miles from the religious centers of Muqdisho and Marka. On the other hand, his successors as heads of the community came from Saramaan, Molimad, and Hakaba, all well upcountry. There is evidence that Ibrahim Hassan himself had made the pilgrimage to Mecca before founding Baardheere, but his successors may not have—their names do not contain the title "Haji" which virtually all Somali pilgrims insert.[44] From this we can infer that ideas of radical reform were being propagated in Somalia itself.

The massive opposition to the reform movement can have several explanations. Many Somalis who may have been unmoved by the religious message of Baardheere were clearly alarmed by the threat it posed to the ivory trade. The missionary Ludwig Krapf noted the importance of this factor in his observations on the neighboring Galla country in the 1850s.[45] In the 1890s the merchants of Luuq who had been victimized by the reformers' army and had later joined Sultan Yusuf's expedition still bitterly recalled the ivory prohibition.[46] Indeed, one of Yusuf's first measures as he sought to restore tranquility to the area after his assault on Baardheere was the revitalization of the ivory trade to Baraawe.[47]

It is also conceivable that there was a "regional" factor involved in the intense resistance to the *jihad*. Although most of the leaders in the Baardheere movement were members of southern Somali clans, there is evidence to suggest that many of their followers were nomads from various Daarood clans and subclans that had recently arrived from the north. Oral traditions do point to an increase in fighting between local clans and northern immigrants in the early 1800s.[48]

44. The successive heads of Baardheere are named by Ugo Ferrandi, "Gli scek di Bardera," pp. 5–7; and also Ferrandi, "Prima spedizione," pp. 202–6.

45. Krapf, *Reisen*, pp. 206–7.

46. Ugo Ferrandi, *Lugh: Emporio commerciale sul Giuba* (Rome, 1903), pp. 227–28.

47. Guillain, *Documents* 3: 186.

48. Corrado Zoli, *Oltre-Giuba* (Rome, 1927), pp. 141–46; Pietro Barile, *Colonizzazione fascista, nella Somalia meridionale* (Rome, 1935), p. 124; Giuseppe

Moreover, traditions of those Daarood now living in Jubaland speak of their mid-nineteenth-century migrations across the Jubba River, which would have placed them in the vicinity of Baardheere precisely during the epoch of the *jihad*'s expansion.[49] The nomadic Daarood, whose faith was not linked to the local cults of the interriver area, were natural allies of the puritanical reformers, particularly when they could cash in on the booty derived from the holy war. If these northern nomads did in fact participate in the *jihad*, it would explain why the reformers enjoyed their greatest success in the Doy and its peripheral villages; for the Doy pastureland had always been something of a no-man's-land attractive to pastoral immigrants from the more arid central Horn. Daarood participation would also explain the vigor of the southerners' response under Yusuf Muhammad whose claimed descent from Muhammad Digil, the recognized ancestor of most southern Somali clans, provided a focus of southern identity against the Daarood.

Whether or not commercial and regional factors bore on the eventual outcome of the *jihad*, it is clear that factors of a political-religious nature militated against Baardheere's success. Because saint worship and the mystical arts had become embedded in the existing political culture of the region, the reformers' attacks on these practices were in essence attacks on the existing political order. Divining, *tacdaar* (involving on occasion frenzied dancing and chanting), and the veneration of clan ancestors were all elements of popular culture. As has been seen, they were important in politics as well as in spiritual affairs. By shunning these practices, the Baardheerans were challenging the sources and symbols of local political authority.

Then, too, Baardheere presented a contrasting model of religio-political leadership. Spiritual authority was clearly not inheritable in Baardheere: the head shaykhs of the community came from five different clans during its twenty-four-year existence. On at least one occasion, an anticipated successor was deemed unworthy to suc-

---

Liprandi, "La residenza di Iscia Baidoa," *La Somalia italiana*, vol. 7, nos. 1–3 (1930), pp. 53–54.

49. E. R. Turton, "The Pastoral Tribes of Northern Kenya, 1800–1916" (Ph. D. thesis, University of London, 1970), pp. 71–75. These traditions are also summarized in I. M. Lewis, "The Problem of the Northern Frontier District of Kenya," *Race* 5 (1963): 48 ff.

ceed.[50] In contrast, Sufi-oriented saints and lineage heads enjoyed their positions of authority largely because of their inherited *baraka* and prestigious patrilines. A system like Baardheere's where leadership was, ideally, based on religious merit and personal zeal for reform was clearly unacceptable to the local wielders of authority.

Moreover, the internal hierarchy of command in Baardheere is evidence that the reformers sought to create a centralized administrative structure by imposing religious taxes and by appointing *khaliifa*s to the regions they conquered. This centralized structure was in direct contrast to the narrower, tomb-centered spheres of influence that local saints had carved out. Baardheere's independent and central religious authority also challenged the very basis of the authority of men like Yusuf Muhammad—that is, an authority deriving not only from a religiously gifted lineage, but also from a series of carefully guarded and locally efficacious "secrets" represented by the "books" of the family.

Thus it is scarcely surprising that Sultan Yusuf perceived the Baardheere movement as a challange to his regional political supremacy. That he was able to mobilize the number of warriors he did attests to the widespread support he enjoyed in the interriver area. We can surmise that most clan leaders and local *wadaaddo* (religious specialists) shared his determination to defend the local variant of Islamic political culture against the radical transformation sought by Baardheere. It is no coincidence that, apart from the districts around Baardheere, the only active support for the *jihad* came from certain elements in the coastal towns. Urbanized Arabs and Somalis were less committed to the practices and premises of the hinterland tradition and hence presumably were more open to appeals for radical reform.[51]

In the guise of a rivalry between two religious leaders—the shaykh of Baardheere and the sultan of Geledi—the Baardheere wars can be seen to represent the conflict between two views of politics and two political systems. The theocracy envisioned by the reformers was

50. Following the death of Abiker Aden Dhurow (ca. 1838), his *wakil*, Mahad Addey, sought to assume a position as head of the community. However, the people of Baardheere elected instead Sherif Abdirahman. Mahad retired to Baraawe, where he finished his days teaching the Quran to children. Ferrandi, "Prima spedizione," p. 204.

51. Christopher, "Extract from a Journal," p. 90; Guillain, *Documents* 3: 37, 142–45.

incompatible with a system of politics based on clanship, lineage *baraka*, and local religious cults. According to one informant, Shaykh Ibrahim of Baardheere had offered the Geledi sultan some religious books and had tried to make a *sameen* (gift of peace) with him based on a common Islamic bond;[52] but Yusuf consulted his own books before marching to Baardheere, and he defeated the reformers with an army drawn from the components of a traditional clan alliance.

Without pushing the analogy too far, the Baardheere polity recalled the religious ideology and theocratic structure of the Ajuraan period, whereas the Geledi confederation represented a religio-political tradition whose roots lay in the post-Ajuraan milieu. In the end, the latter tradition prevailed. Its victory was a mark of the success of the marriage between popular Islam and Somali political culture.

In concluding this chapter, I want to compare three descriptions of the fall of Baardheere. The first was obtained from the shaykhs of a revived (but no longer militant) Baardheere community in 1891 by the Italian explorer Ugo Ferrandi.[53] It is essentially the same account told to I. M. Lewis during his brief visit to Baardheere in the 1950s.[54]

On the day of *khamiis* (Thursday), the second of the month of Mawlud A.H. 1260, [A.D. 1843], the armies of Yusuf Muhammad simultaneously attacked the districts around Baardheere, burning and destroying all. Both Shaykh Abdirahman Sherif and his *naa'ib* Ibrahim Sherif fell while fighting. Ibrahim Sherif was transfixed with the lance of a Laysan warrior [the Laysan were a clan allied with Yusuf], and Abdirahman was no more seen. A legend says that they saw him fly to the sky, which occurred in the village of Marda [a town upriver from Baardheere].

As a result of the battle of Marda, the attackers entered Baardheere only after three days. Thus, the Kablallax (Daarood) inhabitants of Baardheere were able to send away their women and children, who fled toward Anole beyond the Jubba. The [Digil and Rahanwiin] inhabitants did the same, but they fled toward the north, toward Matagassile.

52. *Laashin* Abiker Osman, Afgooye, 3 Oct. 1971; Shaykh Yusuf Muhyeddin, Mereerey, 26 Aug. 1971. According to Shaykh Yusuf Muhyeddin, Sultan Yusuf's response to the gift of books was a letter tacked to the bottom of a sandal (a derogatory gesture) which said, in effect, "May you die well!"

53. Ferrandi, "Prima spedizione," pp. 205–6.

54. "La Communita ('Giamia') di Bardera," p. 37.

The conquerors entered, plundered everything, and set fire to the town. And, thus, for twenty years Baardheere remained deserted.

The second account I obtained from a member of the Eelay clan living near Baydhabo.[55] The Eelay had made up part of the Geledi expedition.

The people of Buur Hakaba and Baydhabo feared the constant magic of the Baardheere diviner, who always foretold when an army was coming to attack the *Iberay* ["the robed ones," as the reformers were known by the upcountry people]. The people went to Afgooye to find one of the Gobroon practitioners. This man they brought to the Buur, and he told them to place some red earth on their camels' backs and to sit backward on their camels.

When the diviner of Baardheere saw the camels, he said, "Those men are still in the region of the red earth [near the Buur] and they are riding in the other direction." In this way the *Iberay* were deceived and defeated.

The final account of the fall of Baardheere was recited by *Laashin* Abiker, a poet of the Geledi.[56]

Part of the secret of the Geledi was to travel on Wednesdays. Commanding the river Jubba near Baardheere was a man called Aw Bahar Aftiin Ali Nurow, who could control the crocodiles of the river. [The name Bahar signifies a member of the group of fisher-ferrymen who are believed to have special powers over river crocodiles.] Yusuf Muhammad called on one of his own *bahar*, Yusuf Osman Baddey, who drove the crocodiles away and permitted the army to cross the river. [For this reason, some informants remembered the war as "Baardheere of the two Yusufs."]

To succeed in the battle, the Geledi made some *tacdaar* with a plant called *saleelimo* [which grows along the Jubba]. They also brought three *haan* [woven baskets] filled with bees which they sent to attack the army of Baardheere. They attacked from all sides and thus Baardheere was destroyed.

55. Mustafa Shaykh Hassan, interviewed in Muqdisho, 12 Aug. 1971.
56. *Laashin* Abiker Osman, Afgooye, 3 Oct. 1971.

It is possible that these three versions of the siege of Baardheere represent merely specific prejudices and perspectives; the first, that of the vanquished and the second and third, that of the victors. In light of what has been said previously, it is not unusual that the Geledi and their allies would attribute their success to the superior *tacdaar* of the Gobroon shaykhs. Nor would one expect that the conquered Baardheerans would view their loss as the result of inferior spiritual reserves; hence the first version deals with the defeat in strictly military terms.

However, the striking contrast between the two versions—which, after all, proclaim the same result—compels the question: Are we not perhaps dealing here with two strains of religious thought, or, to quote Trimingham, two "modes of spiritual outlook"?[57] That of Baardheere is more scholarly, pragmatic, and "international"; that of the Geledi more popular, mystically oriented, and parochial.

While we cannot be certain, we might surmise that the Baardheere jihadists viewed the struggle in classical Islamic terms, as one of "corruption versus reform." Indeed, a few years after the fall of Baardheere, a jihadist sympathizer wrote to the people of Baraawe urging them to throw off their allegiance to the Geledi sultan:

> Now certainly our dead will go to Paradise while theirs will go to Hell, according to God's words: They will be afflicted by the same sorrows as you, but you will be able to hope from God that which they will not be allowed to hope. . . . If you follow the sectarian crowd of the unbeliever Yusuf [of Geledi], there will no longer be bonds between our families. . . . Greet for us your learned ones, who fear God, those whom he does not turn from the true way and who do not join with the sect of that ravenous son of an ass.[58]

The appeal is made in the language of Muslim reform and urges a return to the true way. One cannot imagine the Gobroon shaykhs talking in those terms.

My Geledi informants readily acknowledged that their Sultan Yusuf was accused by the Baardheere shaykh of being the leader of a pack of infidels. However, for the Geledi, who considered themselves Muslims, the choice was not between religious self-reform or

57. Trimingham, *The Sufi Orders in Islam*, p. 11.
58. Guillain has a French translation of the letter, *Documents* 3: 143–45.

moral stagnation. Islam was not at stake in the war; but the prestige of their sultan and their sultan's *tacdaar* was. We might conjecture that the Geledi saw the struggle as a contest between rival Islamic "practitioners," between two repositories of mystical power.

Whereas religious writings from the period—if indeed they exist —would no doubt shed more light on the causes of the war, the evidence from oral traditions provides us with a unique grass-roots perspective. It suggests, I think, that there existed in nineteenth-century southern Somalia at least two distinct strains of Islamic thought and practice. One, informed by currents of reform in the Islamic scriptural tradition, directed its adherents actively to promote administrative, legal, and liturgical change in the wider society. The other, more influenced by the tradition of the saints, saw Islam within the framework of local social relations, that is, as a resource in the constant struggle for material and spiritual security.

For the reformers of Baardheere, the only way to salvation was to follow Quranic imperatives more rigorously. But to their opponents, salvation lay in following the saint, or the sultan, with the most demonstrably powerful *baraka* and *karaamo*. In saying this, we need not assume that one strain of Islam was more pure than another. Rather it is to recognize that there was not a single Somali idea system but several, as the variant traditions tempt us to suggest. The circumstances of the Baardheere *jihad* reveal, among other things, the diverse social forms that Islamic culture could generate and the radically different views that Somali Muslims could hold of their world.

5 Southern Somali Commerce and Economy in the Nineteenth Century

Worldly wealth shifts like the shade of a tree. . . .
Often we see a poor man becoming rich, and a rich man
    becoming impoverished.
    —Excerpts from an anonymous *gabay*

In this chapter, we turn from the world of saints and Sufis to that of traders and entrepreneurs. Specifically, we will look at some of the effects of international trade on Somalia's commercial and economic life during the nineteenth century. I have chosen to focus on developments in southern Somalia because its economy was the most diversified and the sources for studying it most abundant—though they are far from being completely satisfactory. In fact it is only after 1840 that we begin to get enough evidence to describe patterns of exchange and production even in the most rudimentary way.

For much of East Africa, the nineteenth century was a time of flourishing trade and commerce. The rise of the island town of Zanzibar as a major international emporium signaled a new phase in the economic history of that region. By 1830, the island was being regularly visited by European, American, and Asian merchants seeking cloves and sesame from Zanzibar itself, and ivory, horn, and gum copal from the adjacent mainland. The East African slave trade was also reaching its peak at that time: Portuguese, French, and Arab buyers frequented the slave market of Zanzibar in search of cheap labor for mines, plantations, and wealthy households. In response to the growing foreign demand for ivory and slaves, Arab and Swahili traders based at Zanzibar pushed their caravans ever further into the East African interior. By mid-century, commercial expeditions to the great lakes of Central Africa and beyond were common.[1]

The Somali coast, long a part of the western perimeter of the traditional Indian Ocean trading world, also felt the effects of this commercial boom. The towns of the Benaadir[2]—Baraawe, Marka, and Muqdisho—attracted the interest of European and Zanzibari merchants as suppliers of ivory, aromatic woods, animal skins, and, increasingly as the century wore on, agricultural commodities. At the same time, the northern Somali coast acquired more and more importance first as a supplier of meat to the growing British enclave at Aden and then, with the opening of the Suez Canal in 1869, as a strategic strip along the sea route to India. Despite its reputation as a dangerous and inhospitable place for foreigners, Somalia was being drawn, in a new way, into the international economy.

As Somali townsmen and coastal traders became more involved in these emerging patterns of world commerce, their nomadic counterparts in the interior were exposed to new markets for their livestock products and to new opportunities in long-distance caravan trading. Foreign demand also stimulated the small southern Somali agricultural sector, which expanded dramatically by absorbing into its labor force slaves from other parts of East Africa. The traditional Somali weaving industry, facing a challenge from the introduction of

1. Among the recently published studies on the rise of Zanzibar's commercial empire and its impact on East Africa are: Edward A. Alpers, *Ivory and Slaves in East Central Africa* (Berkeley: University of California Press, 1975); C. S. Nicholls, *The Swahili Coast: Politics, Diplomacy and Trade on the East African Littoral, 1798–1856* (New York: Africana Publishing Co., 1971); Frederick Cooper, *Plantation Slavery on the East Coast of Africa* (New Haven and London: Yale University Press, 1977); R. W. Beachey, *The Slave Trade of Eastern Africa* (London: Rex Collings, 1976); Richard Gray and David Birmingham, *Pre-Colonial African Trade* (London: Oxford University Press, 1970); and conference papers reprinted in *African Historical Studies*, vol. 4, no. 3 (1971).

2. Arabs applied the term *benaadir* to the "ports" along the southern Somali coast from Cadale to Baraawe; during the colonial period, Benaadir came to designate a region that included the hinterlands of those ports as well. The term is used here in the latter sense.

mass-produced foreign textiles, responded by seeking less expensive sources of raw cotton along the Shabeelle River. And the concentration of commercial opportunities along the Benaadir drew enterprising Somalis from other parts of the country toward the south and helped to further a process of territorial integration that had been going on for centuries. Although we lack the evidence to measure the scale of these economic changes with quantitative precision, the sources do enable us to sketch out the major historical developments and to outline the dual processes of economic integration and social differentiation associated with the growth of foreign trade in the Peninsula.

The sources used in reconstructing the socioeconomic history of southern Somalia are primarily written ones. They consist largely of the records and observations of a variety of European traders and travelers who frequented the Somali coast in increasing numbers in the last two-thirds of the nineteenth century. On subjects of a strictly commercial nature, Somali oral accounts are of limited value for the period in question. However, they have been used, together with ethnographic data from the early colonial period, to elaborate on the social and political aspects of trade and production.

The Caravan Trade

As we have seen, long-distance caravan trade has long been a part of economic life in the Horn of Africa. How important it was in the early history of Somalia can only be surmised. A number of scholars have taken the existence of numerous ruined and abandoned towns throughout the Peninsula as evidence of a once flourishing inland trade.[3] It is equally plausible, I think, to view these abandoned towns as former administrative centers in the days of the medieval Islamic sultanates.[4] Whatever may have been true in earlier centuries, the nineteenth clearly saw a growth of long-distance caravan trading in many parts of Somalia in response to new demands from the outside world.

3. See, for example, Ali Abdirahman Hersi, "The Arab Factor in Somali History: The Origins and Development of Arab Enterprise and Cultural Influences in the Somali Peninsula" (Ph.D. diss., University of California, Los Angeles, 1977), esp. pp. 142–46, 171–76; J. M. Watson, "The Historical Background to the Ruined Towns in the West of the Protectorate," *Somaliland Journal,* vol. 1, no. 2 (Dec. 1955), p. 123.

4. Cf. chap. 2, pp. 70–72.

By the start of the nineteenth century, the upper Shabeelle
River served as a rough dividing line between two long-distance caravan networks in the Somali Peninsula: the one whose trade flowed
northward through Harar or Dhagaxbuur in the Ogaadeen to the
ports of Seylac (Zeila), Bullaxaar, and Berbera on the Gulf of Aden,
and the other whose routes terminated at the Benaadir towns of
Muqdisho, Marka, and Baraawe.[5] It is the latter system which occu-
pies us here, although the institutions and mechanisms which promoted trade were similar throughout the Somali region.

A considerable proportion of the southern Somali export trade
during the nineteenth century depended on commodities carried
over long distances. By the middle of the century, roughly half of
the Benaadir's exports (in terms of value) consisted of ivory, aromatic woods, gums, and myrhh, with ivory supplying perhaps two-
thirds of the total.[6] It is likely that at one time most Somali ivory
came from areas relatively close to the coast, notably the lower Shabeelle valley. We can surmise, however, that population growth in
the river valley—the result of both immigration and natural increase—had led to the expansion of cultivation and domestic animal
husbandry. Elephant and rhinoceros herds were forced to abandon
the district, and the "ivory frontier" moved steadily upcountry. By
1800, most of the ivory destined for export came from the Jubba and
Shabeelle basins. This necessitated the organization of long-distance
caravan routes.

While the earliest descriptions we have of long-distance trade in
southern Somalia date from the nineteenth century, it is reasonable
to suppose that it began somewhat earlier. Conditions following the

5. The best overview of precolonial trade in the Horn of Africa is provided by
Mordechai Abir in two articles which make essentially the same points: "Caravan Trade
and History in the Northern Parts of East Africa," *Paideuma* 14 (1968): 103–20; and
"Southern Ethiopia," in Gray and Birmingham, *Precolonial African Trade*. Both draw
almost entirely on written sources. Much useful statistical information from these
same sources can be found assembled in two articles by Richard Pankhurst: "The Trade
of the Gulf of Aden Ports of Africa in the Nineteenth and Early Twentieth Centuries,"
Journal of Ethiopian Studies, vol. 3, no. 1 (1965), pp. 36–81; and "The Trade of
Southern and Western Ethiopia and the Indian Ocean Ports in the Nineteenth and Early
Twentieth Centuries," *Journal of Ethiopian Studies*, vol. 3, no. 2 (1965), pp. 37–74.

6. These are crude estimates calculated from the scattered and incomplete
figures given by Charles Guillain, *Documents sur l'histoire, la géographie et la
commerce de l'Afrique orientale*, 3 vols. (Paris, 1856), 2: 530–42 passim, and 3: 148–49,
172–74, 302–27 passim.

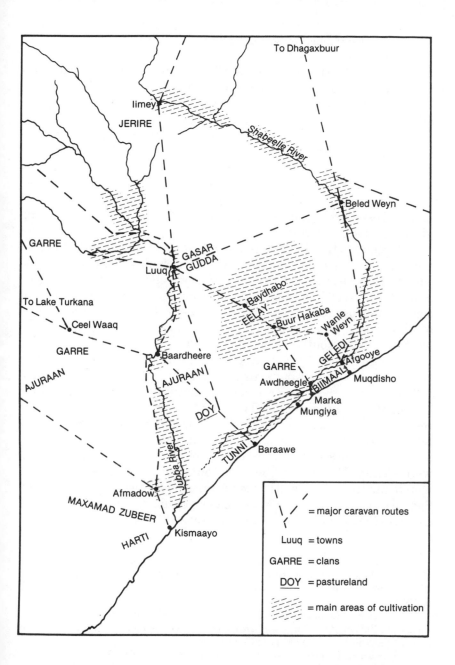

Map 5. Southern Somalia: Ecology and trade, ca. 1850

decline of the Ajuraan state in the mid-seventeenth century may have militated against regular and secure commerce over wide areas. By 1700, however, most of the Rahanwiin clans which today occupy the interriver region had settled into their respective territories. The up-country frontier between Somali and Oromo, the scene of many conflicts during the age of Oromo expansion, was gradually becoming stabilized. Along that frontier there evolved a number of bilingual trading settlements, which were frequently commented upon by later nineteenth-century explorers.[7] Coupled with the integrating force of Islam, these developments could have facilitated the creation of regional exchange networks.

It appears that by 1800 the merchants of Luuq, a small town on the upper Jubba River, enjoyed extensive trading contacts with the surrounding Oromo districts: a European observer reported from Muscat in 1811 that Luuq was sending "immense quantities" of slaves and ivory to the coast near Baraawe.[8] Through the remainder of the century, Luuq retained its position as the most important trading town of the southern Somali interior.

Whatever the extent of pre-nineteenth-century commerce in southern Somalia, new patterns of world production and consumption following upon the Industrial Revolution stimulated the demand for the country's raw materials. These included goat and cow hides (for the shoe and leather industries of Europe and North America); vegetable dyes (for the textile industry); and vegetable oils (for cooking, soaps, and lubricants). From 1830, American and German traders were visiting Baraawe regularly to obtain hides and skins.[9] French merchants from the islands of Mauritius and Reunion put in along the Somali coast to procure beef and dairy products.[10] At the same time, older trade items like ivory, incense, leopard skins, and ostrich feath-

7. Vittorio Bottego, *L'Esplorazione del Giuba* (Rome, 1900), pp. 105–12; P. Maud, "Exploration in the Southern Borderland of Abyssinia," *Geographical Journal* 23 (1904): 568–70; Ugo Ferrandi, *Lugh: Emporio commerciale sul Giuba* (Rome, 1903) p. 316.

8. Reginald Coupland, *East Africa and Its Invaders* (Oxford, 1938), p. 178. Cf. Richard F. Burton, *Zanzibar: City, Island and Coast* (London, 1872), vol. 2, appendix 1, p. 411; and Ferrandi, *Lugh*, pp. 215–17.

9. Norman R. Bennett and George E. Brooks, Jr., eds., *New England Merchants in Africa: A History through Documents, 1802 to 1865* (Boston, 1965), p. 231 n. 40, 475; Guillain, *Documents* 3: 172–73; Coupland, *East Africa*, p. 366.

10. Guillain, *Documents* 3: 162, 172–73.

ers remained important. Ivory in particular continued to provide the impetus for the expansion of the upcountry caravan trade. Its selling price at Muqdisho more than tripled between 1847 and 1890.[11]

By the second half of the nineteenth century, ivory traders from Baraawe were known in Borana country and were reported to be trafficking among the Rendille near Lake Turkana.[12] Other Somalis were actively trading in Konsoland and among the Arbore north of Lake Stephanie.[13] They soon became the major suppliers of imported cotton cloth, metal goods, rice, and sugar to the peoples of southeastern Ethiopia.

These upcountry transactions could be quite complex. For example, to obtain ivory from the elusive hunting populations of the Jubba basin, Somali traders would first have to exchange their cotton cloth for cattle from the Oromo herdsmen of the district. The cattle were then traded to the hunters for ivory. In some areas (such as Konsoland) where good cloth and metal goods were produced locally, Somali traders had to be sure to carry with them more "exotic" items like copper wire, tobacco, or finely fashioned jewelry in order to obtain what they wanted.[14]

In addition to procuring goods for foreign export, Somali traders

11. One can compare the prices for elephant ivory given by Guillain (1847)—12–34 Maria Theresa dollars per *frasila* (approximately 16 kilograms)—with those given by Robecchi-Brichetti and Ferrandi for the years 1891 to 1897—100–150 M.T. dollars per *frasila* for high-quality ivory, and 27–45 M.T. dollars for the inferior grades. The value of hippo teeth and rhinoceros horn appears to have a little more than doubled in this same period, which was the pattern for ivory exports from East Africa generally. See Guillain, *Documents* 2: 533–34; Luigi Robecchi-Brichetti, *Somalia e Benadir* (Milan, 1899), pp. 593–94, 631; Ferrandi, *Lugh*, pp. 353–55. Cf. R. W. Beachey, "The East African Ivory Trade in the Nineteenth Century," *Journal of African History* 8 (1967): 269–90.

12. Beachey, "The East African Ivory Trade," pp. 286–87; Thomas Wakefield, "Routes of Native Caravans from the Coast to the Interior of Eastern Africa," *Journal of the Royal Geographical Society* 40 (1870): 322. In his unpublished diary, Ugo Ferrandi noted that "from Bardera, many go to the court of Afaleta, head of the Boran, and many speak to me of having reached Masai, Rendille, Giangiam." "Prima spedizione Ferrandi in Somalia," typescript memoirs, pp. 119–20.

13. Abir, "Caravan Trade and History," pp. 109–11 and sources cited in same. According to Richard Kluckhorn, "as far as anyone knows the traders working in the Konso area have always been Somalis." "The Konso Economy of Southern Ethiopia," in Paul Bohannan and George Dalton, eds., *Markets in Africa* (Evanston, 1962), p. 417.

14. Abir, "Caravan Trade and History," pp. 113–14; Pankhurst, "The Trade of Southern and Western Ethiopia," p. 38.

also obtained coffee, salt, and nitrate of soda from the Jubba basin and surrounding foothills.[15] These items, along with occasional Oromo slaves, were usually absorbed in local markets along the caravan routes and rarely reached the coast. The most important inland market towns in southern Somalia were Luuq and Baardheere, on the Jubba River; Baydhabo (Baidoa) and Buur Hakaba in the central interriver plain; and Awdheegle and Afgooye along the lower Shabeelle. Since most of these towns were situated in good agricultural country, they were able to supply caravans with foodstuffs and other provisions. In this way, the long-distance caravan trade helped stimulate the local market economy.[16]

Although the inland market centers were small—only the towns along the Shabeelle numbered more than two thousand permanent residents—they were frequented by nomads, farmers, and peddlars from the surrounding districts. In essence, they were small "ports of trade" that offered security and a degree of political neutrality to buyers and sellers from a variety of different clans and locales.[17] This was essential, since long-distance trade in southern Somalia—as in the north—was segmented. Goods originating in the Jubba basin were brought to the towns of Luuq and Baardheere in caravans manned by traders from upcountry clans: Garre, Jerire, and Ajuraan Somali, and Borana Oromo. From the Jubba River towns, Gasar Gudda, Eelay, and Garre traders carried the goods to Baydhabo and Buur Hakaba, to Awdheegle and Afgooye. At these points, the inland traders typically handed over their goods to local brokers or to coastal merchants who might venture inland as far as the lower Shabeelle. No one Somali group monopolized the whole of the long-distance caravan trade; even the ubiquitous Garre seldom took their caravans beyond the river town of Awdheegle. This segmentation of the caravan routes probably explains why neither William Christopher nor Charles Guillain—two mid-century explorers sent to investigate the prospects for increased European trade with Somalia—could obtain

15. Guillain, *Documents* 3: 384–85; Ferrandi, *Lugh*, pp. 355–60.
16. References to internal trade within southern Somalia are found throughout Ferrandi, *Lugh*, esp. pp. 314–68; this work is an invaluable source for the study of late nineteenth-century regional commerce.
17. Ferrandi, *Lugh*, pp. 314–16; see also references in n. 20 below. For the notion of ports of trade, see Karl Polanyi, "Ports of Trade in Early Societies," in George Dalton, ed., *Primitive Archaic, and Modern Economies: Essays of Karl Polanyi* (New York: Anchor Books, 1968), pp. 238–60.

Ferrymen (bahar) *still carry passengers and livestock across the Shabeelle River near Afgooye, the point at which many upcountry trade routes converged in the past.*

Nomads from the area between Baydhabo and Wanle Weyn display the characteristic hair style and carry walking sticks (cul) *and wooden headrests* (barkin) *that mark the rural herdsman.*

from their coastal informants consistent reports of the people and trading centers upcountry.[18]

Given the conditions that prevailed in Somalia, it is not surprising that no single group of indigenous traders dominated all aspects of the long-distance caravan network. The southern Somali commercial system encompassed a region occupied by a vast mosaic of Somali lineages, clans, and confederations, all fiercely independent and most engaged in subsistence pastoralism or agriculture. Each required some access to the major nodes and arteries of commercial exchange; each guarded its right to oversee one leg of the caravan trade as jealously as it guarded its home wells and reserve grazing areas. Tribute—or protection money—exacted from caravans in transit was a source of income for the local community and a means of obtaining scarce goods. In the absence of any large, centralized polity concerned with facilitating long-distance trade, each clan maintained its segment of the operation with its own interests (and those of its allies) in mind. In such circumstances, trade was best conducted through flexible and small-scale exchanges, buttressed by the individual and group alliances characteristic of a basically pastoral society.

Despite the segmentary and decentralized character of long-distance trade in Somalia, certain common institutions spanned the exchange network, insuring the smooth flow of goods across a land inhabited by numerous, frequently hostile clans. One such institution was that of the *abbaan*, or host/protector. Generally a man of prestige and respected lineage in a specific locale, the *abbaan* oversaw the transactions performed by a trader passing through that locale. The *abbaan* negotiated the customs duties and presents expected by clan elders; he saw to the accommodations of the travelers; and he procured guides and camels for the ongoing journey. His also was the

18. Contemporary reports on the routes through Somali country can be found in Guillain, *Documents* 3:175–77; Leon des Avanchers, "Esquisse géographique des pays Oromo ou Galla, des pays Soomali, et de la côte orientale d'Afrique," *Bulletin de la société de géographie*, vol. 4, no. 17 (1859), pp. 153–70; E. G. Ravenstein, "Somali and Galla Land . . . embodying information collected by the Rev. Thomas Wakefield," *Proceedings of the Royal Geographical Society* 6 (1884): 255–73; Ferrandi, *Lugh*, pp. 320–23.

On the difficulties of obtaining consistent reports, see Christopher, "Extract from a Journal by Lieut. W. Christopher, Commanding the H. C. Brig of War *Tigris*, on the E. Coast of Africa. Dated 8th May 1843," *Journal of the Royal Geographical Society* 14 (1844): 80; and Guillain, *Documents* 3: 53.

responsibility for securing reparations for goods stolen from or injuries inflicted upon his client.

The *abbaan* might also fill the role of *dillaal* (broker), or recommend another for that task. It was the *dillaal*'s responsibility to collect products and secure buyers in anticipation of the arrival of a caravan. Traveling merchants frequently left goods on consignment with a trusted *abbaan*, permitting him to keep a share (5–25 percent) of any profits. Exchanges of gifts were common, and it was not unusual for host/trader relationships to persist over many generations. A merchant whose business took him far into the interior required several *abbaan*s for the journey, and thus commercial relationships extended throughout the Somali country.[19]

To be sure, looting along the caravan routes was not uncommon. Bands of armed nomads, operating in the thick bush or barren plains that lay between the major towns and well sites en route, typically demanded a portion of the goods in transit. Having once exacted their price in tobacco, beads, or cloth, however, the marauders might themselves vouchsafe the security of the caravan over the next leg of its journey. Total depredation of the convoy was rare: it would only encourage the caravaneer to select an alternate route for the return journey, perhaps to the benefit of a rival clan. Bandits were, moreover, subject to clan law, and an influential *abbaan* could usually mobilize support for their punishment. Similarly, the *abbaan* had to resist the temptation to betray his client; his reputation as "protector" of trade could easily be sullied by a deceived merchant, who might compose a bitter poem to spread along the caravan routes.[20]

19. During his visit to Muqdisho in 1847, Guillain was assigned an *abbaan* by the elders of Shangaani (*Documents* 2: 506–7, 514, 546). The famous Muslim traveler Ibn Battuta enjoyed a similar reception in Muqdisho five centuries earlier: See G. S. P. Freeman-Grenville, *The East African Coast: Select Documents* (Oxford, 1962), pp. 27–28.

Other contemporary observers of *abbaan*s at work were Georges Revoil, "Voyages chez les Benadirs," 49: 36–37; and Ferrandi, *Lugh*, pp. 285 and 339–41.

For more general discussions of *abbaan*s in the Horn of Africa, see Ernesto Cucinotta, "La proprietà ed il sistema contrattuale nel *Destur* somalo," *Rivista coloniale* 16 (1921): 250–53; and Mordechai Abir, "Brokerage and Brokers in Ethiopia in the First Half of the 19th Century," *Journal of Ethiopian Studies*, vol. 3, no. 1 (1965), pp. 1–5.

20. On banditry and caravan raiding, see Revoil, "Voyages chez les Benadirs," 49: 46–47; 50: 140, 181; Ferrandi, *Lugh*, pp. 326–30. For a comparative discussion from northern Somalia, see I. M. Lewis, "Lineage Continuity and Modern Commerce in

An understanding of the commercial functions of the *abbaan*—well described by Abir in his article on brokerage in the Horn of Africa[21]—should not obscure the fundamentally sociojuridical nature of the institution. The social function of the *abbaan* was to integrate outsiders, for however brief a time, into the clan-community with which they intended to deal. It identified the outsider with a patron and, by extension, with the patron's lineage. Clearly, the *abbaan*'s ability to secure reparations for stolen property or client injury was only as good as the warrior support he could muster. The *abbaan*'s effectiveness thus hinged upon his standing within his own clan. And though particular *abbaan*-client relationships may have grown out of personal or business considerations, they in effect brought one lineage to the support of another. Through the *abbaan*, the client/trader was located in the nexus of clan rights and obligations and thus was insured of the protection due to any kinsman for the duration of his stay in the community.

As might be expected, successful *abbaan*-trader relationships could evolve into more permanent ties between lineages. Reciprocal bonds of exchange and protection were particularly common between Somali clans living along the lower Shabeelle River and Somali or Arab families resident at the coast. Thus the Abikerow lineage of Afgooye district had special ties to the Shanshiiye of Muqdisho, while the Adawiin lineages in the same district had numerous *abbaan*s among the Reer Faqi.[22] In the same way, Biimaal lineages inhabiting the hinterland of Marka traded under the auspices of particular Arab families from that town.[23] The urban Hamarani that were settled in Baraawe divided their inland trade among the five segments of the Tunni confederation.[24] Such corporate commercial alliances were not limited to the coastal districts. Some informants from Afgooye recalled that in generations past, certain lineages from their district

Northern Somaliland," in Paul Bohannan and George Dalton, eds., *Markets in Africa* (Evanston, 1962) pp. 369–70, 380–82.

21. See n. 19 above.
22. Shaykh Mustafa Yusuf, Afgooye, 27 May 1971.
23. Pantano, *La citta di Merca e la regione Bimal* (Leghorn, 1910), pp. 19–20.
24. Colucci, *Principi*, p. 188 n. 1; Giovanni Piazza, "La regione di Brava nel Benadir," *Bollettino della società italiana di esplorazione geografiche e commerciali* (Jan.–Feb. 1909), 3 pts.

enjoyed special commercial and social ties with the Eelay of Buur Hakaba, a small town situated on the caravan route that stretched upcountry from Afgooye.[25] These economic-cum-social connections were frequently marked by the common celebration of religious holidays and lineage-ancestor festivals, and by the exchange of special funereal gifts *(tacas)* following the death of a member of either party. Marriages reinforced commercial alliances. Indeed, one informant described the bond between lineages that exchanged goods on a regular basis as *xidid* ("artery"), the same term used in other contexts to describe a man's relationship to his wife's kinsmen.

Another source of cohesiveness in the trading system of southern Somalia was religion, or rather the protection offered by certain groups of religious to the caravaneer. Prominent in this regard was the Reer Shaykh Mumin lineage, whose members were dispersed along the route which ran from Luuq to Muqdisho. Not only did families of the Reer Mumin have commercial interests in Xamar (the oldest quarter of Muqdisho), Buur Hakaba, and Luuq, but also, as a lineage of religious specialists, they were widely respected and feared for their purported ability to cast the evil eye.[26] The Reer Mumin were successful along the trade routes at least partly because their traditional role as men of religion enabled them to travel freely about the country without fear to their persons or property. In return for fees, they adjudicated commercial disputes or invoked supernatural protection for caravans. Religious sanctions thus assisted the exchange of goods across a politically fragmented region, much the way they did in the Hausa trade diaspora of West Africa.[27]

One noteworthy consequence of this segmented yet well-integrated system of exchange was the almost total exclusion of foreign traders from its operation through most of the nineteenth century. While the merchants of Baraawe were able to negotiate for themselves in the distant interior, coastal Arabs and Indians rarely ventured beyond the market towns of the lower Shabeelle valley. Inland commerce lay entirely in Somali hands until the 1890s, and even then

25. Ali Omar Haji "Goyle," Muqdisho, 24 May 1971; Shaykh Mustafa Yusuf, Afgooye, 27 May 1971.

26. Ferrandi felt that the Reer Shaykh Mumin used their reputation as practitioners of the occult to extort money from itinerant traders: Ferrandi, *Lugh*, pp. 138–39, 242–43, 304.

27. Abner Cohen, *Custom and Politics in Urban Africa* (London, 1969).

only a few Arab traders found their way upcountry.[28] The contrast with the experience of the rest of East Africa, where Arab and Swahili traders established trading posts throughout the Tanganyikan interior as early as 1850, is striking. The difference can perhaps be explained by the fact that long-distance caravan trade in Somalia antedated the commercial diaspora launched from Zanzibar in the 1830s and 1840s, with the result that late-arriving Arab traders could not break into the established web of economic and social institutions that spanned the Somali country. Moreover, those Arab merchants who resided in the Benaadir towns of Somalia and who enjoyed good relations with the Somalis of the interior were predominantly of Hadrami origin.[29] The Omani Arabs who fanned out from Zanzibar in the nineteenth century—and who tended to be Ibadi rather than Sunni Muslims—never acquired comparable influence in the Benaadir hinterland.

To place the southern Somali trade in perspective, it should be emphasized that the quantity of goods which originated in the distant interior was small in comparison to that exported from the rest of Zanzibar's East African dominions. A knowledgeable Italian merchant estimated in the 1880s that Somali products accounted for no more than between one-fifth and one-third of Zanzibar's trade,[30] and this may be somewhat exaggerated. Moreover, the trade within Somalia was always small scale; single caravans rarely numbered more than fifteen or twenty camels. No single Somali trader ever acquired the reputation or wealth of a Tippu Tip or a Mwinyi Kheri; and it is difficult to find evidence in the nineteenth century of any kind of prosperous trading "class" outside of the coastal towns.

There was some significance, however, in the changing composition of the Somali export trade over the course of the nineteenth century. Whereas in the 1840s approximately half of the Benaadir's exports consisted of ivory, aromatic woods, gums, and myrhh (most

28. Christopher, "Extract from a Journal," p. 100; Ferrandi, *Lugh*, p. 140. Ferrandi noted in 1894 that "the Arabs are now beginning to penetrate the interior, formerly closed to them as it was to the Europeans." "Prima spedizione," p. 237.

29. The origins of the urban clans are discussed in Hersi, "The Arab Factor," pp. 235–43; E. Rovatti, "Mogadiscio," *ASMAI*, pos. 87/1, f. 7; Pantano, *La citta di Merca*, p. 13 ff.; G. Cerrina-Ferroni, *Benadir* (Rome, 1911), pp. 28–31. Cf. Enrico Cerulli, *Somalia: Scritti vari editi ed inediti*, 3 vols. (Rome, 1957), 1: 5, 34, 36.

30. Letters of Vincenzo Filonardi, cited in Giuseppina Finazzo, *L'Italia nel Benadir: L'azione di Vincenzo Filonardi, 1884–1896* (Rome, 1966), pp. 141–42.

from upcountry), data from the 1890s reveal that fifty years later these items made up less than one-fourth of the value of total exports from southern Somalia.[31] Durra, sesame products, cotton, and other agricultural exports had assumed new importance. Butter, hides, and livestock on the hoof were also being exported in substantial quantities. Virtually all of the agricultural commodities were grown in the lower Shabeelle Valley, and presumably most of the livestock exports originated from districts close to the coast, though the evidence is not sufficient to argue the latter point with certainty. Nonetheless, there had occurred a marked shift in the center of economic activity in southern Somalia, insofar as production of goods for export was concerned. The next section will examine the forces contributing to that shift and some of the consequences.

The Agricultural Economy of the Lower Shabeelle Valley

While long-distance trade in the Somali interior experienced a steady if unremarkable growth through the nineteenth century, life along the lower Shabeelle River changed dramatically with the increase in foreign trade. The patterns of change owed much to the unique geography of the region. The Somali Benaadir is the only coastal district of East Africa to have for its immediate hinterland a fertile riverine plain. The Shabeelle River runs parallel to the coast for nearly two hundred miles; at some points it lies less than six miles from the sea. Here and there the river banks are higher than the surrounding plain, excellent conditions for irrigated agriculture. South of Jenaale, a large channel branches off from the main riverbed and extends the irrigable land several miles toward the coast.[32] The accessibility and fertility of the Shabeelle valley have made it the source of food for the towns of Muqdisho, Marka, and Baraawe for presumably as long as those towns have existed. Durra has long been the staple crop of the area; some maize was also grown in the nineteenth century.

Oral traditions of the several clans that today occupy the lower Shabeelle valley suggest that the process of Somali settlement of arable riverine land had been going on for several generations before

31. Estimates based on statistics provided in Robecchi-Brichetti, *Somalia e Benadir*, pp. 84, 87, 584–611. See n. 11 above.
32. This channel is known locally as the *Webi Goofka* ("dry river").

1840. In Marka district, an eighteenth-century sultan of the Biimaal clan known as Saddiq Aproone is remembered as having encouraged his pastoral kinsmen to cultivate durra. He went so far as to hire an Indian expert to demonstrate the finer points of irrigated agriculture. Saddiq's successor, Hussein, witnessed the further sedentarization of his clansmen, a process which may have involved the subordination of existing groups of negroid farmers.[33] The actual pattern of Biimaal settlement that was observed in the early twentieth century suggests that the occupation of cultivable land by their ancestors was a systematic process. Each of the four major Biimaal sections, or subclans, held a distinct strip of territory extending from the fertile river bank to the semi-arid coastal dunes. Each of these sectional strips was subdivided over time among the various lineages and *reer*s, usually in proportion to their numbers. The arable portion of the land was held by the lineage until individuals undertook to clear and plant it. Individual occupation of farms became common, the Biimaal say, six to eight generations ago.[34]

Similar traditions of settlement are recounted by the Geledi, who live in the Afgooye district just below the great bend of the Shabeelle.[35] After wandering for several generations through the country, the ancestors of the Geledi found themselves in the vicinity of the Shabeelle. There, as the story goes, a member of the Handab lineage discovered the river by following a white camel which always appeared to be satisfied even when the rest of the herd was suffering from drought. At the point where the camel reached the river, the settlement of Ceelqoode (Elqode) was founded. Then, Shaykh Muhammad Haji Yusuf of the Handab distributed the land to those lineages known collectively as the Tolweyne. The Handab were henceforth

33. These Biimaal traditions were first published by Pietro Barile in 1935 in his *Colonnizzazione fascista nella Somalia* (Rome, 1935), pp. 74–75. Barile apparently gathered information from several informants, though he gives no indication of his sources. The Biimaal elders I talked with confirmed the existence of the personalities and some of the events recorded by Barile; none, however, could match Barile's wealth of detail.

34. Antonio Scarpa, "Della proprieta fondiara in Somalia," *L'Agricoltura coloniale* 17 (1923): 282; Pantano, *La citta di Merca*, pp. 44–45 and map frontispiece.

35. The following information was provided by Abokor Ali Omar, Muqdisho, 14 July 1971, and is part of that local history known to most of the Geledi community. More detailed traditions of the various Geledi lineages were generously made available to me by Virginia Luling, who collected them during two years of field work in the Afgooye district.

known as the *curad* ("first-born") of the Geledi. A second group of lineages, the Yebdaale, settled downriver at a place called Balguurey. As among the Biimaal, each Geledi lineage allocated plots of alluvial land to its individual members.

Other clans throughout the lower Shabeelle region have their own settlement traditions; the distribution of arable land among component lineages appears as a dominant theme in most of them. In surveying the patterns of land tenure prevalent in the cultivable areas of southern Somalia, Massimo Colucci found that in most instances the clan remained the ultimate guarantor of the land, defending it from external aggression. The various lineages comprising the clan had the responsibility of dividing the land and resolving disputes between individuals. Individual clansmen, together with their close relatives or clients, undertook the actual clearing and planting of the land.[36] As far as can be determined, there was always an abundance of cultivable land along the lower Shabeelle River.[37] The major obstacles to increased agricultural productivity were, as I shall argue below, limited manpower and a pervasive pastoral ethic within the politically dominant stratum of Shabeelle valley society.

It is not clear to what extent Biimaal, Geledi, and other Somali clans of pastoral origin actually took up farming and to what extent they simply exploited the labor of groups of client-cultivators previously settled in the area. Throughout the lower Shabeelle region, there existed in the nineteenth century (and probably much earlier) numerous communities of farmers known by a variety of generic names, most connoting servile origins or status.[38] One of these terms,

36. Massimo Colucci, *Principi di diritto consuetudinario della Somalia italiana meridionale* (Florence, 1924) p. 155 ff.

37. Romolo Onor, *La Somalia italiana* (Turin, 1925), pp. 12–14. There is really no way to determine the land-labor ratio for the precolonial period. Early colonial authorities were nearly unanimous in insisting that a shortage of agricultural labor was the major factor preventing the extension of cultivation along the Shabeelle. See the summary in Irving Kaplan et al., *Area Handbook for Somalia*, 2d ed. (Washington, D.C., 1977), pp. 267–70. See also Mark Karp, *The Economics of Trusteeship in Somalia* (Boston, 1960), pp. 79–83, 117–20.

38. Among the terms used in the vicinity of the lower Shabeelle valley were *habash* (apparently derived from an Arabic term that originally referred to a slave from Ethiopia), *ooji*, *addoon*, and *boon* (the same word traditionally used by Somalis to designate the members of certain occupational castes considered inferior). See Virginia Luling, "The Social Structure of Southern Somali Tribes" (Ph.D. thesis, University of London, 1971), pp. 45–47; and Colucci, *Principi*, pp. 213–14. All of these

timo adag ("hard-hairs"), was used to distinguish peoples of apparent negroid origin from the "true" Somalis, who were known as *timo jilicsan* ("soft hairs"), though obvious instances of intermarriage in the past made this a far from clear distinction. Other terms translate more accurately into "slave" or "servant." It is unlikely, however, that all of these farmers were once slaves in the strict sense. Many appear to be descendants of the region's earliest (Bantu-speaking?) inhabitants,[39] and others, Somalis who settled down to farm and who intermarried with their predecessors on the land. These farmers appear to have been incorporated as dependents of later-arriving Somali pastoral clans. They retained their distinctive mode of life (along with certain ritual practices) while becoming progressively integrated into the political and jural communities of their pastoral overlords.

The adoption of client-cultivators by pastoral clans has some similarities with the institution of *sheegad*, through which subordinate pastoral groups were permitted to graze their herds on the land of more powerful clans. Like pastoral dependents, client-cultivators provided warriors for the dominant clan's defense; they received a portion of the spoils of war; they were entitled to blood compensation in cases of homicide or injury; and they participated (with certain restrictions) in the rainmaking and religious ceremonies of the larger confederation.[40]

Unlike pastoral *sheegad*, however, who were always regarded as temporary residents on the land of their patrons, client-cultivators of the lower Shabeelle typically enjoyed uncontested rights to the land they worked, probably because of their prior association with the riverine land, which in any case was of little direct use to their pastoral overlords. They lived in interdependence with the nomads and were not potential competitors for grazing resources, as pastoral clients invariably were. These farming groups, moreover, could not renounce their clientship, for it rested on a position of social rather

---

terms have derogatory connotations and their use is prohibited in contemporary Somalia.

39. This view is held by Cerulli, *Somalia* 2:115–21.

40. This and the following paragraph draw on information provided by Luling, "Social Structure," pp. 47–48, 117–23; Ernesto Cucinotta, "La costituzione sociale somala," *Rivista coloniale* 16 (1921): 493 ff.; and Capt. Casali, "Afgoi" report of 15 May 1910, *ASMAI*, pos. 87/2, f. 17. A number of my informants, who preferred in this instance to remain anonymous, confirmed these descriptions.

than strictly political subordination. Client-cultivators could not (in theory) marry "noble" Somalis; the latter would not eat in the house of a family of servile origins.

By the nineteenth century, these farmers had become an integral part of the economic and social life of the Somali confederations that exercised hegemony in the lower Shabeelle region. All spoke the local Somali dialect, and many, like their pastoral patrons, conserved genealogies, though these rarely exceeded five generations in depth. Their relationship to the neighboring Somali was defined corporately rather than individually. A client lineage typically inhabited and worked the land of a particular *bilis* ("noble") lineage, whose elders in turn represented their clients in Somali clan councils and saw to it that an injured client was fully compensated according to the local *xeer*, or custom. Thus, within the Geledi confederation, a cluster of client groups known collectively as the Aytire were associated with the Tolweyne group of "noble" lineages, whereas those known as the Sabti Umar lived and worked among the Yebdaale moiety.[41] Similarly, along the river behind Marka, each village of client-cultivators was said to "stand with" a particular Biimaal lineage.[42]

Such corporate arrangements did not preclude the formation of individual patron/client ties, as might occur when a Somali "noble" advanced some cows or grain for a dependent's wedding. The indebted client would then be expected to repay his patron with future services, such as house construction or assistance in some commercial venture. For the most part, however, groups of client-cultivators were perceived as augmenting the power and status of the entire clan or clan segment to which they were attached. They provided the clan with additional manpower and productivity. By farming, they left the *bilis* free to raid, trade, and politic—a division of labor that provided the lower Shabeelle region with what was probably the highest overall standard of living in all of the Somali lands.

The mixed agricultural/pastoral economy of the Benaadir hinterland produced a surplus sufficient in most years to supply the small urban populations of the coast with cereal and meat and perhaps to

41. Virginia Luling's evidence suggests that client-cultivators in Afgooye traditionally maintained genealogies distinct from those of the "noble" Geledi; on the other hand, among the nearby Wacdaan, client-cultivators typically adopted the genealogies of their patrons.

42. Pantano, *La citta di Merca,* pp. 76–78.

send a few hundred head of livestock to the Mascarenes annually. Despite nearly ideal natural conditions, however, the Shabeelle Valley appears to have lacked the structural conditions necessary to sustain commercial agriculture on a large scale. Production was geared to meet the domestic needs of the local population, which included storing part of the annual grain harvest in subterranean pits to insure against hard times. To have exploited the commercial potential of the Shabeelle Valley would have required an independent class of agricultural entrepreneurs. I would argue that such a class did not exist before the nineteenth century. Most cultivation was carried out by the groups of client-cultivators described above. The Somali clans that controlled trade, provided security, and dominated decision-making processes in the Benaadir hinterland remained committed to a pastoral ethic and to the view (not unfounded) that herding provided greater long-term security than did farming. Only with the convergence in the nineteenth century of new foreign markets and a ready supply of imported labor were structural conditions altered, making possible the development of a plantation mode of production.

Without exception, Somali informants claim that there occurred a great expansion of cultivation along the lower Shabeelle in the past century. Biimaal traditions tell of the prosperity enjoyed under the late nineteenth-century sultans Hussein Saddiq and Musa Muhammad Hussein.[43] The Geledi speak nostalgically of the days when reserves of durra were measured in terms of *diyehiin* (rectangular pits that held up to 100 quintals, or 10,000 kilograms, of grain) rather than in terms of *gut* (smaller conical pits).[44] I was shown extensive stretches of land, now covered with secondary bush growth lower and denser than that typical of most of the country, which my informants claim had been cultivated in their grandfathers' time.

The "good times" of Somali tradition find confirmation in the accounts of the few European travelers who managed to reach the Shabeelle Valley before 1900. Christopher (1843) claimed, though admittedly without knowledge of earlier Somali agriculture for comparison, that the Benaadir had become the "grain coast for the supply of south Arabia."[45] Guillain (1847), observing the thriving villages along

43. Barile, *Colonizzazione fascista*, pp. 76–77; Ibrahim Ali Subayr, Kilometer 50, 19 Aug. 1971.

44. Abokor Ali Omar, Muqdisho, 18 Mar. 1971.

45. "Extract from a Journal," pp. 87, 97.

the river near Afgooye, commented on the large surpluses that were being harvested from the fertile land with a minimum of effort.[46] Kirk (1873) counted dozens of dhows taking on grain at the ports of Muqdisho and Marka: "until I came here, I never knew there was so much cultivation."[47]

Even more revealing than such impressionistic observations is the fact that new products were being harvested in the interior and marketed along the Somali coast. In the 1840s, sesame had begun to be cultivated intensively in the hinterland; Guillain calculated that merchants could obtain Benaadir sesame for the lowest price in East Africa.[48] Another local product, orchella weed, emerged as a major export of English, French, and German traders in the 1860s.[49] Orchella is a kind of lichen that had been found to produce a purple and crimson dye ideal for coloring silks. By the 1870s, large quantities were being gathered along the Shabeelle. Even as late as 1890, when the discovery of synthetic dyes in Europe had depressed the value of orchella, the Benaadir was exporting over one hundred tons per year.[50]

Yet another product Somali farmers began to cultivate in the mid-nineteenth century was cotton. The story behind its appearance on the local scene is a revealing one. For centuries, Benaadir coastal craftsmen had produced a distinctive cloth known locally as *tomonyo*, or *toob Benaadir*. In narrow courtyards filled with ten or twenty looms stretched across pits hollowed from the earth, servile laborers of wealthy mercantile families worked raw cotton, imported largely from India, into garment-length strips. The Benaadir cloth was not only sold in the towns and bartered upcountry, but also carried by Arab traders to the Red Sea ports and Egypt, where its durability made it competitive with the more colorful imports from India.

Beginning in the 1840s, American traders began to flood the markets of East Africa with mass-produced cotton fabrics from New England mills. A contemporary observer felt that the increasing pop-

46. *Documents* 3: 27 ff.
47. John Kirk, "Visit to the Coast of Somali-land," *Proceedings of the Royal Geographical Society* 27 (1873): 342.
48. *Documents* 3: 315–16.
49. Bennett and Brooks, *New England Merchants*, pp. 518 n. 144, 531, 539–40.
50. Kirk, "Visit," p. 342; Sir H. B. E. Frere, "A Few Remarks on Zanzibar and the East Coast of Africa," *Proceedings of the Royal Geographical Society* 27 (1873): 374; Robecchi-Brichetti, *Somalia e Benadir*, p. 603.

ularity of the *toob Merikaani,* as it was known, would soon drive the Benaadir weavers out of business.[51] To compete successfully with the inexpensive American imports, Somali craftsmen turned to a less costly source of raw cotton—the Benaadir's own hinterland. Whereas in the 1840s cotton fiber seems to have been almost entirely imported,[52] by the 1880s observers found it growing in abundance along the Shabeelle inland from Muqdisho and Baraawe.[53] Donkeys or camels carried the bulk cotton to the coastal towns, where the seeds were removed and the spinning was done.

The cotton may have been a wild variety that grew in Somalia but had not previously been exploited commercially. It may have been introduced by Indian entrepreneurs resident along the coast, or by the Americans themselves.[54] Whatever the origin, the local production of cotton saved the Benaadir weaving industry, which continues down to the present day. In an ironic footnote to the story, it was reported in 1893 that some Indian merchants had rented a German steamer to carry large quantities of raw Benaadir cotton to Bombay.[55]

The production of items like durra, sesame, orchella, and cotton in quantities sufficient to meet the needs of the local market and, to an increasing extent, those of the foreign, was made possible by the importation into the Benaadir of a new supply of agricultural labor: black slaves from the Swahili coast to the south. Limited slave trading almost certainly had been going on for several centuries and consisted chiefly of the export, on a small scale, of Oromo captives to the Middle East.[56] The heyday of the import trade, however, appears

51. Guillain, *Documents* 2: 531–32.

52. Christopher, "Extract," p. 95: Guillain, *Documents* 2: 532, 535; 3: 28.

53. Revoil, "Voyage chez les Benadirs," 49: 35; Robecchi-Brichetti, *Somalia e Benadir,* pp. 83–84, 604 n. 2, 606.

54. The fact that the German explorer Richard Brenner found cotton growing along the Shabeelle River south of Baraawe in 1866 makes it doubtful that the Egyptian expedition of 1875 (which briefly occupied Baraawe and Kismaayo) was a major impetus to Somali cotton cultivation. Otto Kersten, ed., *Baron Carl Claus von der Decken's Reisen in ost Afrika in den Jahren 1862 bis 1865* (Leipzig, 1871), p. 349.

55. Report of Antonio Cecchi summarized in *Documenti Diplomatici: Somalia Italiana (1885–1895)* (Rome, 1895), pp. 19–20.

56. Apart from scattered references in the writings of medieval Muslim and later Portuguese travelers to slave exports from the Horn of Africa (the sources of the slaves almost never specified), we know nothing about the slave trade from Somalia before the nineteenth century. Recent reinterpretations of Somali-Galla movements in

to be linked with the emergence of Zanzibar as a commercial power in East Africa. The earliest dates that can be isolated with any certainty fall around 1800, when Zigua slaves from the Mrima coast were brought to the Bajuni Islands and perhaps to Baraawe.[57] By the 1830s and 1840s, slaves were being carried in Arab dhows to the Somalilands in increasing numbers: six hundred landed at Muqdisho in 1846.[58]

In the 1860s, British naval patrols began to detain slave-laden vessels en route from Zanzibar to the Middle East. East African slavers responded by driving their human cargoes overland from Lamu to the Benaadir, where they were destined for reexport to the north. In 1866 the German explorer Brenner counted six slave caravans in four days passing through Baraawe.[59] Not all of these slaves were reexported, however; Benaadir merchants apparently were selling them in the riverine towns of Awdheegle, Bariirey, and Afgooye. The British consul John Kirk drew attention to this fact in the 1870s, by which time he estimated that ten thousand slaves were crossing the Jubba annually.[60]

Evidence of large numbers of unassimilated slaves in the Benaadir comes from the existence of ex-slave communities along the lower Shabeelle and Jubba Rivers. As early as 1843, an English visitor was cautioned by his Somali hosts about the danger from "the slaves, or rather self-liberated free men of the interior." The secluded community of runaway slaves at Golweyn, he noted, "acknowledge no authority."[61] Late in 1867, the dhow-chaser G. L. Sullivan liberated 322

---

southern Somalia suggest, however, that chronic warfare must have produced at least small numbers of captives for the foreign market. See Hersi, "The Arab Factor," pp. 142–76; Beachey, *Slave Trade*, p. 6; E. R. Turton, "Bantu, Galla, and Somali Migrations in the Horn of Africa: A Reassessment of the Juba/Tana Area," *Journal of African History* 16 (1975): 534–35.

57. Vinigi L. Grottanelli, *Pescatori dell'Oceano indiano* (Rome, 1955), p. 210; and idem, "I Bantu del Giuba nelle tradizioni dei Wazegua," *Geographica Helvetica* 8 (1953): 259.

58. Guillain, *Documents* 2:537.

59. Kersten, *Baron C.C. von der Decken's Reisen*, p. 349.

60. Kirk to the Earl of Derby, *State Papers* 67 (1875–76): 431; cf. Peter Collister, *The Last Days of Slavery* (Dar Es Salaam, 1961), p. 55, where the estimate is made that 12,000 slaves reached Somaliland by the overland route in 1874.

61. Christopher, "Extract from a Journal," pp. 84, 100.

slaves entering and leaving Baraawe. Among those freed were Nyika, Nyamwezi, Yao, Nyassa, Makua, and Ngindo captives.[62] Many of these same groups had been found in small communities along the Jubba River by the von der Decken expedition in 1865. Most had escaped after brief periods of servitude under Somali or Arab masters.[63]

Yet for all those slaves who escaped, it is clear that many more stayed on the land. They helped to augment the agricultural labor force at a time when several major wars—including the Baardheere *jihad* described in the preceding chapter—and a cholera epidemic had taken the lives of many Somalis and their client-cultivators.[64] Most of the newly arrived slaves were either purchased by Somali landholders from Arab traders or were received as payment for debts owed. Unlike the long-established groups of client-cultivators, newly imported slaves had no political or legal rights within the larger community. If a slave was killed, the owner demanded from the murderer not the standard amount of bloodwealth but the market value of the slave. Slaves could be liberated only on an individual basis by their owners.[65] It followed that slaves were considered personal property, the fruits of their labor accruing first to the owner.

The results for the Shabeelle valley economy were dramatic. In less than a generation there was created a new class of dependent labor the deployment of which was not constrained by custom. Slaveholders could turn to commercial agriculture without threatening subsistence production and without disrupting the social fabric that bound patron clans to their client-cultivators. The acquisition of slaves gave their owners a new flexibility in meeting the foreign demand for

62. G. L. Sullivan, *Dhow-Chasing in Zanzibar Waters* (London, 1873), pp. 153–72.

63. Kersten, *Baron C.C. von der Decken's Reisen*, pp. 302–3. See also Grotanelli, "I Bantu del Giuba," pp. 252–53.

64. Apart from the wars associated with the Baardheere *jihad*, there were ongoing hostilities between the two most powerful riverine clans, the Geledi and the Biimaal; see Lee V. Cassanelli, "The Benaadir Past: Essays in Southern Somali History" (Ph.D. diss., University of Wisconsin, 1973) p. 106 ff. Christopher ("Extract from a Journal," p. 92) heard that some 10,000 warriors had already died in the Baardheere campaigns of the late 1830s and early 1840s.

For the cholera epidemic of 1858–59, see James Christie, *Cholera Epidemics in East Africa* (London, 1876), p. 111.

65. For the distinction between rights of first-generation slaves and those of client-cultivators, see Cucinotta, "La costituzione sociale somala," pp. 494–97.

grain, sesame, and orchella. The phenomenon of individual slaveholding also made possible the opening up of new tracts of land specifically for commercial production.

Whether the expansion of cultivation was accompanied by
changes in Somali notions of land tenure is not clear. The point was
much debated in the early colonial literature. Some writers held that
the apparent trend toward individual landholding in the later nineteenth century marked a break with customary practice, which was
seen to involve collective ownership by the lineage group over *adableh* (cultivable land). Others argued that Somali *xeer* had always
recognized a form of individual ownership over cultivated land and
that the expansion of cultivation simply enabled more individuals to
become landholders.[66]

The historian is apparently confronted here with a situation
that was changing over time, and one that was complicated by the
juxtaposition of land occupied by long-standing client-cultivators
and land being newly cleared for commercial agriculture. There is
some evidence to suggest that Islamic *qaaddi*s were called upon
more frequently to witness and record land transactions in the years
after 1900.[67] The growing influence of the *qaaddi*s, who upheld the
Sharia'atic notion that the man who fructifies the land becomes its
owner, may have given the impression to early colonial observers that
the lineage had become correspondingly less important as an arbiter
of land questions, and that individual tenure was increasing.

The entire debate tends to obscure the point that agricultural
land in itself was traditionally of little value to the Somali individual.
The occupation of *adableh* increased neither his status nor his power
within the clan; in fact, possession of cultivable land presumed a
certain status within the clan and a certain number of clients or slaves
to till it. The formal ceremony that preceeded the actual granting of

66. The debate is outlined by Colucci, *Principi,* pp. 209–10. See also Scarpa,
"Della proprieta fondiara," pp. 285–94. A recent reassessment both of the debate and
of changing patterns of land tenure in Somalia is Marco M. G. Guadagni, "Somali Land
Law: Agricultural Land from Tribal Tenure and Colonial Administration to Socialist
Reform" (Ph.D. thesis, University of London, 1979), esp. pp. 56–77.

67. Scarpa, "Della proprieta fondiara," p. 291; Colucci, *Principi,* p. 232; Guadagni, "Somali Land Law," pp. 35–37. The *rahan,* or Sharia'atic mortgage, which
facilitated the buying and selling of land, became increasingly important with the
spread of Islamic *jamaacooyin* (agricultural settlements) throughout the interior
around the turn of the century.

land to an individual—a ceremony marked in most places by the gathering of lineage elders, the offer of a gift by the petitioner, and the demarcation of boundaries—was in essence a confirmation of the individual's good standing within his lineage.[68]

What was important politically—that is, in terms of status and power—was not ownership of the land but one's relationship to the people on it. In a corporate relationship, such as that between client-cultivators and their "noble" overlords, power and status accrued to the group. With the acquisition of slaves by individuals, there was clearly greater scope for the accumulation of personal wealth, and hence of influence, within the clan. One example recorded in tradition is that of Aw Nur Ahmedow of the Geledi clan, Afgooye district. His sizable holdings enabled him to dispense large reserves of grain to his kinsmen during the famine years of the early 1890s. On another occasion, he bought grain from those of his neighbors who were unable to sell it on a glutted market and fed his dependents with it. These acts of largesse won him many adherents, and it is no coincidence that Aw Nur was one of the most influential spokesmen among the Geledi at the time of the colonial occupation. At one point, the Italians even considered recognizing him as the nominal sultan of the Afgooye district, in view of his wealth and prestige.[69]

We must be careful, however, not to exaggerate the impact of slaveholding on the traditional sociopolitical structure of southern Somalia. There is no evidence to suggest that the small group of wealthy slaveowners along the lower Shabeelle developed into an independent political force at the expense of traditional clan leaders. In the first place, the acquisition of slaves occurred along traditional lines of exchange between coast and interior.[70] No individual had a

68. Colucci, *Principi*, pp. 192–97. As Guadagni puts it, "land rights are strictly connected with personal status and with social responsibilities." "Somali Land Law," p. 65.

69. Information provided in interviews with Muhammad Abdullahi Ibrahim, Afgooye, 4 Mar. 1971; Aboker Ali Omar, Muqdisho, 8 Apr. 1971; and Ma'allin Yusuf, Muqdisho, 15 Apr. 1971.

The Italian administrator Giacomo Trevis called Aw Nur a "rich and influential Somali," while Chiesi and Travelli identified him as the "head of Eel-Qode," one of the villages in the Afgooye settlement area. G. Finazzo, *L'Italia nel Benadir*, pp. 457–58; Gustavo Chiesi and Ernesto Travelli, *Le Questioni del Benadir* (Rome, 1904), pp. 198–99.

70. The examples of registered transactions cited by Luigi Robecchi-Brichetti, *Lettere dal Benadir* (Rome, 1904), pp. 31–34, and the documents assembled by Chiesi

monopoly on the trade in slaves or on the alliances that such transactions could produce. Then, too, few landholders had more than
ten or fifteen slaves.[71] This may have been the result of the limited
supply of imported labor. It may also have been the consequence of
another factor: a wealthy individual could freely acquire slaves, but
he still needed to obtain the formal consent of the lineage elders to
obtain land. And though no informants ever said that the lineage
consciously limited the amount of land an individual could occupy,
the fact remains that individual plots in the past rarely exceeded
forty hectares; the average was more like five or ten.[72] The institutionalization of land distribution (with its potential for restricting
plot size) thereby had the effect of limiting the amount of personal
wealth an individual could amass through slave labor. The slave-
owner was induced to channel a portion of his wealth in slaves and
their produce into the lineage. Whether by giving female slaves as
wives to client-cultivators, by loaning slaves to needy kinsmen, or by
contributing surplus grain to wedding feasts, religious festivals, or

---

and Travelli, *Le Questioni,* esp. pp. 37, 317–22, indicate that slaves were often used
as payment for debts owed or as collateral for goods advanced on credit to upcountry
traders.

On the basis of preliminary research into the history of nineteenth-century
Muqdisho, Dr. Edward Alpers has hypothesized that the development of a slave mode
of production contributed to the emergence of a class alliance between the traders of
Muqdisho and the wealthy landholders of the Shabeelle Valley, backed perhaps by the
merchant capitalists of Zanzibar. If the hypothesis is correct, it lends support to our
thesis that the integration of town and country in nineteenth-century Somalia was
accompanied by increasing economic differentiation in the Benaadir region. See Edward
A. Alpers, "Towards a History of Nineteenth Century Muqdisho: A Report on Research
in Progress," paper delivered at the First International Congress of Somali Studies,
Muqdisho, 6–13 July 1980, esp. pp. 5–8.

71. I am indebted to Virginia Luling for information on nineteenth-century
slaveholding among the Geledi of Afgooye district. My informants from Mereerey and
Shalambood also indicated that slaves were fairly evenly distributed among landholders before abolition; they could recall only a handful of individuals who owned more
than a dozen slaves. Compare the similar figures provided by Robecchi-Brichetti on the
number of slaves owned by urban residents in the early twentieth century. *Lettere dal
Benadir,* pp. 68–70, 98–105, 179–203.

72. These figures derive from Virginia Luling's research at Afgooye. None of
my informants from other districts differed drastically with these estimates of plot size.
Here again the absence of any distinct recollection of the amount of land held by one's
forebears suggests that land ownership itself was not the critical measure of one's
wealth or status.

clan rituals, the wealthy landholder remained above all a traditional patron within the lineage. By controlling land distribution, the lineage maintained some control over the disposition of its members' personal wealth.

Finally, there is little evidence to suggest that the few large slaveholders in nineteenth-century Somalia ever became full-time agricultural entrepreneurs. Most, it appears, maintained large herds of livestock, under the care of kinsmen or clients, in keeping with traditional Somali patterns of status and wealth.[73] "Yusuf Roobleh was rich in cattle and slaves," an informant would recall; not, "he was rich in land."[74] Those who purchased slaves typically did so with capital derived from livestock sales or commercial ventures; and they used returns from their investments in commercial cultivation to augment the size of the family herds. Whether the agro-pastoral entrepreneurs of the nineteenth-century Benaadir realized the ultimate vulnerability of plantation agriculture in an era of abolition remains a moot question; but by continuing to invest in pastoralism, they provided themselves with future economic security and established a pattern that has continued into the twentieth century among many Somalis who use part of their earnings from foreign trade to build up their livestock holdings.

The agricultural boom of the nineteenth century almost certainly strengthened the economic position of the riverine clans vis-à-vis their coastal counterparts. The land- and slaveholders of the Shabeelle Valley were critical links in the system of production and trade that supplied the coastal markets, and there is some evidence that they provided credit to small merchants and traders who plied the area between the river and the coast.[75] Control over the supply of commodities demanded by foreign traders also enabled the Shabeelle

73. There is little direct evidence on this point. However, the use of slaves for herding livestock and the apparent ease with which Somali landholders moved back into the pastoral sector following drought and abolition in the late 19th century suggest that pastoralism remained as a "back-up" investment for most Shabeelle valley residents. See Chiesi-Travelli, *Le Questioni,* pp. 97–98, 342; Giogio Sorrentino, *Ricordi del Benadir* (Naples, 1910), pp. 417–19.

74. Colucci observed in the 1920s that the term *hanti,* which in Somali connotes the idea of property, was used by his informants solely with reference to slaves. *Principi,* p. 217, n. 4.

75. See for example *Documenti Diplomatici: Somalia (1899–1905)* (Rome, 1905), Appendix 2, no. 45; Sorrentino, *Ricordi,* p. 145.

valley clans to exercise a certain leverage over politics in the coastal towns.

In the early 1870s, for example, the elders of the Shangaani quarter of Muqdisho opposed the construction of a Zanzibar fortress in their town. Sultan Ahmed of Geledi, at that time still on good terms with the Zanzibar government and eager to demonstrate his influence, threatened to have his allies along the river boycott the Shangaani market if its elders obstructed the plan. The Shangaani leadership soon saw the merit of Ahmed's position, and the garrison was built.[76] Similarly, the Biimaal were not averse to holding back supplies from their riverine farms whenever the townsmen of Marka pursued policies they felt were inimical to their interests. By refusing to transport grain to the coast, they could disrupt the export market, particularly at the end of the southwest monsoon when Arab dhows were preparing for their return to Arabia. Such tactics, used often during the politically turbulent years of the later nineteenth century, came abruptly to the attention of Italian colonials when their garrison in Marka was cut off from food supplies for five months during the summer of 1904.[77]

Throughout the nineteenth century, the sultans of Zanzibar clearly recognized the economic potential of the riverine areas of Somalia. Both Sayyid Said and his son Barghash corresponded with the sultans of Geledi and tried to woo them with gifts; and when the latter proved to be unpredictable allies, the sultans of Zanzibar sought to draw up commercial agreements with Geledi's traditional inland rivals, the Biimaal.[78] However, the Zanzibaris lacked first-hand knowledge of and real influence over politics in the Somali interior. Unable to penetrate the Benaadir hinterland, they had to be content with a nominal presence in the major coastal towns. There they found greater receptivity to their commercial ambitions and secured the right to build a *garesa* (fort) in Marka (in the 1860s), and later in Muqdisho and Baraawe, ostensibly to protect foreign traders. The Benaadir coastal families, always vulnerable to economic sanctions from the hinterland Somali, came increasingly to rely on the power of

76. Muhammad Abdullahi Ibrahim, Afgooye, 4 Mar. 1971; Mustafa Yusuf, Afgooye, 27 May 1971. This episode is also referred to in Rovatti, "Mogadiscio," *ASMAI*, pos. 87/1, f. 7, p. 6.

77. See chap. 6, pp. 224–26.

78. Pantano, *La citta di Merca*, pp. 9–10; Barile, *Colonizzazione fascista*, pp. 90–95.

Zanzibar. It was the approval of town elders that enabled the sultans of Zanzibar to maintain fortified garrisons along the Somali coast through the 1870s and 1880s.[79]

For their part, the Somalis of the Shabeelle Valley were keenly aware of the foreign interest in their new-found agricultural wealth. Guillain was told in 1847 that the local farmers did not attempt to grow sugar, cotton, and indigo—despite the suitability of the environment—because they feared the Arabs would come and take it from them.[80] Sultan Ahmed Yusuf of the Geledi had barred all Zanzibari officials from visiting his territory as his price for assisting Barghash to construct the *garesa* in Muqdisho.[81] On numerous occasions, foreign merchants were discouraged from visiting the Shabeelle Valley because of reported Somali fears that their land would be coveted and eventually seized by outsiders.[82]

Somali fears of territorial dispossession were, as it turned out, well-founded. It was precisely the productive potential of the lower Shabeelle that attracted the keenest colonial interest in Somalia. Impressed by the sizable quantities of cotton that had been marketed at Baraawe, and the recent successes of local tobacco cultivation in the area, an Italian envoy wrote of Muqdisho's hinterland in 1893:

> Given the special circumstances of these people, the state of agriculture is, one can say, truly flourishing; and as soon as improvements in seeds and in agricultural implements are adopted, we can hope for even greater things than have happened in Baraawe.[83]

Another report from the same year stated:

> From what I have been able to observe in the brief time I had to survey the Benaadir interior, I feel that the land is ideally suited to agriculture, especially with a suitable system of irriga-

79. For further details, see Cassanelli, "The Benaadir Past," pp. 110–13.
80. Guillain, *Documents* 3: 28.
81. Mustafa Yusuf, Afgooye, 27 May 1971. Cf. Barile, *Colonizzazione fascista,* pp. 89–90.
82. Finazzo, *L'Italia nel Benadir,* pp. 456–60; Chiesi and Travelli, *Le Questioni,* pp. 197–98; Tomasso Carletti, *Attraverso il Benadir* (Viterbo, 1910), pp. 51, 74. Carletti (p. 51) mentions an Indian merchant who had lived for twenty years in the town of Marka and had never set foot outside its walls for fear of the surrounding Biimaal.
83. Report of G. Lovatelli to the Foreign Ministry, 27 May 1893, Document 77, Appendix 7, in *Documenti Diplomatici: Somalia Italiana (1885–1895)* (Rome, 1895).

tion, which will be easy to realize given the presence of many small rivulets; the soil, not suffocated by the thick tropical vegetation that one typically encounters in the swampy lands south of the equator, can with little expense and effort be prepared for the most varied cultivation; the climate is dry and perfectly healthy, and the heat is tolerable.[84]

Ten years later, a commission sent to investigate the efforts made by the chartered Benaadir Company to abolish slavery in Somalia, submitted the following recommendations.

Our firm conviction is that the future greatness of the Colony [of Somalia] lies in the development of agriculture. There is no longer any question that all of the land from the middle Shabeelle valley to the left bank of the Jubba is susceptible to the greatest agricultural exploitation. . . .

What we have seen while surveying the territory of Baraawe . . . between the Webi Goofka and the Shabeelle River, and beyond the Shabeelle, has provided the basis for our conviction; the agricultural products which flow to the markets of Marka and Muqdisho behind which, all the way to the river, live dense populations of workers, have reinforced and positively confirmed our opinion.

Then, in two paragraphs that future years would show to be more optimistic than prescient, the commissioners wrote:

Nor can one pose any objections regarding labor. Once the problem of slavery is brought under control through uniform laws appropriate to the circumstances . . . it will be easy to utilize the thousands and thousands of arms of this population (of ex-slaves). . . .

This might seem to be . . . only a dream. No. We who write no longer live in an age of easy optimism, of illusions, of dreams. We speak like this because we have seen: because our conviction has been growing day by day with our study of the places and with our research into their resources, and into their nature.[85]

In fact, Italian colonists and officials would find the shortage of manual labor to be the major obstacle to the development of a profita-

84. Cited in Chiesi and Travelli, *Le Questioni*, p. 364.
85. Ibid., pp. 365–66.

ble agricultural colony in Somalia. Most increases in agricultural productivity during the colonial period resulted from intensive capital
investment, improved irrigation technology, or the introduction of
new crops (like bananas and grapefruit), not from any substantial
growth of the agricultural labor force. Colonial officials often had to
resort to forced labor to maintain irrigation works and to clear new
land. While we lack hard statistics from the nineteenth century, it
seems safe to say that total agricultural output in the best years of
that century matched anything that the colonial regime could accom-
plish in the twentieth, even with the improved technology and military
force at its disposal. The nineteenth century revolution in commercial
agriculture in the Benaadir was the product of a unique (and short-
lived) labor supply situation that could not be recreated in the twentieth. Nonetheless, it left its mark on colonial perceptions of the
region's potential and on colonial plans for Somalia's future.[86]

Patterns of Economic Adaptation and Social Change

Most nineteenth-century Europeans were preoccupied with
the slave trade, discussions of which tended to dominate their writings on the economy of southern Somalia (and on East Africa as a
whole). However, the development of a slave-based plantation economy along the lower Shabeelle was only one of many changes that
followed from the incorporation of the Somali hinterland into the
international economy.

For one thing, over the course of the century, the export of
Somali livestock became established as a major commercial enterprise, particularly for those clans whose pastoral migrations season-
ally took them to home wells near the coast. Livestock trading was
scarcely a new feature of Somali pastoral life, but the opening of new
markets in the Western Indian Ocean coupled with improvements in
ocean shipping raised the livestock export business to a new level. The
establishment of a British colony at Aden (in 1839) and the growth of
wealthy foreign communities on Zanzibar and the Mascarenes increased the demand for regular supplies of meat and dairy products,

86. As one scholar sums it up, "Until the outbreak of the war with Ethiopia in
1935, the energies of the colonial government were devoted largely to agriculture and
to public works connected with agriculture." Robert Hess, *Italian Colonialism in
Somalia* (Chicago, 1966), pp. 162–63.

and Somalia was the closest source of secure supply for both areas. In the 1840s, a few hundred head of live cattle were exported from the Benaadir annually. By the mid-1890s, between two and three thousand head were being exported each year, despite the decimation of herds caused by the rinderpest epidemic of 1890–91.[87] The livestock trade in the north experienced a similar growth, with black-head sheep and goats the major items involved.[88]

The rise in foreign demand for Somali livestock prompted some coastal merchants to specialize in the collection and sale of meat on the hoof. In 1847, a merchant of Marka assured the French explorer Charles Guillain that he could provide the latter with two hundred head of cattle within four days for export to the island of Bourbon— this despite the fact that the people of the immediate hinterland had recently fallen on hard times.[89] The wealthy Hindu traders who trafficked in the Gulf of Aden ports rarely dealt in cattle, leaving the livestock trade there to Somali specialists.[90]

In a recent article, Jeremy Swift has described the emergence, during the twentieth century, of a Somali livestock-trading class.[91] While it is difficult to find hard evidence for the presence of such a "class" in the precolonial period (when the livestock trade was considerably smaller than it would become), some of the characteristic class behavior analyzed by Swift can be inferred from our own case study. For example, we have argued that nineteenth-century livestock traders along the Benaadir invested some of their earnings in slaves, just as, in more recent times, exporters of meat-on-the-hoof used their profits to hire paid herdsmen. In both cases, the investors secured labor that was free of traditional kinship obligations. Similarly, the presence of a class of dependent laborers in the nineteenth century enabled slaveholders to turn cultivable land into a source of personal wealth (though we noted the restrictions placed on the accumulation of such wealth). In the twentieth century, an emerging commercial elite used hired labor to sink new wells, enclose grazing areas, and

87. Guillain, *Documents* 2: 532–33; 3: 149, 172–73, 328–29; Robecchi-Brichetti, *Somalia e Benadir*, pp. 84, 87; Onor, *La Somalia italiana*, pp. 266–67.

88. Pankhurst, "The Trade of the Gulf of Aden Ports," pp. 36–81 passim.

89. Guillain, *Documents* 3:149.

90. Pankhurst, "The Trade of the Gulf of Aden Ports," p. 48.

91. "The Development of Livestock Trading in a Nomad Pastoral Economy: The Somali Case," in *Pastoral Production and Society* (Paris and Cambridge, 1979), pp. 447–65. Cf. Alpers, "Toward a History of Nineteenth Century Muqdisho," pp. 6–7.

maintain fleets of trucks to help sustain export operations that were largely independent of traditional communal constraints.[92] The nineteenth-century growth of plantation agriculture can thus be seen as an early manifestation of embryonic capitalist enterprise in Somalia, however limited in scale and duration.

One of the most significant long-term consequences of the economic transformation of Somalia in the nineteenth century was the impetus it gave to population movements within the Peninsula. In particular, the concentration of agricultural and commercial opportunities along the Benaadir acted as a magnet drawing Somalis from the northern and central parts of the country. Guillain noted as early as 1847 that Somalis from Berbera came periodically to Baraawe to obtain cotton goods, grain, cow hides, and silver, all items that had become more abundant with the advent of foreign trade in that region.[93] The same observer recorded an episode in which a wealthy Majeerteen merchant requested permission from Sultan Said of Zanzibar to establish a grain export center at Mungiya, a small enclave on the coast southwest of Marka. The aim of the project was to collect grain from the inland river towns of Golweyn and Buulo Mereerta for export to Arabia. Unfortunately, the enterprising northerner became embroiled in local politics and found his efforts sabotaged by the prepotent sultan of Geledi, who himself sought to control the productive surplus.[94]

In the years that followed, increasing numbers of traders from Hobya and Majeerteenia came in dhows to Marka and to the new town of Kismaayo.[95] Some settled permanently along the Benaadir, joining kinsmen who had arrived there earlier by the overland route. To be sure, many Somalis migrated to the southern coast for reasons other than commerce. Interclan conflicts, the Baardheere religious wars, and Somali-Oromo warfare for control of Jubaland all resulted in the movement of nomadic groups from the interior to the extensive plains southwest of Baraawe. And from the 1880s, Ethiopian military expansion drove countless Somalis out of the southern Ogaadeen toward Jubaland, where the terrain was suitable for the resumption of their

92. Ibid., pp. 462–64.
93. Guillain, *Documents* 3:173.
94. Ibid., p. 76.
95. Cecchi to Ministry of Foreign Affairs, 9 May 1895, Document 90, Appendix 11, *Documenti Diplomatici: Somalia Italiana (1885–1895);* Corrado Zoli, *Oltre-Giuba* (Rome, 1927), pp. 143, 146; Turton, "The Pastoral Tribes," pp. 79–80.

pastoral pursuits.[96] These multiple migrations produced frictions of their own: many of those northern Harti lineages today settled in the Kismaayo area came originally in response to appeals for aid from their kinsmen, who in the 1880s were engaged in a struggle for political supremacy and control of local commerce with elements of the neighboring Maxamed Zubeer clan.[97]

Examples of migration for political reasons notwithstanding, it is clear that potential profits from caravan trading, cattle dealing, and (by the 1880s) gun running remained powerful motivating factors. The Harti, sections of which had long traditions of trading across the Gulf of Aden in the north, came south in great numbers and established themselves as the dominant group of petty traders along the coast between the Jubba and the Tana Rivers.[98] Sections of the immigrant Ogaadeen experimented with grain-growing in the *wadi*s around Afmadow, employing as laborers Oromo who had been captured in the Ogaadeen occupation of Jubaland.[99] In the last two decades of the century, the pastoralists west of the Jubba became major exporters of cattle and hides, enterprises that remain important in the region to this day.[100]

The traditional mobility of the Somali population greatly facilitated its ability to respond to short-term opportunities generated by the rapidly changing conditions of the late nineteenth century. Information on market conditions and political security was disseminated by sailors, caravaneers, and entrepreneurs of various sorts. One such enterprising individual was Ali Naar. A native of the Ogaadeen region, Ali became a prominent merchant in Kismaayo, where he acquired some notoriety by initially opposing Zanzibar's efforts to establish a garrison there in 1881. Later, he gained recognition as a spokesman for Somali businessmen in Kismaayo, and the Italian explorer Luigi Robecchi-Brichetti encountered him trading in Hobya in the 1890s.[101] Widely traveled men like Ali Naar symbolize the increas-

96. Turton, "The Pastoral Tribes," p. 267 ff.

97. Zoli, *Oltre-Giuba*, pp. 154–56; Turton, "The Pastoral Tribes," p. 88 ff.

98. Zoli, *Oltre-Giuba*, pp. 261–66; Turton, "The Pastoral Tribes," pp. 80–82.

99. Turton, "The Pastoral Tribes," p. 204.

100. Peter Dalleo, "Trade and Pastoralism: Economic Factors in the History of the Somali of Northeastern Kenya, 1890–1948" (Ph.D. diss., Syracuse University, 1975), esp. p. 44 ff.

101. For Ali Naar, see Zoli, *Oltre-Giuba*, pp. 153–55; Turton, "The Pastoral Tribes," pp. 92–93; Robecchi-Brichetti, *Somalia e Benadir*, pp. 203–4. For other prominent and widely traveled merchants, see Zoli, *Oltre-Giuba*, p. 263.

ing contacts between northern and southern Somalis that characterized the later nineteenth century, as well as the growing involvement
of Somalis in the world of international commerce.

While Somali nomads and traders were responding to the economic stimuli of world trade, foreign powers were becoming increasingly interested in the commercial and strategic potential of the Horn.
The Benaadir ports were "ceded" to Italy by the sultan of Zanzibar
in 1890, and while Italian forces did not move inland to occupy the
Shabeelle valley until 1908, their efforts to abolish slavery and regu-
late trade along the coast effectively ended the expansion of commercial agriculture in the hinterland.[102] Competition between Italian and
British officials to lure the caravan trade toward ports in their respective spheres of influence on opposite sides of the Jubba exacerbated
interclan rivalries and added to the political uncertainties that hin-
dered commerce. Even more serious for the southern Somali economy
was the expansion of Ethiopian forces into the southern Ogaadeen
and into the plains east of Luuq. Periodic military incursions launched
from Harar and the upper Shabeelle disrupted caravan routes, ham-
pered the movements of petty traders, and created general conditions
of insecurity for farmers, nomads, and merchants alike. Somali pastoralists driven from the Ogaadeen by these same invading armies
began to raid for livestock and caravan goods throughout the interriver area. The result was an overall decline in long-distance trading
activity during the last decade of the century.[103] The events of the
1890s, coupled with foreign efforts to partition the Somalilands into
no fewer than five colonial territories, slowed many of the processes
of economic transformation outlined in this chapter and provided at
least one motive for the fierce resistance posed by Somalis to the
European colonial occupation.

102. See chap. 6 below, pp. 201–7.

103. Ferrandi, *Lugh*, pp. 19–21, 316; Sorrentino, *Ricordi*, pp. 278–79; Turton,
"The Pastoral Tribes," p. 354 ff.; Finazzo, *L'Italia nel Benadir*, pp. 325–26.

6 Local History and Regional Resistance:

The Somali Response to Colonial Occupation in the Benaadir Region, 1870–1910

To the foreigners, show only your strong points;
   To your kinsmen, your weak ones.
      —Somali saying

With the partition of Africa by the European powers at the Congress of Berlin in 1884, the colonial era can be said to have officially begun. The actual occupation of African territory by colonial forces often proved to be a long, drawn-out process that sometimes took several decades. In Somalia, for example, the Italians did not move to occupy the southern interior until 1908, and not until well into the 1920s were they and the British able to "pacify" parts of the northern and central Peninsula.

One reason for the slow pace of European penetration in the Horn was the determined Somali resistance that colonial forces encountered in many locales. The best known of the Somali resistance movements was that led by the famous shaykh, warrior, and poet Muhammad Abdullah Hassan, known to the Europeans of the time as the "Mad Mullah." This charismatic leader was without question the

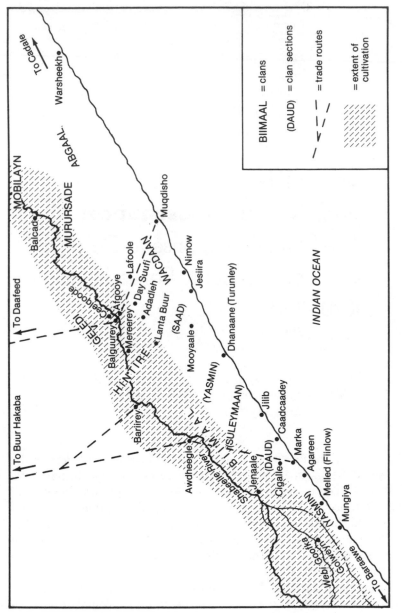

Map 6. *The Lower Shabeelle Valley, 1850–1910*

BIIMAAL = clans
(DAUD) = clan sections
‒ ‒ ‒ = trade routes
▨ = extent of cultivation

To Cadaale

Warsheekh

MOBILAYN

Balcad

MURURSADE

ABGAAL

To Daafeed

Ceelqooda

Day Suufi

Lafoole

Adadleh

Aigooye

WACDAAN

Muqdisho

GEEDI

Balguurey

Mereerey

Lanta Buur

(SAAD)

Nimow

HINTIRE

Mooyaale

Jesiira

(YASMIN)

Dhanaane (Turunley)

To Buur Hakaba

Bariirey

(SULEYMAAN)

Jilib

Caadcaadey

Shabeelle River

Awdheegle

Jenaale

(DAUD)

Cigalle

Marka

Agareen

Melled (Fiinlow)

(YASMIN)

Mungiya

Webi Goofka

Lower Gooleweyn

INDIAN OCEAN

To Baraawe

dominant Somali personality of the early twentieth century; and his twenty-one-year desert war against British, Italian, and Ethiopian forces in northern Somaliland clearly merits the attention it has received from foreign and Somali scholars.[1]

A few recent studies have begun to examine the impact of Shaykh Muhammad's movement elsewhere in Somalia and to show in particular how the Islamic Salihiya order which he led attracted militant supporters in parts of the south.[2] Scholars have noted the existence of independently generated resistance activities in the southern regions, but very little systematic research has been conducted in these areas up till now.

In this chapter I will examine the genesis and nature of anticolonial resistance in the Benaadir region of southern Somalia. By focussing on this region, which was the scene of many of the developments discussed in previous chapters, it is possible to detect certain continuities in the political, economic, and religious patterns that influenced individual behavior and belief. It is also possible to see how various local and regional loyalties, forged in the past, were called into play during the course of the resistance struggle. To the extent that these patterns can be identified and traced over several decades, the resistance period provides a window onto processes of local decision-making and group mobilization that presumably operated in precolonial times as well.

Fortunately, the last decade of the nineteenth century and the

1. For example, Douglas Jardine, *The Mad Mullah of Somaliland* (London, 1923); F. S. Caroselli, *Ferro e fuoco in Somalia* (Rome, 1931); I. M. Lewis, *The Modern History of Somaliland* (London, 1965), chap. 3; R. L. Hess, "The Poor Man of God— Muhammad Abdullah Hassan," in Norman Bennett, ed., *Leadership in Eastern Africa* (Boston, 1968); Brad G. Martin, *Muslim Brotherhoods in Nineteenth Century Africa* (Cambridge, 1976), pp. 177–201; Said Sheikh Samatar, "Poetry in Somali Politics: The Case of Sayyid Mahammad Abdille Hasan" (Ph.D. diss., Northwestern University, 1979); idem, "Maxamad Cabdille Xasan of Somalia: The Search for the Real Mullah," *Northeast African Studies*, vol. 1, no. 1 (East Lansing: Michigan State University, African Studies Center, 1979), pp. 60–76.

On the Somali side, there is Aw Jaamac Cumar Ciise, *Taariikhdii Daraawiishta* (Muqdisho, 1976); Aw Jaamac Cumar Ciise, ed., *Diiwaanka Gabayadii* (Muqdisho, 1974); Axmed F. Cali "Idaaja," *Ismaaciil Mire* (Muqdisho, 1974); Axmed F. Cali "Idaaja" and Cabdulqadir Xirsi "Yamyam," *Dabku Shiday Darwiishkii* (Muqdisho, 1975).

2. Martin, *Muslim Brotherhoods*, esp. pp. 188–89; E. R. Turton, "The Impact of Mohammed Abdille Hassan in the East African Protectorate," *Journal of African History* 10 (1969): 641–57.

first of the twentieth provide the historian with more abundant written and oral documentation than is available for any previous period of Somali history. Colonial military and administrative reports provide a chronological outline of the major events of the occupation together with an external perspective on the forces at work in Somali society around the turn of the century. These sources are particularly valuable because they come from a period before colonial administration was extended to the interior and imposed new constraints on the operation of local politics.

The written evidence is nicely complemented by oral accounts from Somali informants, a few of whom as children had actually lived through the events of the colonial occupation. Recollections of the resistance were still widespread when I visited Somalia in 1971 and, unlike most traditions of earlier events, were rich in nuance and detail. From these testimonies it is possible to discern the complex of personal motives and lineage-group concerns that were operating in Somali society at the time of the colonial conquest, and how these varied from one clan community to another. The combination of oral and written sources thus makes it possible to trace in some detail the interplay of local and external forces during a turbulent period of Somali history.

I will begin with an outline of the major historical developments that preceded the arrival of Italian forces along the southern Somali coast and summarize the circumstances of the colonial occupation itself. I will then examine the resistance through the eyes of four local Somali communities and analyze these case studies in order to draw generalizations from them. I will give particular attention to the divergent local interests that impeded Somali attempts to achieve a wider regional resistance. Finally, I will look at the connections between the southern resistance and the dervish movement of Muhammad Abdullah Hassan and conclude by offering some thoughts on the various levels at which the Somali resistance can be analyzed and understood.

The Background

We can characterize the years from 1870 to 1910 as a time of political disaggregation, economic dislocation, and religious reorientation in the Benaadir region of southern Somalia. The three trends were distinct but interrelated. Whereas the process of religious reorientation went back to the early nineteenth century, the political and economic changes with which we are concerned began to crystallize only after the middle of the century. A knowledge of the consequences of all three developments is essential for understanding the character and course of the later anticolonial resistance activities.

Political Disaggregation

In the forty years following the Baardheere wars of 1840–43 (see chapter 4), the dominant political force in the southern Somali interior was the Geledi clan and its allies. The dramatic victory of Geledi Sultan Yusuf Muhammad over the Baardheere reformers in 1843 propelled him and his immediate successors to a position of military and religious prominence in the interriver area. Yusuf's successful campaign had earned him the allegiance of most of the clans that occupied the triangle of territory between Baraawe, Baydhabo (Baidoa), and the outskirts of Muqdisho; while the religious prestige of his Gobroon lineage gave him an added dimension of authority among the neighboring Digil and Rahanwiin confederations.

Moreover, from their base in the village of Afgooye near the Shabeelle bend, the Geledi sultans could tap two important sources of revenue. Most of the major trade routes from the interior to Muqdisho converged near the river crossing at Afgooye. At that point, the sultans collected transit fees and gifts from caravan traders carrying ivory and incense to the coast. In addition, Afgooye formed one end of an agricultural axis that extended along the lower Shabeelle valley to the plains northeast of Baraawe. From the farming communities along the river, Yusuf and his successors collected tribute in exchange for the protection which Geledi warriors provided. The combination of military, religious, and economic preeminence allowed the Geledi sultans to assert their leadership over this loose confederation of southern clans for several years after the Baardheere episode.[3]

3. For more details on Sultan Yusuf's political activities, see Lee V. Cassanelli, "The Benaadir Past: Essays in Southern Somali History" (Ph.D. diss., University of Wisconsin, 1973), pp. 100–112. See also Virginia Luling, "The Social Structure of Southern Somali Tribes" (Ph.D. thesis, University of London, 1971), pp. 176–86.

However, this interriver confederation was fragile; like most Somali alliances, it depended for its continued existence on shared economic needs, the threat of a common enemy, and strong leadership. During the second half of the nineteenth century, the conditions that had helped generate the confederation changed. In 1848, the legendary Sultan Yusuf Muhammad was killed in a battle with the Biimaal, one of the few Benaadir clans that had failed to acknowledge his authority. Although Somalis seldom attribute military defeat to divine disfavor, they may sometimes interpret major setbacks on the battlefield as evidence of ineffective *tacdaar* (sacred magic) by the leader, who may then suffer a loss of religious prestige. We can infer that this happened after Yusuf's defeat and death at the hands of the Biimaal: there is evidence that at least four clans renounced their position as *raaciye* ("followers") of the Geledi.[4] While Yusuf's son and successor Ahmed succeeded in regaining the allegiance of some of these clans, the fiercely independent Biimaal continued to resist Geledi hegemony along the lower Shabeelle. A series of indecisive skirmishes between the Geledi and the Biimaal over the next several decades culminated in a major encounter at Agareen in 1878, where Sultan Ahmed met a death uncannily similar to his father's thirty years earlier.[5] The battle of Agareen eroded Gobroon prestige still further, and successive sultans of Geledi had neither the religious charisma nor the military power to restore it.

In addition, the absence of any major military threat to the inhabitants of the interriver area obviated the need for maintaining a large-scale military alliance. With the collapse of the Baardheere *jihad*, a region-wide challenge to the established social order had been removed. Beyond this, migrations of northern Somali pastoralists, which had peaked in the middle third of the century, began to subside. These movements of camel and goat nomads across the southern plains had threatened the ecological balance of the area and prompted a number of temporary alliances among the semisedentary clans resident there.[6] By the 1880s, most of the northern nomads had crossed the Jubba River and occupied grasslands on its western bank. The

4. Cassanelli, "The Benaadir Past," pp. 113–14, 119–20.
5. Ibid., pp. 113–14. See also Georges Revoil, "Voyages chez les Benadirs les Comalis, et les Bayouns en 1882–1883," *Le Tour du Monde* 49: 26–27; Pietro Barile, *Colonizzazione fascista nella Somalia meridionale* (Rome, 1935), pp. 94–98.
6. See chap. 2, pp. 77–78.

threat to the southern clans had abated, and the need for large-scale military cooperation correspondingly diminished.

Thus by 1882 a French traveler could report that the Sultan of Geledi had great difficulty controlling his old allies in Daafeed and no longer received tribute from the nearby village of Mereerey. Trade through Afgooye seems to have decreased in the last quarter of the nineteenth century as many caravans diverted their routes through Awdheegle and Marka, in Biimaal territory.[7] An Italian official who visited Afgooye in 1896 noted that Sultan Osman seemed to enjoy complete authority only over his own Geledi community, while he retained some influence over the neighboring Wacdaan and the Tunni of the lower Shabeelle.[8]

On the eve of the colonial occupation of Somalia, then, the one political leader who might have been able to pull together a traditional alliance of southern clans was not in a position to do so. Even at its strongest, the authority of the Geledi sultans had been limited: they never actually ruled over the confederation's constituent clans, and there was no hierarchy of officials through which they could manage the day-to-day affairs of their allies. Rather, a strong sultan had influenced his allies only in his capacity as religious leader and as guarantor of economic prosperity. When alien threats occurred in these spheres of activity, the sultan was a natural rallying point, as his role in the Baardheere wars demonstrated. Had the Italian colonialists therefore directly attacked the religious institutions of the Benaadir, Geledi leadership might again have been invoked by its former allies. But the initial colonial penetration of the area was far more gradual and diffuse than Baardheere religious expansion had been, and far less threatening to the economic security of the nomads than the northern pastoral migrations of the preceding half century had been. Thus it is possible to argue that the early colonial presence was not initially perceived to be as great a danger to the inhabitants of the region as earlier "invasions" had been. What is clear is that a region-wide politico-military alliance that had persisted through much

7. Revoil, "Voyages chez les Benadirs," 50: 177, 182. Cf. Ugo Ferrandi, *Lugh: Emporio commerciale sul Giuba* (Rome, 1903), p. 321, and Luigi Robecchi-Brichetti, *Somalia e Benadir* (Milan, 1899), pp. 635–36. In 1893, Commissioner Lovatelli felt that Marka was the most important commercial town of the Benaadir; see *L'Esplorazione commerciale e l'esploratore* (Milan), 8 (1893): 358–59.

8. Giuseppina Finazzo, *L'Italia nel Benadir: L'Azione de Vincenzo Filonardi 1884–1896* (Rome, 1966), pp. 458–59.

of the nineteenth century was not reactivated during the period of the colonial occupation. The Italians did not have to face a powerful traditional alliance of southern Somali clans.

Economic Dislocation

At the same time that the major political confederation in southern Somali was coming apart, the economic order was undergoing strains from two directions. In the interior, a newly reunited and well-armed Ethiopian state was beginning to expand into the lowlands east and south of Shewa. By the 1880s, Ethiopian forces were raiding the farming villages along the upper Shabeelle and exacting tribute from nomads at their dry-season watering sites. As we have seen, these raids also seriously disrupted the lowland long-distance caravan trade.[9] By partially redirecting the flow of goods from trade and tribute toward the highland economy, the Ethiopian military presence cut into the profits of the lowland traders. As long-distance trade became a riskier enterprise, Benaadir coastal merchants restricted the quantity of goods advanced to upcountry caravaneers, and the overall level of commercial activity began to decline. The first Europeans to visit the commercial center of Luuq on the upper Jubba River heard local merchants complain that trade had fallen off as a result of the prevailing conditions of insecurity in the region.[10]

The declining prosperity of long-distance trade was only one aspect of the economic dislocation that characterized the last quarter of the century. Along the lower Shabeelle River, agricultural production suffered from a crisis brought on partially by foreign attempts to abolish the slave trade. The antislavery campaign began in earnest, as far as the Somalis were concerned, when Barghash became sultan of Zanzibar in 1870. Urged on by his European advisers, Barghash issued an ordinance in 1873 proclaiming the end of slave trading in all

9. For examples of the impact on local communities of Ethiopian raids see A. D. Smith, "Expedition through Somaliland to Lake Rudolf," *The Geographical Journal* 8 (1896): 120 ff.; Prince Nicolas D. Ghika, *Cinq mois au pays des Somalis* (Geneva, 1898), pp. 63, 142–45; E. Ruspoli, *Le spedizioni Ruspoli: Lettere di D. E. Ruspoli e di E. Dal Seno* (Rome, 1893), p. 11. Cf. Richard Pankhurst, "The Trade of Southern and Western Ethiopia and the Indian Ocean Ports in the Nineteenth and Early Twentieth Centuries," *Journal of Ethiopian Studies*, vol. 3, no. 2 (1965), pp. 41–42.

10. Ferrandi, *Lugh*, pp. 19–21, 316; Pankhurst, "The Trade of Southern and Western Ethiopia," pp. 41–42.

of Zanzibar's dominions. The decrees of 1876 further prohibited the conveyance of slaves by land and forbade slave caravans from approaching the coast.[11] To enforce his decrees along the Benaadir, Barghash ordered his governors to construct *garesa*s (fortified residences) in the major towns and sent additional soldiers to staff them.

A contemporary chronicler recorded the impact of the Zanzibar decrees by contrasting the resultant situation with a perhaps idealized picture of earlier times.

> [In the old days] . . . when the slaves arrived the buyers acquired them on fixed terms and set them to work in the fields harvesting maize; with the earnings received from their agricultural labor, the contracted debt was paid. . . .
>
> But in the time of Barghash ibn Said in 1290 [1873] the Christians prohibited the people of the coast from transporting slaves and from acquiring them; this was a very serious development for the area. Anyone with slaves sold them in cash at a price of 60 to 70 thalers. These slaves had come secretly by way of land; but when the Christians learned that the Arabs carried slaves overland, they compelled Barghash ibn Said to order the governors of the towns, whenever they discovered anyone arriving in town with slaves brought overland, to seize the slaves and whatever money and possessions [the slaveholder] had and to jail him for six months. . . . Barghash administered all these decrees, and so the slave routes were interrupted. This happened in the year 1292 [1875–76]. Nevertheless the people continued to sell slaves as in times past; and the slaves were purchased at inflated prices. This continued until 1300 [1882–32].[12]

The decrees and the Zanzibari attempts (however half-hearted) to enforce them drove up the cost of slaves. Along the Benaadir a male slave valued at 15–30 thalers in the 1840s cost 40 thalers in the 1860s and 70–100 thalers after 1875.[13] The chronicler also suggests

11. The various ordinances are detailed in Reginald Coupland, *The Exploitation of East Africa* (London, 1939), pp. 182–234.

12. From a variant version of the "Book of Zanj" translated from the Arabic by Cerulli, *Somalia: Scritti vari editi ed inediti,* 3 vols. (Rome, 1957), 1: 353–54. The translation into English is mine.

13. Based on figures in William Christopher, "Extract from a Journal by Lieut. W. Christopher, Commanding the H. C. Brig of War *Tigris,* on the E. Coast of Africa. Dated 8th May 1843," *Journal of the Royal Geographical Society* 14 (1844): 102;

that credit became difficult to obtain and that more slaves had to be purchased in cash. One can infer from these developments that only wealthy merchants and landholders could continue to acquire slaves readily. The limited evidence available suggests that many small farmers were compelled to rely on the largesse of the wealthy to obtain slaves or, that failing, to abandon commercial agriculture altogether. Some even returned to full-time pastoralism.[14]

While abolitionist efforts never succeeded in totally cutting off the supply of slaves to the Benaadir, they did make it easier for escaped slaves to find refuge. Settlements of runaway slaves had been reported in southern Somalia as early as the 1840s.[15] After 1875, the presence of British antislave naval patrols off the coast and Zanzibari *garesa*s along the coast encouraged an even greater movement of runaways toward the secluded bush country along the lower Jubba and Shabeelle Rivers. In some places, dynamic ex-slave leaders organized the refugees into protected villages whose reputations as havens spread throughout the Benaadir. By 1890, for example, the remarkable ex-slave Nassib Bunda—dubbed by one colonial author an "African Spartacus"—could claim at least nominal authority over some twenty thousand escaped or emancipated slaves in Goshaland, along the lower Jubba; while a smaller federation of ex-slave villages had consolidated in the Avai region along the lower Shabeelle. By the end of the century, these new settlements had secured recognition from Zanzibar and from the European authorities and were beginning to export small quantities of foodstuffs to coastal markets.[16]

Charles Guillain, *Documents sur l'histoire, la géographie et le commerce de l'Afrique orientale*, 3 vols. (Paris, 1856), 2: 537; Otto Kersten, ed., *Baron Carl Claus von der Decken's Reisen in ost Afrika in den Jahren 1862 bis 1865* (Leipzig, 1871), 2: 320; Robecchi-Brichetti, *Somalia e Benadir*, p. 210; Vittorio Bottego, *L'Esplorazione del Giuba* (Rome, 1900), p. 338; and Ferrandi, *Lugh*, p. 358.

14. Ugo Ferrandi, "Prima spedizione Ferrandi in Somalia," typescript memoirs, pp. 104–5; Lovatelli to Minister of Foreign Affairs, Rome, 27 May 1893, *Documenti Diplomatici: Somalia Italiana (1885–1895)*, Appendix 7, Document 77. Both sources report that many members of the Tunni clan in the hinterland of Baraawe were compelled to abandon their farmlands in part because a rival clan further up the Shabeelle River had diverted a major irrigation channel.

A number of my informants in Afgooye and Marka recalled that with the end of slavery their grandfathers or fathers left the land and took up pastoralism.

15. Christopher, "Extract from a Journal," p. 84.

16. For details on the escaped slave communities, see Lee V. Cassanelli, "Social Constructs on the Somali Frontier: Ex-Slave Communities in Nineteenth-Century

The flight of slaves from river plantations coupled with the abandonment of agriculture by small farmers who could no longer obtain servile labor brought to an end a half-century of economic expansion in the Shabeelle Valley. While subsistence farming continued among the older communities of client-cultivators and, increasingly, within newly founded religious settlements (see below), large-scale commercial production declined almost everywhere in the Benaadir.[17]

Even nomads were not immune from the economic crisis of the late nineteenth century. A major rinderpest epidemic devastated cattle herds in the fertile Doy region, leaving vast stretches of pasture "whitened with bones."[18] Several years of poor rainfall through the 1890s only aggravated the situation by impoverishing clan resources and prompting nomadic raids on neighboring herds.[19]

The seeming decline of productivity in all spheres of Benaadir economic life in the closing years of the century had important political ramifications. One was a diminution of the tribute that had customarily (if only sporadically) flowed to such regional authorities as the sultans of Geledi. The loss of manpower to the ex-slave villages and to the new religious settlements (jamaacooyin) along the rivers meant a corresponding decrease of agricultural surplus; declining trade meant decreasing customs revenues. The sultan of Geledi, unable to extract the wealth from outside his own clan that had allowed him a certain independence of action, lost much of his regional power and influence, with consequences that have already been described.

Thus in the last two decades of the nineteenth century, the economic troubles Somali traders, farmers, and nomads were experiencing go some way toward explaining the political fragmentation outlined in the previous section. In turn, the political and economic malaise may have aided the spread of new religious organizations—the Islamic tariiqas, or brotherhoods—which seemed to offer some solutions to the problems of the day.

Somaliland," in Igor Kopytoff, ed., *The Internal African Frontier* (Philadelphia, forthcoming).

17. See n. 14 above.

18. Ugo Ferrandi, *Da Lugh alla costa* (Novara, 1902), p. 39.

19. Extract from a report by Commissioner G. Sorrentino, Appendix 6, Document 76, *Documenti Diplomatici: Somalia Italiana (1885–1895)*.

Religious Reorientation

The remarkable spread of Islamic *tariiqa*s to the Somali interior in the late nineteenth century can be considered a new phase in the centuries-long process of Islamization in the Horn. Its antecedents can be found in the lives of the saints, who introduced Islamic custom and ritual to the rural countryside; and in the reformist zeal represented by the Baardheere shaykhs, who sought to refashion the social order around them. However, in contrast to the saints, who worked as individuals within the local communities of Somalia, the *tariiqa*s were organizations whose leaders had close ties to the major centers of Islamic learning in the Middle East. And while the spread of the *tariiqa*s stemmed from the same impulse toward religious revitalization that had inspired the Baardheere reformers, they were more concerned with individual self-improvement than with social reformation, though their communal organization was not without its revolutionary social implications.

The most important *tariiqa*s in Somalia were the Qadiriya, Ahmediya, and Salihiya. Each offered a "way" toward closer communication with God and sought to institute distinctive liturgical, communal, and doctrinal practices to help its adherents achieve that closer union. The *tariiqa*s were introduced into Somalia by Somalis who had studied in Arabia and who returned home as *khaliifa*s, the designated representatives of the order's mother house. The *khaliifa*s in turn appointed a number of local shaykhs to supervise religious activities in the individual settlements (*jamaacooyin*) that sprang up throughout the country.

Most *jamaacooyin* in the south were established in cultivable districts. Occasionally, tracts of abandoned land were granted by clan elders to the founding *khaliifa* or shaykh; in other instances, the settlements occupied border territory disputed by two neighboring clans and thus provided a solution acceptable to both parties.[20] Membership in the religious settlements typically consisted of the shaykh

---

20. Beled-el-Amin ("Town of Peace"), founded by Shaykh Uways about 1890 in the vicinity of Mereerey, is an example of the former. Information provided by Muddey Haji Geeley, 31 May 1971, Muqdisho. The settlement was described some years later by Franco Monile, *Africa Orientale* (Bologna, 1933), pp. 134–36. Other examples of *jamaacooyin* founded under various circumstances are provided by Cerulli, *Somalia* 1: 200–204; 3: 168–76.

and his adepts, who devoted themselves to farming and to teaching
and prayer, and a larger number of participants from nearby clans
who might take part in Friday worship and in periodic religious celebrations. Although structurally distinct from the clan, a settlement
sometimes drew a majority of the members of a neighboring clan into
its religious activities; more commonly in the years before 1900, two
or three *jamaacooyin* representing different *tariiqa*s competed
within a single district for adherents.[21]

Probably the most influential of the *tariiqa*s in southern Somalia (in terms of numbers of adherents) was the Qadiriya, which had
a branch in the coastal town of Baraawe by the late eighteenth century.[22] About 1880, Shaykh Uways bin Muhammad al-Baraawi and his
disciples began to establish small settlements along the lower Shabeelle River and in the dry-land farming country beyond Baydhabo.
Likewise the Ahmediya, initially founded by Ahmed ibn Idris al-Fasi,
spread to Somalia in the 1860s, though most of its settlements date
to the period after 1880.[23] The Ahmediya was particularly popular in
the Marka region (where Shaykh Ali Maye was its best-known leader)
and in the area between Daafeed and Baydhabo (where Shaykh
Muhammad Wa'esle and Shaykh Hassan Ma'allin worked to propa-
gate it).

The third major *tariiqa* in Somalia was the Salihiya, whose most
famous adherent was Muhammad Abdullah Hassan. Under the leadership of Shaykh Muhammad, the Salihiya became after 1899 the
most militant of the Somali *tariiqa*s, urging its followers to take up
arms against the colonial infidels. While the Salihiya had its greatest

21. Cerulli, *Somalia* 1:191–95. A good example of an instance where an entire
clan associated itself with the *tariiqa* of its head shaykh is provided by David Marlowe,
"The Galjaal Barsana of Central Somalia: A Lineage Political System in a Changing
World" (Ph.D. diss., Harvard University, 1963), p. 92ff.

22. For information on the spread of the Qadiriya I am indebted to Sherif Herow
Hassan Aliow of Baydhabo, Omar Isa Haaq of Afgooye, and Aw Jama Omar Isa of the
Academy of Somali Studies, Muqdisho. For Shaykh Uways, see also Brad G. Martin,
"Muslim Politics and Resistance to Colonial Rule: Shaykh Uways b. Muhammad al-
Ba'rāwī and the Qādirīya Brotherhood in East Africa," *Journal of African History*
10 (1969): 471–86; and Cerulli, *Somalia* 1: 187–88, 196–97.

23. My sources on the Ahmediya, apart from Cerulli, *Somalia* 1:190–95, are
Omar Isa Haaq of Afgooye, Shaykh Abdullahi Hassanow of Dhanfurur, and Sherif
Aliow Abdi Nur of Baydhabo. The founding dates of the various *jamaacooyin* are
listed in an unpublished report to the United Nations Trusteeship Council which was
provided to me by the late Alphonso A. Castagno. It was prepared in 1953 and 1954.

impact in the north of the Peninsula, it also had a considerable following in the south.[24] Muhammad Guled, for example, established a number of Salihiya-affiliated settlements along the middle Shabeelle River; and Shaykh Abdi Abiker "Gafle"—one of the best-known resistance leaders in the south—belonged to the Salihiya order in the Marka district.

The rapid diffusion of the *tariiqa*s was not unique to Somalia; similar developments occurred throughout the Islamic world at this time. However, conditions in late-nineteenth-century Somalia were particularly conducive to their growth. Apart from providing the means by which Somalis could express a more formal commitment to Islam, the *tariiqa*s represented a form of communal solidarity over and above clan and territorial ties. Moreover, *tariiqa* shaykhs offered an alternate source of leadership at a time when traditional politico-religious authorities seemed unable to cope with political and economic disorder.

Beyond this, the *tariiqa*s' new agricultural settlements tended to absorb many of the recently displaced members of Somali society: exslaves, impoverished farmers, and others who had suffered losses of status or wealth following the warfare, drought, and livestock epidemics of the late nineteenth century. Several of the *tariiqa* shaykhs themselves—notably Shaykh Uways of the Qadiriya and Muhammad Guled of the Salihiya—were reputedly men of non-noble origins.[25] By providing within their settlements a degree of economic security and a sense of community, the shaykhs were able to attract many of the marginal elements of southern Somali society to the brotherhoods.

For the most part, the *tariiqa*s in the south played only a limited role in the subsequent Somali resistance to colonial occupation. While several prominent individuals with *tariiqa* affiliation formed part of the militant opposition, the *tariiqa*s as a whole were more concerned with communal agriculture and worship than with radical political action. The reasons for their stance, which will be elaborated in the general analysis following the case studies, seem closely related to the structure and leadership that has been outlined. Having taken root in the turbulent closing decades of the century, the *tariiqa* settlements appeared to be seeking a peaceful environment in which

24. Turton, "The Impact of Mohammed Abdille Hassan," esp. pp. 647–49.
25. Cerulli, *Somalia* 1: 187, 189.

they could pursue the practice of their faith. Situated in the interstices of clan society and drawing their initial membership largely from its marginal elements, they did not have the military ethos or warrior strength to pose a serious threat to colonial forces. And despite the potential for transcending parochial clan allegiances inherent in *tariiqa* organization, most of their leaders came from "client" groups or from small religious lineages. They had spent long periods of study outside the country. As a result, they could not be expected to have large followings of Somali warriors from the more powerful pastoral clans. Thus their potential for military opposition was limited, a fact not lost, as shall be seen, on the early colonial authorities.

Summary

On the eve of the colonial occupation, then, southern Somali society was attempting to adjust to several profound changes. The breakup of a major political confederation, the disruption of production and trade, and the spread of new religious institutions were region-wide processes that affected virtually all elements of society. To the traditional clan divisions characteristic of Somali life had been added new cleavages between rich and poor, former patron and ex-slave, and even between followers of different religious orders. Disunity, of course, was not new to the Somali scene; the commercial and political links that had been built in the nineteenth century were fragile strands overlaying a profoundly faction-ridden society. That society was now being threatened by foreign powers who sought to exploit Somali disunity for their own ends.

Colonial Aims and Actions, 1870–1908

The Zanzibar Sultanate

We have seen how Zanzibari efforts to control commerce along the Benaadir and to abolish the slave trade led Sultan Barghash (1870–88) to erect forts in the major towns of the Somali coast. Not surprisingly, some of the earliest outbreaks of Somali anticolonial activity were directed against these symbols of Zanzibari authority. The Zanzibari-staffed garrison in Marka had been built in the 1860s, apparently at the request of some of the elders of that town. In 1873,

Somalis in the Marka district began a campaign of harrassment against the Zanzibari *askari*s (soldiers) there, making it unsafe for the latter to venture beyond the walls of their fortress. Hostility peaked in 1876, when Biimaal warriors attacked and killed the *wali* (governor) and his contingent of forty *askari*s on the road between Marka and Muqdisho.[26]

Further south, anti-Zanzibari sentiments were equally strong. When in 1875 Egyptian Khedive Isma'il sent a naval expedition to the southern Somali coast to challenge Zanzibar's tenuous suzerainty there, local Somali leaders welcomed the new arrivals. After the Zanzibari *wali* of Baraawe was forced to flee, some Somalis no doubt hoped that the Egyptians would reinstitute the slave trade. Others saw the Egyptians as potentially useful allies against an apparent Zanzibari-British effort to dominate the Somali coast. However, after only three months, the khedive abruptly recalled the expeditionary force. The ousted Zanzibari governor returned to his post and promptly arrested several local Somalis, who were sent to jail in Zanzibar. A year later, hostilities surfaced again in Baraawe: some Zanzibari *askari*s were killed, and Sultan Barghash was forced to construct a *garesa* for his troops in that normally peaceful Somali town.[27]

Even in Muqdisho, where Barghash had managed to build a large *garesa* through the good offices of Sultan Ahmed Yusuf of Geledi, Zanzibari representatives were far from secure. Today the old fortress is a museum; in it, one can still observe the slot in the floor of the second story receiving room through which the *wali* heard petitions from Somali residents. He apparently felt it unsafe to mix with the people in the courtyard below. The French traveler Georges Revoil summed up the tenuous position of Zanzibar's authority along the Somali coast in the 1880s with the observation, "The towns of the littoral are in a perpetual state of siege."[28]

The first Italians along the Benaadir inherited the problem of Somali discontent over foreign intervention in local trade and politics. Zanzibar's new sultan, Khalifa, had "ceded" the coastal towns to Italy

26. Georges Revoil, *Voyage au Cap des Aromates* (Paris, 1880), pp. 60–62; "Estratto dal diario di Ugo Ferrandi," *Bollettino di l'esplorazione commerciale e l'esploratore* (1895), p. 74 ff.
27. Revoil, *Voyage au Cap des Aromates*, pp. 61–62; Georges Douin, *Histoire du Règne du Khédive Ismail*, vol. 3, no. 3, pp. 680–84.
28. "Voyage chez les Benadirs," *Le Tour du Monde*, 49: 22.

in 1890, even though they were hardly his to cede. In April of that year, two Italian soldiers were killed as they disembarked to reconnoiter the northern Benaadir town of Cadale. Sultan Khalifa disclaimed all responsibility for the presence of "infidels" along the Somali coast. However, Italian authorities who later investigated the incident found that the local Somalis were extremely hostile toward the Zanzibari regime and may have mistaken the Italian envoys for Germans, who were perceived as allies of the Omani sultan.[29]

The Ethiopians

Even before the Italians began to take steps to assert control over their new possessions, another well-armed power was threatening Somali society from the west. Ethiopian King Menilek, having consolidated his power in the Shewa highlands, began to seek out livestock and manpower in the lowlands to the southeast. When Egyptian forces abandoned the Islamic city of Harar in 1885, Menilek moved in. In January 1887, he personally led an army against the forces of the Harari emir Abdullahi and defeated them on the plains outside the walled town. Thus even before Menilek was crowned emperor of Ethiopia (in 1889), Harar had become a symbol of Ethiopian expansion into the Somali Peninsula.

Using Harar as a base, expeditions of armed Ethiopian warriors on horseback set out to exact tribute from the Oromo and Somali populations to the south. By the mid-1890s, these raids were reaching the Shabeelle basin and beyond. In 1896, Ethiopian forces reached the outskirts of Luuq on the upper Jubba River.[30] Earlier such military forays had been disruptive to trade; in an age of colonial expansion, they assumed even more menacing proportions.

29. The sailors who landed at Cadale were instructed to claim friendship with the sultan of Zanzibar. Survivors of the affair stated that the Somalis feared a German landing. Insofar as the sultan of Zanzibar and the Germans were on good terms at the time, the attack may well have been intended as a rebuff to Sultan Khalifa. Moreover, one cannot rule out the complicity of that sizable group of Arabs who were growing increasingly discontent with their waning influence both in Zanzibar and along the Somali Benaadir. They fomented opposition to the new order along the Somali coast throughout the 1890s. See the extract from a report of naval Commander Amari to the Ministry of Marines dated 30 April 1890 in *Documenti Diplomatici*, no. 28. Cf. Finazzo, *L'Italia nel Benadir*, pp. 214–17.

30. Finazzo, *L'Italia nel Benadir*, pp. 311–12.

As far away as the Benaadir Coast, Somalis were aware of the Ethiopian threat. In a report which followed the assassination in 1897 of an Italian official in Marka, one of the reasons given for Somali discontent was "a general uneasiness caused by rumors of an Amharic invasion."[31] Such rumors proved well founded; in the spring of 1905, an Ethiopian force estimated at several thousand well-armed horsemen pushed down the Shabeelle Valley to the environs of Balcad, about a day's march from Muqdisho.[32] A Somali poet in the Afgooye area recorded the episode in the following verses.

When I was still a young man
Into the world I loved the Amhara came
They came from Jigjiga and the confines of Awdal
Crossing the Ogaadeen, they killed many from the
    Karanle
They used guns against the people of Imaan Cumar
They killed many from the Jidle and Jajeele.
[Then] they arrived at Jiiciyow and at the banks of the
    Webi.

When they reached Jibbirrow they were attacked;
The Muslims confronted them and fighting began;
In the country near Yaaqle
The Mobilayn stood firm and fought with them,
The magic of the Gobroon defeated them.
[But] when the Amhara left the infidels appeared,
Coming from every corner of the world. . . .[33]

The poem indicates that the threat of Ethiopian expansion was felt even by those living in the Benaadir hinterland, and that some Somali clans actually engaged in combat with the invading forces. It also suggests that the Ethiopians were initially perceived to be a greater danger than the Italians, who at that time were still confined to their enclaves along the coast. It soon became clear, however, that the Italians had imperial designs on the country as well, and that their

31. The report is quoted in Giorgio Sorrentino, *Ricordi del Benadir* (Naples, 1910), pp. 77–81.
32. Giuliano Bonacci, "Gli Abissini nella Somalia," in idem., *La nostra politica coloniale* (Rome, 1908), pp. 42–46.
33. Recorded in an interview with *Laashin* Anshooley Osman Aliow, Muqdisho, 31 July 1971.

presence was far more permanent than that of the Ethiopian raiders. It appeared that any resistance struggle the Somalis would have to wage would be on two fronts.

The Italians

The danger of Italian colonization seems to have been clear to some Somali leaders at least as early as 1895, when the sultan of Geledi told a visiting colonial official that his people feared that Europeans would seize Somali farmland once they saw how productive it was.[34] Somali suspicions about the Italians resulted partly from the fact that the Italians appeared to be continuing Zanzibar's policies: attempting to tax trade, to establish military garrisons along the coast, and to suppress the slave trade. But beyond this, the Italians posed further problems: they were Christians, they were apparently cooperating with other colonial powers in the area, and (unlike the Zanzibaris) they continued to send expeditions of exploration to the Somali interior. Given these potential dangers, it is remarkable that the Italians managed to stay on as good terms as they did with most Somali clans in the first decade of their presence.

The early years of Italian activity in Somalia have been well documented elsewhere.[35] The following summary stresses only those aspects of Italian colonial policy that most directly affected Somali life in the years before 1908.

From 1893 to 1896, the Italian presence was limited to a small garrison of soldiers at Luuq on the upper Jubba River, and to a few traders along the coast. The Italian outpost at Luuq had been established in 1895 to gather information on Somali trade in the region and to protect Italian interests in the face of Ethiopian claims to the area. While the Italians posed as defenders of the Somalis, they did little to protect the nomads and farmers of the interior against continued Ethiopian raids. Somalis upcountry had to rely on their own resources to defend themselves.

Along the Benaadir coast, the Italian presence consisted of the representatives of the Royal Italian East African Company, popularly (and appropriately) known as the Filonardi Company. Vincenzo Filonardi was a Roman trader who had been active in Zanzibar and East

34. Finazzo, *L'Italia nel Benadir,* pp. 456–60.
35. Robert Hess, *Italian Colonialism in Somalia* (Chicago, 1966), chaps. 1–4.

Africa for almost a decade. He had considerable knowledge of the Benaadir, its peoples and their customs. Known as Aw Filo within the local merchant community—*Aw* is a term of respect typically applied to Somali elders—Filonardi managed to sign treaties of friendship with representatives of several hinterland clans. These treaties essentially pledged Somali loyalty to the company administration in recognition of its "just laws" and the prosperity it had helped restore in the wake of the disastrous drought and rinderpest epidemic of the early 1890s.[36]

Filonardi also made efforts to establish a commercial code which combined elements of Italian and Islamic law. This code was administered by local *qaaddi*s (Islamic legal experts); while it had the effect of extending the *qaaddi*s' influence in the coastal areas, it had little effect in the interior. In fact, Filonardi and his associates rarely ventured into the countryside; when they did, it was strictly for commercial reasons.

Unfortunately for Filonardi, his pioneering efforts in Somalia made little impression on his own countrymen. He received little moral or material support from an Italian government still uncertain about what sort of colonial policy to pursue. Despite Filonardi's appeals for more time and money to consolidate his operations, his company was allowed to collapse in financial failure.[37]

Perhaps because of the Filonardi Company's limited intervention in Somali affairs, there was only one notable incident of Somali hostility between 1893 and 1896. That occurred on 11 October 1893, the day the Italian flag was first raised over the *garesa* in Marka. A Somali attacked and killed an Italian soldier; he in turn was killed with three shots from a "Wetterly" gun.[38]

Eighteen ninety-six marked a turning point in Somali-Italian relations. Somali oral tradition remembers the year as *Axad Shekki* (the "Sunday year of Cecchi"). Antonio Cecchi was an ardent expansionist who for some time had been urging the Italian government to take over the Benaadir concessions. In seeking to promote his own

36. A list of these treaties is given in *Documenti Diplomatici*, pp. 229–37. The standard treaty agreement can be found in Finazzo, *L'Italia nel Benadir*, pp. 293–94.

37. The story of the Filonardi years is told with much sympathy and great detail by Finazzo, *L'Italia nel Benadir;* a more concise, less personal account is Hess, *Italian Colonialism in Somalia*, chap. 2.

38. Gustavo Pesenti, "I Martiri della Somalia," *Rivista coloniale*, vol. 2, no. 1 (July 1914), p. 10.

version of Italian power in Somalia, Cecchi upset the fragile commercial arrangements that Filonardi had constructed. He replaced Filonardi's influential Hadrami interpreter with Arabs of his own choosing, returned an unpopular Italian resident to Marka, and sent soldiers to the lower Jubba area to try to force Somali caravaneers to unload their wares at Baraawe rather than at the British-held ports of Kismaayo and Goobweyn.[39]

Cecchi's presence also resurrected Somali fears of territorial dispossession, which had for at least fifty years been part of the supposed xenophobia of the country. Several European visitors in the later nineteenth century had commented on Somali suspicions that their best agricultural land would soon be coveted and seized by foreigners.[40] Thus it did not escape public attention when a cousin of Cecchi visited the Benaadir in 1895 to investigate the possibilities for commercial agriculture. There soon followed talk of growing cotton on Italian plantations along the Shabeelle.[41]

Finally, Cecchi appeared to symbolize colonial aggressiveness in the distant interior. In 1895, the Italian Geographical Society had dispatched Vittorio Bottego to explore the sources of the Jubba River;[42] and in 1896, Ugo Ferrandi arrived to establish a garrison at Luuq.[43] The latter move was intended as a response to the threat posed by Ethiopian expansion. In the fall of 1895, an Ethiopian expedition under the command of Dedjazmatch Wolde Gabre reached the environs of Luuq. When the Ethiopians returned the following year, the Benaadir was rife with rumors that the invaders intended to march to the Indian Ocean and return with seashells for the emperor.[44]

The perceived "Ethiopian menace" was one of the factors that prompted Cecchi to seek an Italian alliance with the Somalis of the southern hinterland. In November 1896, he and a score of Arab *askari*s set out to meet with the presumably influential sultan of Geledi. It was the first colonial attempt to penetrate the interior with a military contingent, and it ended disastrously for the Italians. Cecchi's expedi-

39. Finazzo, *L'Italia nel Benadir*, pp. 324–28, 353–54.
40. Guillain, *Documents* 3: 28; Finazzo, *L'Italia nel Benadir*, pp. 456–60; Gustavo Chiesi, *La Colonizzazione europea nell'Est Africa* (Turin, 1909), pp. 445, 460.
41. Hess, *Italian Colonialism in Somalia*, pp. 54–56.
42. Bottego, *L'Esplorazione del Giuba*.
43. His experiences are recorded in *Lugh*.
44. Finazzo, *L'Italia nel Benadir*, pp. 311–12.

tion was besieged and most of it destroyed at a place called Lafoole, along the Muqdisho-Afgooye road, by Somali warriors of the Wacdaan clan.[45] The "Lafoole Massacre," as the Italian press called it, came less than a year after the humiliating Italian defeat at Adwa in Ethiopia. It contributed to the withering of Italian colonial resolve; not for another decade would colonial forces again attempt to reach the Shabeelle Valley. Indeed, it was three years before the Italian government moved to ratify a pending charter for a new trading company that was to take up the burden of Somalia.

The discontent that produced Lafoole led to further anticolonial incidents along the coast. In Baraawe, Haji Shaykh Abbas railed against his Somali compatriots and called them "women" for allowing the Italians free movement there. Further north, in Warsheekh, a government *askari* was accosted as he stepped outside the garrison.[46] And in Marka, a young Somali, Omar Hassan Yusuf, assassinated the Italian Resident, Giacomo Trevis. According to local accounts, Omar emerged after praying in the small mosque of Shaykh Osman "Marka-yaalle" and knifed the "infidel" Trevis as he walked along the beach.[47] Although there was no proof, Italian officials believed that Omar was part of a massive anticolonial conspiracy. A report filed by the acting governor tried to assess the factors that had provoked the assassination. Among them, he decided, were religious fanaticism, Trevis's disdainful treatment of slaveholding notables, antagonism aroused by the resident's policy of compulsory labor, and the aforementioned rumors of an Ethiopian invasion.[48]

In the decade following the Lafoole incident, the Italians remained at the coast, their colonial policy marked by uncertainty and indecision. Their only major venture into the interior was the establishment of a garrison of Arab soldiers at Baardheere in 1902. Until 1905, the coast was administered by a series of "Benaadir Company" officials supported by a small contingent of Italian military officers. Under the company's troubled rule, a few new treaties of friendship

45. See below, pp. 209–10, for the Wacdaan role in the Lafoole ambush. The reasons for the Cecchi mission are outlined in *Ufficio Storico: Somalia*, vol. 1, *Dalle origini al 1914* (Rome, 1938), p. 79. The Geledi sultan himself was clearly aware of the Ethiopian danger: see *Documenti Diplomatici*, no. 84.

46. Finazzo, *L'Italia nel Benadir*, pp. 279, 325, 369.

47. Interview with Haji Isma'il Ali Omar, Shaykh Hassan Ma'allin, and Ali Hassan Muhammad at Shalambood, 20 Nov. 1977.

48. Sorrentino, *Ricordi del Benadir*, pp. 77–81

were signed with clan elders; some modest public works projects were initiated in the major towns; and government *askari*s were posted to guard coastal wells and market places in an effort to prevent further antigovernment incidents.[49]

There also occurred during this period a subtle shift in Italian policy. Filonardi had cultivated the friendship of the urban inhabitants of the coast by using them as interpreters and counselors and by supporting the *qaaddi*s. He largely ignored the affairs of Somalis in the interior. Beginning, ironically, with the arrival of the archcolonialist Cecchi and continuing under his successors, Filonardi's policy was modified to woo the interior clan leaders. To this end, selected elders resident in the hinterland received government stipends, and fugitive slaves were restored to landholders on condition that they be treated as salaried laborers. The new policy—it does not seem to have been explicitly formulated—worked to the detriment of the coastal Arabs. They lost not only influence with the new regime but also many of the benefits that they had derived from their role as middlemen in the export trade, because most revenue now went directly into the coffers of the Benaadir Company.[50]

In Marka, Somali and Arab fears of a colonial vendetta were intensified by the infamous Ashraf episode. Several families of these widely respected religious notables had long been suspected by the Italians of having had a hand in the Trevis assassination and in an attempt on the life of his successor. A complex series of events led to the arrest of five Ashraf leaders, among them the well-known *qaaddi* Sherif Osman. The prisoners were sent to the *garesa* prison in Muqdisho, where, under mysterious circumstances, all five perished. Their fate was soon known along the entire East African coast; in Zanzibar it became common to say that those who entered the prisons of the Benaadir left only as corpses.[51]

In its early years, the Benaadir Company adopted a policy of gradualism on the slavery issue, in the belief that limited colonial

49. Hess, *Italian Colonialism*, pp. 64–84.

50. According to one colonial observer in 1901, Italian unpopularity resulted from "more than hatred of religion or race . . . the rancor which the Arab merchants feel towards us." *Ufficio Storico* 1: 94. The preceding analysis is pieced together from the *Ufficio Storico* and from Hess, *Italian Colonialism*, passim.

51. The evidence for this "travesty of justice" is brought out in the very frank report of Gustavo Chiesi and Ernesto Travelli, *Le Questioni del Benadir* (Milan, 1904), esp. pp. 159–63.

manpower and the desire for economic stability precluded any drastic measures to eradicate slavery. In 1902, however, several visiting journalists accused the company of acquiescing in the continuation of slavery; the resulting scandal led to an official investigation of company personnel and ultimately to the promulgation of three new ordinances. The final one, issued on 15 April 1904, outlawed all forms of servitude and sought to impose strict controls on the number of hours, the payment, and the treatment of exslaves who stayed on the land.[52]

Within a fortnight, Biimaal warriors clamped a blockade on the roads leading into Marka. Government troops sent out from Muqdisho to relieve the besieged town were attacked on three separate occasions during their march along the coast. These battles marked the beginning of an extended period of conflict between Biimaal and Italian forces.[53] The imposition of the blockade and subsequent Biimaal assaults upon the property of urban merchants suggest that the pendulum of colonial favoritism had swung back again toward the coast. This was in fact true; the commission investigating the slavery issue had relied heavily on testimony from Arab and Somali townsmen, who were only too willing to supply information and regain some of their lost influence with colonial authorities. Thus, some of them were perceived by their rural countrymen as collaborating with the new regime and hence became subject to retaliation.

This second period of anticolonial violence, acted out chiefly by the Biimaal clan, lasted until late 1905. Then Biimaal attacks ceased. Nomads and farmers attended the markets of Marka and Muqdisho in increasing numbers.[54] When 1906 passed without any major disturbances, Italian authorities began to feel that the "few rebellious elements" had retired for good to the interior. The colonial government was also relieved to know that the dervish threat along the northern confines of their colony had been removed: in 1905 Muhammad Abdullah Hassan had signed a treaty with British and Italian representatives and was living peacefully with his followers in the

52. The slavery issue is discussed in Hess, *Italian Colonialism*, chap. 3 and 4. An Italian government investigation resulted in the publication of the aformentioned report by Chiesi and Travelli, *Le Questioni del Benadir*. See also A. Perricone-Viola, "La liberazione degli schiavi nel vecchio Benadir," *Rivista delle Colonie*, vol. 10, no. 8 (1936), pp. 882–86, for a summary of the various colonial ordinances.

53. *Ufficio Storico: Somalia* 1: 114–16. See below, pp. 225–28.

54. G. Cerrina-Ferroni, "Situazione generale della colonia," 23 Mar. 1906, *ASMAI*, pos. 87/1, f. 6.

Nugaal Valley.[55] From the Italian viewpoint, the situation had improved considerably.

Then, in February 1907, two thousand Somalis attacked an Italian regiment at Turunley (Dhanaane), along the coast north of Marka. This battle marked the beginning of a third wave of violence which would last (as far as the Benaadir was concerned) for more than three years. Unlike the anticolonial outbreaks of 1896–97 and 1904–5, Turunley does not appear to have been provoked by any specific colonial action; rather it expressed a general and widespread reaction to the ever-growing presence of foreigners on Somali soil. The sporadic violence which followed the battle of Turunley was more extensive geographically than either of the earlier outbreaks had been. It also was the first time firearms were used by the Somali resisters, a factor of particular significance, as we shall see.

The third wave of anticolonial activity forced the Italian government to reassess its policy of limited action in Somalia. An observer had noted that, despite the presence of some 2,100 government soldiers in 1907, the colony's security was no better than it had been at the time of Filonardi (with 300 soldiers), of Governor Dulio (600 soldiers in 1902), or of Commissioner Mercatelli (1,200 soldiers in 1904).[56] The need for colonial security coupled with the desire for a more productive local economy finally led the Italian government to the decision that a few strident voices had been urging from the beginning: Italy would occupy the hinterland. After a series of Somali attacks on government installations and on the herds of the government's Somali allies, Italian troops in August 1908 were dispatched to the interior.

The Somali Response, 1896–1908:
Four Case Studies

Like the Italians, the Somalis viewed the Lafoole incident as a watershed in the history of the relationship between the two countries. Throughout the Benaadir, from Warsheekh to well south of Marka, 1896–97 is remembered as *Axad Shekki* (the "Sunday year of Cecchi"). The Biimaal date the beginning of their twelve-year re-

55. See below, pp. 247–48.
56. *Ufficio Storicio: Somalia* 1: 137.

sistance at *Axad Shekki*. The Italian bombardment of the small coastal village of Nimow in retaliation for Cecchi's death marked the first such colonial action against a Somali civilian population. It is clear from colonial reports and from Somali oral recollections that Lafoole precipitated a response from all the districts of the hinterland.

It is difficult to generalize about the Somali response to the situation in 1896. Each district felt the impact of the colonial presence in a different way. Each had been conditioned by social and economic dislocation to a different degree, and local political circumstances varied considerably. Looking at the overall picture, the years from 1897 to 1907 were marked by a wait-and-see approach by the Somalis, which corresponded to the Italian hesitancy to take decisive action. The decade saw diplomatic approaches attempted by both sides and occasional, usually isolated, acts of violence. Throughout this period of tense mutual restraint—broken only by the eighteen months of open Biimaal hostility in 1904–5—Somali society was reassessing its resources in light of the changes and challenges outlined above.

The following detailed case studies will give some idea of the complexity of forces at work in Somali society during the early years of colonial intrusion. Where possible, I will examine the particular personalities and local interest groups that contributed to the formulation of clan policy and speculate on the various motives of those who sought accommodation with the colonial power and those who chose to resist militarily. (The general analysis resumes on p. 228.)

(1) Geledi

In the first part of this chapter, we noted how the Geledi confederation headed by the Gobroon shaykhs of Afgooye had lost much of its cohesiveness as the nineteenth century drew to a close. The succession of Osman Ahmed in the 1880s brought to the Geledi sultanate a man of lesser ambitions and more limited political skills than his illustrious forebears. Osman, for example, did nothing to punish the Biimaal when they blockaded a branch of the Shabeelle River and thus caused severe hardship to Geledi's agricultural allies downriver.[57] During Osman's reign, numerous former allies and sub-

---

57. The Webi Goofka ("dry river") was a branch of the Shabeelle River which irrigated the land between the main riverbed and the coastal dunes. It began just below the village of Kaytoy and reentered the main watercourse northeast of Baraawe.

jects began to assert their independence from Geledi leadership; and the religious heads of nearby Mereerey began to extend their influence over populations once loyal only to the Gobroon.[58]

Despite these setbacks, Osman's inherited *baraka* (grace) as a member of the Gobroon lineage was still respected by many ordinary Somalis in the region. We have seen how Gobroon *tacdaar* was given much of the credit for warding off an Ethiopian invasion that had threatened the Shabeelle valley in 1905.[59] In the mid-1890s, Osman's army had still been strong enough to defeat their traditional Hintire rivals down the river.[60] And Cecchi apparently felt that Osman remained a force to be reckoned with, for the ill-fated Lafoole expedition had originated with Cecchi's scheme for an Italian-Geledi alliance.

The Italian investigation of the Lafoole incident produced conflicting evidence about the complicity of the Geledi in the affair. Acting-Governor Dulio felt that the young men of Geledi were fiercely opposed to the Italian presence, whereas their elders wanted some sort of accommodation. The authorities had received a letter from the wealthy landholder Aw Nur Ahmedow disclaiming Geledi involvement in the attack on Cecchi's expedition; but at the same time reports reached Muqdisho that a hostile shaykh was drawing large crowds in Balguurey and Ceelqoode (Elqode). The governor could only conclude that Sultan Osman had known of the plans for the attack at Lafoole but had restrained his followers from taking part.[61]

In fact, the sultan was in a difficult position. Within his own Gobroon lineage, advisers were urging him to stand against the Italians and so restore his prestige among nearby clans who were fearful

---

Whether a natural depression or a man-made channel, the Webi Goofka had enabled segments of the Tunni clan to cultivate large tracts of previously arid land in the later nineteenth century. The damming of the Goofka by the Biimaal in the 1880s forced many of the Tunni off the land. See Chiesi and Travelli, *Le Questioni*, pp. 97–98; "Lovatelli al Ministero degli Affari Esteri," 27 May 1893, in *Documenti Diplomatici*, no. 77.

58. Group interview with elders of Mereerey, 26 Aug. 1971; cf. Revoil, "Vogages chez les Benadir," 50: 177, 182.

59. See line 13 of poem, p. 200 above.

60. Hintire traditions recall a series of battles with the Geledi in the 1880s and 1890s, and acknowledge having lost one of them (group interview, Mereerey, 23 May 1971). This is probably the same battle which Ugo Ferrandi heard about and described in his memoirs ("Prima spedizione," p. 34).

61. Sorrentino, *Ricordi del Benadir*, pp. 32–34.

of the foreigners. Geledi's long-time allies the Wacdaan had apparently acted independently at Lafoole; and they had been assisted by a handful of warriors from the Murursade, also Geledi allies. Now, the Wacdaan were beginning to blockade the caravan routes that ran through their territory to the coast. Osman's uncle and others felt that if the sultan wavered in his resistance, Gobroon authority would be weakened for good.[62]

Many from the Adawiin lineage, whose religious prestige among the Geledi was second only to the Gobroon's, preached a policy of nonaccommodation. The Adawiin shaykhs were in close contact with Somali and Arab scholars of Muqdisho; already several Arabs had fled that town in protest against the presence of the infidels.[63] The Adawiin apparently shared many of the same feelings.

To the still amorphous group of opposition one could add some of the merchants and traders of the Herabow, Muhammad Subis, and Reer Haji lineages, who enjoyed commercial and matrimonial ties with the large trading families of Muqdisho.[64] These townsmen had become disillusioned with the Italians after the departure of Filonardi and the demotion of his Arab interpreter.[65] Their anticipated loss of influence and profits colored the attitudes of their Geledi (and other) allies in the interior.

On the other side were those, still the majority in Afgooye, who

62. This and much of what follows emerged from a series of interviews with Abokor Ali Omar of Afgooye. He in turn had consulted a number of Geledi elders, many of whom I subsequently met to corroborate their accounts. Among the most knowledgeable about the initial period of Italian contact were Muhammad Abdullahi, Ali Omar Haji "Goyle," Ma'allin Yusuf Muhammad, and Hussein Abdi Gaduud.

Where possible, I have cited written colonial sources as additional evidence. On Gobroon advice to Sultan Osman, see Tomasso Carletti, *Attraverso il Benadir* (Viterbo, 1910), pp. 73–74. Carletti was told by a relative of Sultan Osman that the sultan was in fact a friend of the government but that he was receiving "bad counsel" from those who said that the Italians intended to take Geledi's land and women and to destroy their mosques. See also Cerrina-Ferroni, *Benadir*, p. 42.

63. One of the most prominent Muslim scholars to flee the environs of Muqdisho was Shaykh Abokor Mukhdaar, who emigrated to Warsheekh. Interview with Omar Isa Haaq, Muqdisho, 17 Mar. 1971.

64. Information supplied by Shaykh Mustafa Yusuf to Abokor Ali Omar. Cf. Cerrina-Ferroni, *Benadir*, pp. 23–31.

65. The possible involvement of Abobaker bin Awood, Filonardi's erstwhile assistant, in the events of Lafoole is discussed by Finazzo, *l'Italia nel Benadir*, p. 349 ff.

counseled neutrality until Italian motives could be determined. Prevalent in this group were wealthy landholders and merchants, many from the prestigious Abikerow lineage. Men like Aw Nur Ahmedow and Mahmud Abtiow continued to correspond with the Italian authorities in the years between 1896 and 1907, urging them to avoid rash actions and protesting the Geledis' peaceful intentions. These men of wealth had an influence over their clansmen quite out of proportion to their numbers. Such influence was largely the result of the patronage that they had dispensed in the difficult years following the abolition of slavery and the flight of smaller farmers from the land. During the famine years of 1890–95, those with large reserves of grain had helped supply the less fortunate. Aw Nur Ahmedow was even said to have distributed supplies on credit to small traders and shopkeepers without demanding interest.[66] Thus it is not difficult to see how such individuals, having many kinsmen in their debt, could command widespread support for whatever political decisions they made.

Clearly there was an element of self-interest in the pacific posture of the wealthy. They feared the possibility of an Italian expropriation of riverine lands and the abolition of slavery. At the same time, they wanted to avoid divisiveness within their own society, which could threaten their position by driving client-cultivators into the new religious settlements or exslave villages. The combination of self-interest and public concern emerges in the following excerpted letter written to an Italian government investigator shortly after the Lafoole attack. The writers sought to strike a bargain: the return of an escaped slave for a pledge of peace.

A letter sent to dear and honorable friends, to the grand Commandante, to consul Dulio, and to our friend Haji Ahmed.

May God protect all. . . .

We have sent this letter with a courier from the Matan tribe for the purpose of obtaining the return of the slave who fled to Muqdisho, in exchange for a gun [taken presumably in the Cecchi attack] which we send to you with the courier.

When the slave is returned we will summon the heads of Geledi and discuss the question of peace.

66. Ali Omar Haji "Goyle," 8 Apr. 1971. For colonial references to this influential merchant, see Finazzo, *L'Italia nel Benadir,* pp. 292–93, and Carletti, *Attraverso il Benadir,* p. 184.

We do not wish evil nor the ruin of our town, and we will seek to recover the material lost by that expedition of whites [Cecchi's] insofar as our strength permits.

I am a lieutenant of the Government and under the protection of its flag and you will find me always at your side; honor me by restoring the slave, thus making a good impression on the other heads [of Geledi].

To our dear friend, our light, Haji Ahmed. . . .

Let your voice be heard by the consul.

Help me to make a good impression [by returning the slave] and I will take upon myself the task of persuading the heads of Geledi to come to you as a sign of complete submission. . . .

From the hands of your friend and shaykh, Nur Haji Ahmedu, and of the shaykh Mahmud Abtiow.[67]

Nur and Mahmud clearly wanted to preserve political stability. As their letter suggests, the only means of realizing that objective was persuasion through the institution of the *shir*, or assembly of all adult males. To carry weight in such an assembly, they needed to demonstrate their ability to recover slaves that had sought refuge with the Italian authorities. More cautious than many of their youthful kinsmen, men like Nur and Mahmud used the means at their disposal to wring whatever concessions they could from the new regime.

We must assume that Sultan Osman himself considered the possibility of shoring up his waning power through an alliance with the Italians. Yet he was the head of a large community of divergent interests, and the fact that the Italians had withdrawn after the Lafoole affair gave him little confidence in their support at that time. Consequently, he remained noncommittal for several years. He had ignored Cecchi's request for a meeting just before the latter's abortive expedition;[68] now he temporized. Even after visiting Muqdisho and speaking with the governor in 1902, he continued to mistrust the Italians and was mistrusted by them. As late as 1906 he was suspected of conniving with Somali resisters who sought to cross his territory to visit the mullah in the north.[69]

A further episode that occurred in the Afgooye district during this period deserves mention. In the late 1890s, a *jamaaca* of the

67. Sorrentino, *Ricordi*, pp. 192–93.
68. Finazzo, L'Italia nel Benadir, p. 343.
69. Cerrina-Ferroni, *Benadir*, p. 42.

Ahmediya way was established in Geledi territory. Its leader was Shaykh Abiker Ali Jelle, a member of the sultan's own Gobroon lineage. When Abiker began to preach outright opposition to the colonials sitting threateningly on the coast, he was forced by the Geledi elders to leave the district.[70] The Geledi never joined the order in great numbers. The reason, I was told, was that the Geledi felt that participation in the *tariiqa* would sap their military strength.[71] Of those who had joined the Ahmediya community, several left with Abiker. Their response was typical of many pious Muslims who chose to emigrate to the bush rather than confront the infidels.

Thus the lines were being drawn among the Geledi in the face of the colonial menace. A letter from the sultan and elders of Geledi to the Italian governor outlined their concerns in 1903.

> After we lived for years with our custom [of slavery], the government of Zanzibar came to our land and prohibited their importation and exportation by sea; but in the cities and fields they could not prevent the trade. The [Filonardi] Company, which governed for three years, restored fugitive slaves. So did [Governor] Dulio, who passed seven tranquil years among us. In [January] 1903 a ship of war reached Muqdisho to impede slavery. After this, we received only money [for the slaves] and no longer the restitution of the slaves. We have awaited the government's consideration of this matter.
>
> The inhabitants of the interior are in great agitation. Part of them, weak and poor, pray for the coming of Shaykh Muhammad bin Abdullah and invoke him day and night. Others think of emigrating to other places. And all this is caused by the great sentiment regarding the slaves. From the time of my grandfather—67 years now—we have always had cordial relations with the Christians.
>
> The government has kept seven of our slaves and sent them away on a boat, while our elders lament![72]

Some elders who visited Muqdisho in November 1903 protested:

---

70. Abokor Ali Omar, Muqdisho, 2 Feb. 1971. This may be the same "rebellious shaykh" mentioned in an Italian report of 1904: "Telegram from Acting-Governor DeVita to the Italian Consul in Zanzibar," 13 Oct. 1904, *ASMAI*, pos. 66/4, f. 43.

71. *Laashin* Abiker Osman, Afgooye, 23 Sept. 1971. See below pp. 238–39.

72. Chiesi and Travelli, *Le Questioni*, pp. 272–73.

We have protected the trade routes and remained faithful for fourteen rainy seasons [since *Axad Shekki*]. Now our slaves don't get returned; ill will grows among our people, especially among the poor who, having only a few slaves, when these flee, lose all means of earning a living and don't know whether to leave or stay.[73]

When the Italians finally decided to occupy Afgooye in 1908, there were, as one of my informants analytically put it, three groups of opinion in the district.[74] Sultan Osman, who had suffered a final humiliating defeat at the hands of the Hintire in *Axad Mereerey* (1903–4), was prepared to receive the Italian forces openly. Most of the Geledi followed him. A second group, of which Aw Nur Ahmedow and Shaykh Muhammad Ibrahim were probably typical, accepted the colonial arrival with little enthusiasm. For the sake of order, they coexisted with the infidels but in several instances were clearly uncooperative. The influential Nur refused Italian offers to become titular head of all Geledi; Muhammad Ibrahim refused to order his lineage members to work at clearing roads and suffered temporary exile as a result.[75]

A third group, many of them early followers of Shaykh Abiker Ali Jelle, expressed their hostility more dramatically. They fled from Afgooye when the Italians occupied that town.[76] Others, including Ahmed Uways Baahuur, Aw Abdullahi Ibrahim Birkin, and Abdi Gaduud joined the dervishes and fought with guns against their own clansmen. I was told that twenty-eight members of the Geledi community eventually joined the dervish movement[77]—a small but significant number from a clan generally considered to have collaborated with the colonial occupation.

73. Ibid., p. 353.
74. This was precisely the way a Somali informant described it to me. Muhammad Abdullahi, Muqdisho, 25 Feb. 1971.
75. The Geledi claim that Shaykh Muhammad Ibrahim was deported to Bender Kassim on the northern Somali coast for a year to reprimand him for his noncooperation. I could not corroborate this in colonial records.
76. Shaykh Abiker Kassim, who had been a follower of the Ahmediya Order, went to preach against the infidels among the Mobilayn, who lived north of the Geledi. He was killed in a religious or personal dispute by a follower of the Salihiya Order. See "Notizario per l'anno 1909," *ASMAI*, pos. 66/6, f. 63.
77. Information provided by Muhammad Abdullahi and Baahuur Haji Ahmed Uways Baahuur, Muqdisho, 17 May 1971. Both were sons of dervishes.

(2) Wacdaan

Between Afgooye and Muqdisho lay about twenty-five kilo-
meters of thick brush and scrub grass. In the late nineteenth century,
the area was inhabited by the camel-keeping Wacdaan clan, who had
been close allies of the Geledi for the preceding hundred years.[78] In
the middle of the century, a number of Wacdaan had turned to farming; this helped to reinforce their political union with the Geledi, for
the two groups shared land, markets, and credit facilities in the district between the river and the coast.

Two factors bearing heavily on Wacdaan attitudes toward the
colonial presence were the internal struggle for leadership, and the
economic dislocation brought about by the abolition of slavery and by
the famine years of 1889–95. Most Wacdaan farming appears to have
been done by slaves imported to Somalia after 1840; there is little
evidence that Wacdaan pastoralists had large numbers of traditional
client-cultivators typical of such riverine clans as the Geledi.[79] Thus
abolition had more severe consequences for Wacdaan farm labor than
it did for Geledi's. The dry years of the 1890s only exacerbated the
economic situation: it was reported in 1898 that one-half of the Wacdaan population had been forced to abandon its home territory for
pastures further inland.[80] Apart from weakening their bonds with the
Geledi, these developments, we can surmise, made the Wacdaan extremely fearful of any further threat to their land and well-being.
They were, moreover, the first inland Somalis whose territory was
actually invaded by colonial soldiers at the time of the Cecchi expedition.

One of the most influential leaders among the Wacdaan was the
learned Shaykh Ahmed Haji Mahhadi. He was not a Wacdaan but a
member of the Bendabo lineage of Muqdisho. He had lived there most
of his life, teaching alongside such renowned Muslim scholars as

78. For details on the Wacdaan-Geledi alliance, see Luling, "Social Structure,"
pp. 174–76.
79. For the most part, Wacdaan slaves adopted the genealogies of their patrons,
a common practice among slaves of recent venue. In contrast, Geledi client-cultivators
maintained independent (if relatively shallow) genealogies, reflecting their longer permanence in the area. Personal communications from Virginia Luling.
80. Acting-Governor Dulio to the Ministry of Foreign Affairs, 21 Apr. 1899,
ASMAI, pos. 66/4, f. 41.

Shaykh Sufi and Shaykh Mukhdaar.[81] Like the latter, he found coexistence in a town which housed infidels intolerable, and he chose to retire to the small coastal enclave of Nimow, a little south of Muqdisho. There he set up a small *jamaaca*—some say it followed the Qadiriya way—which attracted several of the local inhabitants. When Nimow was shelled by an Italian warship in retaliation for the Cecchi ambush, Ahmed Haji fled to Day Suufi (in the heart of Wacdaan territory) where he intensified his preaching against the infidels. As late as 1907, the acting Italian governor considered him "the most listened-to propagandist in this area of the Shabeelle. Even the Geledi turn to him rather than to their own sultan for religious counsel."[82]

One of the Wacdaan leaders apparently influenced by Ahmed Haji was Hassan Hussein, titular head of the largest subsection of the Wacdaan clan, the Abubakar Moldheere. The Abubakar Moldheere were the most numerous and hence the most militarily powerful section of the Wacdaan in the late nineteenth century. They inhabited the bush country between the river and the coastal dunes, including the villages of Nimow and Day Suufi. Hassan Hussein is remembered as one of the first Wacdaan to oppose the Italians; warriors from his lineage were prominent among the forces that attacked Cecchi at Lafoole.[83] Likewise, it was spokesmen for the Abubakar Moldheere who most strenuously urged the blockade of caravan routes to Muqdisho.

The other sizable section of the Wacdaan, the Mahad Moldheere, inhabited the clan territory contiguous to Afgooye and the fertile lands around Adadleh. Their interests coincided more with those of the agricultural Geledi. However, their smaller numbers gave them less influence in Wacdaan clan councils, which came to assume greater importance for policymaking as the Wacdaan began to act independently of the Geledi. While the Mahad Moldheere apparently cooperated in the Lafoole siege—at that time, the Wacdaan stood as one, I was told[84]—their leader Abiker Ahmed Hassan subsequently struck an independent diplomatic stance.

81. On Ahmed Haji, I received information from the contemporary Somali historian Aw Jama Omar Isa, Muqdisho, 15 Mar., 1971; Aw Abdullah Hassan, Afgooye, 16 Oct. 1971; Hussein Abdi Gaduud, Muqdisho, 17 May 1971.

82. Cerrina-Ferroni, *Benadir*, p. 36.

83. Sorrentino, *Ricordi*, pp. 60–63; Carletti, *Attraverso il Benadir*, p. 171.

84. Aw Abdullah Hassan and Aw Osman Abdullah, Afgooye, 16 Oct. 1971.

In 1899, the Italian authorities sought to persuade the Wacdaan to submit peacefully to the government. They demanded that forty hostages surrender to the authorities in Muqdisho as a sign of Wacdaan submission.[85] Only the Mahad Moldheere responded. Their leader, Abiker, became a stipended official, which enhanced his standing among those of pacific persuasion. The Abubakar Moldheere refused to send the twenty representatives demanded of them and for some years remained openly defiant of Italian authority. They continued to attack caravans and occasionally to boycott the market of Muqdisho. There is some evidence to suggest that feuding within the Wacdaan increased after this rift between the two major lineages.[86]

The conciliatory initiatives of the leaders of the Mahad Moldheere toward the colonial government bore some political fruit. For although Hassan Hussein and the Abubakar Moldheere resigned themselves to accommodation with the Italians after 1908, their section received fewer stipended positions than the numerically smaller Mahad Moldheere did. Moreover, the stipends they received were smaller than those of the Mahad Moldheere officials.[87] In the early 1960s, a man of the Mahad Moldheere was recognized as titular head of all the Wacdaan.[88] I could not ascertain if this had been true throughout the twentieth century.

While factionalism goes some way toward explaining the dual response of the Wacdaan to colonial occupation, it should not be assumed that anticolonial feeling ran strictly along sectional lines. Individuals from both sections continued to participate in resistance activities and, after their leaders submitted to Italian authority, joined the southern dervishes. The best-remembered dervishes from the Wacdaan were Barghash Yusuf, Muhammad Geedi, Ali Omar

85. Dulio to Ministry of Foreign Affairs, 21 Apr. 1899, *ASMAI*, pos. 66/4, f. 41.

86. Several informants told me that at one time the Wacdaan were more strongly united; and Virginia Luling (personal communication) recorded the comment of an informant to the effect that in the time of the Italians feuding among the Wacdaan increased as traditional *diya* payments were unable to keep the peace. Cf. Carletti, *Attraverso il Benadir*, pp. 164–77, passim.

87. "Ruolo dei Capi e Cadi stipendiati," *Bollettino Ufficiale della Somalia italiana* 5 (31 Aug. 1914): 6–7. The list reveals 9 Abubakar Moldheere stipended against 15 Mahad Moldheere, the average stipend being 20 percent smaller.

88. Aw Osman Abdullah of Afgooye supplied this information to Abokor Ali Omar.

Garrarey, and the brothers Muhammad and Mustafa Hussein.[89] It
does not appear that Hassan Hussein, head of the Abubakar Moldheere section, ever became a dervish.[90] Nor did the fiery Bendabo
shaykh Ahmed Haji Mahhadi. Ahmed Haji's son Muhammad, however, was a well-known southern follower of the "Mad Mullah."
He went a step further than his father by interpreting the anticolonial religious message as a call to take up arms against the infidel invaders.[91]

(3) Hintire

Like the nearby Geledi, the Hintire were a clan of mixed
pastoralists and farmers. They occupied a compact stretch of territory
flanking the Shabeelle River town of Mereerey.

Although the Hintire were considered *raaciye* ("followers") of
the Geledi sultan from the early nineteenth century and had supported him in the Baardheere campaign of 1843, they themselves
claim that their ancestors never accepted the religious supremacy of
the Gobroon shaykhs. In the middle of the nineteenth century, the
recognized leader of the Hintire was Shaykh Madow Mahad, who
claimed descent from the legendary Shaykh Hassan Buraale.[92] This
claim to a noble religious ancestry was enhanced by Madow's imbib-
ing of advanced religious learning at Baraawe, at that time a major
center of Sufi learning for all southern Somalia.[93] According to Hintire traditions, it was this higher education that enabled Madow to
surpass even the Gobroon shaykhs in knowledge of the mystical arts.
The religious rivalry between Shaykh Madow and Shaykh Ahmed

89. Aw Abdullah Hassan, Afgooye, 16 Oct. 1971. Carletti noted that some Wacdaan who had submitted to the Italian government at the coast felt betrayed when the
Italians occupied their land, and they responded by joining the dervishes. *Attraverso
il Benadir*, pp. 175–77.

90. He was receiving a stipend in 1914.

91. Aw Abdullah Hassan, Afgooye, 16 Oct. 1971; Cerrina-Ferroni, *Benadir*,
p. 37.

92. The following information comes from traditions related to me by Ahmed
Shaykh Osman, grandson of Shaykh Abow Yunis of Mereerey. A number of traditions
had been recorded in a manuscript in the possession of Shaykh Abow Yunis and are
generally well known among the Hintire. For references to Shaykh Hassan Buraale,
see pp. 109–10, 125, 133.

93. Baraawe had been attacked by the Baardheere reformers who opposed the
excesses of popular Sufism.

Yusuf of Geledi—who is also said to have studied at Baraawe as a young man—is the subject of numerous anecdotes, some in the form of Sufi stories extolling the superior insight of one or the other.[94]

Although the Hintire could not hope to match the warrior strength of the Geledi, Madow's religious esteem proved helpful to the Geledi, at least initially. When Ahmed Yusuf became sultan of Geledi in 1848, Madow is said to have given him some land as a sign of friendship and a token of their school days together at Baraawe.[95] And the Hintire claim that the prestige of their shaykh aided Ahmed in regaining the loyalty of many clans that had defected after the Biimaal victory over his father in 1848.[96] However, at the same time, Madow was acquiring a religious following of his own, notably among the Hober clan of Daafeed, a district where the Gobroon shaykhs had been dominant for several generations.[97] Limited political cooperation between these neighboring clans thus did not prevent competition between their leaders for spiritual ascendancy. Without some awareness of this traditional religious rivalry, the particular response of the Hintire to the colonial occupation would be less understandable.

Madow was succeeded as head shaykh of the Hintire by his eldest son Ashir, who from all accounts was every bit as gifted as his father. Ashir was truly a man of religion; where his father had combined the roles of shaykh and *islao* (politico-military head), Ashir gave the responsibilities of managing day-to-day affairs to one of his kinsmen, though he continued to be regarded by outsiders as spokesman for the Hintire.[98] Ashir had little sympathy for the military exploits

94. This recalls the competition between Sultan Yusuf Muhammed and the shaykhs of Baardheere as portrayed in the tradition of the interriver clans—a competition between two purveyors of spiritual power. See chap. 4, pp. 142–46.

95. Information contained in the mss. of Shaykh Abow Yunis. Cf. chap. 3, n. 6.

96. For a list of the clans allied to the sultan of Geledi, and of those who declared their independence after the battle of Caadcaadey in 1848, see Cassanelli, "The Benaadir Past," pp. 119–20.

97. The Hober are the only segment of the Shan Daafeed (the "Five Daafeed") that claim affiliation with the Hawiyya clan family, the remaining four generally being grouped with the Rahanwiin. Significantly, the Hober appear to have been the only component of the Daafeed cluster which did not follow the Geledi sultan into battle against Baardheere. *Laashin* Abiker, Afgooye, 23 Sept. 1971; group interview with elders of Daafeed, Wanle Weyn, 27 Nov. 1977.

98. Until very recently there had existed among the Hintire both an *islao* and a head shaykh. In 1970 the revolutionary government abolished honorific titles, replacing them with the more egalitarian term *Aw*, a word signifying "respected elder."

of his Geledi neighbors; when Sultan Ahmed Yusuf tried to mobilize a large army to attack the Biimaal in 1878–79, Ashir refused to allow his people to participate.[99] This refusal appears to have marked the end of whatever cooperation had existed between the two clans. During the last two decades of the century, there occurred a number of skirmishes between the warriors of the Hintire and Geledi. The verdicts were mixed, although the Hintire won a last-minute victory in a battle in 1903–4, which proved to be the last between these riverine rivals.[100]

This background of antagonism toward the Geledi influenced the initial Hintire response to the "Italian problem." Immediately after the battle of Lafoole in 1896, the Wacdaan sent a courier to Mereerey to solicit Shaykh Ashir's support in their continuing struggle with the colonials. The courier asked Ashir to use his spiritual influence to help defeat the infidels. The Hintire leader refused on the grounds that the Wacdaan had assisted the Geledi in earlier battles with his clan. Ashir abruptly spurned the Wacdaan's conciliatory offer of a gift of one hundred cows; the messenger is said to have ridden off without a parting word.[101]

Shaykh Ashir's position toward the colonials remained consistent throughout his lifetime and gives the lie to all simplistic views of Somali resistance. He felt that the Hintire, as good Muslims, should go to war only if their territory were invaded.[102] This policy he had applied in his dealings with other Somali clans as well. He had declined to participate in Sultan Ahmed's aggressive campaigns against the Biimaal. He had counseled patience when his militant son and other kinsmen wanted to raid Geledi herds and seize land in dispute between the two clans. And as late as 1904, when acts of open resistance were becoming commonplace in the Benaadir, a colonial informer reported

99. Traditions say that Ashir recited the prayer over the dead for Sultan Ahmed even before Ahmed departed for the battlefield, where he lost his life. Accounts of the battle of Agareen were recorded by Revoil, "Voyages chez les Benadirs," 49: 25–27; Ferrandi, "Prima spedizione," pp. 244–46; and Barile, *Colonizzazione fascista,* pp. 96–98.

100. The Geledi themselves admit losing the battle of *Axad Mereerey* ("the Sunday [year] of Mereerey") because one of their warrior contingents attacked prematurely. The dating of a year by the battle suggests that it was one of the more important events that year (1903–4).

101. This episode is recorded by Sorrentino, *Ricordi,* p. 158, who obtained it from a Somali informant.

102. I heard this from a number of Hintire informants.

that Ashir refused to join the resisters: it was claimed that the shaykh would encourage his followers to take up arms only if the Italians moved inland and directly threatened Mereerey.[103]

While Ashir sought to avoid endangering the lives of his kinsmen, he nonetheless wanted nothing to do with the infidels. He consistently rebuffed messengers sent to him by the Italian authorities.[104] Even his Somali enemies praised his nonaccommodating stance. A poet of Afgooye, recording the attitudes of the various southern clans toward the foreign invaders, said

> Ra'dhige Cashir Madow Caalin Mahad
> Racyinimo aas diiday.
>
> The writer of "R," Ashir Madow Alin Mahad
> Refused to take the road to damnation
> [By receiving the infidels].[105]

Yet Ashir was aging, and his sons had begun jockeying for succession to his position of authority. At his death in May 1907, the three sons of his youngest wife decided to take a stance that was openly hostile to the Italians.[106] These three sons did not enjoy as much influence in Hintire clan councils as did Ashir's older children. It is also possible that they had been excluded from Ashir's political inheritance, for his eldest son, Muhyeddin, had become head shaykh of Mereerey while the second oldest, Isma'il, had assumed the leadership of the Hober at Daafeed. As a result, the three junior sons may have sought increased prestige and power by taking an independent stand on the colonial issue. The three began cooperating actively with the ever-growing group of Benaadir resisters, and Mereerey soon became a major center for the gathering of dervish recruits. Those Hintire who chose to fight still invoked the name of their deceased leader: oral accounts recall how one warrior rose during a *shir* and vowed that he would never offer an infidel the hand he had used to greet Shaykh Ashir.[107]

103. Monti to Governor, 7 June 1904, *ASMAI,* pos. 66/4, f. 43.
104. Sorrentino, *Ricordi,* p. 299 ff.
105. *Laashin* Abiker Osman, Afgooye, 23 Sept. 1971.
106. The sons were Hassan, Hussein, and Abow Yunis. Abow Yunis was still living in Mereerey during my visits in 1971.
107. The warrior's name most commonly mentioned was Ahmed Gabay. This paragraph and the following one summarize information collected in interviews with Ahmed Shaykh Osman, Shaykh Yusuf Muhyeddin, and *Laashin* Baley Aliow Mukh-

At the news of his father's death, another son, Abokor—soon to become the most famous—returned to Mereerey from the upper Shabeelle, where he had been assisting some kinsmen in their struggle against Ethiopia's imperial armies. Already at this time Abokor was a declared dervish; nonetheless, he counseled his kinsmen to observe his late father's dictum and refrain from following the example of the three younger brothers. Only when the Italians began to march inland in August 1908 did Abokor and his brothers reach an accord: they decided to oppose the occupation with arms. The town of Mereerey was one of the few places along the Shabeelle which met the Italians with a united show of force. More than seventy Hintire perished in a field outside the town, which was later burned to the ground. Several of those involved in the fighting were self-proclaimed supporters of the northern dervish leader Sayyid Muhammad Abdullah Hassan, among them Hussein Muhammad Yahiyow, nephew of Abokor Ashir, and Ibrahim Sha'ayb, who fired the first shot with a newly acquired musket.[108] A local poet recalled the battle some years later:

> Abokor Ashir Madow said, I will not hoist the [infidels'] flag;
> The Hintire preferred death to disgrace.
> When the infidels came thundering into Mereerey,
> We saw many young men confront the barrels of guns;
> They were fired upon and silenced forever.
> We saw many people wearing mourning cloths,
> And many children who became orphans.[109]

(4) Biimaal

In the last of our case studies, we examine the best-known example of southern Somali resistance—that of the Biimaal of Marka district. By now it should be apparent that many factors influenced the decisions to resist or to accept colonial authority. The same politi-

---

daar, Mereerey, 25 May 1971; and from interviews with Muddey Haji Geeley and Isaq Muhammad, Muqdisho.

108. The battle was described for me in considerable detail by Isaq Muhammad, Muqdisho, 20 Sept. 1971, and Shaykh Yusuf Muhyeddin, Mereerey, 25 May 1971. The Italian account of the encounter is in Gino Macchioro, *Relazione sulla Somalia italiana per l'anno 1908–1909* (Rome, 1910), p. 8.

109. *Laashin* Anshooley Osman Aliow of Califow.

cal and personal motives that we have observed in the preceding cases were also operating in the Biimaal community, and in the account which follows one can sense the anguish and uncertainty that must have been felt by many Somalis around the turn of the century. Yet there is little question that the resistance in Marka district was the fiercest and most prolonged in the Benaadir. This is not surprising in light of the earlier history of the Biimaal; their continual struggle against many enemies had given them a cohesiveness and a military organization far tighter than that of most other southern Somali clans.

The Biimaal consisted of four territorial sections spread along the coastal dunes between Jesiira and Mungiya and extending inland to the farmlands along the Shabeelle.[110] Each of these sections was represented by a number of religious authorities known generally as *macallimiin* and by a number of politico-military figures known as *malaakh*s and *amaanduulle*. In times of crisis, leaders from all four sections would gather in *shir* to work out a common policy of action. While traditionally the Biimaal recognized an official called *ugaas* who was titular religious head of the entire clan, his role was mainly one of summoning clan assemblies and of bestowing his blessings on the final decisions that were reached.

Throughout the nineteenth century the Biimaal had stood together to defend their territory and their independence against encroachments by the powerful sultans of Geledi; both Yusuf Muhammad and his son Ahmed Yusuf lost their lives in battle against the Biimaal. These proud nomads had also firmly resisted the sultan of Zanzibar's growing influence in Marka by ambushing the governor of that town together with forty *askari*s in 1876.[111] Marka was the major commercial outlet for Biimaal livestock and for the grain produced by their slaves and client-cultivators along the nearby Shabeelle; and they carefully guarded their access to it. When occasional differences arose between Biimaal leadership in the interior and the old Arab and Somali families of Marka—who were always more interested than the Biimaal in establishing relations with foreign powers

110. Virtually all we know about traditional Biimaal social and political organization was recorded by Gherardo Pantano, *Nel Benadir: La citta di Merca e la regione Bimal* (Leghorn, 1910), pp. 41 ff. Pantano's monograph provides the ethnographic fragments from which the information in this paragraph is drawn.

111. Barile, *Colonizzazione fascista*, pp. 94–96; Ugo Ferrandi, "I Biemal," *L'Esplorazione commerciale e l'esploratore* (Milan), vol. 10, no. 3 (1895), pp. 122–24.

—the Biimaal would hold up food supplies to the townsmen or divert their exports to smaller outlets along the coast. These boycotts proved extremely effective in assuring Biimaal influence in urban politics, as the Italians would learn in 1904. The respect accorded to the Biimaal by the inhabitants of the Benaadir is well summed up in the following Hawiyya proverb.

> I went to raid unripe durra in the tribe of the Gaaljacal.
> I went to raid cooked beans in the tribe of the Abgaal.
> I went to raid valor in the tribe of the Biimaal.[112]

With the arrival of the Italians at the coast in 1890, Biimaal leaders were in almost constant *shir* in an effort to coordinate their plans. The Italian government always viewed them as its most determined opponent; colonial policy was geared from the beginning to try to divide the Biimaal leadership and thus divide the opposition. Given this policy, it is remarkable that the people of Marka district remained united for most of the period between 1890 and 1908; and, as we shall see, when a majority of the clan leadership felt that further resistance was useless (toward the end of 1908), the entire community came together to give its consent in a remarkable display of renewed unity.

After the Lafoole episode, several Biimaal sections boycotted the market of Marka to express their support for the Wacdaan action. The northern Biimaal collaborated with Hassan Hussein of Lafoole in cutting off land communications between Muqdisho and Marka. This action forced the Italians to occupy the coastal town of Jesiira. It was shortly thereafter that the Italian resident of Marka, Giacomo Trevis, was assassinated by a young Biimaal warrior. In colonial circles, it was believed that the Saad (the northernmost section) were responsible for the murder.[113]

Trevis's successors attempted to mollify the Biimaal leadership. The influential elder Haji Ali Isa was promised a stipend of 120 thalers annually.[114] The attempted bribe did not work, however; Haji Ali continued to demand that the government replace residents he disliked and that they restore escaped slaves to their rightful owners. In 1903, just before his death, Ali Isa wrote to the Italian consul:

112. Cerulli, *Somalia* 2: 264.
113. Sorrentino, *Ricordi*, p. 82.
114. Chiesi and Travelli, *Le Questioni*, pp. 274–75, and Document 42.

Our slaves have fled to Marka. . . . We asked restitution from [resident] Monti; he sent us to Governor Dulio. We can do nothing without our slaves. You [Sapelli] are supposed to be our protector, and if you leave your subjects without slaves, the land will fall into ruin, and your administration will fall into ruin.[115]

The first occasion for united Biimaal action followed upon the government's antislavery decrees of 1904. Their action seems to have been directed as much against the perceived collaboration of the townsmen of Marka as it was against the colonial government.[116] Early in April 1904, Biimaal leaders met in *shir* and decided to blockade the port of Marka from the interior. The blockade was timed to coincide with the beginning of the southwest monsoon, which virtually cut off access to Marka by sea. Throughout the summer of 1904, Somali lookouts stood perched on the dunes outside the town "within shouting distance of its walls." By June, the town was facing starvation and the population of Marka had dwindled from some five thousand to less than half that number.[117] A relief column of colonial *askari*s sent out from Muqdisho was attacked three times en route and suffered considerable losses. Among the forty-five Biimaal dead in the encounters was the famous warrior-poet Jibril Ma'allin Barrow, who had been an outspoken foe of the Italians since the *shir* of *Axad Shekki* (1896).[118]

The news of the battles spread quickly through the interior. Several of the central Biimaal, whose farming villages stood not far from Marka, wanted to approach the government to negotiate; but they refrained out of respect for the mourning period following the burial of the Biimaal dead. In early June, a local *shir* was called at Cigalle, on the sand hills behind Marka. There took place a debate between two *macallimiin*, one urging an outright attack on Marka, the other advising caution until all the Biimaal could be consulted. It was agreed to call another meeting and in the meantime to secure support from surrounding clans.[119] When the southwest monsoon

115. Ibid., pp. 275–76.
116. See above, p. 206.
117. Vice-resident of Marka DeVito to Governor Sapelli, 28 May 1904, *ASMAI*, pos. 66/4, f. 43; Monti to Consul-General at Zanzibar, 29 June 1904, *ASMAI*, pos. 66/4, f. 43.
118. Interview with Ibrahim Ali Subayr, Muqdisho, 11 Aug. 1971. Cf. "Notes of various informants," 28 May 1904, *ASMAI*, pos. 66/4, f. 43.
119. Monti to Governor Sapelli, 7 June 1904, *ASMAI*, pos. 66/4, f. 43.

began to lessen in late September, the blockade of Marka was partially lifted. Italian forces immediately occupied the dunes above the town and constructed a *zariba* at Cigalle.

At this point some Biimaal elders began to counsel accommodation with the ever-more threatening foreigners. The autumn rains were promising a good harvest and many landholders wanted to be able to sell their agricultural surpluses at the coast. In addition, the northern Biimaal, early opponents of the colonial presence, were reluctant to march on the foreign outpost at Jesiira. They feared that the Italians would retaliate by poisoning their coastal wells. A number of tentative attempts were made to establish contact with Italian authorities; through the first six months of 1905, the Italian Resident at Marka received several Biimaal delegations bearing letters protesting their loyalty.[120] These first public rifts in Biimaal unity prompted a poet to compose lines which subsequently became famous throughout southern Somalia:

> Reer Jannow waa jid galeen
> Reer Jaaximow iska jooga.
>
> People of Heaven have found their way [by making war]
> People of Hell, stay where you are [in submission].[121]

The *macallimiin*, I was told, fiercely opposed all efforts at peaceful coexistence. For them, the infidel towns had to be avoided at all costs. In January 1905, religious leaders sparked an attack on the Italian garrison at Cigalle. In this battle, Haji Abdi Abiker "Gafle" came to the attention of the Italian authorities. Although wounded in the leg, he managed to escape and for the next fifteen years remained a leading opponent of Italian rule in the Benaadir. He provides a good example of the role played by religious leaders in the Biimaal resistance. Before the Italian arrival, he had been a well-known teacher of religion. After making the pilgrimage to Mecca, he became a representative of the Salihiya order in the Marka district. It is extremely

120. For a possible interpretation of these gestures of accommodation, see below pp. 247–48. Several of my informants recalled that the Biimaal felt threatened by the Italian occupation of their coastal wells. Ibrahim Ali Subayr and others, "Kilometer 50," 19 Aug. 1971. Cf. Sapelli to Consul, 27 Feb. 1905, *ASMAI*, pos. 66/4, f. 44.

121. This poetic fragment was recited for me by Ibrahim Ali Subayr, Muqdisho, 11 Aug. 1971, and Ali Ahmed Yerow, Jenaale, 24 Oct. 1971.

Salah "Abooye" (front left) and friends pose for a picture in Shalambood following a group interview.

likely that Abdi "Gafle" was the individual who provided the initial links between the Biimaal resistance and the northern dervish movement of Shaykh Muhammad Abdullah Hassan. Colonial officials viewed him as one of their main antagonists and a major source of disruption along the Benaadir.[122]

After the battle of Cigalle, it appears that all of the Biimaal elders met at a great *shir* in Mooyaale to assess the situation. Up until this point, the clan had relied on its own resources to combat colonialism—but it was becoming clear that they were no match for the superior firepower of the Italians. Thus, at the *shir* of Mooyaale, it was decided to send a delegation of five hundred warriors and religious spokesmen to the mullah's headquarters in the north. This was

122. Information about Haji Abdi Abiker "Gafle" was provided to me by Haji Isma'il Ali Omar of Shalambood, 20 Nov. 1977; he showed me a manuscript which included a brief biography of Haji Abdi Abiker. The governor of the colony in 1906–7 asserted that Haji Abdi was well acquainted with Shaykh Muhammad's successes in the north, which provided him with a "ready audience" among the Biimaal. Cerrina-Ferroni, *Benadir*, p. 53.

a decisive step in the history of the resistance: it must have been difficult for the proud Biimaal to seek aid from outside, but eventually the skeptics were brought into agreement. Supplies were collected throughout the area and the delegation departed. Oral accounts remember the four leaders of the group as Malak Abdi Tur'ay, Shaykh Jemaal Ma'allin Hassan, Muhammad Mursal, and Bilaw Ageede.[123]

The next major battle between Biimaal and colonial forces occurred at Turunley in February 1907. It was a disaster for the Somali side. Several hundreds lost their lives, including, according to several accounts, ten brothers from the same family.[124] After this catastrophe, a second delegation was sent north to Ilig, with the intention of obtaining firearms. In the meantime, the first delegation returned with three hundred guns. By the late summer of 1907, the Biimaal were ready to make their last stand.

Turunley was not the last battle to be fought by a large Biimaal army. They battled colonial forces for three hours at Jilib in March 1908. Two thousand warriors confronted more than five hundred colonial troops at Fiinlow (Melled) in July of the same year, in the famous battles of *Sabti iyo Axad* ("Saturday and Sunday"). But by the autumn of 1907, the Biimaal resistance had merged with a larger anticolonial movement. Somalis throughout the Benaadir remember the year 1907–8 as *Khamiis Daraawiish* (the "Thursday Year of the Dervishes"). It was the dervish movement that picked up the scattered remnants of the various local resistances and in so doing left a considerable legacy of its own. We will examine the *daraawiish* of the Benaadir in the concluding section of the chapter, following a general analysis of the four local resistance movements that have just been described.

An Analysis of Local Resistance in the Benaadir

The preceding case studies represent only a fraction of the dozens of Somali clans and districts that were faced with the problem of colonial occupation. Still, they give us some appreciation of the

123. Haji Isma'il Ali Omar, Ali Hassan Muhammad, Shaykh Hassan Ma'allin, Hussein Osman Hassan, Marka, 21 Nov. 1977.
124. Turunley was described for me by the informants listed in n. 123; cf. Cerrina-Ferroni, *Benadir*, pp. 80, 102–3.

problems faced by the Somalis as well as an idea of the various alternatives open to them at the end of the last century. In this section I will make some generalizations about these local responses to colonial invasion, with the understanding that historical research in other districts may modify any conclusions reached.

When discussing resistance and accommodation, it is important to select the proper units of analysis. It is often assumed that certain clans opposed the colonials while others readily allied with them. Our case studies show, however, that there were differences of opinion within every clan. Among the seemingly pro-Italian Geledi, for example, there existed several undercurrents of anticolonial feeling—notably within the *jamaaca* of Abiker Ali Jelle and within certain traditional religious lineages and trading families. The Wacdaan, who were united at the battle of Lafoole, later split along lineage lines, the leader of one segment favoring peace and the other continuing a guerilla-style opposition. The Hintire of Mereerey provided yet another variation. Most agreed that the Italians presented a threat: the debate was whether to ignore them (Shaykh Ashir's position) or take up arms against them (the three younger sons' position); whether to pose a "resistance of the mind" or one of the hands.[125]

The point here is that within each Somali community there were groups with different personal, religious, and political interests; it would be surprising had it been otherwise. Somali society was like any other in producing some individuals who acted chiefly for motives of personal gain or political ambition. There were those who genuinely felt that making peace with the colonial powers was in the long run the best way to insure the safety and integrity of their kin community; and there were those who were prepared to sacrifice their property, their family unity, and even their lives in resisting the colonial intrusion. To speak of entire clans as either "resisters" or "collaborators" is obviously to misrepresent the historical situation.

Having said this, it is equally important to realize that each of the communities we have studied tried to achieve some sort of consensus on the colonial problem. The members of each clan met frequently in *shir* to debate the issues and to persuade others to their viewpoints. Thus, in the early days of the colonial presence, most clans were able to present a united front. As the war of attrition with the Italians

125. Cf. Robert Rotberg and Ali Mazrui, *Protest and Power in Black Africa* (New York, 1970), Introduction, p. xviii.

ground on, however, rifts in Somali unity began to appear, and the colonials were quick to exploit these divisions. Our case studies suggest four sets of reasons for the inability of local Somali communities to sustain a united front: (1) within each clan, there were divergent economic and social interests that were accentuated by colonial policy; (2) within each district, there were differences of religious opinion which made it difficult for Somalis to unite strictly on the basis of a common Islamic religion; (3) within each community, competition for political influence (often along traditional lines) led to the emergence of factions which sometimes supported different approaches to the colonial problem; (4) eventually, there developed a new force—the dervishes—which gave the militant opponents of colonialism an alternative to local resistance and which drew them away from identification with strictly clan interests. We will examine each of these factors in greater detail.

Economic Interests

In the first section of the chapter, we saw that the late nineteenth century was a time of economic dislocation throughout much of Somalia. Many merchants who had grown wealthy through their involvement in the caravan trade began to lose money as trade routes from the interior were made increasingly unsafe by Ethiopian raids and Somali banditry. Those merchants who blamed foreigners for their economic decline were naturally more vocal in their opposition to colonialism. Such was true, for example, with certain coastal families and some of the merchants of Afgooye.[126] On the other hand, some traders and businessmen felt that their losses could be recovered by establishing commercial contacts with the new foreign rulers, who might provide new markets for the export of Somali products.

In addition, some of the farmers along the Shabeelle Valley who supplied grain to the inhabitants of Marka and Muqdisho felt that a policy of resistance would cut off their access to these coastal markets and remove a source of income. One reason for the breakdown of Biimaal unity after the successful blockade of 1904 was the desire of some families in the immediate hinterland to resume trade with that

126. See above, p. 210.

town. Nomads as well as farmers had to be concerned with their economic well-being; although the northern Biimaal were among the earliest opponents of Italian occupation, they were also the most vulnerable to colonial retaliation, since from Jesiira the Italians could prevent them from using the coastal wells in the dry season.

A crucial economic issue was the question of slavery. Most colonial officials felt that their effort to end slavery was the main reason for the resistance of the southern Somali clans.[127] By using this argument, the Italians justified their presence while conveniently ignoring the fact that they were also threatening the Somalis' political autonomy and territorial integrity. It is no coincidence that the Wacdaan and Biimaal posed the first concerted opposition to the colonial presence. Both had been early victims of Italian firepower: the Biimaal at Marka in 1893 and the Wacdaan at Nimow in 1897. These jolting experiences were a direct result of the fact that Biimaal and Wacdaan territory extended to the ocean littoral; and thereafter, though confined to the coast, the Italians were perceived as occupying clan territory.

Nonetheless, there was some truth to the idea that Somali slaveholders were among the earliest opponents of colonial administration. The letters cited in the preceding section testify to the declining productivity of agriculture which Somali spokesmen attributed to the loss of slave labor. Particularly hard hit were small farmers and those who had obtained imported slaves in the mid-nineteenth century: many Wacdaan fell into this category. In contrast, riverine communities like the Geledi and Hintire contained large populations of long-resident client-cultivators who had been partially assimilated by the dominant population and who, as a consequence, were more likely to remain on the land despite emancipating legislation. Thus, while both Geledi and Hintire experienced a declining labor supply, economic life in Afgooye and Mereerey was less disrupted than it was among Biimaal and Wacdaan. This fact may help account for the more pacific posture initially assumed by the first two clans when confronted with the Italian presence.

Finally, some of the wealthier slaveholders did not hesitate to

127. Chiesi and Travelli, *Le Questioni*, pp. 265–76 passim; the various appendixes in their report also contain letters from colonial officials who expressed this opinion. Cf. Hess, *Italian Colonialism*, pp. 87–89, 97–99.

deal with the colonial authorities in an effort to preserve their dominant positions. A few were prepared to accept colonial rule in exchange for the restoration of their slaves and recognition of their authority. Although the number of Somalis with large slaveholdings was small, they were typically individuals who had close ties to coastal merchants and who were able to communicate directly with the Italians at the coast. This made it appear that they were a major force in Somali society.

The colonial authorities did not hesitate to exploit these "class" differences, however weak they were. They did so in two ways, which may appear contradictory but which nonetheless helped to further their policy of divide and rule. On the one hand, they gave moral and material support to individuals and communities which protected former slaves, such as certain religious *jamaacooyin* and leaders of escaped-slave settlements.[128] At the same time, colonial officials tried to woo the big landholders who had owned slaves by promising them government stipends. The colonials assumed they could win the wealthy over to the cause of "colonial order and stability." To some extent they were successful.

Thus there seems to be little question that economic interests divided Somali society, though in ways not always predictive of subsequent behavior toward the colonialists. Wealthy slaveholders interested in maintaining their investments, poor farmers forced to abandon commercial farming after abolition, and exslaves eager to preserve their newly found freedom could not be expected to cooperate against a common enemy. Still, the colonial policy of divide and rule did not always work. The famous exslave Nassib Bunda, initially regarded as a bulwark of colonial pacification along the lower Jubba, spent his last years in rebellion against colonial authorities; it is even reported that he corresponded with the dervish leader Muhammad Abdullah Hassan in the north.[129] One can also cite the example of the wealthy Aw Nur Ahmedow of Afgooye who, according to oral accounts, refused to accept government offers of the chiefship of Afgooye district.[130] The very fact that Aw Nur was wealthy gave him the capacity to act independently in the face of colonial efforts to buy his support.

128. See below, p. 237.
129. Chiesi, *La Colonizzazione europea,* pp. 631–34.
130. Abokor Ali Omar, Muqdisho, 8 Apr. 1971.

Religious Interests

Religious leaders stood in the forefront of the anticolonial resistance in southern Somalia. We have noted the role played by Ahmed Haji Mahhadi among the Wacdaan, and the active part taken by the *macallimiin* in all of the Biimaal-Italian battles. Shaykh Ashir of Mereerey, though not a man of violence, refused to deal with the Italians; and many of the religious leaders of Afgooye were dissatisfied with their sultan's attempts to negotiate with the foreigners.

Much of the Somali poetry that grew out of the resistance movement reflects this religious dimension. Most Somalis are familiar with the famous lines of the anonymous poet quoted earlier:

> People of Heaven have found the way [by making war].
> People of Hell, stay where you are [in submission].

Another poet of Afgooye was equally graphic.

> When [the colonials] came to Shangaani and occupied it
> And the compound of Shaamow 'Amuud was taken by
>   force,
> The people met and conferred at Weliyow Cadde.
> The Biimaal are holy fighters of whom I need say
>   nothing:
> For five years and five months they fought.
> Let the foul [uncircumcised] infidels be castrated![131]

Finally, a Biimaal poem composed after the construction of an Italian fort at Fiinlow, southwest of Marka, seems to portray the struggle for the homeland in religious terms:

> Now Fiinlow has been settled by infidels;
> Who will shed his blood for it?
>
> Now Fiinlow is occupied by infidels;
> Who will hurl spears at them?
>
> Fiinlow is my home.
> Why should I flee when strangers appear?[132]

131. *Laashin* Anshooley Osman Aliow, Muqdisho, 31 July 1971.
132. This poem was recited for me by a number of informants in the Marka district, although they could not identify the author.

Oral recollections and colonial writings make it clear that most of the religious opposition to colonialism came from traditional men of religion. These authorities, known generally as *wadaaddo,* were the respected practitioners of sacred magic *(tacdaar)* and divining *(wardi)* who could be found throughout Somali society. In addition to performing the usual religious services, they acted as consultants to clan elders and helped insure clan prosperity through their ritual blessings, prognostication, and political mediation. The *macallimiin* among the Biimaal, and lineages of religious specialists such as the Sheekhal and Reer Shaykh Mumin, who could be found in dispersed communities throughout the Benaadir, were examples of such local religious authorities.[133]

From the outset, Italian authorities were aware that the *wadaaddo* posed a threat to their plans for pacification. Sorrentino, the commissioner who investigated the causes of the Lafoole massacre, reported on the rumored activities of a hostile Sheekhal leader named Abobaker Yerow.

> To render our weapons harmless, he practiced a bit of sorcery, killing a goat and a snake; he said that he had read in the sacred books that this sorcery would always assure victory to the Wacdaan.[134]

Commissioner Sorrentino also learned that

> The Wacdaan wish to march at once on Muqdisho; but Abobaker Yerow is opposed, saying that they were not yet under good auspices; not this Friday but perhaps the next would be more propitious.[135]

Among the Biimaal, he felt that

> The religious are those who make up the worst element; by distorting the law of Muhammad, they preach religious hatred. I do not believe that their control over the masses is such as to enable them to stir an entire clan to revolt; at the same time, they can through their preaching prompt a few fanatics to commit

133. For a discussion of the various roles played by these religious specialists, see chap. 4, pp. 122–35.

134. Sorrentino, *Ricordi,* p. 119.

135. Ibid., p. 143.

crimes such as those which victimized Talmone and Trevis in Marka.[136]

During the Biimaal blockade of Marka in 1904, the Italian Resident wrote:

> The Biimaal have given some two thousand thalers to their Mohallim [sic] to practice their witchcraft, to make our soldiers leave the country, and to prevent our guns from firing.[137]

Finally, after the battle of Turunley (1907), the colonial authorities learned from informants how the Biimaal had prepared their attack.

> The Ugas performs the rite of *tadach* [sic]; he writes the appropriate Quranic verses on tablets . . . then he pours water over the future combatants—it is so miraculous as to render the warriors invincible to bullets. . . . The Ugas orders the departure [of the army] after fixing the day and hour of the *shirib* [war march to the accompaniment of chanted prayers].[138]

From the repeated references to what are clearly the practices of *tacdaar* and *wardi,* it is apparent that the Italian nemeses were none other than the traditional religious specialists.

In addition to the *wadaaddo,* there was another group of holy men in the Benaadir who wielded some influence during these years. These were the *khaliifa*s and shaykhs of the various Sufi orders which, as we noted earlier, were beginning to spread throughout Somalia in the late nineteenth century. At first glance it might appear that the *tariiqa*s offered great potential for mass opposition, particularly when local clan unity began to break down. Not only did the religious brotherhoods provide a structure and a leadership to focus pan-tribal loyalties, but they also provided an ideology which could confront the infidels on a basis common to all Somalis, regardless of clan. Muhammad Abdullah Hassan's *jihad,* it may be recalled, began as a movement of Salihiya reform.

---

136. Ibid., p. 420. In interviews with Ibrahim Ali Subayr, "Kilometer 50," 19 Aug. 1971, and Haji Isma'il Ali Omar, Marka, 20 Nov. 1977, I was told that it was the unity of the *macallimiin* which kept the Biimaal together in their resolve to oppose Italian power.

137. "Monti al Ministero degli Affari Esteri," 29 June 1904, *ASMAI,* pos. 66/4, f. 43.

138. Gustavo Pesenti, *Danane nella Somalia italiana* (Milan, 1932), pp. 33–35.

Throughout the Benaadir, however, the *tariiqa*s had little to do with the active opposition to colonialism. There seem to be several reasons for this. First, many of the *tariiqa* leaders were not inclined to seek radical political reform. They sought to spread their new liturgical practices by peaceful rather than militant means. The agricultural settlements *(jamaacooyin)*, which we have seen to be important social institutions, were refuges that favored coexistence with the political authorities, be they Somali or foreign. Second, there was not one but three "Ways" competing for the loyalty of the people: Qadiriya, Ahmediya, and Salihiya. It is evident that the *tariiqa*s, despite a common commitment to Islam, spent much of their energies debating points of dogma and practice and thereby weakening their potential as a unifying force.[139] Even Muhammad Abdullah Hassan did not completely escape *tariiqa* partisanship: a number of his writings were clearly concerned with demonstrating fallacies in the Qadiriya practice of *tawassul* (the intercession by saints in a man's prayers to Allah).[140] To be sure, he did preach against those who associated with infidels, whatever their *tariiqa* affiliation. Nevertheless, his intellectual position on the controversial religious issues of the day was not shared by all Muslims; as a result, we can conclude that some Islamic leaders opposed Muhammad Abdullah Hassan for theological reasons. It was not that many *tariiqa* leaders were antinationalist; rather they were more concerned with religious questions than with political ones.

A final reason why the new *tariiqa*s failed to assume a leading role in the resistance (with a few exceptions which will be mentioned below) may have to do with the humble backgrounds of many of the *tariiqa* leaders and their early adherents. Men like Shaykh Uways and Shaykh Muhammad Guled came from client agricultural communities rather than powerful nomadic clans.[141] They had spent considerable time outside of Somalia studying religion and were not influential in local politics. Many of their early followers were drawn from the less fortunate segments of Somali society—destitute farmers, former slaves, and social outcasts. While a leader like Muhammad Abdullah Hassan was able to combine the qualities of shaykh and

139. See, for example, Cerulli, *Somalia* 1: 195–200; 3: 171–74.
140. See Martin, *Muslim Brotherhoods*, pp. 197–201.
141. Cerulli, *Somalia* 1: 187, 189

warrior in his dervish movement, I suggest that many Somali warriors did not follow the leadership of these southern *tariiqa* shaykhs simply because they were not of "noble" origins.

The Italian authorities were quick to recognize the *tariiqa* leaders as potential political allies. The same Sorrentino who complained about the militant *wadaaddo* among the Biimaal and Wacdaan proposed to give money to the founders of *tariiqa* settlements in order to secure "the benevolence of the Religious Head and of his adepts."[142] The government hoped that the shaykhs would, if nothing else, maintain neutrality in the anticolonial campaign. Several *tariiqa* members openly professed their support of Italian authority as a way to avoid bloodshed among fellow Muslims; a few even assisted the colonial cause by helping to spread the news of Shaykh Muhammad's supposed excommunication from the Salihiya Order by Muhammad Salih in 1909.[143]

Not all *tariiqa* adherents in the Benaadir were Italian partisans. We have mentioned the outspoken anticolonialism of Haji Abdi Abiker "Gafle" (Salihiya), Ahmed Haji Mahhadi (possibly Qadiriya), and Abiker Ali Jelle (Ahmediya). However, in most oral recollections these men are exceptions. Said one old man:

> Yes, it is true that Abdi Abiker and Haji Weheley [another Ahmediya leader] were active in the Biimaal resistance. But they were unusual—most *tariiqa* followers minded their own affairs during the Biimaal-Italian wars.[144]

Perhaps the most characteristic example of the position taken by *tariiqa* leaders in southern Somalia at the turn of the century was that of Shaykh Uways. Suspected of opposition by the Italians,[145] eventually killed by the followers of Muhammad Abdullah Hassan,[146] he is remembered by most Benaadir Somalis as a good and learned preacher of Islam who traveled unarmed throughout the country looking for places to establish new religious settlements.

142. Sorrentino, *Ricordi*, p. 337.
143. Macchioro, *Relazione... per l'anno 1908–1909*, pp. 19–20. Omar Isa Haaq, in an interview in Muqdisho on 17 Mar. 1971, recalled how many shaykhs set themselves up as heads of *jamaacooyin* in order to draw stipends from the colonial government.
144. Ibrahim Ali Subayr, "Kilometer 50," 19 Aug. 1971.
145. Cerrina-Ferroni, *Benadir*, p. 44.
146. Cerulli, *Somalia* 1: 188.

Local Political Interests

In addition to the economic and religious sentiments that divided Somalis during the period of resistance, there also existed within each local community certain political cleavages which cannot be explained solely in terms of the colonial problem. That is, within each clan certain factions that had traditionally competed for status and authority often took different positions on the colonial question. They may have been equally suspicious of the foreigners, but considerations of internal power and prestige drove them to adopt diverse tactics.

An example may help to illustrate the point.[147] In Afgooye in the late 1890s, an Ahmediya *jamaaca* was set up on the margins of Geledi territory by Abiker Ali Jelle. Abiker was a member of the Gobroon lineage to which the sultan of Geledi also belonged. Abiker may have been able to attract a small following to his *jamaaca* by virtue of the prestige he enjoyed as a member of the Gobroon. But he also claimed to possess additional *baraka* as a master of the Ahmediya "Way." In essence, he was setting himself up as a religious authority in competition with the Geledi sultan, whose prestige, as we have noted, was declining at this time.

The colonial issue became a test of the religious authority of Abiker (and his *tariiqa*). When the people of Afgooye found themselves face-to-face with the Italian menace, they recall that Abiker urged them to oppose the extension of Italian influence. By taking this position, Abiker placed himself (wittingly or unwittingly) in direct opposition to Sultan Osman, who had adopted a wait-and-see attitude toward the foreigners. The resulting competition for followers between the two leaders clouded the resistance issue and even reversed the general pattern whereby traditional leaders tended to oppose and *tariiqa* shaykhs to accept the colonial presence. Ultimately, Geledi's elders forced Abiker and his militant followers to leave Afgooye. Oral sources said that only a few Geledi ever joined the *tariiqa* since they felt that such a move would sap the community's military strength. That military strength, as we have seen, was always associated with the religious powers of the Gobroon sultans. If the people had joined the *tariiqa,* whose religious legitimacy derived from a different source, they would have been denying the supremacy of the sultan's

147. The following incident is alluded to above, pp. 212–13.

authority. The majority of the residents of the Afgooye were not prepared to go this far. Thus we can hypothesize that when the Geledi opted against Abiker Ali Jelle's position, they were opting specifically for their sultan's traditional authority and not necessarily for Italian rule. The Italian issue simply provided the occasion for the resolution of the religious conflict (and perhaps of a Gobroon intralineage conflict).

This type of factionalism clearly influenced policymaking elsewhere in the Benaadir. In Mereerey, as we noted, the three sons of Shaykh Ashir's youngest wife urged members of their community to take the initiative and attack the colonial forces stationed along the coast. This was a break with their father's policy, which had always been one of strictly defensive warfare. Ashir had insured the continuation of his policy by selecting his eldest son as his successor. The three younger sons, having been excluded from major leadership roles among the Hintire, sought to acquire influence by taking independent action. Thus, differing opinions on what measures to take against the infidels mirrored the competition for power and prestige within the clan. Similarly, the eventual break between the two sections of the Wacdaan should be understood in the context of the smaller section's waning influence in clan councils. By choosing to make peace with the colonials, the smaller group assured itself of increasing influence when and if colonial rule was established. This does not mean that one group was more realistic or more pragmatic than the other but rather that for the Somalis of the early twentieth century, internal politics were as important as external ones.

Alongside these ongoing traditional rivalries, however, each local Benaadir community had a deep-seated impulse to maintain cohesion and political unity. One example should suffice to make this point. We saw how, shortly after the Biimaal blockade of Marka was lifted in 1904, some sections of that community began to explore ways of negotiating with the powerful foreigners. This created rifts in the once-united Biimaal leadership. Haji Abdullah Ali Isa, son of the man who had opposed the Italians on the slavery issue, sent a letter to the government in 1905.

> We [the Biimaal] were the strongest [of the Somali] under the governments of Zanzibar and Filonardi, but with Badolo [who became resident of Marka in 1900] things changed and many spies divided us.

He added:

> On Thursday, we will meet with all the Daud [one Biimaal sec-
> tion] at Kaytoy and send some elders with a cow to the Suleyman
> and Yasmiin [other sections] to make peace, which is our ancient
> custom.[148]

This offering was intended to heal the growing divisions within the
Biimaal clan. To Abdullah Ali Isa, disunity was a greater evil than
submission to the Italians. Biimaal oral sources say that once the
Biimaal decided that they could not defeat the superior Italian weapons, they agreed to make peace as an entire community. We can
surmise that this was less an act of friendship toward the foreigners
than a gesture made to preserve Biimaal unity. It shows a commitment by these local Somali communities to stand together even in the
face of adversity.

In retrospect, the weakness of these early resistance movements
in the Benaadir was their parochialism. Confined by tradition, still
wary of traditional Somali enemies, each clan tried to meet the colonial dangers with its own limited resources. Only toward the end of
1905 did certain Benaadir leaders begin to see the futility of fighting
as small, local armies. Then there began a new phase of the southern
resistance: the *daraawiish* would soon make their appearance in the
lower Shabeele Valley.

The Daraawiish in the Benaadir, 1905–8

The word dervish (*darwiish*, pl. *daraawiish*) has generally
been associated with a member of a Sufi religious order. In Somalia,
the British and Italians applied the term to the followers of Shaykh
Muhammad Abdullah Hassan, the famous poet and resistance leader.
The shaykh himself called his followers *daraawiish* rather than
Somali to signify a brotherhood that transcended clan affiliations.
Initially, these followers were members of Ina Abdullah's Salihiya
order.[149]

148. "Haji Abdalla Issa al Residente di Merca," 10 Apr. 1905, *ASMAI*, pos. 66/4,
f. 44.
149. Muhammad Abdullah Hassan is often referred to by Somalis as Ina Abdullah Hassan, which simply means "son of Abdullah Hassan."

In the Benaadir, the term *darwiish* as used by most of my oral informants had a slightly different meaning. *Darwiish* referred not to the follower of a particular Islamic *tariiqa* but to a militant opponent of colonial rule. The oral testimony I received suggested that a *darwiish* was characterized by his (1) possessing a gun; (2) being a follower of Muhammad Abdullah Hassan, having received his blessing either in person or from one of his designated lieutenants; and (3) leading an adventurous life of raiding, warfare, and living off the land.

Possession of a gun was uncommon even in the active years of dervish activity in the south (1907 and after); there were probably never more than between three and four hundred firearms in Somali hands in all the Benaadir. The gun (usually an Italian Wetterly or a Turkish rifle; occasionally a pistol) gave the carrier a special status; virtually all of my informants took delight in recalling the names of those of their kinsmen who possessed guns at the time of the occupation. The southern dervishes had among their number at least two men who knew how to repair the weapons.[150]

Since virtually every non-Italian gun that turned up in Somali hands came from one of the camps of Muhammad Abdullah, the term *darwiish* became synonomous with a follower of the shaykh—though as shall be seen the southern dervishes had their own leadership. After the battle of Turunley in February 1907, contacts between southern and northern resisters increased. It is said that at least ten or fifteen warriors from every sizable village in the Benaadir journeyed to the Nugaal to try to acquire firearms. One was the father of the ten young men killed at the battle of Turunley; another was Abokor Ashir, son of the Mereerey Shaykh Ashir Madow. Those who sought guns at the camp of the mullah did not always succeed. I was told that one man by the name of Daahir Elow Keeley of the Hintire was not given a gun; rather than returning to his home empty-handed, he killed himself before the eyes of the shaykh's followers.[151]

As much by circumstance as by choice, the southern *daraawiish* were a wandering army. As more and more clan elders reached agreement with the Italians after 1905, the more dogged opponents of colonial rule were forced to abandon their home villages and roam about with others of the same persuasion. The acquisition of guns

150. Muddey Haji Geeley, Muqdisho, 16 May 1971.
151. Ibid., 9 June 1971.

enabled the *daraawiish* to modify traditional Somali military strategy. During the years of strictly local resistance, large numbers of kinsmen armed with spears would surround and assault a *zeriba* or a troop of enemy soldiers in march. The dervishes, on the other hand, made quick hit-and-run raids, first in one district, then in another.[152] They were not a cluster of kinsmen defending a given territory; they were a mobile commando unit defending their own independence. Colonial retaliation was difficult against such guerilla tactics. After the Italians moved inland in 1908, dervish warriors continued to raid the grain stores and the herds of Somalis who had submitted to the alien regime. Because of such tactics, several of my informants characterized the *daraawiish* as nothing more than vagrant *shuufta* (bandits).

It should be pointed out that the *daraawiish* were by no means the only Somalis who continued to resist after 1905. Segments of the Biimaal, for example, continued their own running battle with the invaders, mounting large-scale assaults against them at Turunley (1907), Jilib (March 1908), and Shalambood (July 1908).[153] In the last two battles, it appears that some *daraawiish* fought alongside those armed with traditional weapons. Only after 1908 did the *daraawiish* form the majority of those who fought openly against the Italians. Even then, the number of *daraawiish* in the Benaadir probably never exceeded two thousand.[154] Their importance lay less in their numbers than in their multiclan composition and in their links to the wider movements of anticolonial resistance in the Horn of Africa.

The dervish legend may take on more substance with a look at the history of one of the leaders of the Benaadir resistance, Abokor Ashir "Saa'amawaayo."[155] Third-born son of the respected Shaykh

152. Ibrahim Ali Subayr, "Kilometer 50," 19 Aug. 1971. Cf. Macchioro, *Relazione*, pp. 5–7, 11–12.

153. The last is remembered by Somalis as the battle of *Sabti iyo Axad* ("Saturday and Sunday"). Over the two-day period, some 2,000 Biimaal confronted 500 government soldiers. According to *Ufficio Storico: Somalia* 1: 147, the Biimaal suffered 1,000 warriors killed or wounded. The Italians subsequently named the site Vittorio d'Africa.

154. This is a crude estimate made from oral accounts and Italian assessments; the number does not include the firearms in the possession of the dervishes on the upper Shabeelle near Beled Weyn.

155. The following narrative draws on information collected in interviews with Abdelqadir Abokor Ashir, sole surviving son of "Saa'amawaayo," on 10 Aug. 1971, at Dundumey, near Wanle Weyn; Muddey Haji Geeley, Muqdisho, 31 May 1971; Shaykh

Ashir of Mereerey, Abokor learned the mystical arts of *tacdaar* and *wardi* from his father. Preferring the adventurous life of a warrior, however, he chose not to become a *wadaad*. Like many youths of his time, Abokor and his comrades spent much of their energy in raiding livestock; a favorite target was Mereerey's neighbor and sometime rival, the Geledi. Abokor was so successful in his raids that he acquired the unusual nickname "Saa'amawaayo" ("the time never fails"), which referred to his instinct for making military forays at precisely the right time to insure success. From all indications, his adventurousness caused his religious father some concern and, no doubt, many sleepless nights.

Always eager for action, Saa'amawaayo and some of his companions journeyed to the Hiiraan, near the upper Shabeelle, in *Sannad Isniin* (1904–5).[156] There they aided some distant kinsmen in opposing the attempts of Ethiopian forces to take tribute from the area. Shortly after, it is said, Aboker journeyed to the camp of Muhammad Abdullah Hassan, who was then settled at Ilig, and there took the title of *darwiish*. He received a handgun, a horse, and the long white robe characteristic of the followers of the shaykh.

At the death of his father in 1907, Saa'amawaayo returned to Mereerey where, as we have seen, he counseled his half-brothers against taking rash actions against the Italians. At this time it appears that Saa'amawaayo was more concerned with Ethiopian aggression than with Italian expansion. He returned a second time to the Hiiraan front. Only when he learned of the Italian occupation of Mereerey did he return to the Benaadir.

With him was the Shabeelle *darwiish* Yusuf Adil, whom he had assisted in the fight against Ethiopian troops. Another comrade in arms was Haji Ahmed Uways Baahuur, a *wadaad* from Afgooye. That Haji Ahmed and Saa'amawaayo, from rival clans, should be remem-

---

Yusuf Muhyeddin, Mereerey, 26 Aug. 1971, and Isaq Muhammad, Muqdisho, 20 Sept. 1971.

Abokor is mentioned in the written account of Cerrina-Ferroni, *Benadir*, p. 43; and Macchioro, *Relazione*, p. 20. He was considered one of the more prominent dervish leaders in the retrospective account of Caroselli, *Ferro e fuoco*, pp. 171–72, 176, 188, 191–93. The fragments summarized by Caroselli do not contradict Somali recollections of Saa'amawaayo's whereabouts at different periods of his life.

156. It is said that Saa'amawaayo's initial motivation in making the journey was to acquire arms to help the Hintire in their periodic clashes with the neighboring Geledi.

Shaykh Abdelqadir, last surviving son of the southern dervish leader Abokor Ashir "Saa'amawaayo," holds book of family records. With him is one of his sons.

bered in oral accounts as close friends shows how the dervish movement had become a pan-tribal affair. Along with other resisters from the Biimaal, Wacdaan, Geledi, and Hintire, these men continued to harrass farmers and herders who had come within the Italian sphere of influence. Meeting in various places, attacking at unpredictable times, the *darawiish* sustained their resistance in the Benaadir until 1910. By then nearly four thousand Italian troops had occupied Balcad and were looking upcountry toward Wanle Weyn and Maxaddey. As a result, many *daraawiish* surrendered their arms and returned home. Some, however, continued to fight from the Hiiraan, where in 1913 the uncle of Muhammad Abdullah Hassan had occupied and fortified Beled Weyne.[157] Saa'amawaayo, it is said, returned again to Mereerey in *Sannad Isniin* (1911–12). But life under colonial rule was not agreeable to him; he died some years later near Buur Hakaba, supposedly on his way to find further adventure across the Italian-Ethiopian border.

While Abokor Ashir Saa'amawaayo was widely known as the leader of the dervish resistance in the Benaadir, there were other well-known personalities in its various districts. Among the Biimaal, Haji Abdi Abiker "Gafle" enjoyed a great reputation as a clever and persistent thorn in the colonial side. It was he who urged the Somalis to break the dikes along the lower Shabeelle in order to flood the surrounding plains and make it impossible for Italian forces to reach the river.[158] Barghash Yusuf was the most prominent dervish from the Lafoole area, and Yusuf Adil along the mid-Shabeelle. These men coordinated dervish activities and provided the otherwise amorphous group with a recognizable continuity.

The multiclan composition of the dervish "army" has been mentioned. Even those clans considered most receptive to colonial rule—the Geledi, Abgaal, and Begeeda—surrendered some of their members to the lure of the dervishes. Equally interesting was the sociological makeup of the group. It appears that neither age nor former mode of livelihood restricted membership in the *daraawiish,* though they generally tended to be men of fighting age (twenty to fifty years) and the nature of their resistance forced them to abandon whatever wealth they had.[159]

157. F. S. Caroselli, *Ferro e fuoco in Somalia* (Rome, 1931), pp. 207–8.
158. Macchioro, *Relazione*, p. 20.
159. According to one informant, a certain wealthy farmer named Yusuf Robleh who lived at Anooley (near Mereerey) put his harvest and his family herds at the disposal of the dervishes in the area. He also sent a number of his slaves to Shaykh

It is difficult to know if the southern dervishes had as their goal anything as grand as "national independence." Certainly Muhammad Abdullah Hassan conceived of his struggle in national terms, as indicated by his numerous poems and letters to foreign officials.[160] Unfortunately, none of the southern dervish leaders left comparable documents; we can only hypothesize that those who visited the shaykh in person knew of his long-range goals. Many of the Benaadir *daraawiish*, like Haji Abdi Abiker and Saa'amawaayo, were well-traveled. They obviously knew that the colonial threat was more than just a local matter, and consequently they had a wider "national" perspective than most of their kinsmen.

Religious reform does not seem to have been a major preoccupation of the southern dervishes, nor do they appear to have been united by any one *tariiqa*. Oral sources suggest that some of the Benaadir dervishes switched their affiliation from Qadiriya or Ahmediya to Salihiya in the course of the struggle. Some, however, simply became dervishes without joining a *tariiqa*.[161] In fact, many of the resisters came from a background influenced more by the traditional *wadaaddo* than by the *tariiqa* shaykhs. Saa'amawaayo enjoyed his reputation as a practitioner of *tacdaar* to the end of his life. Abdi Abiker "Gafle," it was said, could turn bullets into water; and Shaykh Muhammad had to persuade his skeptical followers at Ilig that Haji Ahmed Uways Baahuur was a good ally to have in spite of his being suspiciously regarded as a powerful *wadaad*.[162] The resistance movement in the Benaadir was anti-foreign and anti-infidel, but it was not revolutionary in an Islamic sense. In retrospect, the major historical significance of the Benaadir dervishes was their role in linking south-

---

Muhammad to care for the livestock taken by the dervishes in raids. Interview with Muddey Haji Geeley, Muqdisho, 31 May 1971.

A more cynical informant said that any person of wealth who refused to support the dervishes when they approached an area would have his land and stock confiscated by the guerillas. Ibraahim Ali Subayr, Muqdisho, 11 Aug. 1971.

160. See, for example, B. W. Andrzejewski and I. M. Lewis, *Somali Poetry* (Oxford, 1964), p. 66 ff.; letters in *Ufficio Storico: Somalia* 1: 315–17; and Caroselli, *Ferro e fuoco*, passim.

161. *Laashin* Anshooley Osman Aliow, Muqdisho, 31 July 1971; Ibrahim Ali Subayr, "Kilometer 50," 19 Aug. 1971; Abdullahi "Begedow," Ceelqoode, 19 Oct. 1971; Ali Ahmed Yerow, Jenaale, 24 Oct. 1971. It was said that Saa'amawaayo switched his affiliation from Ahmediya to Salihiya after his visit to Sayyid Muhammad.

162. Baahuur Haji Ahmed Uways Baahuur, Afgooye, 17 May 1971.

ern Somalia, both strategically and emotionally, with Muhammad Abdullah Hassan's resistance in the north.

As early as 1902 the Italians had recognized the possibility of an alliance between southern dissidents and the "Mad Mullah's" movement in the British-occupied north. Indeed, letters from Somali elders had encouraged colonial fears; they threatened to invite the shaykh south if the Italians did not leave them alone.[163]

But only in late 1904 does evidence point to actual contact between southern resisters and their northern counterparts. The head shaykh of Baardheere had sent a letter to Shaykh Muhammad. The Biimaal *shir* of Mooyaale decided to send their delegation to Ilig.[164] Saa'amawaayo is said to have gone to the northern dervish camp late in *Sannad Isniin* (mid-1905). Thus it appears that the first link between south and north was forged on the initiative of the southerners themselves, though the historian must suspect that the shaykh had himself considered the possibility of a southern alliance.

The curious lull in Somali anticolonial activity in the south between October 1905 and February 1907 can be explained if one regards this period as the time when northern and southern Somali leaders were preparing a coordinated plan of resistance. In March 1905, Muhammad Abdullah Hassan signed the treaty of Ilig. This granted him and his dervish followers a tract of land in the Nugaal in exchange for his promise to keep the peace.[165] Somali historians have long argued that this apparent accommodation with the infidels was only a ploy on the part of the shaykh to buy time, to allow him to regroup his forces and to secure new allies. Evidence from Benaadir sources substantially supports this view. The years 1905–7 witnessed the visits of several southern delegations to the dervish headquarters at Ilig. During this time, many Benaadir militants became *daraawiish*. Guns first began to appear in the south. And the shaykh wrote his *Risalat al-Bimal* ("Message to the Biimaal") in which he proclaimed the necessity of *jihad* against the infidels.[166]

163. Caroselli, *Ferro e fuoco*, p. 166 n. 2. See also the letter from the elders of Geledi above, p. 213.

164. Sapelli to Consul, 26 Dec. 1904, *ASMAI*, pos. 66/4, f. 44.

165. The background to the signing of the Treaty of Ilig is discussed in Hess, *Italian Colonialism*, pp. 133–34.

166. Martin, *Muslim Brotherhoods*, pp. 196–97. Italian suspicions of anticolonial subversion during the treaty period are discussed in A. Gaibi, "Il Mullah: Breve storia di un falso Messia," *Rivista coloniale* 22 (1927): 208–13.

Furthermore, although the dervishes refrained from anti-European activities from 1905 to 1907, they were not entirely inactive. On the Ethiopian front the dervish warrior Nur Bora was organizing opposition to Amhara military expansion.[167] This was also the time when Saa'amawaayo went to the Hiiraan to fight on the western front. Common concern over the Ethiopian menace, therefore, helped reinforce the emerging sense of unity between north and south.[168]

The Italians must have felt that the settlement of Ilig had gained them a permanent ally when, after the Biimaal attack at Turunley in February 1907, Muhammad Abdullah Hassan sent a public letter to the Biimaal leaders condemning their rash action.[169] However, at the very same time the shaykh was secretly receiving a Biimaal delegation, to whom he confided his plans. What they were emerged some months later when several hundred Biimaal—along with members of other clans—made the trek to the Nugaal. The travelers were provided with some eighty guns and a message of encouragement to be given to Haji Abdi Abiker "Gafle" on their return. A Biimaal envoy interrogated some years later by the Italian authorities in Marka gave the following eyewitness account.

> Before we left, the Mullah called us together within his *zariba*
> . . . and said: Now return to your homes; remain good Muslims;
> do not approach the Government; be always its enemy. Having
> said this, he had a Quran brought in from which he read that the
> Islamic religion calls on the good Muslim to keep his distance
> from the infidel; as for the Christian, he must always oppose
> him.[170]

Shortly after this episode, Shaykh Muhammad broke the treaty of Ilig by invading Hobya.

167. Chiesi, *La Colonizzazione europea,* pp. 585–86.

168. An anonymous Italian report noted: "The Mullah will attack the Benadir only when he is sure internal conditions in Ethiopia will paralyze their forces." "Considerazioni sul territorio della colonia e piu specialmente sulla frontiera nord," *ASMAI,* pos. 87/2, f. 27.

169. An Italian translation is found in *Ufficio Storico: Somalia* 1: 133.

170. This very interesting document, an eyewitness account of a southern Somali's experience in Shaykh Muhammad's camp, confirms traditions collected in northern Somalia regarding delegations from the Benadir. (Personal communication from Muusa Galaal.) "Interrogazione di *Zuber Ali,*" contained in a report of the Resident of Marka, Vitali, to the Acting Governor, *ASMAI,* pos. 66/6, f. 63.

In the Benaadir, what began as a few incidents not unlike those which the Italians had experienced before suddenly erupted into a widespread campaign of violence. In February 1908, two stipended Somali officials were killed near Jilib. A few days later an Italian

Monument in Muqdisho to Shaykh Muhammad Abdullah Hassan, leader of the dervish resistance and "father of Somali nationalism."

officer was killed in an attack on his installation by Somalis armed with guns. Raids against leaders friendly to the colonials were stepped up. When the period of closed coast arrived, some fifty dervishes initiated another blockade of Marka and took part in the bloody encounter of *Sabti iyo Axad.* Elsewhere, followers of Yusuf Adil armed with guns were attacking the previously neutral clans east of Baardheere; and Jumbo at the mouth of the Jubba River was threatened by an alliance of surrounding clans.[171]

In June 1908 Governor Carletti wrote to the Ministry of Foreign Affairs.

> We cannot afford to delay our move inland, since it will be difficult to occupy the river when the rebels who left over two months ago return with guns from the Mullah Muhammad.[172]

To give added weight to his pleas for decisive government action, Carletti attached a letter from the sultan of Geledi written earlier that month.

> The Biimaal have abandoned their territory and the major part —around 4000—are in voyage to the Mullah. Only the old men, women, and children remain. Even among the Hintire only a few remain. . . . You must make war without any delay. Don't remain inactive. . . . Your enemies won't obey your orders and say, "We will obey only Shaykh Muhammad Abdullah. . . ."
>
> Hintire, Biimaal, Wacdaan, Jambelul, Daud, and Mobilayn amount to more than 100,000 [*sic*]. If their messengers return with arms, they will all stand against us and the territory will be lost, since they desire only war.[173]

While the letter almost certainly exaggerates the number of Somalis who actually left to contact the mullah in the north, it does give an idea of the extent to which the resistance had become pan-tribal. A united resistance is precisely what the colonials feared.

Therefore, in August 1908, auxiliary soldiers under Italian command marched inland to the Shabeelle. They raised the flag at Bariirey; they fought with valiant Somalis for several hours outside of

171. Macchioro, *Relazione,* pp. 5–10; Cerrina-Ferroni, *Benadir,* pp. 67–69.
172. "Carletti al Ministero degli Affari Esteri," 29 June 1908, *ASMAI,* pos. 66/4, f. 47.
173. Ibid.

Mereerey; then their forces marched triumphantly into Afgooye. The colonial occupation of the interior had begun, prompted by the events of the "Year of the Dervishes."

Conclusion

Looking back over the forty years covered by this chapter, one can observe a definite growth in the scale and scope of anticolonial activity in the Benaadir. From the localized outbursts against the Zanzibari *garesa*s in the 1870s, Somali opposition grew to include whole districts during the anti-Italian activities of 1896–97 and 1904–5; then it expanded to the entire Benaadir in the years 1907–10. The political groupings involved also changed over time. Only one section of the Biimaal (the Suleymaan) seems to have been responsible for ambushing and killing the Zanzibari *wali* Salim bin Yaqub in 1876; a small group of Bravanese had attacked *askari*s in that town after the Egyptians left in 1876. In contrast, in 1896 the entire Wacdaan community had carried out the Lafoole attack; and as we have seen, the Biimaal were united from 1896 until their blockade of 1904. By 1907, the *daraawiish* were enlisting supporters from virtually every clan in the Benaadir. The scale of the resistance had clearly grown.

In addition, we can suggest that the ideology of the resistance was transformed in the course of the Somali struggle. Opposition to Zanzibar had been motivated by concern over the possibility of a socioeconomic crisis—the abolition of slavery and the inevitable decline of agricultural productivity—though Somali reactions to Barghash's political pretensions no doubt played a part. By the Italian period, the threat of territorial dispossession was of major concern to the resisters; that is almost certainly why the Wacdaan and Biimaal were the earliest Benaadir clans to take up arms—their lands were the first to be invaded. The resistance thus assumed a politico-territorial dimension, clan-wide *shir*s being the sign of this wider concern. The Italians also brought out the element of religious opposition for the first time—unlike the Zanzibaris, they were infidels.

Although the colonial occupation of clan lands was a powerful impetus to clan unity, such unity was not gained without a struggle. As has been seen, economic concerns, religious differences of opinion, and local politics frequently overshadowed the colonial issue, making united action on this level difficult.

Thus it was the dervish movement which, for all its apparent diffuseness, took the resistance a step further. By bringing together in its ranks rich and poor, nomad and farmer, *wadaad* and warrior from all clans, it embodied all aspects of the earlier phases. Ideologically, too, the dervish resistance went a step further. For unlike the Somali actions of the earlier phases, the militant activities of the dervishes were not localized responses to specific colonial provocations. Dervish actions were themselves provocations, challenging an alien culture to respond. The dervishes in the Benaadir sought to take the initiative away from the foreigners. They appeared to be asserting their absolute refusal to compromise with any form of colonial subjugation; they opposed Somali clan leaders who did submit.

Many of the dervishes, as we have seen, were extraordinary individualists. Saa'amawaayo was something of a prodigal son and an inveterate adventurer. Haji Ahmed Uways Baahuur, the mention of whose name always drew a chuckle of recognition from my informants, was an eccentric *wadaad*. And Haji Abdi Abiker "Gafle," who forever limped after being injured at Cigalle in 1904, connived against the Italians until the early 1920s; then, nearly seventy and almost blind, he told the Italian commissioner that he wanted to return home and die peacefully in the place of his birth, near Lanta Buur.[174]

These were clearly unconventional men. In asserting their right to live free of foreign domination, they frequently violated the conventions of their own society. Attacking their own kinsmen's herds, burning villages, extorting supplies from the rich—these acts took the Somali warrior ethic beyond its acceptable social limits. They even fought using guns—the weapons of the infidel.[175] While they claimed they were defending that which was most traditional in Somali life, their actions severed them from their clans and threw them together

---

174. See n. 122 above.

175. One colonial official described the strategy of the dervishes in this way:

[Shaykh Muhammad] . . . has many thousands of horsemen. For them he needs arms and ammunition, and these can only be obtained through the exchange of animals—hence the continued raids [on livestock]. His means are always the same: he seizes the clan notables who are still not his declared followers and takes possession of all that belongs to them. When they promise to obey him, they are freed to collect their goods. If they please Mohammed Abdullah Hassan, he gives them a share of the booty and keeps the rest for his followers.

Ernesto Cucinotta, "Le scorrerie del Mullah," *Rivista coloniale* 6 (1909): 191–93.

in a pan-Somali movement that was quite untraditional. Only in this way were they able to transcend the limits of the old order and point the way to a new and revolutionary one.

It can be argued that there was no other path open to the militant opponents of colonial rule after 1905. The individual clans could not sustain a militant opposition; the *tariiqa*s were not inclined to pose one. From this perspective, the dervishes were simply those few men from each locale who opposed accommodation longer than the rest. They were unwilling to concede the futility of struggling against superior arms and a foreign power determined to occupy the land.

Still, it seems more than coincidental that few of the militant dervishes participated in the colonial administration after they surrendered their arms. None of those who lived into the 1920s and 1930s, to my knowledge, participated in the stirrings of modern political nationalism, though future research may modify this assertion. The significance of their resistance lay more in their valor and their decision to prolong their individual freedoms than in the creation of any proto-nationalist movement. Perhaps more than anything else, the dervishes in the Benaadir represented a form of resistance that asserted Somali cultural integrity in the face of an increasingly pervasive alien presence. The tangible benefits they achieved were few. Yet the values they expressed and the memories they left became part of the consciousness that would later sustain the growth of modern Somali nationalism.

Afterword

The story of the southern Somali resistance is an appropriate place to conclude this study of precolonial Somalia for several reasons. In the first place, the relatively abundant evidence available from the time of the colonial occupation makes it possible for the historian to analyze in some detail the operation of clan, religious, and embryonic class loyalties that for earlier periods can only dimly be discerned. In the course of the resistance struggle, alliances were forged and rivalries revived along a number of lines, many of which were seen to extend well back into the past. If the analysis is accurate, we can say that Somali society—far from being politically undifferentiated, religiously unified, and socially homogeneous in the late precolonial period—consisted of many diverse and overlapping interest groups, and that membership in these groups made a difference in the way individuals perceived and acted in their world.

At the same time, the evidence suggested that neither clan, nor class, nor religious group analysis alone could account for all of the political alignments that emerged during the resistance period. The interplay of numerous cross-cutting loyalties evident in the years after 1870 should alert the historian to the importance of examining Somali society from a number of analytical perspectives, particularly for periods when the data are much thinner.

The events of the resistance also reveal patterns of regional interaction which, as I have argued, characterized many aspects of the Somali experience in the precolonial period. Although decision-making remained localized at the level of the clan or village assembly, individuals, information, and firearms moved readily across clan lines and supported a striking if short-lived movement of regional opposi-

254

tion to the Europeans. The dervish call for unity and for a resistance that transcended parochial interests was the ideological expression of this wider regional initiative. In their own time, to be sure, the dervishes were often characterized as bandits and treated by their countrymen as social misfits. Yet their very existence suggests a society that was becoming aware of itself as a unity without yet being united. The common fund of historical experience in the Peninsula had begun to find expression in a movement that combined religious, political, and cultural strains in its struggle for identity.

Still, for all that the resistance period can reveal to us about the formative processes of the past, it has to be seen in retrospect as a transitional era in Somali history. For with the imposition of colonial rule in the early twentieth century, new forces came into play which altered both the objective conditions of Somali society and Somali perceptions of that society. These forces—the establishment of colonial administrations, the creation of new markets and job opportunities, the extension of roads and government services into the interior —contributed to the territorial integration of Somalia on a scale unprecedented in precolonial times. These changes also contributed to the growing political consciousness of the people, as Somalis throughout the Peninsula became aware of a common colonial condition. This enlarged consciousness found expression in the Somali political parties that emerged after World War II.

The forces of the twentieth century sometimes simply accelerated processes of regional integration that were already underway. The incorporation of rural Somalia into the wider world economy, stimulated as we saw by the livestock, slave, and grain trades of the nineteenth century, now reached its final stage. In the south, the Italian colonial government granted agricultural concessions to European farmers along the Shabeelle in an effort to promote the production for export of cotton, fruits, and vegetables. British efforts to secure regular supplies of Somali livestock for their growing colony in Aden drew more northern Somali pastoralists into the export trade, while Somalis along the Jubba began to smuggle camels and cattle across the border to new markets in colonial Kenya.[1]

1. For contemporary discussions of the prospects and problems of Italian plantation agriculture in the early twentieth century, see G. Ferrari, *Il basso Giuba italiano e le concessioni agricole nella Goscia* (Rome, 1911); R. Onor, *La Somalia italiana* (Turin, 1925); G. Scassellati-Sforzolini, *La Società Agricola Italo-Somala in Somalia* (Florence, 1926); and frequent articles in the periodical *L'Agricoltura coloniale*

Colonial policies also furthered, perhaps unwittingly, the religious integration of Somalia. In their efforts to "pacify" the Somali interior, the Italians enlisted the assistance of local Somali shaykhs, many of them representatives of the various Islamic *tariiqa*s that had first made their appearance in the second half of the nineteenth century. The shaykhs were provided with government stipends and administrative backing to encourage them to establish small religious settlements in remote districts beyond direct government control. This attempt to co-opt a segment of the religious leadership in Somalia clearly facilitated the diffusion of the *tariiqa*s. By the 1920s, virtually every Somali was at least nominally affiliated with one or another of the major orders, and Governor Riveri could express concern over the prospect of a new religious revival that would unite Somalis across clan lines in opposition to the colonial regime.[2]

The colonial period also brought some important discontinuities, as well as new forms of regionalism. European efforts to establish "law and order" led to the creation of rudimentary district administrations and locally conscripted militia units that linked rural Somali communities to a central government for the first time. The partition of the Somalilands meant that northern Somalis were drawn, however gradually, into an English-speaking legal and educational tradition, while their counterparts in the south learned to cope with the Italian language and (from 1923) with Fascist discipline. These experiences produced new sets of regional loyalties which the rise of militant Somali nationalism after World War II would only partially submerge.

Moreover, the Italian government's decision to emphasize agricultural development in the interriver area and not to interfere with

published by the Istituto Agricolo Coloniale Italiano of Florence beginning in 1907.

For the livestock trade from British Somaliland, see Richard Pankhurst, "The Trade of the Gulf of Aden Ports of Africa in the Nineteenth and Early Twentieth Centuries," *Journal of Ethiopian Studies*, vol. 3, no. 1 (1965), pp. 36–63, where official Protectorate Reports are summarized.

The most comprehensive study of Somali trade in Kenya during the early colonial period is Peter Dalleo, "Trade and Pastoralism: Economic Factors in the History of the Somali of Northeastern Kenya, 1890–1948" (Ph.D. diss., Syracuse University, 1975).

2. The best study of the historical development of the *tariiqa*s in early twentieth-century Somalia is still Enrico Cerulli's "Note sul movimento musulmano nella Somalia," originally published in 1923 and included in *Somalia: Scritti vari editi ed inediti*, 3 vols. (Rome, 1957), 1: 177–210. For Riveri's report, see Carlo Riveri, *Relazione annuale sulla situazione generale della colonia*, 1920–21 (Mogadiscio, 1921), esp. pp. 16–17.

the pastoral sector produced something of a dual economy in the south. Italian planters and officials replaced the embryonic class of Somali agro-pastoral entrepreneurs that had emerged in the nineteenth century. The cultivating peoples of the south were absorbed increasingly into a wage and market economy, benefiting perhaps more than any other sector from colonial development schemes. Apart from some of the northern clans that engaged in livestock trading with Aden, most Somali pastoralists remained on the margins of the export sector until the 1950s, when demands for meat from the oil-rich Middle East produced something of a commercial revolution in Somalia. Thus the economic dominance of Somali pastoralism, which had characterized most of the precolonial period, gave way in the first half of the twentieth century (at least in the south) to a territorial economy where agriculture provided the main link to world trade.[3]

Finally, the colonial period witnessed the emergence of a small group of Western-educated Somalis versed in modern notions of nationalism and self-determination. This group ultimately channeled the growing political consciousness of their countrymen into a movement for territorial independence. By organizing territory-wide political parties and appealing to pan-Somali sentiments, they enlarged the scale of interaction to the national level. On the political front, at least, one can argue that the twentieth century inaugurated a new phase in the evolution of Somali identity. Patterns of Somali-wide interaction came to the fore; national organizations, movements, and ideologies provided the dominant motifs.

Nonetheless, there is evidence to suggest that patterns of regional interdependence forged in the precolonial period persisted well into the present century. I am not thinking here simply of the regional character of many post–World War II political parties, which scholars agree often reflected north/south, pro-British/pro-Italian, and clan-family cleavages within the Somali population.[4] I am also thinking of

3. The structural characteristics of the Somali economy during the colonial period are analyzed by Mark Karp, *The Economics of Trusteeship in Somalia* (Boston, 1960).

4. On the nature and characteristics of the postwar Somali political parties, see I. M. Lewis, "Modern Political Movements in Somaliland," *Africa* 28 (July 1958): 244–61, and 28 (Oct. 1958): 344–63; and A. A. Castagno, "The Political Party System in the Somali Republic: A Balancing Coalitional Approach," in James Coleman and Carl G. Rosberg, Jr., eds., *Political Parties and National Integration in Tropical Africa* (Berkeley, 1964).

Five-point star on the Somali flag is said to symbolize the five regions into which the Somali nation was divided during the colonial period. It has been the goal of post-Independence Somali governments to reunite the people under one flag.

those persisting commercial and social networks that continued to underpin rural life in the Horn. For despite the existence of international territorial boundaries separating the territories of British Somaliland, Italian Somaliland, and the Ethiopian Ogaadeen, pastoral nomads continued during the twentieth century to move back and forth across political frontiers in order to exploit their traditional rainy-season pastures and wells. Italian reports from the 1920s and 1930s provide substantial evidence of trade and pastoral movement across their soon-to-be-contested border with Ethiopia. Nomads whose home wells were situated in the mountains of British Somaliland continued to cross into the Ethiopian-occupied Hawd after each spring rain. It was even reported in the 1950s that Somalis from the southern Ogaadeen often drove their livestock more than five hundred miles overland to the port of Berbera (rather than to the nearer Indian Ocean ports of Muqdisho and Marka) to take advantage of higher prices and traditional trading allies along the northern littoral.[5]

Religious pilgrimages, too, carried Somalis across territorial borders through the twentieth century. The tombs of Shaykh Hussein of Bale and of the ancestors of Daarood and Isxaaq attracted Somalis from many parts of the Peninsula; while Ogaadeen Somalis often began their pilgrimages to Mecca by trekking overland to the ports of British Somaliland or Djibouti.[6]

Finally, the refugee crisis of the late 1970s provides striking testimony about how regional ties of kinship and alliance survived the colonial partition of the Horn. Since 1978, literally hundreds of thousands of Somali refugees from the Ethiopian side of the border have been absorbed within Somalia (excluding those received in government-operated refugee camps), most of them by nomadic families

5. Regio Governo della Somalia, *Direttive per l'oltre confine* (Mogadiscio, 1932); John A. Hunt, *A General Survey of the Somaliland Protectorate, 1944–1950* (Hargeisa and London, 1951), esp. p. 152 ff.; Leo Silberman, "Somali Nomads," *International Social Science Journal,* vol. 11, no. 4 (1959); Irving Kaplan et al., *Area Handbook for Somalia,* 2d ed. (Washington, D.C., 1977), pp. 272–77; T. W. Box, "Nomadism and Land Use in Somalia," *Economic Development and Cultural Change,* vol. 19, no. 3 (1971), pp. 222–28.

6. I. M. Lewis, "Sufism in Somaliland: A Study in Tribal Islam," *Bulletin of the School of Oriental and African Studies* 17 (1955): 590–97; Ali Abdirahman Hersi, "The Arab Factor in Somali History: The Origins and Development of Arab Enterprise and Cultural Influences in the Somali Peninsula" (Ph.D. diss., University of California, Los Angeles, 1977), pp. 39–41.

with long-standing ties of kinship or mutual assistance with the immigrants. Such examples suggest that the modern bonds of citizenship have not replaced older networks of cooperation and solidarity, networks which continued to operate below the level of colonial administration throughout the twentieth century.

If regional processes of adaptation and integration have to some extent been superseded by national ones in recent times, clearly the former have not been entirely eclipsed. While this is not the place to elaborate on this point, one final example may illustrate the continuity I have in mind. As everywhere in colonial Africa, new employment opportunities in twentieth-century Somalia attracted rural Somalis to the major centers of economic activity. This is a process which, as we noted in chapter 5, had already begun in the nineteenth century. After 1910, many Somalis joined the colonial police force or local militias. Others came to the towns as interpreters, clerks, or petty traders. Still others went even further, taking up employment as seamen in the maritime trade, as truck drivers or tea-shop operators in East Africa, or (more recently) as drivers and pipeline workers in the Middle East. One of the most striking features of this Somali diaspora is the extent to which it remained linked to the local pastoral economy. A considerable share of the overseas earnings of these enterprising individuals was traditionally sent back to kinsmen in the interior. And as numerous observers have noted, many of these "travelers" ultimately returned to Somalia to invest their new income in livestock and livestock-related enterprises.[7]

The consequences of the diaspora for pastoral development, for the accumulation of wealth, and for the exercise of political influence in those regions of the country from which the travelers came, would form the subject of another study. However, it might be fruitful to view these developments within the context of the "regional resource systems" sketched out in the second chapter. From the viewpoint of the rural nomadic family, I would suggest, kinsmen employed overseas were regarded as supplementary sources of income, as insurance against hard times in the pastoral economy, and as the link with new resources, just as pastoral neighbors, townsmen, and agricultural allies had been in times past. Indeed, we might view the twentieth-century diaspora as the Somalis' attempt within a new political and

7. Hunt, *A General Survey*, p. 121; I. M. Lewis, *A Pastoral Democracy* (London, 1961), pp. 32, 269–70. This is a phenomenon that clearly merits further study.

economic order to extend the old regional resource system outwards, to seek new ways of promoting the pastoral enterprise. Clearly the experiences of work and travel overseas expanded Somali economic horizons and no doubt produced strains in group relations; but they need not automatically imply a complete break with the adaptive strategies of the past. New opportunities could often be perceived in traditional terms.

Indeed, I have tried to argue throughout this book that the legacy of the past is best regarded as a series of ongoing processes of adaptation to the natural, social, and political environment of the Horn. As the environment (in its broadest sense) changed, adaptation produced new institutions, networks, and ideologies; but these were always conditioned by the loyalties, beliefs, and perceptions of what went before.

The persistence of this legacy is perhaps most clearly seen in the challenges which face Somalia's contemporary leaders, challenges that are often clearly dilemmas. How, for example, does a government create an agriculturally self-sufficient society from a nation of nomads whose long struggle against the environment has proven time and again the resiliency of a pastoral existence? How can it sedentarize a population for whom regional mobility is an ingrained way of life? How are the proud descendants of once-powerful clans to be incorporated into the political leadership of a state determined to abolish "tribalism" and equalize opportunity? How is the deeply rooted but regionally focused tradition of Somali Islam to be marshalled in the creation of a modern socialist society? And how is the great legacy of Somali oral tradition to be preserved for posterity when some of its best examples consist of poetic diatribes by one clan's poets against members of another clan or region? Whether the forces which shaped Somali society in the past will continue to shape its future depends in large measure on how these questions are answered.

Appendix A
Comments on the Collection and Use of Somali Oral Sources

The oral material used in this study was collected during two periods of field research in southern Somalia: the first for ten months in 1971 and the second for some four months in 1977. In the course of both visits, my assistants and I interviewed about 120 Somali informants in a variety of settings and circumstances. Some of the interviews were taped and transcribed; others were recorded by hand. Because I was learning the Somali language as I went along, an interpreter was present at all interviews. The dialects spoken in the southern Somali interior posed considerable difficulties even for the most linguistically astute English-educated Somalis, most of whom were from the north. Consequently, I was most fortunate to locate three assistants and interpreters who had been born in the south and were interested in its history. Since they had been educated for the most part in Italian, which I also knew, much of our translating and transcribing was done initially in that language and later, at my leisure, rendered into English.

Since I wanted to write a regional history, I sought out informants from about a dozen clans scattered throughout southern Somalia. Identifying them was mainly the result of advice from students, scholars, and government officials who came from the various districts in which the clans were located. There are in Somalia no professional oral historians comparable to the hereditary *griot*s of

Mali and Senegal or to the *iggawen* (poet-musicians) of the western Sahara. Nevertheless, virtually every clan or village community had its recognized historical experts. These might be clan elders, shaykhs, or even young men who by inclination or temperament have imbibed more local history than their peers. Sometimes a single individual was considered by his kinsmen as the authoritative repository of the clan's history. More often, however, an individual would be knowledgeable in some areas of tradition while deferring to a kinsman in another. An informant would frequently tell me, "If you want to know more about the first Europeans who came to this district, you must talk to so-and-so"; or, "Shaykh Muhammad can tell you about the history of the Ajuraan in this area." By consulting each informant about other potential sources, I built up a list of experts throughout the interriver area.

Because of the uncertain political conditions which prevailed in Somalia in both 1971 and 1977, I was limited in my rural travel to the major towns and settlements of the south. This was not a serious handicap, however, as most Somalis, unless they were very old, were willing to travel to Shalambood or Wanle Weyn or Muqdisho to meet me, using the occasion to visit relatives and friends as well. Most often one of my assistants or a previous informant would make the initial contact, explain my objectives, and arrange for me to meet the party in question. In a few instances, my assistants were sent to record testimonies from informants who lived in areas that were inaccessible to foreigners. In this way, I managed to contact and interview most of the individuals on my list.

As most of my informants were over forty years of age and seldom still engaged in the day-to-day herding of livestock, it was not difficult to arrange even several meetings over the course of a few months. When I myself traveled upcountry, I carried sugar or tea to offer as gifts to my informants and a Polaroid camera so that I might leave family photographs with my hosts. The photographs proved very popular. When the informants came to me, I gave them a few shillings to cover the cost of bus or truck transport and meals, and that was usually adequate compensation.

By the time of my visit in 1977, a Somali Academy of Arts and Sciences had been established in Muqdisho and had in residence several dozen traditional poets and historians to assist researchers. However, only a handful of these men came from the regions on which my research was focused, and so I found it convenient to continue making my own contacts with the help of local elders and officials. A list of those informants who provided the most useful information for the current study can be found at the end of Appendix A.

When initially planning my research, I had intended to interview as many informants as possible on an individual basis. As it turned out, much of the oral information I collected came from group interviews. This seemed to be the way the Somalis preferred it. Whenever they had a choice, my informants would ask to include Abdi X or Hussein Y in the interview. This was partly because, I think, the transmission of knowledge in Somalia is considered a public act: it is history about the group and therefore ought to be done by the group. Suspicion about my motives may also have played a part. Informants sought to assure the community that nothing divisive or detrimental was being related.

But even beyond this, Somalis seemed to recognize that individual memories are limited and prone to error. Many of the events I sought to reconstruct required information that could only be supplied by a number of sources. In a society where, traditionally, ill-timed words or misinformed accusations could spark a feud, elders were constantly reminding their kinsmen to speak cautiously and accurately. There is a Somali proverb: "Whoever does not make sure of what he says is worse than a liar."

Consequently, about two-thirds of the interviews I conducted involved two or more informants, most in groups of three or four. On those few occasions where up to a dozen people participated, it was normally only two or three who carried the conversation, the others simply nodding assent or supplying points of detail. Even when an informant came into a settlement from an outlying area, he was typically joined by a few kinsmen and the local shaykh. Together we would share some tea and perhaps bread dipped in sesame oil; then the interview would proceed.

As might be expected in a group interview, my informants frequently sought to obtain a consensus on their account of past events. However, the search for consensus did not prevent situations where the participants openly disagreed. For most subjects, there existed no "official" version, and lively discussions sometimes arose about the

sequence of events leading up to, for example, a past encounter between two clans, or about the names of the most prominent elders
involved in negotiating an alliance. I recall a few instances in which
the local shaykh was asked to consult his "books" to help establish
when a particular mosque was first built, or in what year a prominent
saint died.[1] It was not uncommon, after a period of friendly debate,
for the participants to defer to the opinion of the most respected elder
or *haji* present. At times, however, the group would acknowledge
that they were not sure of the answer and ask me to return later after
they had consulted other elders.

A few informants proved to be highly knowledgeable about
certain episodes in the past, and I usually tried to arrange follow-up
interviews with them in a private setting. Informants interviewed
individually tended to be a bit more candid about the ins-and-outs of
intraclan politics, but rarely did their testimonies contradict the
thrust of what I had obtained from the group interviews. Indeed,
while informants from a particular family or lineage might seek to
cast the most favorable light possible on their forebears' actions,
they were perfectly well aware that a persistent researcher could
ask the same questions of informants from the "other side." As a
result, I seldom encountered conflicting versions of the *outcomes* of
past disputes or feuds; only the *motives* of historical personalities
or the *causes* of past events were subject to divergent interpretations. Thus I came to have considerable confidence in the substance
of the traditions collected in the group interviews and in the actual-
ity of events said to have happened several generations ago. On the
other hand, causes, motives, and sequential relationships almost always had to be inferred from the circumstances described in the
various testimonies.

1. These "books" or collections of Arabic manuscripts typically contained religious writings, hagiographies of saints, and bits of Islamic law, though I was told that
sometimes they contained written versions of the community's most important traditions. It appears that many such local traditions were written down in the early part
of the twentieth century, perhaps in response to colonial efforts to record the indigenous histories of their new administrative districts. Until an Arabic scholar can conduct
a systematic survey of these scattered manuscript collections—no easy task in light of
the way they are jealously guarded by the religious families that keep them—there is
no way of knowing whether they can add significantly to the corpus of local traditions
that have been transmitted orally.

The Nature and Interpretation of Somali Oral Traditions

While Somali stories *(sheekoyin),* proverbs *(maahmaah, odhaah),* [2] and the many genres of traditional poetry *(gabay)* [3] frequently contain information useful to the historian, most of the oral material used in this study belongs to that category which Somalis call *taariikh,* or "history." The term, derived from the Arabic, refers simply to the recounting of past events. In Somali conversation it is typically qualified by a noun or noun substantive, so that one has *taariikhdii daraawiishta* ("the history of the dervishes") or *taariikhdii Suldaan Yuusuf Maxamad* ("the history of Sultan Yusuf Muhammad"). The term *taariikh* is also applied by Somalis to historical accounts that have been written down in Arabic or in European languages or, more recently, in the new Somali script. Whether oral or written, *taariikh* is almost always a prose narrative, introduced by some phrase like *"Waqtii hore"* ("In earlier times") or *"Waqtii Axmed Yuusuf"* ("In the time of Ahmed Yusuf").

The oral traditions that I collected in the field can almost all be characterized as informal, episodic, and stylistically simple. There are in Somalia no epic narratives and virtually no formalized traditions of the sort found in many centralized states of precolonial Africa. In contrast to classical Somali poetry, which follows strict rules of meter and alliteration and typically contains ornate and richly nuanced turns of phrase, *taariikh* usually consists of spare, direct narrative related by an informant in his own words. Most individual testimonies were made up of several episodes strung together and punctuated with occasional explanation and commentary, or by the recitation of a proverb or poetic fragment purportedly composed at the time of the event or in commemoration of it. The following testimony taken from

2. *Maahmaah* are alliterated proverbs; like the traditional poetry from which they are frequently extracted, they must contain at least two words per line that begin with the same vowel or consonant sound. *Odhaah,* which can be translated "sayings," need not be alliterated.

3. The term *gabay,* though commonly used to describe poetry in general, more accurately refers to the best-known genre of classical Somali poetry, which contains 14–16 syllables per line. Many *gabay* are famous for their stylistic elegance, rich allusions, and topical significance.

an elderly religious notable of the Saramaan district of southern Somalia is typical in its style and content:

More than two hundred years ago there lived in the upper Jubba area two great tribes, the Laysan and the Oormale. The leader of the Laysan was Malak Issak Hassan Dinnow. He established settlements in the Saramaan area. The leader of the Oormale was Malak Nur Foday, and his encampments were built in Herrarey Yiffey in the Ard Madow area. The wars between them continued more than seven years.

Their religious leaders (Ashraf) tried to prevent bloodshed, but the Laysan leader did not heed their advice and continued to fight. The Ashraf leaders said that he would continue to suffer defeat for ignoring their counsel. In fact Malak Issak was defeated in seven important battles.

His chief advisers told him that he must end the war because the people were being killed. There were not enough of them remaining to tend the animals and to sow the fields. They had to increase the numbers of their men in order to fight.

But Issak Hassan Dinnow only scoffed and laughed at them. He said: My people the Laysan are divided into two parts, Bari and Horsi [east and west]. My part is the Bari. If the Horsi refuse to fight, the Bari and I will continue the war. If the Bari refuse to fight, my family and I will continue the war. And if my own family refuses me, my servant and I will continue the war.

The people were surprised and also inspired by his bravery. They continued to follow him again. Then an old man said, "My leader, you must listen to my advice. You must not forget to give to the elders of the Ashraf one hundred young camels, so that they will be content and reconsider what they told you before."

The people voiced their approval and Issak paid the one hundred camels to the Ashraf together with one hundred horses. The heads of the Ashraf were content and said to Issak, "Go, you will conquer your enemy." Issak then took his warriors and attacked the followers of Nur Foday.

By using magic and the Quran, Nur had set up a horn attached to a tall tree to warn his people whenever enemies approached. But this time the horn did not sound, so the Laysan entered his settlement with ease.

Then three servants were sent into Nur's settlement. Issak's own servant was braver than the others. The three met Malak Nur himself, who was washing the body of his daughter who had recently died. He thought the the three visitors were members of his own settlement, and asked them to take up his daughter and carry her to the place of burial. But Issak's servant threw his spear into Nur's breast. Nur Foday tried to swallow his ring, but the servant plucked it from his mouth and put it on his own finger.

Then he brought the body of Nur Foday to his leader and chanted:

> "Whether the God who created you is merciful, or casts
>   you into hell, it is not my lot to know;
> (All I know) is that Nur Foday was stricken down (by a
>   spear in) his breast."

This brave action inspired the Laysan to revenge and they drove the Oormale from the country, except for those they took captive to tend the animals and farms. The leader of the Laysan Issak Hassan Dinnow then recited the following poem:

> "Until the sky becomes warm the only thing that falls is
>   dust;
> "I have become warmer and warmer, and now my rain
>   has fallen."

The large area of Ard Madow once belonged to the Oormale, but today it belongs to the Laysan. The soil there is good, and the farmers of upper Jubba prosper from it still.[4]

There are several other variants of the tradition of the Laysan-Oormale wars extant in southern Somalia. The one cited was provided by Sherif Aden Yusuf, whose Ashraf ancestors figure prominently in the account of Malak Issak Hassan's ultimate success. Despite the informant's concern to demonstrate the historical importance of the Ashraf in the Saramaan area, his testimony contains references to places and personalities that can be corroborated from other sources. When analyzed alongside other variants, Sherif Aden's account has considerable historical importance even while it serves the special interests of his lineage.

4. Sherif Aden Yusuf, Saramaan; recorded by Muhammad Rinjele, 15 July 1971.

I should also like to call attention to the poetic fragments that occur in Sherif Aden's testimony and, for that matter, in many of the traditions I collected. Since lines of poetry are memorized and transmitted more readily in Somali society than unalliterated prose narratives, the poetic fragments often serve as mnemonic devices to help individuals recall entire episodes in their clan's history. In fact, it appears that one of the major ways the society transmits historical episodes is in the form of explanations or commentaries accompanying popular poetry. To make the meaning of a poetic fragment clear to succeeding generations, the circumstances which gave rise to its composition must be recounted. Thus poetry serves both to commemorate events and to assist in passing them on as part of tradition.

Throughout Somalia there are very few formal occasions on which historical traditions are routinely recounted. An exception is religious holidays and saints' feast days. During these celebrations, as we noted in chapter 4, the gathering of pilgrims occasions the exchange of stories about the lives of the saints or, at festivals honoring clan ancestors, the retelling of the founding of the clan. Even here, however, formal recitations are rare, and the passing on of historical information is largely incidental to the praying and celebration.

There is one other category of ritual celebrations that can occasion the public recitation of historical narratives. These celebrations occur in areas where group solidarity appears to derive more from historical alliances than from genealogical proximity, and they seem to be confined mainly to southern Somalia. As we have seen previously, many of the territorial groupings in the interriver zone consist of clans and lineages of diverse origins that occupied the land at different times. Frequently with the aid of religious intermediaries—like the Ashraf mentioned in the foregoing tradition—these diverse groups coalesced into confederations that shared farm and pasture land in their districts. In these districts it is not uncommon to find annual celebrations, often in conjunction with the Somali New Year, that expressly commemorate the solidarity of the confederation. The reader may recall from chapter 4 the legacy of the saint Omar "Arag": every year his ancestors preside over the gathering of representatives from the Saramaan cluster and ritually share out water which has been poured over wooden Quranic tablets. Such rituals of reaffirmation also occur among the Shanta Aleemo, the "five branches" of the Daafeed tribal cluster around Wanle Weyn. And in the Afgooye district, the annual *Istuunka* ("stick fight") is the occasion for the reciting of poetry that celebrates, among other things, the historic alliance of the Geledi and Wacdaan. In all these cases, the recollection of historical events is one aspect of the celebration.

Apart from the saints' days and clan festivals, however, Somali oral traditions are for the most part transmitted by elders in small family settings, or passed from older youths to their younger siblings during the long days spent tending the herds. Under these conditions, it is not surprising that the oral historical legacy consists primarily of episodic fragments that are widely known but rarely retold systematically.

In this book, I have used several different types of oral accounts which for purposes of discussion can be divided into the following three categories: *(1)* clan histories, which include origin stories, migration narratives, and accounts of alliances, wars, and the settlement of lands; *(2)* histories of locales, including eteological tales, town histories, and etymological narratives; and *(3)* personal histories, which include episodes from the lives of famous warriors or clan leaders and, more typically, of saints.

Clan and lineage traditions are the richest sources for cultural and social history, since they report events that helped to forge and to sustain group identity and that define the clan's relations with other groups in the wider society. Certain episodes that deal with events in the remote past—clan-origin stories, for example—are the most stylized. While folklorists might classify these as myths, Somalis include them in the category of *taariikh,* history. The following account of the formation of the Geledi clan is typical.

Omar Diin came to Adari from Arabia after a disagreement with his countrymen. At Adari he married a Hawiyya girl and had a son called Muhammad, who was an ancestor of Ajuraan. Then he arrived in the *doy* [a general name for the red-earth region of southern Somalia] and married a Digil girl, who was the daughter of a great sultan. She was childless because a serpent had lodged in her womb. Omar Diin cured her by applying a salve of clarified butter *(subag)* which had been warmed over a fire *(dab)* and served in a ladle *(qaarsin).* The serpent was driven out.

The girl's father said *"Galad ii galow,"* that is, you have done me a great favor, and hence Omar Diin's descendants took the name Geledi.

The couple then had two sons who were named Dab and Qaarsin. The descendants of Dab occupied Afgooye, while the descendants of Qaarsin remained in the Upper Jubba area.[5]

In her excellent study of the Afgooye community, the anthropologist Virginia Luling includes a more detailed version of this tradition, one which provides the names of the sultan and his daughter and many of the places where Omar Diin's descendants settled. Yet her version is a composite, pieced together, as she acknowledges, from many different testimonies. As she says, and as I can testify from similar experiences in other districts, each informant relates the origin story in ways reflective of his own current status and experience: some are full of magic and odd detail, others more "rationalized" and prone to suppress details the teller feels are improbable.[6] While the tradition clearly contains many elements that are "improbable," all its variants serve to affirm the existence of relations between the Geledi of Afgooye district and the upcountry clans between Baydhabo and Luuq. If the origins of these relations as described in the tradition are suspect, their historical reality is confirmed by the widespread support that the Geledi Sultan Yusuf Muhammad was able to muster during his impressive expedition against the reformers of Baardheere in 1843 (see chapter 4). It is this historical reality that clan traditions illuminate, however fantastic their form may appear to the outsider.

Another example, also from the history of the Geledi, further demonstrates the nature of the historical content in these traditions.

The descendants of Dab wandered over many places; but in two they remained for a long time. One section, those who came to be called the Tolweyne, settled near the river. They were led then by Aw Isma'il, who gave his name to the settlement. They sunk wells and blessed them, and the people multiplied. So rapidly did their numbers increase that the sultan who dominated the region ordered the well to be covered over with dirt.

While most of their livestock was without water, one white camel seemed to always be satisfied. A member of the Handab

5. Interview with Abokor Ali Omar, Muqdisho, 24 June 1971.
6. See Virginia Luling, "The Social Structure of Southern Somali Tribes" (Ph.D. thesis, University of London, 1971), pp. 26–37.

lineage followed her one day and found the [Shabeelle] river. The people moved to the riverbank and founded Ceelqoode.

The second group, headed by Shaykh Aw Jirow, was called the Yebdaale. They settled at the place called Balguurey.[7]

Here, tradition clearly reflects the contemporary social structure: the neighboring settlements of Ceelqoode and Balguurey are today the centers of the two moieties of the Geledi clan. While there is no way to corroborate the historical primacy of the Handab in the settlement of Afgooye, they are recognized today as the *curad* ("first-born") lineage in the community. We also know that the Shabeelle valley was indeed dominated by a powerful sultanate before the Geledi became ascendant in the eighteenth century (see chapter 3), and we can infer from the tradition that the Geledi were subordinate to it for a time. Finally, we probably are safe to conclude from the evidence in the tradition that the Geledi were not a recognizable unity at the time of their movement into the Shabeelle valley, and that only after the expulsion of the Silcis sultanate did the confederation as we know it begin to coalesce.

While traditions of origins and settlement can, if understood in context, point up probable factors that influenced the historical formation of groups, there is little question that they often do so in a form susceptible to folklore analysis. Many motifs in the traditional history of the Geledi appear in the traditions of other clans. Some of the most common are claims to descent from an Arab immigrant; discovery of a suitable place to settle, often with the assistance of an animal; and expulsion of a wild animal or (on occasion) of a human tyrant.[8]

Clan traditions also record the formation of alliances with neighboring clans, accounts of notable battles, or efforts to overcome a particular period of hardship for the community. The following account provides some vivid details on a battle fought in the early 1840s between the Hareyn clan and an army of zealous Islamic reformers based in the religious settlement of Baardheere (cf. chapter 4):

As the army of Baardheere approached the Hareyn country, they dispatched their spokesmen to demand the submission of

7. Interview with Abokor Ali Omar, Muqdisho, 24 June 1971.
8. Cf. Ugo Ferrandi, *Lugh: Emporio commerciale sul Giuba* (Rome, 1903), p. 211, who records the tradition of a wounded elephant leading the Gasar Gudda to the small peninsula on the Jubba River where they founded the town of Luuq.

the Hareyn. The Hareyn elders asked for four days to consider the demands. Meanwhile they offered 300 camels to feed the visiting army. During those four days, messengers from the Hareyn were sent to all the surrounding tribes, saying that if they refused to support the Hareyn against the "robed ones" [as the religious zealots were known for their long white *futas*] these tribes too would be crushed by the Baardheerans. The messengers went disguised as women, complete with robes and jewelry. As the other tribes gathered, they formed a long battle line with the Hareyn toward the center and slightly behind the front. When the four days were up, the Hareyn leaders refused the offer to submit peacefully and challenged the robed ones to fight. In the skirmishes which followed, the Hareyn lost the fewest men, keeping their warriors in reserve. When the other tribes were exhausted, the Hareyn reserves were strong and they pursued the robed ones all the way to Baardheere. It is said that the wild animals of the plains scattered before the fleeing Baardheerans and their pursuers. When they reached the Jubba River, the inhabitants saw the animals in flight and knew that the robed ones had been defeated.[9]

Here, although the tradition functions partly to embellish the history of the Hareyn, we have a description of an episode whose outcome conforms with what is known about the fate of Bardheere from external sources. While some of the more colorful details may be suspect as historical evidence, they are so unique to this account in its many variants that they ought not to be dismissed out of hand.

A second category of oral traditions—which I have labeled traditions of locale—purports to explain the origins and historical significance of certain ruined walls and fortifications; the names given to particular grazing areas or wells; or the reasons for demarcating boundaries at certain points. Such traditions are not central to the maintenance of group identity and cohesion, but they frequently provide information suggestive of patterns of historical interaction between neighboring groups, or of the sequence of different clans that may have occupied a given locale in the past.

There is a place not far from Afgooye called Lafagalle, which means "the bones of the Galla." This goes back to an uncertain

9. Interview with Mustafa Shaykh Hussein, Muqdisho, 12 Aug. 1971.

time, though the old men say it was a year in which two enemies threatened the Geledi. The *Gaal waranleh* ("Galla with spears") approached from the regions of Abyssinia, and the Abgaal came from the northeast. People recall it was the time for the harvest and all the *tub* (stubble) was left in the fields after the grain had been cut.

The Geledi called on the *tacdaar* [magic which renders an enemy impotent] of their shaykhs to help them make a deal with the Abgaal. They allowed the Abgaal to eat their fill of the grain that had been stored up from the harvest, and then the Abgaal left the area. So the Geledi had only to face the Galla threat. They fought with them all the way to Lafagalle where many hundreds of the Galla are said to have perished.[10]

Another example:

Madax-gooy means "cut head." The Ogaadeen people used to inhabit the area around Madaxgooy. They fought constantly with the Eelay. The Eelay once defeated them and pursued them all the way to Afmadow. However, the pursuers were struck with smallpox, and when the Ogaadeen learned of their weakness, they retook their old territory. At Madaxgooy a bloody battle took place, and the head of an Eelay warrior named Mahhadi was severely wounded. For two days he hid in a baobab tree. On the third day, an Ogaadeen nomad found him and killed him, and from that time the place was called Madaxgooy.[11]

What I have called personal traditions are most typically laudatory accounts of warriors or hagiographic accounts of saints. They tend to be concerned with personalities that have been important in the formation, consolidation, or defense of a clan or village community. In saint stories, several of which are included in chapter 4, the traditions often have the quality of didactic, exemplary, or Sufi mystical parables.

For individuals who lived within the past 100 to 150 years, I was often able to obtain specific details about their personalities, about specific decisions they took, or (for saints) about the religious schooling they had. Somalis are astute observers of individual physical

10. Interview with Ma'allin Yusuf Nur, Muqdisho, 22 July 1971.
11. Interview with Mustafa Shaykh Hussein, Dipartimento Culturale, Muqdisho, 12 Aug. 1971.

characteristics and behavioral traits—as witnessed by the many unique nicknames (*naanay*s) given to individuals by their peers—and this is reflected in the anecdotal personal traditions. Much of the information in chapter 6 on the Somali resistance drew from recollections about prominent individuals.

Personal traditions are also useful to the historian because they provide some indication of the motives which Somalis attribute to individuals who take unusual actions.

> Ahmed "Gole" of the Omar Mahmud clan moved with his family out of the Majeerteen region to settle with the Maxamad Zubeer clan beyond Dhagaaxbuur. This occurred about 150 years ago. The reason was a quarrel which he had with a less important *wadaad* [religious specialist] who had once been a pupil of "Gole." When many of his own kinsmen sided with the *wadaad,* Gole decided to leave his home area. He took his family, and now his descendants number close to 200.[12]

In attempting to generalize about the time depth of Somali oral traditions, I can say that detailed personal traditions are rare beyond 150 years, though accounts of the lives of many seventeenth- and eighteenth-century saints have no doubt been recorded in Arabic manuscripts and therefore have survived longer. Certain battles which seem to have occurred in the mid- to late eighteenth century— between the Laysan and the Oormale, between the Geledi and the Silcis—are still vividly remembered, presumably because they were instrumental in securing the victors undisputed possession of their present territory. Traditions surrounding the Baardheere wars of the 1830s and 1840s are, as we have seen, widespread in southern Somalia, though less significant conflicts from the same century have left few memories. A number of natural catastrophes that occurred in the past—droughts, locust invasions, smallpox epidemics—often are given specific names, but few are remembered for more than three or four generations.

I have already commented on the unusual time depth of traditions associated with the Ajuraan sultanate (chapter 3). The Ajuraan were dominant in the sixteenth and seventeenth centuries; and while it is not uncommon for Somalis to tell stories about tyrants from the remote past, the Ajuraan episodes have the aura of historicity about

12. Muusa H. I. Galaal, Muqdisho, 6 Oct. 1977.

them. While there is no way of knowing for certain, I would speculate that the Ajuraan tradition has been so well preserved because it was generated in a truly epochal period in the history of the peoples of the region. Events like those associated with the Ajuraan involved the consolidation of clans and the creation of numerous new alliances and enmities. While many of these intergroup relationships no longer survive, the very scale of the Ajuraan confederation insured that at least some some political bonds or rivalries would persist. Those that did helped keep alive the Ajuraan tradition, which must represent one of the "great events" of southern Somali history.

Somali Oral Tradition as History and Process

It should by now be apparent to the reader that I have regarded Somali oral traditions not simply as expressions of culture and belief but also as suitable evidence for use by historians. At the same time, I do not consider them direct evidence from the past but rather as living interpretations of historical experience. I have also suggested that traditions must be treated carefully: they cannot be lifted from the culture in which they are rooted or from the particular social situations in which they are transmitted. The oral record must be studied alongside the social groups whose identity it embodies and helps to reinforce. And it goes without saying that traditions are most useful to the historian when used in conjunction with other available oral and written evidence.

I am aware that most oral documents are susceptible to different types of scholarly analysis, among them functional, structural, and existential. However, I believe that these different modes of analysis are not mutually exclusive—that, for example, recognizing the political functions of a tradition does not automatically render it useless as a piece of historical evidence. The fact that certain traditions are remembered and others (presumably) forgotten is almost certainly a "function" of their relative political or social importance to the group that remembers (or forgets) them. But those traditions which are preserved, even for the most self-serving of reasons, may well have historical foundations. At the very least, such foundations cannot be ruled out a priori.

The fact that accounts are altered or embellished from one generation to the next, in accordance with the philosophical or political outlook of each, does not make them ahistorical. The very fact that traditions are reconstructions of the past suggests, if anything, a concern to make that past real and meaningful. This, after all, is the purpose of all historical interpretation, academic or otherwise. Particularly in a society like the Somali, in which there are no officially sanctioned histories, one should expect to find different evaluations of the same event, be it the religious wars of Baardheere or the causes of the Ajuraan downfall. The need continually to explain such phenomena indicates the ongoing reality of the event in the historical consciousness of the people. That reality may be refracted by the different perspectives of those who reflect on it; but it is not denied.

To pursue this line just a bit further, we can take the example of the saint stories. The fact that these are embellished with accounts of miraculous feats and physical transformations does not, of course, mean that the saint never lived or never affected the peoples who remember him. Indeed, one cannot understand the historical importance of saints without taking into account popular beliefs about their miraculous powers. It is precisely the belief in their unusual powers that gives the saints their place in Somali tradition and that gave them their importance in the past. Even the most reductionist of analyses must deal with reasons for the saints' centrality in the social history of Somalia, and Somali tradition offers as good a place as any to begin the search for those reasons.

However, having said all this, I think it is simplistic to approach Somali oral traditions as if each contained an objective "kernel" of historical truth to which has adhered countless folk motifs, literary elaborations, didactic morals, and political twists; and to see the oral historian's only task as that of peeling away the accretions to discover the historical kernel. Traditions need to be regarded as interpretive wholes, whose form and content reflect a variety of processes operating concurrently on them. In any generation, people are preserving, transmitting, elaborating, utilizing, and reflecting upon traditions—and often doing all simultaneously. Different kinds of traditions succumb, so to speak, in different degrees to the exigencies of each process. Some origin narratives, for example, have become so stylized, and some religious stories so utilized for didactic purposes, that the historical happening has become incidental to their preservation. On the other hand, the existence of multiple interpretations of the Baardheere *jihad* never obscures the historical event that remains the heart of the tradition.

I make these assertions about the fundamental historicity of

Somali oral traditions not on faith but on the basis of my observations of how Somalis see and interpret real events. There is definitely a sense of history in Somali society. Their genealogical system, though primarily concerned with defining the range of contemporary social relationships, and always subject to manipulation through telescoping or artificial lengthening, nonetheless is concerned with establishing primacy: primacy of birth, of settlement, of conversion to Islam. Hence it is concerned with time. Similarly, the Islam which almost all Somalis profess is a religion rooted in history. Its saints lived in real time, its legal precedents derived from historical experience. In the Arabic hagiographies written about Somali saints, important events like miracles are usually reported along with the names of persons who provided the original testimony and who transmitted it orally.[13] These *isnaad*s, or chains of transmitters, are intended to authenticate the reported events in an historically verifiable framework. And finally, the importance in Somali life of topical political poetry, which survives over time despite the disappearance of the circumstances that gave rise to its composition, helps sustain a sense of history.

If that sense of history differs from our own, it is nonetheless grounded in the Somali belief that social realities are not simply revealed paradigms for all time but rather the outcome of real events, real people, and real struggles over land, wells, and power. That each Somali generation seems to relive many of the same types of events often makes the specificity of historical traditions suspect, and gives them at times a kind of exemplary or idealized cast. Yet I have tried to show that as social relationships on the ground change over time, traditions themselves change. It is the oral historian's task to study not only the processes of history but also the processes of tradition. The shaping of Somali society is equally a shaping by Somali society.

Selected Oral Informants

The following is a list of those Somali informants who in 1971 and 1977 provided the most useful data for the subjects discussed in this study. Many were interviewed more than once, either singly or in groups. I have not included the names of many who participated in group interviews and who may have added a point or

---

13. Personal communication from B. W. Andrzejewski, School of Oriental and African Studies, University of London.

two to the main testimony; the omission of their names in no way
qualifies my appreciation for their help.

Each source is listed with his approximate age at the time of the
interview, his place or places of residence, and a note on the nature
of the information he supplied. The transcriptions of informants'
names here and throughout the book are anglicized, even though
some individuals now prefer to write their names in the new Somali
orthography.

1971

Shaykh Abdelqadir Abokor Ashir, 81, Dundumey (Daafeed). Sole
    surviving son of the southern dervish leader Abokor Ashir
    "Saa'amawaayo"; provided information on his father, the
    dervishes, the Ajuraan.
(Islao) Abdullah Hassan, 68, Afgooye. Wacdaan resistance.
Ma'allin Abdullahi Abdirahman Aden, 70, Muqdisho and Tagal
    Molimad. Baardheere wars, early saints.
Shaykh Abdullahi Hassanow, 84, Dhan-furur. History of the
    Ahmediya Order in Somalia.
Abokor Ali Omar, 35, Ceelqoode and Muqdisho. Abokor served as
    both informant and assistant in recording Geledi history.
Laashin Abiker Osman, 75, Ceelqoode. Silcis period, Baardheere
    wars.
Ahmed Shaykh Osman, 30, Mereerey. My assistant and translator
    of written documents in the possession of Shaykh Abow
    Yunis of Mereerey. Hintire history.
Ali Ahmed Yerow, 70, Jenaale. Biimaal resistance, dervishes.
Ali "Begedow," 55, Anooley. Reciter of poems composed during
    the Italian occupation; Ajuraan history.
Ali Omar Haji "Goyle," 77, Ceelqoode. Silcis period; trading
    partnerships in the past.
Sherif Aliow Abdi Nur, 61, Baydhabo. A *khaliifa* in the Ahmediya
    Order, Aliow provided many details on its history and on the
    history of the Salihiya Order.
Shaykh Aliow Mahad Emed, 65, Bulow Eelay. Ajuraan history.
Laashin Anshooley Osman Aliow, 73, Califo. Dervish history.
Shaykh Abdullahi Muhammad Osman, better known as Abdullahi
    "Begedow," 68, Danyeerey and Ceelqoode. A founder of one
    of the first political parties in Somalia, he provided

information on early Italian activities along the Shabeelle valley.

Baahuur Haji Ahmed Uways Baahuur, 60, Balguurey. Son of the Geledi *darwiish* Ahmed Uways Baahuur.

Laashin Baley Aliow Mukhdaar, 77, Mereerey. Hintire resistance.

Shaykh Omar Isa Haaq, 75, Afgooye. History of the Qadiriya and Ahmediya Orders.

Sherif Herow Hassan Aliow, 82, Baydhabo. History of the Qadiriya.

Ibrahim Ali Subayr, 65, Kilometer 50. Biimaal resistance.

Shaykh Jama Omar Isa, 50, Muqdisho. This well-known Somali historian provided much background information on Somali resistance during the colonial period.

Ma'allin Yusuf Nur, 62, Afgooye. Early Italian activities among the Geledi.

Muhammad Abdullahi Ibrahim Birkin, 65, Afgooye. The dervishes in the Afgooye district.

Sherif Haji Muhammad Ali Ibrahim Jennay, 70, Tagal Molimad. Early history of Baydhabo region.

Muddey Haji Geeley, 73, Muqdisho. Ajuraan; Hintire resistance.

Mustafa Shaykh Hassan, 40, Muqdisho and Baydhabo. Then a member of the Dipartimento Culturale, Mustafa knew many oral traditions regarding the Baardheere *jihad.*

(Islao) Osman Abdullah, 83, Afgooye. Wacdaan resistance, life of Ahmed Haji Mahhadi.

Salah "Abooye," 77, Shalambood. Biimaal and Hintire resistance.

Shaykh Yusuf Muhyeddin, 69, Mereerey. Ajuran, Hintire history; the dervishes in Mereerey.

1977

Haji Abdullahi Shaykh Ibrahim, 74, Wanle Weyn. Daafeed history, Baardheere wars.

Abba Ali Muhammad Ahmed, 55, Marka. History of Marka, Ajuraan.

Shaykh Aqib Abdullahi Jama "Qumbihaali," 50, Muqdisho. A member of the Somali Academy, Shaykh Aqib provided information on Somali religious customs and beliefs.

Ali Hassan, 50, Marka. Biimaal resistance.

Shaykh Hassan Ma'allin, Shalambood. Biimaal resistance.

Haji Isma'il Ali Omar Haji Mumin, 77, Shalambood. Information on
the life of resistance leader Haji Abdi Abiker "Gafle."

Abba Muhammad Ahmad, 77, Marka. History of mosques of
Marka, Ajuraan ruins.

Muusa Haji Isma'il Galaal, 70, Muqdisho. Invaluable source of
background information on Somali pastoralism, weather lore,
astrology, religion.

Haji Muhammad Ma'allin Osman, 60, Wanle Weyn. Daafeed
history.

Sa'id Osman Kenadid, 53, Muqdisho. A member of the Somali
Academy, Sa'id provided data on the history of Hobya
district.

Haji Yahya Ma'allin Aden, Wanle Weyn. Religious history of
southern Somalia, including Baardheere wars.

Appendix B
Glossary of Somali and Arabic Words

abbaan: host, patron, protector
abtirsiinyo: genealogy
adableh: cultivable (usually irrigated) land
afguri: dialect or subdialect
amaanduulle: leader of a raiding party
aqal: nomadic house
arbaca: Wednesday
askari: soldier, usually noncommissioned
asraar: sacred mysteries
axad: Sunday
aziimo: sacred knowledge
baraka: holiness, grace, inherent spiritual power
bilis: of noble ancestry (cf. *boon*)
boon: of low status or nonnoble ancestry (cf. *bilis*)
boqor: title equivalent to sultan, the designated leader of a clan or
   confederation
ceel: well
curad: "first born"; used in southern Somalia to designate a
   lineage believed to have been the first to settle an area
darwiish (pl. *daraawiish*): generally, a member of a Sufi order; in
   Somalia, a follower of the Salihiya leader Muhammad
   Abdullah Hassan
dayr: season of light rains (Somali autumn)

dibi: "bull"; used to designate terrain suitable for the breeding and rearing of cattle

dikri: spiritual exercises, often including repetitive chants and prayers, designed to make God present to the believer; each Islamic order has its distinctive *dikri*

dillaal: commercial broker

diya: traditional "bloodwealth," a form of compensation for injury or insult, usually paid or received collectively

doy: "red earth" pastureland

emir: a commander of the faithful; military leader in a theocratic state

gaal: a non-Muslim; infidel

gabay: poetry; also, a particular genre of classical Somali oral poetry

garesa: fort or fortified residence

geel: camels

gibilcaad: "white-skin," a term attributed to persons of purported Arab ancestry living in distinct communities in parts of southern Somalia

gu: the main rainy season (Somali spring)

haan: woven basket, typically used to store milk

imam: "leader of the faithful," typically the head of a theocratic polity

islao: traditional leadership title found particularly among Hawiyya clans of south-central Somalia; frequently bestowed on the brothers or relatives of the clan leader and involving political or military responsibilities

isnaad: chain of witnesses or authorities who authenticate an Islamic tradition

isniin: Monday

jamaaca (pl. *jamaacooyin*): an Islamic religious settlement or congregation headed by a shaykh

jihad: holy war

jiilaal: long dry season between *dayr* and *gu* (Somali winter)

karaamo: charismatic gifts, typically including the ability to work miracles

khaliifa: individual designated by the founder or head of an Islamic brotherhood to supervise the brotherhood's activities in a particular country or region

khamiis: Thursday

laashin: a clan poet

loox: fragment of bark or wood on which Quranic verses are written

maahmaah: alliterated proverb

macallin (pl. *macallimiin*): religious teacher or scholar [as part of an anglicized name, Ma'allin]

malaakh: in some clans, a title connoting military leadership [as part of an anglicized name, Malak]

marti: guest, company

meher: traditionally, the bridewealth paid by a husband to his wife's lineage members; in contemporary usage, the personal gift of the groom to his bride

naa'ib: the representative or deputy of a government, frequently a territorial governor in a theocratic state

odhaah: saying

qaaddi: an Islamic judge or legal expert

raaciye: "followers"; the subjects of a sultan or state

reer: an extended family or lineage segment; by extension, any group that lives or acts in common, e.g., a herding unit

saab: a conical wicker basket, typically used to support other containers

sabti: Saturday

sameen: conciliatory gift

sannad: year; Somali years are traditionally named for the day of the week on which they begin (e.g., *sannad Isniin,* a Monday year)

shaykh: Islamic teacher; man of religion

sheegad: lineage group or segment that attaches itself to another, usually in a dependent relationship

sheeko: story, folk tale

sherif: title given to a member of the Ashraf, purported descendants of the Prophet Muhammad

shir: clan meeting, assembly (usually of adult males)

shuufta: bandit

sixir: magic, sorcery

siyaaro: religious pilgrimage; visit for the purpose of making offerings at the tomb of a deceased saint or ancestor

subag: clarified butter

taariikh: history

tacas: gift of condolence given to the family of the deceased *tacdaar:* sacred magic directed toward a difficult task, commonly employed in a military encounter

tariiqa: a "Way"; an Islamic order, brotherhood

tawassul: the intercession by saints on behalf of those who pray to God

toob: length of cloth; by extension, the ankle-length robe into which it is made

ugaas: traditional leadership title, equivalent in some clans to that of sultan

waber: title given to clan leader in some Hawiyya clans

wadaad (pl. *wadaaddo*): religious specialist

wakil: representative of an Islamic leader, often the head of a mosque

wali: governor, guardian (as of a sultan's domains)

war: shallow pool or depression where rainwater collects

wardi: revelations; mystical enlightenment bestowing the capacity to divine or foresee the future

wazir: a minister (typically in a theocratic government)

xeer: customary law

xidid: "artery"; one's wife's kinsmen

xirmo: prohibition; restriction on a grazing area during certain seasons

xoog: strength; force

zariba: fortress or enclosure, often of thorn bush

Bibliography

Unpublished Sources

Archival Documents

The major unpublished documents used in this study were scrutinized during two six-week periods of research at the *Archivio storico dell'ex Ministero dell'Africa Italiana (ASMAI)*. The archives are located in the Ministry of Foreign Affairs in Rome and fall under the supervision of the *Comitato per la Documentazione dell'Opera dell'Italia in Africa*. This committee has produced a catalogue of the archive's holdings, which can be consulted at *ASMAI*. Each shelf *(posizione)* contains the reports and correspondence of a particular period, beginning in the 1880s. The holdings are well organized, though some of the folders are incomplete.

The colonial archives of Somalia were partly destroyed during World War II when the British occupied the country. Some documents, I understand, were sent to London where they are not yet available to the public.

The Garesa (now National) Museum in Muqdisho contains samples of some of the earliest treaties signed between European and Somali leaders as well as some exchanges of correspondence, commercial documents, and religious manuscripts, all in Arabic. Unfortunately many of the items listed in the Museum Catalogue (Mogadiscio, 1934) were lost during World War II.

Several unpublished reports on Somali grazing patterns, livestock management, and water resources were consulted at the *Centro di Documentazione* of the Istituto Agronomico in Florence, and in the library of the United Nations Food and Agricultural Organization (UNFAO), Rome.

Theses, Manuscripts, and Conference Papers

Alpers, Edward A. "Towards a History of Nineteenth Century Muqdisho: A Report on Research in Progress." Paper presented at the First International Congress of Somali Studies held in Muqdisho, Somalia, 6–13 July 1980.

Cassanelli, Lee V. "The Benaadir Past: Essays in Southern Somali History." Ph.D. diss., University of Wisconsin, 1973.

Castagno, Alphonso A. "The Development of the Expansionist Concepts in Italy (1861–1896)." Ph.D. diss., Columbia University, 1956.

Dalleo, Peter. "Trade and Pastoralism: Economic Factors in the History of the Somali of Northeastern Kenya, 1890–1948." Ph.D. diss., Syracuse University, 1975.

Ferrandi, Ugo. "Prima spedizione Ferrandi in Somalia." Typescript memoirs. Entry no. 777 in the National Museum Library, Muqdisho.

Galaal, Muusa H. I. "Stars, Seasons and Weather in Somali Pastoral Traditions." Personal copy.

Guadagni, Marco M. G. "Somali Land Law: Agricultural Land from Tribal Tenure and Colonial Administration to Socialist Reform." Ph.D. thesis, School of Oriental and African Studies, University of London, 1979.

Hersi, Ali Abdirahman. "The Arab Factor in Somali History: The Origins and Development of Arab Enterprise and Cultural Influences in the Somali Peninsula." Ph.D. diss., University of California, Los Angeles, 1977.

Luling, Virginia. "The Social Structure of Southern Somali Tribes." Ph.D. thesis, University of London, 1971.

Marlowe, David H. "The Galjaal Barsana of Central Somalia: A Lineage Political System in a Changing World." Ph.D. diss., Harvard University, 1963.

Samatar, Said Sheikh. "Poetry in Somali Politics: The Case of Sayyid Mahammad Abdille Hasan." Ph.D. diss., Northwestern University, 1979.

Turton, E. R. "The Pastoral Tribes of Northern Kenya: 1800–1916." Ph.D. thesis, University of London, 1970.

Published Sources

Bibliographical Aids

Bibliografia somala. Muqdisho: Scuola Tipografica Missione Cattolica, 1958. Prepared by the Chamber of Commerce, Industry, and Agriculture of Somalia (2,000+ entries).

Castagno, Margaret. *Historical Dictionary of Somalia.* Metuchen, N.J.: Scarecrow Press, 1975. Bibliographical section contains 675 entries.

Johnson, John William. "A Bibliography of the Somali Language and Literature." *African Language Review* 8 (1969): 279–97.

Lewis, I. M. "Bibliography" and "Supplement." *Peoples of the Horn of Africa.* London: International African Institute, 1969.

Marcus, Harold G. *The Modern History of Ethiopia and the Horn of Africa: A Select and Annotated Bibliography.* Stanford: Hoover Institution, 1972. Particularly helpful for nineteenth-century travelers' accounts.

Palieri, Mario. *Contributo alla bibliografia e cartografia della Somalia italiana.* Rome: Istituto Coloniale Fascista, n.d. (probably ca. 1935). Lists many obscure journal articles from nineteenth and early twentieth centuries.

Salad, Mohamed Khalief. *Somalia: A Bibliographical Survey.* Westport, Conn.: Greenwood Press, 1977. Contains ca. 4,000 entries published up through 1972.

Official Government Publications

Beginning in the 1890s, the Italian Parliament and the Ministry of Foreign Affairs published periodical reports, collections of documents, and monographs on Somalia. Many contain information on Somali society and local political leaders during the period just prior to the colonial occupation.

Bollettino Ufficiale della Somalia italiana, no. 5 (Aug. 1914). Includes detailed list of stipended government headmen and *qaaddi* s.

Camera dei Deputati. *Documenti diplomatici presentati al Parlamento italiano dal Ministro degli Affari Esteri: Somalia italiana (1885–95).* Rome: Tipografia della Camera dei Deputati [hereafter TCD], 1895.

———. *Documenti diplomatici . . . : Somalia italiana (1899–1905).* Rome: TCD, 1905.

————. *Documenti relativi alle condizioni ed all'amministrazione del Benadir.* Rome: TCD, 1903.

Carletti, Tommaso. *Relazione sulla Somalia italiana per l'anno 1907–08.* Rome: TCD, 1910.

Cerrina-Ferroni, G. *Benadir.* Rome: Ministero degli Affari Esteri, 1911. Provides political information on Somali clans most involved in resisting Italians.

Chiesi, Gustavo and Ernesto Travelli. *Le Questioni del Benadir: Atti e relazione della Commissione d'inchiesta della Società del Benadir.* Milan: Bellini, 1904. Contains numerous interviews with Somali leaders on issues of slavery and agriculture.

Commando del Corpo di Stato maggiore. *Riporto operazioni militari.* Bulletins nos. 7–13 (May 1903–May 1904). Rome: Ufficio Coloniale, 1903–4.

————. *Ufficio Storico: Somalia.* Vol. 1, *Dalle origini al 1914.* Rome: Tipografia Regionale, 1938. Contains detailed maps and several appended documents.

Corso, Francesco. *Le residenze di Balad e di Audegle.* Monografie e rapporti coloniali, no. 2. Rome: Tipografia Nazionale, 1912.

De Martino, G. *Relazione sulla Somalia italiana per l'anno 1910.* Rome: TCD, 1911.

Gasparini, Jacopo. *Le popolazioni fra il Gheledi e lo Sciaveli.* Monografie e rapporti coloniali, no. 5. Rome: Tipografia Nazionale, 1912.

Macchioro, Gino. *Relazione sulla Somalia italiana per l'anno 1908–09.* Rome: TCD, 1910. Describes colonial occupation of lower Shabeelle valley.

Regio Governo della Somalia. *Direttive per l'oltre confine.* Gubernatorial circular no. 400. Muqdisho: Stamperia della Colonia, 1932.

Riveri, Carlo. *Relazione annuale sulla situazione generale della colonia, 1920–21.* Muqdisho: Ufficio del Governo, 1921. Good overview of developments during World War I.

Russo, Enrico. *La residenza di Mahaddei-uein.* Memorie e monografie coloniali: serie politica no. 5. Rome: Istituto Coloniale Italiano, 1919.

Zoli, Corrado. *Oltre-Giuba.* Rome: Sindicato Italiano Arti Grafiche, 1927. Contains important historical traditions of nineteenth-century Daarood migrations.

Contemporary Works (Travelers' Accounts, Memoirs, Monographs)

Barbosa, Duarte. *A Description of the Coasts of East Africa and Malabar in the Beginning of the Sixteenth Century.* Trans. by E. J. Stanley. London: The Hakluyt Society, 1866.

Bennett, Norman R. and George E. Brooks, Jr., eds. *New England Merchants in Africa: A History Through Documents, 1802 to 1865.* Boston: Boston University Press, 1965. These letters and memoirs are useful for tracing commercial developments along the southern Somali coast.

Bonacci, Giuliano. *La nostra politica coloniale.* Rome: Tipografia di Attilio Friggeri, 1908.

Bottego, Vittorio. *L'Esplorazione del Giuba.* Rome: Società Editrice Nazionale, 1900. First eyewitness description of Luuq.

Carletti, Tommaso. *Attraverso il Benadir.* Viterbo: Agnesotti, 1910. Knowledgeable account by an ex-governor of Somalia.

Christie, James. *Cholera Epidemics in East Africa.* London: Macmillan and Company, 1876. Useful review of known trade routes in the 1860s and 1870s.

Christopher, William. "Extract from a Journal by Lieut. W. Christopher, Commanding the H. C. Brig of War *Tigris*, on the E. Coast of Africa. Dated 8th May 1843." *Journal of the Royal Geographical Society* 14 (1844): 76–103. Earliest written account of Geledi society and the impact of the Baardheere wars.

Ferrandi, Ugo. "I Biemal." *L'Esplorazione commerciale e l'esploratore* (Milan) 10 (1895): 74–77, 122–24.

———. *Da Lugh alla costa (Apr. 1897).* Novara: Arturo Merati, 1902.

———. *Lugh: Emporio commerciale sul Giuba.* Rome: Società Geographica Italiana, 1903. Magnificent study of the Gasar Gudda clan and of regional trade by the resident of Luuq in 1896–97.

———. "Gli scek di Bardera." *Bollettino della Società africana italiana* 11 (1892): 5–7.

Ferrari, G. *Il basso Giuba italiano e le concessioni agricole nella Goscia.* Rome: Bernardo Lux, 1911. Economic life along the Jubba in the early 1900s, with some historical traditions.

Freeman-Grenville, G. S. P. *The East African Coast: Select Documents.* Oxford: Clarendon Press, 1962.

Ghika, Prince Nicolas D. *Cinq mois au pays des Somalis.* Geneva: George et Co., 1898.

Guillain, Charles. *Documents sur l'histoire, la géographie et le commerce de l'Afrique orientale.* 3 vols. Paris: Arthus Bertrand, 1856. Invaluable for mid-nineteenth century political and economic situation along the Benaadir, with useful summary of earlier history; contains earliest recorded versions of some Somali oral traditions.

Kersten, Otto, ed. *Baron Carl Claus von der Decken's Reisen in ost Afrika in den Jahren 1862 bis 1865.* With accounts by R. Brenner and Th. Kinzelbach, 1866 and 1867. Leipzig: C. F. Winter, 1871.

Useful first-hand descriptions of Jubba River and coastal society in the 1860s.

Kirk, John. "Visit to the Coast of Somali-land." *Proceedings of the Royal Geographical Society* 27 (1873): 340–43.

Krapf, J. L. *Reisen in ost Afrika.* 2 vols. Korntal: The Author, 1858. Some notes on the Bardheere wars.

Leon des Avanchers. "Esquisse géographique des pays Oromo ou Galla, des pays Soomali, et de la Côte orientale d'Afrique." *Bulletin de la Société de Géographie,* vol. 4, no. 17 (1859), pp. 153–70. Including trade routes to southern Ethiopia.

———. "Missionaire au pays de Gera." *Bulletin de la Société de Géographie,* vol. 5, no. 12 (1866), pp. 163–74.

Manzoli, G. "La colonia del Benadir." *L'Italia coloniale,* vol. 3, no. 1 (1902), pp. 39–71. Good description of economic life.

Pantano, Gherardo. *La citta di Merca e la regione Bimal.* Leghorn: S. Belforta, 1910. Important contribution to Biimaal ethnography.

Paulitschke, Philipp. *Ethnographie nordost Afrikas: Die geistige Cultur der Danakil, Galla, und Somali.* Berlin: Dietrich Reimer, 1896. Selections on Benaadir need to be treated with caution.

Piazza, Giovanni. "La Regione di Brava nel Benadir." *Bollettino della Società italiana di esplorazione geografiche e commerciali* (Jan.–Feb. 1909). 3 pts.

Ravenstein, E. G. "Somali and Galla land . . . embodying information collected by the Rev. Thomas Wakefield." *Proceedings of the Royal Geographical Society* 6 (1884): 255–73.

Revoil, Georges. *Voyage au Cap des Aromates.* Paris: E. Dentu, 1880. Describes Somali-Zanzibar relations during the 1870s.

———. "Voyages chez les Benadirs, les Comalis, et les Bayouns en 1882–1883." *Le Tour du Monde,* vols. 49, 50, 56 (1885 sq.). Despite inaccuracies, a useful account of life in Afgooye during late precolonial period.

Robecchi-Brichetti, Luigi. *Lettere dal Benadir.* Milan: Società Editrice, "La Poligrafica," 1904. Impressionistic letters with some statistics by an ardent abolitionist.

———. *Somalia e Benadir.* Milan: Carlo Aliprandi, 1899. On the whole, a perceptive account of economic and social life in the early 1890s.

Sorrentino, Giorgio. *Ricordi del Benadir.* Naples: Francesco Golia, 1910. Sent to investigate the Lafoole ambush of 1896, Sorrentino discovered much about Somali activities through the use of informants.

Sulivan, G. L. *Dhow-Chasing in Zanzibar Waters.* London: Dawson's, 1967. (Originally published 1873.) Benaadir slave trade.

Von Schickh, Lt. Chevalier. "Report on the Disasters That Have
    Happened to the Expedition of the Baron Charles von der Decken."
    Proceedings of the Royal Geographical Society 10 (1866): 91–102.

Secondary and Anthropological Works

The following list is limited to those books and articles that
were most valuable for this study. Works of a general or comparative
nature, such as those on pastoralism in other societies, are cited in the
relevant footnotes and are not listed here.

Abir, Mordechai. "Caravan Trade and History in the Northern Parts of
    East Africa." *Paideuma* 14 (1968): 103–20.
———. "Southern Ethiopia." In Richard Gray and David Birmingham,
    eds., *Pre-Colonial African Trade.* London: Oxford University
    Press, 1970. These are good overviews of trading patterns from the
    Red Sea, Gulf of Aden, Benaadir, and Swahili coasts to southern
    Ethiopia.
Andrzejewski, B. W. "The Veneration of Sufi Saints and Its Impact on the
    Oral Literature of the Somali People and on Their Literature in
    Arabic." *African Language Studies* 15 (1974): 15–54.
Andrzejewski, B. W., and I. M. Lewis. *Somali Poetry.* Oxford: Clarendon,
    1964. The introduction and poems provide a good background to
    Somali economic and religious life.
Barile, Pietro. *Colonizzazione fascista nella Somalia meridionale.*
    Rome: Società Italiana Arti Grafiche, 1935. Despite the title, the
    work provides many historical traditions that are extremely valuable
    when controlled by other sources.
Benardelli, Gualtiero. "L'Anello dell'Imam: Leggenda di El Uergadi."
    Somalia d'Oggi, vol. 1, no. 1 (1956), pp. 24–25.
———. "Uno scavo compiuto nella zona archeologica di Hamar Gerjeb nel
    territorio di Meregh durante l'agosto 1932." *Somalia d'Oggi,* vol. 2,
    no. 1 (1957), pp. 28–35.
Box, Thadis W. "Nomadism and Land Use in Somalia." *Economic
    Development and Cultural Change,* vol. 19, no. 3 (1971), pp.
    222–28.
Bozzi, Luigi and G. A. Triulzi. "Osservazioni sugli animali domestici
    allevati in Somalia." *Rivista di agricoltura subtropicale e
    tropicale,* vol. 47, nos. 7–9 (1953), pp. 266–94.
Braukämper, Ulrich. "Islamic Principalities in Southeast Ethiopia Between
    the Thirteenth and Sixteenth Centuries." *Ethiopianist Notes,* vol. 1,
    no. 1 (Spring 1977), pp. 17–56; and vol. 1, no. 2 (Fall 1977), pp. 1–44.

Caroselli, F. S. *Ferro e fuoco in Somalia.* Rome: Sindicato Italiano Arti
    Grafiche, 1931. Perceptive study of the dervish movement,
    particularly as it affected the Italian colony.
Cassanelli, Lee V. "Migrations, Islam, and Politics in the Somali Benaadir,
    1500–1843." In Harold Marcus, ed., *Proceedings of the First United
    States Conference on Ethiopian Studies, 1973.* East Lansing:
    Michigan State University African Studies Center, 1975.
Cerulli, Enrico. *L'Islam di ieri e di oggi.* Rome: Istituto per l'Oriente,
    1971. A collection of the author's articles on Islam.
————. *Somalia: Scritti vari editi ed inediti.* 3 volumes. Rome: Istituto
    Poligrafico dello Stato, 1957, 1959, 1964. Cerulli's articles and
    papers, collected here, have provided the groundwork for most
    modern linguistic, ethnographic, and historical research on the
    Somalis.
Chiesi, Gustavo. *La colonizzazione europea dell'est Africa.* Turin:
    Unione Tipografica Torinese, 1909. A massive work of synthesis but
    without footnotes or references to sources.
Chittick, H. Neville. "An Archaeological Reconnaissance in the Horn: The
    British Somali Expedition, 1975." *Azania* 11 (1976): 117–33.
————. "An Archaeological Reconnaissance of the Southern Somali
    Coast." *Azania* 4 (1969): 115–30.
Colucci, Massimo. *Principi di diritto consuetudinario della Somalia
    italiana meridionale.* Florence: Società Editrice "La Voce," 1924.
    Scholarly study of the social organization of southern Somali clans
    and of the various forms of land tenure in the south.
Cucinotta, Ernesto. "Delitto, pena, e giustizia presso i Somali del
    Benadir." *Rivista coloniale* 16 (1921): 14–41.
————. "La proprietà ed il sistema contrattuale nel *Destur* somalo."
    Rivista coloniale 16 (1921): 241–64.
————. "La costituzione sociale somala." *Rivista coloniale* 16 (1921):
    389–405, 442–56, 493–502.
————. "La scorrerie del Mullah." *Rivista coloniale* 6 (1909): 191–93.
Curle, A. T. "The Ruined Towns of Somaliland." *Antiquity* 11 (1937):
    315–27.
Doresse, Jean. *Histoire sommaire de la Corne orientale de l'Afrique.*
    Paris: Librarie Orientaliste Paul Geuthner, 1971.
Drysdale, John. *The Somali Dispute.* London: Pall Mall Press, 1964.
Fantoli, Amilcare. *Contributo alla climatologia della Somalia.* Rome:
    Ministero degli Affari Esteri, 1961. Meteorological data from the
    early 1900s.
Finazzo, Giuseppina. *L'Italia nel Benadir: L'azione di Vincenzo
    Filonardi, 1884–1896.* Rome: Ateneo, 1966.
Fleming, Harold C. "Baiso and Rendille: Somali Outliers." *Rassegna di*

studi etiopici 20 (1964): 35–96. Important historical reconstruction from linguistic evidence.

Gaibi, A. "Il Mullah: Breve storia di un falso Messia." *Rivista coloniale* 22 (1927): 200–226.

Galaal, Muusa H. I. *The Terminology and Practice of Somali Weather Lore, Astronomy, and Astrology.* Muqdisho: The Author, 1968.

Girace, Alfonso. "Mogadiscio Cento Anni Fa." *Corriere della Somalia,* vol. 5, no. 110 (10 May 1954), p. 5. A comment on historical ruins in Muqdisho.

Grottanelli, Vinigi L. "I Bantu del Giuba nelle tradizioni dei Wazegua." *Geographica Helvetica* 8 (1953): 249–60.

———. "The Peopling of the Horn of Africa." In H. Neville Chittick and Robert I. Rotberg, eds., *East Africa and the Orient: Cultural Syntheses in Pre-Colonial Times.* New York: Africana Publishing Co., 1975. Good synthesis of the available evidence.

———. *Pescatori dell'Oceano Indiano.* Rome: Cremonese, 1955. Detailed study of the Bajuni of the southern Somali coast, with a historical chapter on the peopling of the adjacent mainland.

Heine, Bernd. "Notes on the History of the Sam-Speaking People." Staff Seminar Paper No. 9, Department of History, University of Nairobi (Kenya), 12 January 1977, cyclostyled, 14 pp.

———. "The Sam Languages: A History of Somali, Rendille, and Boni." *Afroasiatic Linguistics,* vol. 9, no. 2 (1978), pp. 1–93. Excellent review of the current state of linguistic research.

Hess, Robert L. *Italian Colonialism in Somalia.* Chicago: University of Chicago Press, 1966. Particularly good on the early years of Italian rule in Somalia.

———. "The Poor Man of God—Muhammed Abdullah Hassan." In Norman Bennett, ed., *Leadership in Eastern Africa.* Boston: Boston University Press, 1968.

Hunt, John A. *A General Survey of the Somaliland Protectorate, 1944–1950.* Hargeisa and London: Crown Agents for the Colonies, 1951.

Kaplan, Irving et al. *Area Handbook for Somalia.* 2d ed. Washington, D.C.: U. S. Government Printing Office, 1977.

Karp, Mark. *The Economics of Trusteeship in Somalia.* Boston: Boston University Press, 1960. Important analyses of Somali pastoral and agricultural economies in the twentieth century.

Konczacki, Z. A. "Nomadism and Economic Development of Somalia." *Canadian Journal of African Studies,* vol. 1, no. 2 (1967), pp. 163–75.

Laitin, David. *Politics, Language, and Thought: The Somali Experience.* Chicago: University of Chicago Press, 1977.

Lewis, Herbert S. "The Origins of the Galla and Somali." *Journal of*

African History 7 (1966): 27–46. Important reinterpretation of the Somali migrations.

Lewis, I. M. "La Communità ('Giamia') di Bardera sulle rive del Giuba." *Somalia d'Oggi,* vol. 2, no. 1 (1957), pp. 36–37.

———. "Dualism in Somali Notions of Power." *Journal of the Royal Anthropological Institute of Great Britain and Ireland,* vol. 93, no. 1 (1963), pp. 109–16.

———. "The Dynamics of Nomadism: Prospects for Sedentarization and Social Change." In Theodore Monod, ed., *Pastoralism in Tropical Africa.* London: International African Institute, 1975.

———. "From Nomadism to Cultivation: The Expansion of Political Solidarity in Southern Somalia." In Mary Douglas and Phyllis Kaberry, eds., *Man in Africa.* London: Tavistock, 1969. Contrasts social organization in north and south.

———. "Historical Aspects of Genealogies in Northern Somali Social Structure." *Journal of African History* 3 (1962): 35–48.

———. "Lineage Continuity and Modern Commerce in Northern Somaliland." In Paul Bohannan and George Dalton, eds., *Markets in Africa.* Evanston: Northwestern University Press, 1962.

———. *The Modern History of Somaliland.* London: Weidenfeld and Nicolson, 1965.

———. "Modern Political Movements in Somaliland." *Africa* 28 (July 1958): 244–61, and 28 (Oct. 1958): 344–63.

———. "Notes on the Organization of the 'Ise Somali." *Rassegna di studi etiopici* 17 (1961): 69–82. Example of the use of Sufi literature in praise of Somali ancestors.

———. *A Pastoral Democracy.* London: Oxford University Press, 1961. Classic study of northern Somali social organization.

———. *Peoples of the Horn of Africa.* London: International African Institute, 1955, 1969. Thorough combing of the sources and large bibliography make this an extremely useful, if disjointed, ethnographic survey.

———. "The Problem of the Northern Frontier District of Kenya." *Race* 5 (July 1963): 48–60. Summarizes migration traditions of Kenya Somali.

———. "Shaikhs and Warriors in Somaliland." In Meyer Fortes and Germaine Dieterlen, eds., *African Systems of Thought.* London: Oxford University Press, 1965.

———. "Sharif Yusuf Barkhadle: The Blessed Saint of Somaliland." *Proceedings of the Third International Conference of Ethiopian Studies held at Addis Ababa (1966).* Vol. 1. Addis Ababa: Institute of Ethiopian Studies, 1969. Example of widespread legends of holy men.

————. "The Somali Conquest of the Horn of Africa." *Journal of African History* 1 (1960): 213–30. Good statement of the traditional interpretation of direction of Somali migrations.

————. *The Somali Lineage System and the Total Genealogy.* London: Crown Agents, 1957.

————. "Sufism in Somaliland: A Study in Tribal Islam." *Bulletin of the School of Oriental and African Studies* 17 (1955): 581–602, and 18 (1956): 146–60.

Lewis, I. M., ed. *Abaar: The Somali Drought.* London: International African Institute, 1975.

Liprandi, Giuseppe. "La residenza di Iscia Baidoa." *La Somalia italiana,* vol. 7, nos. 1–3 (1930), pp. 45–58.

Martin, Brad G. "Mahdism, Muslim Clerics, and Holy Wars in Ethiopia, 1300–1600." In Harold G. Marcus, ed., *Proceedings of the First United States Conference on Ethiopian Studies, 1973.* East Lansing, Mich.: African Studies Center, Michigan State University, 1975.

————. *Muslim Brotherhoods in Nineteenth Century Africa.* Cambridge: Cambridge University Press, 1976. Chapters on Shaykh Uways of the Qadiriya and Shaykh Muhammad Abdullah Hassan of the Salihiya.

————. "Muslim Politics and Resistance to Colonial Rule: Shaykh Uways b. Muhammad al-Barāwi and the Qādirīya Brotherhood in East Africa." *Journal of African History* 10 (1969): 471–86.

Moreno, Martino M. *Il somalo della Somalia: Grammatica e testi del Benadir, Darod, e Dighil.* Rome: Istituto Poligrafico dello Stato, 1955.

Onor, Romolo. *La Somalia italiana: Esame critico dei problemi di economia rurale e di politica economica della colonia.* Turin: Fratelli Bocca, 1925. Excellent analyses of pastoral and agricultural economies in the early twentieth century.

Pankhurst, Richard. "The Trade of Southern and Western Ethiopia and the Indian Ocean Ports in the Nineteenth and Early Twentieth Centuries." *Journal of Ethiopian Studies,* vol. 3, no. 2 (1965), pp. 37–74.

————. "The Trade of the Gulf of Aden Ports of Africa in the Nineteenth and Early Twentieth Centuries." *Journal of Ethiopian Studies,* vol. 3, no. 1 (1965), pp. 36–63.

Perricone-Viola, A. "La liberazione degli schiavi nel vecchio Benadir." *Rivista delle colonie* 10 (1936): 882–86.

Pesenti, Gustavo. *Danane nella Somalia italiana.* Milan: L'Eroica, 1932. Participant in the Biimaal-Italian wars discusses, among other things, Somali military tactics and organization.

Pirone, Michele. *Sguardo alla società somala e ai suoi problemi in generale.* Pt. 3 of idem, *Appunti di sociologia generale.* Muqdisho: Istituto Universitario della Somalia, 1965. Good ethnographic sections reflect the author's long first-hand experience in Somalia.

———. *Appunti di storia dell'Africa.* Vol. 2, *Somalia.* Rome: Edizioni "Ricerche," 1961. Provocative survey of Somali history.

———. "Leggende e tradizione storiche dei Somali Ogaden." *Archivio per l'antropologia e l'etnografia* 84 (1954): 119–28.

Provenzale, Francesco. *L'Allevamento del bestiame nella nostra Somalia.* Rome: Bertero, 1914. The best early study of Somali transhumance, livestock management, and traditional nomenclature.

Puccioni, Nello. *Antropologia e etnografia delle genti della Somalia.* 3 vols. Bologna: Nicola Zanichelli, 1936. Volume 3 contains important data on Somali material culture.

Rosetti, Carlo. *Tre note sulla città di Mogadiscio.* Rome: Istituto Coloniale, 1907.

Russo, Enrico. "Il Mullah ed i suoi seguaci nella Somalia italiana." *Rivista coloniale* 17 (1920): 344–62.

Samatar, Said S. "Maxamad Cabdille Xasan of Somalia: The Search for the Real Mullah." *Northeast African Studies,* vol. 1, no. 1 (1979), pp. 60–76.

Scarpa, Antonio. "Della proprietà fondiara in Somalia." *L'Agricoltura coloniale,* vol. 17, no. 8 (1923), pp. 281–94. Land tenure in southern Somalia.

Swift, Jeremy. "Pastoral Development in Somalia: Herding Co-operatives as a Strategy Against Desertification and Famine." In Michael Glantz, ed., *Desertification.* Boulder: Westview Press, 1977.

———. "The Development of Livestock Trading in a Nomad Pastoral Economy: The Somali Case." In L'Équipe écologie et anthropologie des sociétés pastorales, eds., *Pastoral Production and Society.* Paris: Maison des Sciences de l'Homme; Cambridge: Cambridge University Press, 1979.

Touval, Saadia. *Somali Nationalism: International Politics and the Drive for Unity in the Horn of Africa.* Cambridge, Mass.: Harvard University Press, 1963.

Trimingham, J. *Islam in Ethiopia.* London: Frank Cass, 1965. Useful overview of history of Islam in the Horn of Africa.

———. *The Sufi Orders in Islam.* London: Oxford University Press, 1971. Little specifically on Somalia, but valuable for structure and practice of *tariiqa*s in general.

Turnbull, Richard. "The Darod Invasion." *Kenya Police Review* (Oct. 1957), pp. 308–13.

Turton, E. R. "Bantu, Galla, and Somali Migrations in the Horn of Africa:

A Reassessment of the Juba/Tana Area." *Journal of African History* 16 (1975): 519–37.

———. "The Impact of Mohammed Abdille Hassan in the East African Protectorate." *Journal of African History* 10 (1969): 641–57.

———. "Kirk and the Egyptian Invasion of East Africa in 1875: A Reassessment." *Journal of African History* 11 (1970): 355–70.

Watson, J. M. "The Historical Background to the Ruined Towns in the West of the Protectorate." *Somaliland Journal,* vol. 1, no. 2 (Dec. 1955), pp. 120–25.

Index

University of Pennsylvania
Publications in
Ethnohistory

Lee V. Cassanelli, *The Shaping of Somali Society:*
   Reconstructing the History of a Pastoral People,
   1600–1900